Understanding and Using

Microsoft® Excel 5.0

Steven C. Ross
Associate Professor of Management Information Systems
Western Washington University

Stephen V. Hutson
Microcomputer Coordinator
Rampage Clothing Company

WEST PUBLISHING COMPANY
Minneapolis/St. Paul • New York
Los Angeles • San Francisco

WEST'S COMMITMENT TO THE ENVIRONMENT

In 1906, West Publishing Company began recycling materials left over from the production of books. This began a tradition of efficient and responsible use of resources. Today, up to 95 percent of our legal books and 70 percent of our college and school texts are printed on recycled, acid-free stock. West also recycles nearly 22 million pounds of scrap paper annuallythe equivalent of 181,717 trees. Since the 1960s, West has devised ways to capture and recycle waste inks, solvents, oils, and vapors created in the printing process. We also recycle plastics of all kinds, wood, glass, corrugated cardboard, and batteries, and have eliminated the use of Styrofoam book packaging. We at West are proud of the longevity and the scope of our commitment to the environment.

Production, Prepress, Printing and Binding by West Publishing Company
Project Management by Labrecque Publishing Services

 Text is Printed on 10% Post Consumer Recycled Paper

Microsoft® and Windows™ are either registered trademarks or trademarks of Microsoft Corporation in the United States and/or other countries. Screens are reprinted with the permission of Microsoft Corporation. All rights reserved. Reprinted by permission.

Copyright ©1995 by WEST PUBLISHING COMPANY
                    610 Opperman Drive
                    P.O. Box 64526
                    St. Paul, MN 55164-0526

All rights reserved
Printed in the United States of America
02 01 00 99 98 97 96 95   8 7 6 5 4 3 2 1

Library of Congress Cataloging-in-Publication Data

Ross, Steven C.
    Understanding and using Microsoft Excel 5.0 / Steven C. Ross, Stephen V. Hutson.
        p.   cm. (The Microcomputing series)
    Includes index.
    ISBN 0-314-04626-7 (soft)
    1. Microsoft Excel for Windows. 2. BusinessComputer programs. 3. Electronic spreadsheets.
I. Hutson, Stephen V. II. Title. III. Series.
HF5548.4.M523R6736   1995
650'.0285'5369 — dc20   94-5365
                                                                                           CIP

British Library Cataloguing-in-Publication Data. A catalogue record for this book is available from the British Library.

Contents

Preface, xiii
Publisher's Note, xvi
About the Authors, xxii

Fundamental Spreadsheet Operations — 1

UNIT 1 / THE WINDOWS ENVIRONMENT — 2

Learning Objectives	2
Important Commands	3
Introduction to Microsoft Windows and Excel	3
The Keyboard	3
The Mouse	9
Windows and Dialog Boxes	10
Guided Activity 1.1: Starting Windows and the Program Manager	12
Guided Activity 1.2: Touring Windows Using the Mouse	13
Guided Activity 1.3: Touring Windows Using the Keyboard	16
Guided Activity 1.4: Starting Excel Using the Mouse	18
Guided Activity 1.5: Starting Excel Using the Keyboard	21
File Manager	22
Guided Activity 1.6: Using the File Manager	24
Launching Excel from DOS	28
Review Questions	29
Key Terms	30
Documentation Research	30

UNIT 2 / THE EXCEL WORKBOOK — 31

Learning Objectives	31
Important Commands	32
The Spreadsheet Concept	32
Excel Window Tour	33
Excel Commands	38
Heads-Up Computing	40
File Commands	40
Shortcut Menus	43
Entering Information into a Workbook	43
Guided Activity 2.1: Entering Text and Constant Values	46
Guided Activity 2.2: Entering Formulas	50
Guided Activity 2.3: Using Multiple Sheets in a Workbook	52
Backup	53
Guided Activity 2.4: Retrieving and Backing Up Files	54
Exercise 2.1: Harold's G.P.A.	56
Exercise 2.2: The Perfect Job (I)	57
Exercise 2.3: A Check Register (I)	58

Exercise 2.4: Business Mileage (I) 58
Exercise 2.5: Form 1040EZ (I) 59
Exercise 2.6: Things to Do (I) 60
Review Questions 61
Key Terms 61
Documentation Research 62

UNIT 3 / OPERATORS AND FUNCTIONS — 63

Learning Objectives 63
Important Commands 64
Arithmetic Operators 64
Guided Activity 3.1: Using Operators 67
Functions 69
Using the Help Window 78
Guided Activity 3.2: Using Functions 83
Guided Activity 3.3: Using the Help System 85
Exercise 3.1: More Fun with Functions 86
Exercise 3.2: The Lottery Winner 87
Exercise 3.3: A Check Register (II) 88
Exercise 3.4: Business Mileage (II) 88
Exercise 3.5: Form 1040EZ (II) 88
Exercise 3.6: Buford Fencing Company (I) 89
Review Questions 90
Key Terms 91
Documentation Research 91

APPLICATION A / POOR RICHARD'S (I) — 92

UNIT 4 / CHANGING THE APPEARANCE OF THE WORKBOOK — 94

Learning Objectives 94
Important Commands 95
Ranges as a Concept 95
Edit Commands 98
Insert Commands 99
Format Commands 100
Styles 109
Guided Activity 4.1: Using Numeric and Date Formats 111
Guided Activity 4.2: Using Styles and Templates 114
Exercise 4.1: Date and Currency Formats 116
Exercise 4.2: The Perfect Job (II) 117
Exercise 4.3: A Check Register (III) 117
Exercise 4.4: Business Mileage (III) 118
Exercise 4.5: Form 1040EZ (III) 118
Exercise 4.6: Things to Do (II) 118
Exercise 4.7: Buford Fencing Company (II) 118

Review Questions 119
Key Terms 119
Documentation Research 119

UNIT 5 / PRINTING THE WORKBOOK 121

Learning Objectives 121
Important Commands 122
Page Setup 122
Setting and Removing Page Breaks 127
Printer Setup 127
Print Preview 129
The Print Command 129
Using the Tools | Options Command with Printing 130
Guided Activity 5.1: Printing the Workbook 131
Exercise 5.1: Printing a Header 132
Exercise 5.2: A Check Register (IV) 133
Exercise 5.3: Business Mileage (IV) 133
Exercise 5.4: Form 1040EZ (IV) 133
Exercise 5.5: Things to Do (III) 133
Exercise 5.6: Buford Fencing Company (III) 134
Review Questions 134
Key Terms 134
Documentation Research 134

APPLICATION B / POOR RICHARD'S (II) 135

Intermediate Worksheet Operations and Graphics 137

UNIT 6 / CLIPBOARD COMMANDS AND OUTLINE OPERATIONS 138

Learning Objectives 138
Important Commands 139
Copy and Paste 139
Guided Activity 6.1: Making Preliminary Entries in the Workbook 140
Guided Activity 6.2: Copying from One Cell to Another Cell 140
Guided Activity 6.3: Copying from One Cell to Several Other Cells (I) 142
Guided Activity 6.4: Copying from One Cell to Several Other Cells (II) 143
Fill Command 145
A Keyboard Shortcut 145
Guided Activity 6.5: Adding Formulas 145
Guided Activity 6.6: Copying from a Range to a Cell 146
Guided Activity 6.7: Copying from a Range to a Range 148
General Rules for Copying 149
Cut and Paste 150
Dragging 150
Guided Activity 6.8: Moving a Range with Cut and Paste 151

Guided Activity 6.9: Performing a Sensitivity Analysis 152
Copy and Paste vs. Cut and Paste 153
Edit | Paste Special 153
Inserting Copied (or Cut) Cells 154
Pasting Multiple Copies 154
Guided Activity 6.10: Special Pasting Procedures (I) 154
Guided Activity 6.11: Special Pasting Procedures (II) 155
Outlining a Workbook 156
Guided Activity 6.12: Outlining a Worksheet 158
Exercise 6.1: A Sales Workbook (I) 160
Exercise 6.2: The Perfect Job (III) 161
Exercise 6.3: A Check Register (V) 162
Exercise 6.4: League Standings (I) 162
Exercise 6.5: Business Mileage (V) 163
Exercise 6.6: Gas Mileage (I) 163
Review Questions 164
Key Terms 164
Documentation Research 165

UNIT 7 / CELL REFERENCE AND CALCULATION — 166

Learning Objectives 166
Important Commands 167
Cell References 167
Guided Activity 7.1: Cell References 171
Recalculation 172
Guided Activity 7.2: Recalculating 175
Calculating with Displayed Values 177
Guided Activity 7.3: Calculating with Displayed Values 177
Exercise 7.1: Sales by State 178
Exercise 7.2: A Sales Workbook (II) 180
Exercise 7.3: Gas Mileage (II) 180
Review Questions 180
Key Terms 181
Documentation Research 181

APPLICATION C / COMPOUND INTEREST (I) — 182

UNIT 8 / CHARTS — 184

Learning Objectives 184
Important Commands 184
Steps in Creating a Chart 185
Worksheet Preparations 186
Insert | Chart Command 190
Guided Activity 8.1: Making Your First Charts 203
Selecting Items in a Chart 204
Editing the Data Series Formulas in a Chart 205

Enhancing the Chart	205
Exporting a Chart	211
Printing a Chart	211
Guided Activity 8.2: Charting RB Company Data	212
Guided Activity 8.3: Adding Optional Features to the Charts	216
Exercise 8.1: Charting State Sales Data	218
Exercise 8.2: The Perfect Job (IV)	219
Exercise 8.3: A Sales Workbook (III)	219
Exercise 8.4: Gas Mileage (III)	219
Exercise 8.5: League Standings (II)	219
Review Questions	219
Key Terms	220
Documentation Research	220

APPLICATION D / THE HOTEL MANAGER — 221

UNIT 9 / WORKBOOK TOOLS — 222

Learning Objectives	222
Important Commands	223
Spell Checker	223
Solving for a Desired Result	224
Guided Activity 9.1: Using the Goal Seek Tool	225
Solving Complex Problems	225
Guided Activity 9.2: Using the Solver	227
Managing Scenarios	230
Guided Activity 9.3: Using the Scenario Manager	230
Auditing Worksheets	232
Guided Activity 9.4: Auditing a Worksheet	234
Exercise 9.1: Finding an Interest Rate	235
Exercise 9.2: A Sales Workbook (IV)	236
Exercise 9.3: Pleasant Cove Marina (I)	236
Exercise 9.4: Pleasant Cove Marina (II)	238
Review Questions	238
Key Terms	238
Documentation Research	238

Advanced Workbook and Database Operations — 239

UNIT 10 / DATA COMPUTATION OPERATIONS — 240

Learning Objectives	240
Important Commands	241
Creating a Range of Values	241
Guided Activity 10.1: Copying the Data Disk	245
Guided Activity 10.2: Creating a Range of Values	246
Guided Activity 10.3: Creating a Trend Series	249

The AutoFill Handle — 250
Guided Activity 10.4: Using the AutoFill Handle — 252
Guided Activity 10.5: Adding a Custom List — 253
One-Variable Table — 255
Guided Activity 10.6: Creating a One-Variable Table — 256
Two-Variable Table — 257
Guided Activity 10.7: Creating a Two-Variable Table — 258
Using Array Formulas — 259
Guided Activity 10.8: Using Array Formulas — 260
Exercise 10.1: Compound Interest Revisited — 261
Exercise 10.2: A Sales Workbook (V) — 261
Exercise 10.3: A 401(k) Plan — 261
Review Questions — 262
Key Terms — 263
Documentation Research — 263

UNIT 11 / DATA SELECTION OPERATIONS — 264

Learning Objectives — 264
Important Commands — 265
Terminology — 265
Sorting — 266
Guided Activity 11.1: Sorting — 268
Specification of Criteria — 269
Filtering Records — 272
Guided Activity 11.2: Performing Database Operations — 276
Guided Activity 11.3: Using Combined Criteria — 278
Creating Subtotals in a Database — 279
Guided Activity 11.4: Creating Subtotals — 280
Creating a Pivot Table — 280
Guided Activity 11.5: Creating a Pivot Table — 284
Database Statistical Functions — 284
Guided Activity 11.6: Using Database Statistical Functions — 286
A Data Distribution Table — 287
Guided Activity 11.7: Computing a Data Distribution Table — 288
Using a Data Form — 289
Guided Activity 11.8: Using a Data Form — 290
Exercise 11.1: More Database Exercises — 290
Exercise 11.2: The Perfect Job (V) — 291
Exercise 11.3: A Check Register (VI) — 291
Exercise 11.4: League Standings (III) — 292
Exercise 11.5: Business Mileage (VI) — 292
Exercise 11.6: Things to Do (IV) — 293
Exercise 11.7: Software Inventory (I) — 293
Exercise 11.8: A Statistical Problem — 293
Review Questions — 293
Key Terms — 294

Documentation Research   295

APPLICATION E / PREDICTING THE FUTURE   296

UNIT 12 / ADVANCED WINDOWING AND PREFERENCE OPERATIONS   298

Learning Objectives   298
Important Commands   299
Customizing Your Display   299
Document and Cell Protection   307
Using Undo and Repeat   308
Guided Activity 12.1: Using Undo   309
Displaying and Customizing Toolbars   310
Graphic Items on the Workbook   312
Guided Activity 12.2: Creating an Illustrated Workbook   315
Using Controls in Worksheets   316
Guided Activity 12.3: Using Controls in a Worksheet   317
Windows and Panes   319
Guided Activity 12.4: Using Workbook Windows and Panes   323
Range Names   324
Find and Replace Commands   328
Example: Using Advanced Windowing Commands   329
Example: Global Range Names   330
Guided Activity 12.5: Using Advanced Features   331
Exercise 12.1: Using Range Names in Formulas   332
Exercise 12.2: The Perfect Job (VI)   333
Exercise 12.3: Search and Replace   333
Exercise 12.4: Gas Mileage (IV)   333
Exercise 12.5: Software Inventory (II)   333
Review Questions   334
Key Terms   334
Documentation Research   334

APPLICATION F / SPRING BREAK: FLORIDA OR BUST   335

UNIT 13 / ADVANCED FILE OPERATIONS AND DATA INTERCHANGE   337

Learning Objectives   337
Important Commands   338
Data Disk File Types   338
File Commands   339
Moving and Copying Data from One Workbook to Another   342
Guided Activity 13.1: Manipulating Files   343
Linking Workbooks by Formula   345
Guided Activity 13.2: Linking Workbooks by Formula   347
Consolidating Data   348
Guided Activity 13.3: Consolidating Data   349

The Workbook as a Consolidation Tool	351
Guided Activity 13.4: Using Workbooks	352
Exchanging Data with Other Applications	354
Data	Text to Columns and ASCII File Importation	357
Guided Activity 13.5: Practicing File Import and Export	359
Links Between Excel and Other Windows Applications	359
Guided Activity 13.6: Embedding an Object	362
Exercise 13.1: Consolidating Data from Two Workbooks	365
Exercise 13.2: Linking Workbooks	366
Exercise 13.3: Snow Data	367
Exercise 13.4: Gas Mileage (V)	367
Review Questions	367
Key Terms	368
Documentation Research	368

UNIT 14 / ADVANCED FUNCTIONS — 369

Learning Objectives	369
Lookup Tables	369
Guided Activity 14.1: Building a Lookup Table	372
Logical Expressions	372
Examples	374
Guided Activity 14.2: Using Logical Functions	376
String Reference, Manipulation, and Functions	377
Cell and Range Reference Functions	379
Advanced Mathematical Functions	380
Exercise 14.1: Assigning Grades	382
Exercise 14.2: Computing Minimum Payments	382
Exercise 14.3: Catch the Wave	383
Exercise 14.4: Form 1040EZ (V)	383
Exercise 14.5: Dice (I)	384
Review Questions	385
Key Terms	385
Documentation Research	385

UNIT 15 / MACRO COMMANDS AND CUSTOMIZATION — 386

Learning Objectives	386
Important Commands	387
Macro Commands	387
Guided Activity 15.1: Recording a Macro	388
The Visual Basic Toolbar	389
Editing with the Recorder	390
Guided Activity 15.2: Editing a Macro with the Recorder	392
Guided Activity 15.3: More Editing by Recording	392
Guided Activity 15.4: Manually Editing a Macro	396
Running Command Macros	397

Guided Activity 15.5: Creating a Button-Operated Macro	401
Guided Activity 15.6: Creating a New Menu Item	402
User-Defined Commands	402
Global Macros	402
Guided Activity 15.7: Creating a User-Defined Command	403
Visual Basic Terminology	404
Visual Basic Help	405
Exercise 15.1: Running Macros	406
Exercise 15.2: Transpose Command	407
Exercise 15.3: Business Mileage (VII)	407
Exercise 15.4: Dice (II)	407
Review Questions	408
Key Terms	408
Documentation Research	408

UNIT 16 / VISUAL BASIC PROGRAMMING — 409

Learning Objectives	409
Using Control Structures in a Procedure	410
Variables in Visual Basic	412
Guided Activity 16.1: A Statistical Problem Revisited	413
Custom Functions	415
Guided Activity 16.2: Defining a Custom Function	416
Interactive Procedures	419
Guided Activity 16.3: Creating an Interactive Procedure	421
Collections Revisited	422
Custom Dialog Boxes and Menu Items	422
Guided Activity 16.4: Enhancing an Interactive Procedure	425
Debugging Macros	426
Exercise 16.1: A Check Register (VII)	428
Exercise 16.2: Business Mileage (VIII)	428
Exercise 16.3: Form 1040EZ (VI)	428
Review Questions	428
Key Terms	428
Documentation Research	429

APPLICATION G / POOR RICHARD'S (III) — 430

APPENDIX A / ANSWERS — 438

Answers to Checkpoints	438
Answers to Review Questions	440

APPENDIX B / EXCEL VERSION 5 FUNCTIONS — 443

Mathematical Functions	443
Financial Functions	446
Date and Time Functions	448

Statistical Functions	449
Database and List Management Functions	452
Choice Functions	453
Logical Functions	454
Matrix Functions	455
Text String Manipulation Functions	455
Cell and Range Reference Functions	456
Engineering Functions	457
DDE/External Functions	459

APPENDIX C / EXCEL VERSION 5 COMMANDS — 460

Application Control Menu	460
Document Control Menu	460
File Menu	461
Edit Menu	462
View Menu	463
Insert Menu (Workbook)	463
Format Menu (Workbook)	465
Tools Menu	465
Data Menu	467
Window Menu	468
Help Menu	468
Insert Menu (Chart)	469
Format Menu (Chart)	469
Info Menu	470

INDEX — 471

Preface

> *If you had no power of calculations you would not be able to calculate on future pleasure, and your life would be the life, not of a man, but of an oyster.*
>
> Socrates

Understanding and Using Microsoft Excel 5.0 is about calculating with personal computers—specifically, with the popular program Excel. Calculation is a fundamental aspect of the analysis of data, and the business student and professional must be a skillful analyst if he or she is to be a successful manager. Not only is the Excel package a powerful analysis tool in its own right, it is also a good tool for learning about data analysis in general.

Why This Book?

There are many books available that discuss Excel 5. Why, then, would anyone write another book? We decided to do so because our students as well as our colleagues at several universities desired a book that was tailored to the way personal computing is taught at the college and professional level. We could find no book designed for use in academic and workshop settings. We saw a need for a book that would present concepts and skills as well as provide activities, applications, and questions for practice and teaching purposes. *Understanding and Using Microsoft Excel 5.0* is such a book.

Our goal was to support the efforts of the instructor by providing the essential facets of the software, with activities and exercises, to reinforce and evaluate the student's learning experience. Examples are drawn from the fields of business administration and economics to illustrate how the software can be used in other course work and in the daily tasks performed by business professionals. The Instructor's Manual provides supplementary materials and suggestions for integrating this book with other course materials.

This book serves a different role than the reference manuals furnished with the Excel 5 software. Those manuals, while comprehensive, often are difficult to read and fail to provide adequate examples. Accordingly, we sought to provide instruction in fundamental, intermediate, and advanced operations, supporting it with substantial reference material. When more detailed information is required, the user will have a significant foundation for finding and using it.

Finally, *Understanding and Using Microsoft Excel 5.0* is a member of THE MICROCOMPUTING SERIES published by West Publishing Company. It can be used alone, in combination with other books in the Series (listed in the Publisher's Note, on page xvi), or as a supplement to any other book in a course in which a knowledge of Excel 5 is required.

How to Use This Book

You should complete the first five units in the order presented. With that background, the material in the remainder of the book can be covered in the order that suits you best. The more work you do on the computer, the better you will learn the topics. At a minimum, you should complete the Guided Activities with each unit. We strongly encourage you also to work through the Exercises and Applications. Each activity and exercise is designed to illustrate points made in the previous units, and many contain additional material that is best presented during a computer session.

Each unit contains the following features:

LEARNING OBJECTIVES the knowledge and skills addressed in the unit.

IMPORTANT COMMANDS the commands to be covered, which will later serve as a quick reference to the contents of the unit.

COMPUTER SCREENS figures depicting the steps and results of most commands.

GUIDED ACTIVITIES step-by-step, hands-on illustrations of the operations discussed in the unit. The activities contain Checkpoints, which ask questions as you work to develop further your knowledge and skill level. The answers to the Checkpoints are found in Appendix A.

EXERCISES additional computer work designed to challenge your knowledge of the material presented in the unit. Some of these have specific instructions, while others provide less guidance.

REVIEW QUESTIONS questions designed to test your understanding of the material presented. The answers to selected Review Questions are contained in Appendix A.

KEY TERMS a list of the important terms and concepts discussed in the unit. This list is designed for review and self-test.

DOCUMENTATION RESEARCH exercises that require you to use the software publisher's documentation to learn more about the commands and functions discussed in the unit.

Additional features of this book are as follows:

APPLICATIONS seven exercises spread throughout the book that provide additional practice using the material presented. These are designed to be more challenging than the Guided Activities and Exercises.

EXCEL 5 FUNCTIONS this appendix contains a list and short discussion of each Excel 5 function.

EXCEL 5 COMMANDS this appendix contains a list and short discussion of each Excel 5 command.

INDEX the index covers commands, functions, symbols, and other topics. It is designed to allow you to locate the relevant information quickly.

QUICK REFERENCE this reference is placed at the back of the book, where you can easily refer to it.

THE STUDENT DATA DISK the data disk, included in the Instructor's Manual, contains the files needed as input for the Guided Activities, Exercises, and Applications.

A Note of Thanks

- To our parents, Verne and Luann Hutson and Charles and Edythe Ross, who filled us with a love of math and a desire to learn;

- To Nancy Hill-Whilton of West Publishing, and to Lisa Auer of Labrecque Publishing Services, who guided us in the development of an effective manuscript;

- To the reviewers of previous editions of the manuscript: Haw-Jan Wu, Whittier College; John Walker, New Mexico State University; Sandra Rittman, Long Beach City College; Mark Workman, Frank Phillips College; Gary Armstrong, Shippensburg University; Michelle Lenox, Nashville State Technical College; and Leonard Gorney, King's College;

- To our wives, Meredith Ross and Brenda Hutson, who endured the phone calls and the "crazy times";

- To Dawn and Dayna Hutson: may God richly bless you;

- To Kelly and Shannon Ross: may your red skies be at night.

We hope each of you is pleased with the final product.

S.C.R & S.V.H.
Bellingham, Washington and Canyon Country, California
August, 1994

Publisher's Note

This book is part of THE MICROCOMPUTING SERIES. This popular series provides the most comprehensive list of books dealing with microcomputer applications software. We have expanded the number of software topics and provided a flexible set of instructional materials for all courses. This unique series includes five different types of books.

1. *West's Microcomputing Custom Editions* give instructors the power to create a spiral-bound microcomputer applications book especially for their course. Instructors can select the applications they want to teach and the amount of material they want to cover for each application—essentials or intermediate length. The following titles are available for the 1995 Microcomputing Series custom editions program:

Understanding Information Systems

Management, Information, and Systems: An Introduction to Information Systems

Understanding Networks

DOS (3.x) and System

DOS 5 and System

DOS 6 and System

Microsoft Windows 3.0

Microsoft Windows 3.1

Microsoft Windows 95

WordPerfect 5.0

WordPerfect 5.1

WordPerfect 6.0

WordPerfect for Windows (Release 5.1 and 5.2)

WordPerfect 6.0 for Windows

Microsoft Powerpoint 4.0

Microsoft Word for Windows Version 1.1

Microsoft Word for Windows Version 2.0

Microsoft Word for Windows Version 6.0

PageMaker 4

PageMaker 5.0

Lotus 1-2-3 Release 2.01

Lotus 1-2-3 Release 2.2

Lotus 1-2-3 Release 2.3

Lotus 1-2-3 Release 2.4

Lotus 1-2-3 Release 3

Lotus 1-2-3 for Windows Release 4

Lotus 1-2-3 for Windows Release 5

Microsoft Excel 3

Microsoft Excel 4

Microsoft Excel 5.0

Quattro Pro 4

Quattro Pro 5.0 for Windows

Quattro Pro 6.0 for Windows

dBASE III Plus

dBASE IV Version 1.0/1.1/1.5

dBASE IV Version 2.0

Paradox 3.5

Paradox 4.5 for Windows

QBasic

Microsoft Visual Basic

Microsoft Access 1.1

Microsoft Access 2.0

For more information about *West's Microcomputing Custom Editions*, please contact your local West Representative, or call West Publishing Company at 512-327-3175.

2. General concepts books for teaching basic hardware and software philosophy and applications are available separately or in combination with hands-on applications. These books provide students with a general overview of computer fundamentals including history, social issues, and a synopsis of software and hardware applications. These books include *Understanding Information Systems*, by Steven C. Ross, and *Management, Information, and Systems: An Introduction to Information Systems*, by William Davis.

3. A series of hands-on laboratory tutorials (*Understanding and Using*) is software specific and covers a wide range of individual packages. These tutorials, written at an introductory level, combine tutorials with complete reference guides. A complete list of series titles can be found on the following pages.

4. Several larger volumes combining DOS with three application software packages are available in different combinations. These texts are titled *Understanding and Using Application Software*. They condense components of the individual lab manuals and add conceptual coverage for courses that require both software tutorials and microcomputer concepts in a single volume.

5. A series of advanced-level, hands-on lab manuals provides students with a strong project/systems orientation. These include *Understanding and Using Lotus 1-2-3: Advanced Techniques Releases 2.2 and 2.3*, by Judith C. Simon.

THE MICROCOMPUTING SERIES has been successful in providing you with a full range of applications books to suit your individual needs. We remain committed to excellence in offering the widest variety of current software packages. In addition, we are committed to producing microcomputing texts that provide you both the coverage you desire and also the level and format most appropriate for your students. The Executive Editor of the series is Rick Leyh of West Educational Publishing; the Consulting Editor is Steve Ross of Western Washington University. We are always planning for the future in this series. Please send us your comments and suggestions:

Rick Leyh
West Educational Publishing
1515 Capital of Texas Highway South
Suite 402
Austin, TX 78746
Internet: RLEYH@RESEARCH.WESTLAW.COM

Steve Ross
Associate Professor/MIS
College of Business and Economics
Western Washington University
Bellingham, Washington 98225-9077
Internet: STEVEROSS@WWU.EDU

We now offer these books in THE MICROCOMPUTING SERIES:

General Concepts

Management, Information, and Systems: An Introduction to Information Systems
by William Davis

Understanding Information Systems
by Steven C. Ross

Understanding Computer Information Systems
by Paul W. Ross, H. Paul Haiduk, H. Willis Means, and Robert B. Sloger

Understanding and Using the Macintosh
by Barbara Zukin Heiman and Nancy E. McGauley

Operating Systems/Environments

Understanding and Using Microsoft Windows 95
by Steven C. Ross and Ronald W. Maestas

Understanding and Using Microsoft Windows 3.1
by Steven C. Ross and Ronald W. Maestas

Understanding and Using Microsoft Windows 3.0
by Steven C. Ross and Ronald W. Maestas

Understanding and Using MS-DOS 6.0
by Jonathan P. Bacon

Understanding and Using MS-DOS/PC DOS 5.0
by Jonathan P. Bacon

Understanding and Using MS-DOS/PC DOS 4.0
by Jonathan P. Bacon

Networks

Understanding Networks
by E. Joseph Guay

Programming

Understanding and Using Visual Basic
by Jonathan Barron

Understanding and Using QBasic
by Jonathan Barron

Word Processors

Understanding and Using WordPerfect 6.0 for Windows
by Jonathan P. Bacon

Understanding and Using WordPerfect for Windows
by Jonathan P. Bacon

Understanding and Using Microsoft Word for Windows 6.0
Emily M. Ketcham

Understanding and Using Microsoft Word for Windows 2.0
by Larry Lozuk and Emily M. Ketcham

Understanding and Using Microsoft Word for Windows (1.1)
by Larry Lozuk

Understanding and Using WordPerfect 6.0
by Jonathan P. Bacon and Robert G. Sindt

Understanding and Using WordPerfect 5.1
by Jonathan P. Bacon and Cody T. Copeland

Understanding and Using WordPerfect 5.0
by Patsy H. Lund

Desktop Publishing

Understanding and Using PageMaker 5.0
by John R. Nicholson

Understanding and Using PageMaker 4
by John R. Nicholson

Spreadsheet Software

Understanding and Using Microsoft Excel 5.0
by Steven C. Ross and Stephen V. Hutson

Understanding and Using Microsoft Excel 4
by Steven C. Ross and Stephen V. Hutson

Understanding and Using Microsoft Excel 3
by Steven C. Ross and Stephen V. Hutson

Understanding and Using Quattro Pro 6.0 for Windows
by Lisa Friedrichsen

Understanding and Using Quattro Pro 5.0 for Windows
by Larry D. Smith

Understanding and Using Quattro Pro 4
by Steven C. Ross and Stephen V. Hutson

Understanding and Using Lotus 1-2-3 Release 5
by Steven C. Ross and Dolores Pusins

Understanding and Using Lotus 1-2-3 for Windows Release 4
by Steven C. Ross and Dolores Pusins

Understanding and Using Lotus 1-2-3 Release 3
by Steven C. Ross

Understanding and Using Lotus 1-2-3 Release 2.3 and Release 2.4
by Steven C. Ross

Understanding and Using Lotus 1-2-3: Advanced Techniques Releases 2.2 and 2.3
by Judith C. Simon

Understanding and Using Lotus 1-2-3 Release 2.2
by Steven C. Ross

Understanding and Using Lotus 1-2-3 Release 2.01
by Steven C. Ross

Database Management Software

Understanding and Using Microsoft Access 2.0
by Bruce J. McLaren

Understanding and Using Microsoft Access 1.1
by Bruce J. McLaren

Understanding and Using Paradox 4.5 for Windows
by Larry D. Smith

Understanding and Using Paradox 3.5
by Larry D. Smith

Understanding and Using dBASE IV Version 2.0
by Steven C. Ross

Understanding and Using dBASE IV
by Steven C. Ross

Understanding and Using dBASE III Plus, 2nd Edition
by Steven C. Ross

Integrated Software

Understanding and Using Microsoft Works for Windows 3.0
by Gary Bitter

Understanding and Using Microsoft Works 3.0 for the PC
by Gary Bitter

Understanding and Using Microsoft Works 3.0 for the Macintosh
by Gary Bitter

Understanding and Using Microsoft Works 2.0 on the Macintosh
by Gary Bitter

Understanding and Using Microsoft Works 2.0 on the IBM PC
by Gary Bitter

Understanding and Using ClarisWorks
by Gary Bitter

Presentation Software

Understanding and Using Microsoft Powerpoint 4.0
by Karen Young

Combined Books

Essentials of Application Software, Volume 1: DOS, WordPerfect 5.0/5.1, Lotus 1-2-3 Release 2.2, dBASE III Plus
by Steven C. Ross, Jonathan P. Bacon, and Cody T. Copeland

Understanding and Using Application Software, Volume 4: DOS, WordPerfect 5.0, Lotus 1-2-3 Release 2, dBASE IV
by Patsy H. Lund, Jonathan P. Bacon, and Steven C. Ross

Understanding and Using Application Software, Volume 5: DOS, WordPerfect 5.0/5.1, Lotus 1-2-3 Release 2.2, dBASE III Plus
by Steven C. Ross, Jonathan P. Bacon, and Cody T. Copeland

Advanced Books

Understanding and Using Lotus 1-2-3: Advanced Techniques Releases 2.2 and 2.3
by Judith C. Simon

About the Authors

Steven C. Ross holds a B.S. degree in History from Oregon State University and M.S. and Ph.D. degrees in Business Administration from the University of Utah. He is an Associate Professor of Management Information Systems at Western Washington University, Bellingham. His previous positions were as Associate Professor of Information Systems at Montana State University, Bozeman, and Assistant Professor of Management at Marquette University in Milwaukee. His responsibilities include the introduction of microcomputers into the primary computer courses and the integration of computer applications thoughout the curriculum.

Dr. Ross is the Consulting Editor for THE MICROCOMPUTING SERIES. In this capacity he advises both West Publishing Company and the authors on pedagogical, creative, editorial, design, and marketing issues. He is the author or coauthor of a dozen articles dealing with information management and education, and this is one of 25 books on microcomputing that he has written or edited. Two of his books in this series have been translated into French. He also consults with businesses of all sizes to integrate microcomputers into their managerial operations. His teaching and consulting experiences have provided ample material for this book.

Stephen V. Hutson is the Microcomputer Coordinator for Rampage Clothing Company, a leading manufacturer of high fashion women's and misses' clothing. His responsibilities include the instruction of staff in computer applications for the company's several facilities, the installation and maintenance of microcomputers and local area networks, the design of computer-generated reports, and database and macro programming. He holds a B.A. degree in Bible from Central Bible College in Springfield, Missouri. His experience with computers in the business world provides practical examples for this book.

Fundamental Spreadsheet Operations

UNIT ONE The Windows Environment
UNIT TWO The Excel Workbook
UNIT THREE Operators and Functions
UNIT FOUR Changing the Appearance of the Workbook
UNIT FIVE Printing the Workbook

■ **PART ONE** is the first of three parts in this manual. In this part we cover fundamental information that you must know to use Excel and to construct useful workbooks. We discuss how Excel uses the keyboard and the mouse, the screen display, and the spreadsheet concept.

With that background, we address the types of cell entries, how to enter and edit information in cells, and how to save workbooks to and retrieve workbooks from disk storage. Then we teach you how to use Excel arithmetic and functions to enter information into a workbook. This part includes an introduction to some of the more commonly used editing and formatting commands. The final topic concerns printing the workbook.

The application exercises in this part guide you through the development of a simple workbook. At the conclusion of the application exercises, you will have had a good introduction to working with Excel. The remainder of this manual prepares you to accomplish more sophisticated tasks.

Which Release of Excel Are You Using?

This book was written specifically for Version 5 of Excel. Many of the features have not changed from one version to the next, however, so the knowledge you gain from this book is generally applicable to all versions of Excel.

The Windows Environment

This manual is devoted to the task of manipulating and presenting numerical data in Excel. The major tool provided by Excel for this purpose is the workbook. Before the fun of creating workbooks can begin, you must learn how to launch Microsoft Excel from the Windows Program Manager and how Excel uses the keyboard.

Learning Objectives

At the completion of this unit you should know

1. how Excel uses the keyboard keys,
2. how to access a menu in the Windows environment,
3. how to interpret various mouse cursor shapes,
4. common mouse terminology,
5. the various elements of a dialog box,
6. the functions of the various parts of a window,
7. the functions you can perform with the File Manager.

At the completion of this unit you should be able to

1. start Windows,
2. navigate the Program Manager with the mouse or keyboard,
3. launch Excel from Windows or from DOS,
4. access a menu with either the mouse or keyboard.

Important Commands

>EXCEL (DOS command)
>
>File | Exit
>
>File | New
>
>WIN (DOS command)

Introduction to Microsoft Windows and Excel

Windows is an easy-to-learn and easy-to-use method of computing. Its use of color, pictures, and other graphical items helps novice users learn how to accomplish their work. Windows is also a powerful software system that sophisticated users can utilize to great advantage. The major advantages of the Windows environment are as follows:

- It allows the computer to use installed memory to the greatest advantage.
- Its graphical interface provides a consistent "look and feel" to Windows applications, allowing the user to leverage the experience from one application to many others.
- It allows the user to work on several projects at the same time and to transfer results of one effort (say, a spreadsheet graph) into another (say, a report or memo).

Excel is Microsoft's premier product for working with numbers and presenting those numbers, either in a table or a graph. With Excel you can do the following:

- Calculate simple and complex formulas
- Prepare attractive output with the results of the computations
- Graph the results
- Perform what-if analyses to determine the effect of various business strategies
- Perform simple database functions, such as sorting items and counting those items that meet certain criteria (for example, how many orders did we have that were over $1,000?)
- Create simple applications for use by those who are not computer literate

The Keyboard

In this section we describe typical personal computer keyboards. Other keyboards are similar, although placement and color of specific keys and the text or characters used to identify the key might vary slightly. The IBM and other personal computers have over 80 keys, about 40 more than most typewriters. Many of the extra keys have symbols or mnemonics rather than characters. To minimize confusion, we use the following conventions in this module to refer to specific keys.

Keys other than the numeric keys have their names spelled out inside a frame to represent their appearance on the keyboard (for example, [F1], [Home], [Shift]).[1] The following keys are commonly used in Excel data entry and DOS commands:

[Tab] This key is usually to the left of the "Q" key, with two arrows pointing in opposite directions on it.

[Shift] There are two [Shift] keys, usually to the left and right of the bottom row of letter keys, with open arrows that point up. This key allows the selection of ranges of cells when used in combination with the arrow keys. We will discuss the concepts of ranges and range selection in Unit 4.

[Backspace] This key is at the top of the keyboard, with an arrow pointing left.

[Enter] This key has a bent arrow pointing down and left. It is sometimes called the Return key.

[←], [↑], [→], [↓] This set of keys on the right of the keyboard is known as the arrow or cursor keys. Note that [←] and [Backspace] are two different keys and that they do different things. Some keyboards have a separate keypad containing only the arrow keys.

Multiple Key Combinations

Most people know how to use [Shift] on a typewriter to produce a capital letter: hold down [Shift] while pressing the letter key. On a computer, the [Ctrl] and [Alt] keys work in combination with other keys, like [Shift]. To type [Alt][M], hold down [Alt], press [M], and then release both keys. When instructed "press [Alt][F], [X]" (note the comma separating the two letter keys), you would press [Alt] and [F] simultaneously, then release both and press [X].

Function Keys

The function keys are placed across the top or on the left of the keyboard. Excel assigns uses to all the function keys; templates are available from third-party vendors that identify these keys. (Your organization might attach the template, or a copy, to the keyboard; if this has not been done, mark the location of Table 1.1 so that you can quickly refer to it as you use this module.) We will frequently identify these function keys (and function keys in combination with [Alt], [Shift], or [Ctrl]) as keyboard shortcuts. We will identify these in this module by their function key name—for example, [F1].

---

[1] On some keyboards, the [Tab], [Shift], [Backspace], and [Enter] keys are inscribed with both symbols and words; on other keyboards, only with symbols.

FIGURE 1.1
Excel Help window

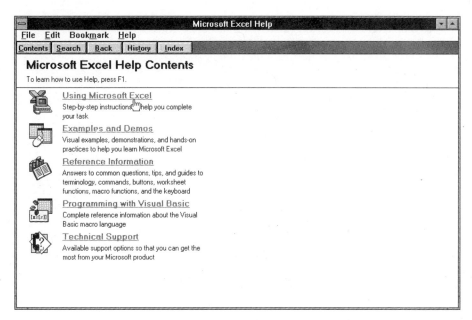

Three of the keys are immediately useful:

[F1] Opens the Help window, illustrated in Figure 1.1. When you have had enough help, you press [Alt][F], [X] to exit Help and return to the workbook.

[F2] Allows you to edit the contents of the cell under the cursor. Press the [Enter] key when finished editing.

[F5] Takes you to a specific place on the workbook.

Other function keys are discussed as needed in later units. See Table 1.1 for a complete list.

TABLE 1.1
Excel function key assignments

KEY	FUNCTION
[F1]	Help
[F2]	Edit (activate formula bar)
[F3]	Paste Name
[F4]	Edit I Repeat
[F4] (when editing a formula)	Toggle Reference Type (from absolute to mixed to relative)
[F5]	Edit I Go To
[F6]	Next Pane
[F7]	Tools I Spelling
[F8]	Toggle Extend Selection (on or off)
[F9]	Calculate all sheets in all open workbooks
[F10]	Activate Menu Bar (same as [Alt])

TABLE 1.1
(continued)

KEY	FUNCTION
F11	Insert I Chart (as new sheet)
F12	File I Save As
Shift F1	Context-sensitive Help
Shift F2	Insert I Note
Shift F3	Function Wizard
Shift F4	Find Next
Shift F5	Edit I Find
Shift F6	Previous Pane
Shift F8	Toggle Add Mode (on or off)
Shift F9	Calculate active sheet
Shift F10	Activate Shortcut Menu
Shift F11	Insert new sheet
Shift F12	File I Save
Alt F4	Control I Close (Excel application window)
Ctrl F2	Display info window
Ctrl F3	Define Name
Ctrl F4	Control I Close (document window)
Ctrl F5	Control I Restore (document window)
Ctrl F6	Control I Next Window
Ctrl F7	Control I Move (document window)
Ctrl F8	Control I Size (document window)
Ctrl F9	Control I Minimize (document window)
Ctrl F10	Control I Maximize (document window)
Ctrl F11	Insert new Excel 4.0 macro sheet
Ctrl F12	File I Open
Ctrl Shift F3	Create Names
Ctrl Shift F4	Find Previous
Ctrl Shift F6	Previous Document Window
Ctrl Shift F12	File I Print

Numeric Keypad Keys

The set of keys on the right side of the keyboard is known as the numeric keypad keys or number pad keys. On some keyboards, they appear in two places, both by themselves and also combined with the numeric keypad.

Key	Description
[←], [↑], [→], [↓]	Moves the active cell one cell left, up, right, or down. If you try to move beyond the edge of the screen, the screen will shift so that the cell can be viewed. You cannot move up from row 1, left from column A, down from row 16,384, or right from column IV.
[Home]	Moves the active cell to the left-most cell of the current row, for example, column A.
[Ctrl][Home]	Moves the active cell to the cell address corresponding to the upper-most and left-most active cells of the worksheet, usually cell A1.
[PgUp]	Moves the active cell up one screen, approximately 20 rows.
[PgDn]	Moves the active cell down one screen.
[Ctrl][PgUp]	Moves the active cell to the previous sheet in the workbook.
[Ctrl][PgDn]	Moves the active cell to the next sheet in the workbook.
[End]	Enters *end mode* when used with other cell movement keys. Press [End], then press one of the arrow keys or the [Home] key. (Do not hold down [End] while pressing the other key; release it first.) The END indicator in the lower-right corner of the window will display. When in end mode, pressing [Home] moves the active cell to the cell that intersects at the right-most occupied column and lower-most occupied row. If the active cell is in the middle of a range of occupied cells, the arrow keys, pressed in end mode, move the active cell to the end of that occupied range in the direction of the arrow. If the active cell is at the end of a range of occupied cells, or if the active cell is unoccupied, the arrow keys, pressed in end mode, move it to the next occupied range in the direction of the arrow. When in end mode, pressing [Enter] moves the active cell to the last occupied column in the current row.

The [Shift] key can be used in combination with each of the above keys in end mode to extend the selected range. When you press any of the above keys (including [End]), or press a key to begin data entry, you will leave end mode. Experiment with end mode to see how it works.

Key	Description
[Ctrl][End]	Selects the lower-right cell of the worksheet. This is identical in effect to pressing [Home] while in end mode. Note that using the [End] key in this combination does not initiate end mode.
[Del]	Deletes the character under the cursor in edit mode. This key is also used as a shortcut key to enter the Edit	Clear command.

Other Keys and Conventions

Several other keys are assigned special functions in Microsoft Excel:

Key	Description
[Num Lock]	Puts the keypad in numeric mode. To use the number pad keys as arrow keys in this mode, you must hold down [Shift].

Key	Description
`Backspace`	Erases the character to the left of the cursor in either input or edit mode.
`Scroll Lock`	When `Scroll Lock` is engaged, the arrow keys move the worksheet instead of the active cell; try it!
`Esc`	Use `Esc` to undo (cancel) an entry, or to cancel either a menu or a dialog box.
`Tab` or `→`	Moves the active cell one cell to the right and accepts any entry in the previous cell.
`Shift``Tab` or `←`	Moves the active cell one cell to the left and accepts any entry in the previous cell.
`Ctrl``→`	If the active cell is in the middle of a range of occupied cells, this key combination moves the active cell right to the end of that occupied range. If the active cell is at the end of a range of occupied cells, or if the active cell is unoccupied, this moves it right to the next occupied range. This is identical in effect to the action of the arrow key in end mode.
`Ctrl``←`	If the active cell is in the middle of a range of occupied cells, this key combination moves the active cell left to the beginning of that occupied range. If the active cell is at the end of a range of occupied cells, or if the active cell is unoccupied, this moves it left to the next occupied range. This is identical in effect to the action of the arrow key in end mode.
`Ctrl``↑`	If the active cell is in the middle of a range of occupied cells, this key combination moves the active cell up to the beginning of that occupied range. If the active cell is at the end of a range of occupied cells, or if the active cell is unoccupied, this moves it up to the next occupied range. This is identical in effect to the action of the arrow key in end mode.
`Ctrl``↓`	If the active cell is in the middle of a range of occupied cells, this key combination moves the active cell down to the end of that occupied range. If the active cell is at the end of a range of occupied cells, or if the active cell is unoccupied, this moves it down to the next occupied range. This is identical in effect to the action of the arrow key in end mode.
`PrtSc`	Sends a snapshot of the screen to the *Clipboard*, a temporary storage place common to all Windows applications. This snapshot can then be *pasted* to (inserted in) other Windows applications, such as Word for Windows or Paintbrush.

Windows menu commands are accessed by pressing `Alt`, followed by the underlined letters of each menu option (we will not print the underlining in this book, however) or by clicking on the commands with the left mouse button. This book will alternate between mouse and keyboard usage—usually denoted by mouse and keyboard icons in the margin—unless there is a valid reason to explain both methods. When a series of commands is required, they are listed with a | symbol separating them; for example, File | Save As means select the File command, then select the Save As command. Feel free to substitute mouse movements for keyboard commands, and vice versa, to learn both methods as you complete the Guided Activities and Exercises.

The Mouse

As a Windows application, Excel makes very extensive use of a mouse. Our experience reveals that students have widely varying reactions to using a mouse for the first time. Although you can duplicate most Excel functions with the keyboard, you will find Windows applications much easier to use if you invest the effort necessary to become proficient in using a mouse.

Mouse Terminology

Several terms are used to describe different mouse activities, each of which has a special function and will produce a specific result.

Click or point-and-click means to point the mouse cursor at a particular object on the screen and press the left mouse button. This generally has the effect of selecting the item.

Right-click means to point the mouse cursor at an object and press the right mouse button. This generally has the effect of calling up a menu of commands that are specific to that object.

NOTE *The center mouse button, if your mouse has one, has no effect in Excel.*

Double-click means to point the mouse cursor at an object and press the left mouse button twice within a second without moving the mouse. (The speed necessary to effect a double-click is adjustable in the Windows Control Panel.) This generally has the effect of selecting the item and pressing [Enter].

Drag means to point the cursor at an object, press the left mouse button, move the cursor to another place on the screen while holding the left mouse button down, and then let go of the button. One common use of dragging in Excel is to select a range of cells.

NOTE *If you are left-handed, the mouse can be configured so that the right button is the primary one. This is accomplished through the Windows Control Panel | Mouse command. This book will use the term left mouse button to refer to the button configured as the primary button.*

Mouse Cursor Shapes

Carefully observing the *mouse cursor* will provide a wealth of information about the current status of Excel. The common cursor shapes discussed below indicate the status of the object that the mouse is over and, many times, tell what Excel is doing or can do with the object.

The most common shape of the mouse cursor is an arrow pointing up and left. The mouse is now in *selection mode*. In Excel, the mouse cursor will take this shape when it is on the menu bar, the toolbar, the scroll bars, and other areas of the window. (See Unit 2 for a discussion of the Excel window.)

When the mouse cursor is moved into an Excel worksheet, it will take the shape of a cross. The mouse is now in *cell mode*. The mouse can be used to select a cell or range of cells.

When the computer is busy calculating or performing disk activity, the mouse cursor will take the shape of an hourglass. You must wait until the computer is done before you can continue.

If you move the mouse cursor between the column or row labels, or to the border of a window, the cursor will take the shape of a two-headed arrow. The mouse is now in *sizing mode*. You can use a dragging technique to change the width of columns, the height of rows, or the size of windows.

Whenever you select one of the graphical item icons on the toolbar, or select the fill handle of a cell, the cursor will take the shape of crosshairs. The graphical item is drawn by dragging the mouse through the area to be covered by the graphic.

The last mouse cursor shape you will see in Excel is the I-beam. You will see this shape if you place the cursor in the formula bar. The mouse is now in *edit mode*. It is easy to insert this mouse cursor between two letters or numbers to edit an entry or formula.

Windows and Dialog Boxes

The Windows Program Manager, illustrated in Figure 1.2, is designed to make the complex syntax and command lines of DOS (disk operating system) as simple as "point-and-click." However, as simple as Windows is to manage, you must have a basic familiarity with the elements of a window. Notice, in Figure 1.2, that every window has a border, a title bar, a Control Menu box, a Minimize button, and either a Maximize or a Restore button. Each of these features provides a function to the window.

You can resize the window by dragging the *border*.

You can move the window by dragging the *title bar*.

You can reduce the window to a small icon by clicking the *Minimize button*.

You can cause the window to fill the screen by clicking the *Maximize button*. This button is available only when the window is not maximized.

You can restore the window to its original size by clicking the *Restore button*. This button is available only when the window is maximized.

You can call up a Control menu to perform all of these functions by clicking on the *Control Menu box*.

You can access hidden parts of a window by clicking the *scroll bar*. You can make fine adjustments by clicking on the arrows at either end of the scroll bar, or make larger adjustments by clicking on the scroll bar itself. You can make adjustments relative to the window size by dragging the *scroll box* (the button next to the arrow at the left of the illustration). Scroll bars can be both horizontal and vertical.

Two Types of Windows

Throughout this book we will refer to various types of windows. The two most important types are application windows and document windows. Other types of windows are variations on these. An *application window* contains a program, such as Excel or Word. A *document window* contains a specific workbook in Excel, a document file in Word, and so on. Excel, like many Windows applications, allows you to work with more than one document (workbook) at once. The *program group* windows (for example, Main) in the Program Manager are also classified as document windows.

Using Dialog Boxes

A *dialog box* is the standard Windows method of communicating with the user. Many commands require additional information; a dialog box is a way of requesting the needed information and relaying that information back to the application. Figure 1.3 shows a sample dialog box (Excel's Tools | Options dialog box), which illustrates most of the types of controls that you will find in a dialog box.

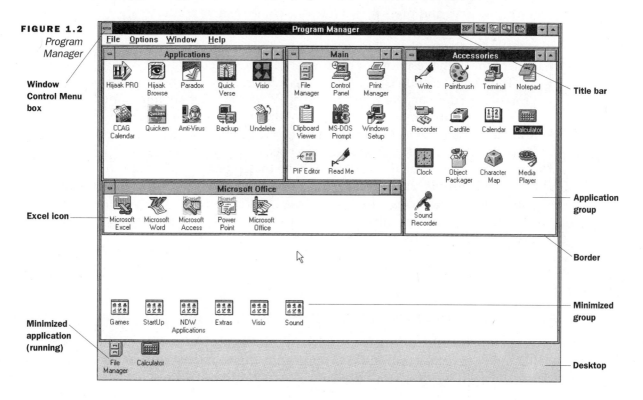

FIGURE 1.2 Program Manager

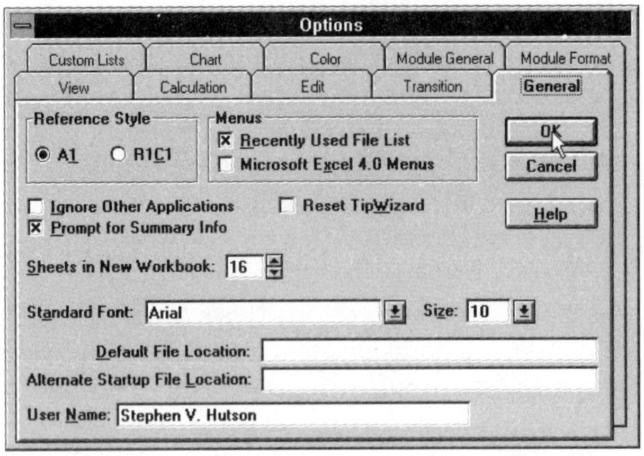

FIGURE 1.3
Sample dialog box

The tabs at the top of the dialog box give it the appearance of an index card file. Concentrating the information in each dialog box allows Excel to have more features without overloading the main menu. If you are working from the keyboard, press [Ctrl][Tab] to move from one card to another. Press [Tab] to move from one control to another within the same card.

The Reference Style section of this dialog box contains **radio buttons** (also called option buttons). These provide a list of *mutually exclusive* choices; one and only one of the selections can be chosen.

The Standard Font and Size options contain **drop-down list boxes**. Clicking on the arrow beside the box (or pressing [Ctrl][↓] from the keyboard) causes a list of choices to be presented. Click on the desired selection, or position the highlight with the arrow keys and press [Enter]. Only one choice can be made.

The File Location and User Name sections contain **text boxes**. Type the desired response in the text box. Text boxes can be linked to list boxes; in these cases, you can either type in the response or choose it from the list box.

The Menus section is a group of **check boxes**. The Ignore Other Applications, Prompt for Summary Info, and Reset TipWizard choices are ungrouped check boxes. In both cases, you may select as many of these as you wish by clicking in the box; an X in the check box means that the item is selected. Click again to deselect an item. From the keyboard, select or deselect a check box by pressing [Spacebar].

The buttons along the right side of the dialog box (OK, Cancel, and Help) are **command buttons**. OK closes the dialog box and sends the responses back to the application. Cancel closes the dialog box, ignoring any changes you may have made, and cancels whatever command opened the dialog box. Help opens a Help window that explains the choices in the dialog box.

GUIDED ACTIVITY 1.1

Starting Windows and the Program Manager

Point-and-click only works with a mouse. Because it is always wise to know at least two ways to accomplish a desired goal, this Guided Activity shows how to navigate through the Program Manager *without* the aid of a mouse.

The procedure for starting Windows varies from place to place, and perhaps from computer to computer. In this Guided Activity, we discuss a typical procedure for hard disk and network systems; if necessary, your instructor will describe any differences for your particular school or organization. To start Windows, you need a computer that has Windows installed on the hard disk or network.[2] When you get ready to save your work, you will need a formatted disk to hold the files you create.

1. Reset or turn on the machine, as appropriate. Remember to enter the date and time, if prompted.

2. Type WIN and then press [Enter] to load Windows. The Program Manager should be the active window on the display (see Figure 1.2). When you start Windows, there will normally be at least three application groups (Main, Accessories, and Games) on the screen. These may be open windows or minimized. One of the program groups will be the active program group, usually denoted by a different color title bar and border.

3. To move from one window to another, press [Ctrl][Tab]. Notice that the title bars and/or borders change color to indicate the active window.

4. To access the window Control menu for the active program group, press [Alt][-] (hyphen). If the current active window is maximized or minimized, restore it to normal size by pressing [R] for Restore. If the window is already normal sized, minimize it by pressing [N]. Note that the N is underscored in the Control | Minimize command name.

5. Access the window Control menu again, and maximize the window by pressing [X] for Maximize. Finally, access the window Control menu one more time, and give the necessary command to restore the window to its original state.

6. Exit Windows by pressing [Alt][F], [X] (File | Exit Windows). When you see the Exit Windows dialog box, press [Enter] to complete the action.

GUIDED ACTIVITY 1.2

Touring Windows Using the Mouse

At this point, you should be looking at the DOS prompt (A:> or C:>). If you do not have a mouse or prefer to use the keyboard, skip to Guided Activity 1.3.

1. Follow the instructions in Guided Activity 1.1 to load Windows.[3]

2. Click on the title bars of various windows. Notice that each window becomes the active window, just as when you pressed [Ctrl][Tab] earlier. Move the windows around the screen by dragging their title bars.

---

2 If your copy of Windows has not been installed, read the Microsoft Windows *User's Guide* booklet that is in the Windows package. Installation is normally performed by the person who owns or is responsible for the software.

3 If your copy of Excel has not been installed, read Chapter 1 of the *User's Guide* that is in the Excel package. Installation is normally performed by the person who owns or is responsible for the software.

3. Click on one of the words on the menu bar at the top of the screen. You will see the various drop-down menus and the options within them. Similar functions are grouped together. Certain menu options are followed by an ellipsis (…); this is your cue that selecting that option will bring up a dialog box. Clicking on an option without an ellipsis will immediately perform that function. Other options may be "grayed out." These options are unavailable, generally because they need some object selected before they can function.

4. Move the mouse cursor to the border of a window. The cursor will change to a double arrow. Drag the border inward and then outward to resize the window. Move the cursor to the corner of the window. As you drag the border, notice that you can resize the window both in height and width.

5. During this step, you will open the Excel application and minimize it, then size the Program Manager so that you can see minimized applications. Next, you will examine a typical Excel dialog box. Finally, you will alternate between the Program Manager and Excel, then close Excel.

   a. Activate the program group containing Excel. (By default, this icon is placed in a group named Microsoft Office, as shown in Figure 1.4; however, it may be in a group with a name like Excel or Windows Applications.) If the program group is minimized, restore it by double-clicking on it. Open Excel by double-clicking on it. Notice that it resides in its own window on top of the Program Manager. Minimize Excel by clicking the Minimize button.

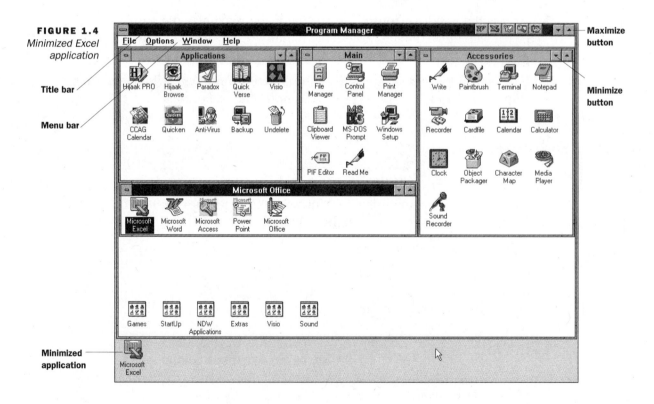

FIGURE 1.4
Minimized Excel application

    b. If the Program Manager is maximized, click the Restore button. Resize the Program Manager window so that about one inch of the desktop is showing at the bottom of the screen. Your screen should look like Figure 1.4.

    c. Double-click on the Excel icon to bring it to the forefront. Notice that it occupies the same size and position as it did before minimizing.

    d. Click on Edit | Find (or press [Alt][E], [F]). The dialog box you are looking at has several of the common features of a dialog box. It contains a text box that allows you to type information needed by the command. The check box labeled Match Case gives you the option of only finding words that match the capitalization of the word(s) in the Find What text box. The check box labeled Find Entire Cells Only lets you prevent Excel from finding cells that contain text in addition to what is in the Find What text box. The Search and Look in list boxes let you determine how and where Excel will search for your requested text. There are also four command buttons—one labeled Find Next to accept the choices and execute the command, one labeled Close to leave the command without executing it, one labeled Replace to change the dialog box to the Edit Replace dialog box, and one labeled Help to open a Help window concerning this command. Now that you have seen a sample dialog box and its contents, click on Close to prevent making any unwanted changes.

    e. Now, to close Excel, click on File, then on Exit. If you typed anything in Excel, you will see a window asking whether you want to save the changes. Click No.

6. To the right of the title bar in the active program group are two buttons: one is a down-pointing arrow, and the other is either an up-pointing arrow or a double arrow, depending on whether or not the program group window is already maximized. These are the Minimize, and Maximize or Restore buttons. If the program group window is maximized, the arrow at the far right will be a double arrow (the Restore button); clicking on it will restore it to its standard size. If the program group is already at its standard size, the far-right arrow will be a single arrow pointing up. Clicking on this Maximize button will cause the program group to fill the entire screen. Clicking on the Minimize button will reduce the program group to a small icon at the bottom of the Program Manager window. Double-clicking on an icon will restore it to a window. Try experimenting with all the possible combinations.

7. Drag the title bar of one of the program groups to where part of the window is hidden on the upper-left portion of the screen. Scroll bars will appear on the right and lower portions of the screen. These scroll bars are navigational aids that are used consistently throughout all Windows applications. They can be used in three ways:

    a. Click on the arrows at the ends of the scroll bar. The window will move one line up, down, left, or right. This movement is identical to pressing the keyboard arrow keys.

b. Click on the scroll bar beside any scroll box. The window will move one screen up, down, left, or right. This movement is identical to pressing [PgUp] or [PgDn] when [Scroll Lock] is pressed. However, the scroll bars give you the added versatility of moving the workbook horizontally.

c. Drag the scroll box to any place on the scroll bar. The window will move proportionally to where the scroll box is placed on the scroll bar.

Once you learn the proper use of the scroll bars, they will rapidly become an indispensable method of navigating through any Windows application.

8. If you are not continuing on to the next Guided Activity, exit Windows by clicking on File | Exit. Click OK when you see the Exit Windows dialog box.

GUIDED ACTIVITY 1.3

Touring Windows Using the Keyboard

At this point, you should be looking at the DOS prompt (A:> or C:>).

1. Follow the instructions in Guided Activity 1.1 to load Windows.

2. Move the windows around the screen by giving the Move command from the application Control menu. To do this, press [Alt][-] (hyphen), [M]. The cursor will become a cross with arrowheads. Press the arrow key pointing in the direction you want to move the window. Each press of the arrow key will move the window a distance determined by your settings in the Windows Control Panel. Press [Enter] to complete the move. Note that if the window is maximized (occupying the full screen), the Move command will be "grayed out" (unavailable).

3. Access the menu by pressing [Alt]. You can then drop down the menu by pressing the underlined letter in the menu item's name. *Note that the underlined character is not always the first letter of the name.* You can press [Alt] *either* in combination with the first letter of the menu item *or* as a sequence. After the desired menu has dropped down, simply press the underlined letter of the command you wish to select. For example, [Alt][F], [X] will exit Windows. You can press [Alt] at the same time as the [F], or you may press [Alt], then [F], then [X].

4. Resize a window by invoking the Size command from the window Control menu. Press the arrow key that is pointing toward the side of the window that you want to change. Then press the arrow key that points in the direction that you want to move it. For example, if you want to make a window smaller by bringing in the right side, press [→] once; then press [←] until the right side of the window is where you want it to be. Press [Enter] to stop sizing the window.

5. During this step, you will open the Excel application and minimize it, then size the Program Manager so that you can see minimized applications. Next, you will examine a typical Excel dialog box. Finally, you will alternate between the Program Manager and Excel, then close Excel.

a. Move between windows by pressing [Ctrl][Tab]. When you reach the program group containing Excel (usually Microsoft Office, but it may be something like Excel or Windows Applications), move within the program group by pressing the arrow keys. When Excel is highlighted, press [Enter] to start the application. Minimize it by pressing [Alt][Spacebar] to access the application Control menu and then pressing [N] to give the Minimize command.

b. If the Program Manager is maximized, press [Alt][Spacebar], then [R], to restore the window size. Then resize the Program Manager window so that about one inch of the desktop is showing at the bottom of the screen. Do this by pressing [Alt][Spacebar], then [S]. Notice the change in the shape of the cursor. Press [↓] to indicate that you are going to size the lower border, then press [↑] about eight times to achieve the desired size. Press [Enter] to accept the size change. Your screen should look like Figure 1.4.

c. Press [Alt][Tab] to change to Excel. Hold [Alt] and press [Tab] until the Excel icon and "Microsoft Excel" appear in the panel in the middle of the screen. Release [Alt] when the application you want appears.

NOTE *This is a very valuable keyboard shortcut. You can quickly change between applications by holding down [Alt] and then repeatedly pressing [Tab] until the desired application comes to the forefront.*

d. Press [Alt][E], [F] to give the Edit | Find command. The dialog box you are looking at has several of the common features of a dialog box. It contains a text box that allows you to type information needed by the command. The check box labeled Match Case gives you the option of only finding words that match the capitalization of the word(s) in the Find What text box. The check box labeled Find Entire Cells Only lets you prevent Excel from finding cells that contain text in addition to what is in the Find What text box. The Search and Look in list boxes let you determine how and where Excel will search for your requested text. There are also four command buttons—one labeled Find Next to accept the choices and execute the command, one labeled Close to leave the command without executing it, one labeled Replace to change the dialog box to the Edit Replace dialog box, and one labeled Help to open a Help window concerning this command. Now that you have seen a sample dialog box and its contents, click on Close to prevent making any unwanted changes.

e. To close Excel from the keyboard, press [Alt][F], [X]. If you typed anything in Excel, you will see a window asking whether you want to save the changes. Press [N].

6. On the keyboard, the Minimize, Maximize, and Restore commands are available from the application Control menu. Access this menu by pressing [Alt][-] (hyphen). A very useful shortcut is mentioned in the preceding note: the [Alt][Tab] combination will toggle between all open windows, whether normal size, maximized, or minimized. When you release [Alt], the program that appears in the panel in the center of the screen will be restored and will become the active window.

18 PART ONE FUNDAMENTAL SPREADSHEET OPERATIONS

7. If you are not continuing on to the next Guided Activity, exit from Windows by pressing [Alt][F], [X]. When you see the Exit Windows dialog box, press [Enter].

GUIDED ACTIVITY 1.4

Starting Excel Using the Mouse

This Guided Activity introduces you to Microsoft Excel.

1. If you are not continuing from Guided Activity 1.2, open Windows as described in Guided Activity 1.1. Click on the program group containing Excel, as shown in Figure 1.5. If this group is minimized, double-click to restore it. Double-click on the Excel icon.

2. As the program is loading, you will see the copyright screen.

3. Next, you see an empty Excel workbook, as shown in Figure 1.6—you are in a *workbook window*. Cell A1 is highlighted by a thick border. In Excel, there are three cursors: one in the formula bar that shows where you are making an entry, a mouse cursor that allows you to choose menu items and perform other navigation chores, and a third cursor in the workbook window that shows which cell is active. The latter cursor is also called the *active cell*.

4. Press the arrow keys to move the active cell around the workbook. Note that you cannot move up from row 1 or left from column A.

5. Press [Ctrl][Home]. The active cell should be cell A1.

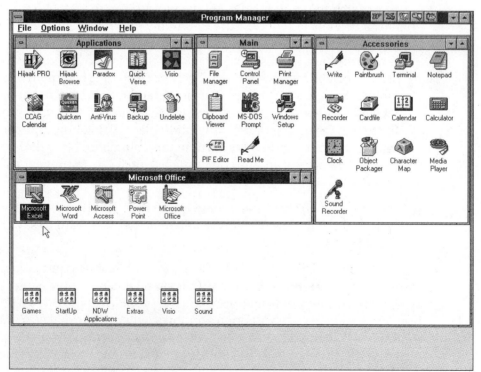

FIGURE 1.5
Program Manager with Excel selected

FIGURE 1.6
Excel window

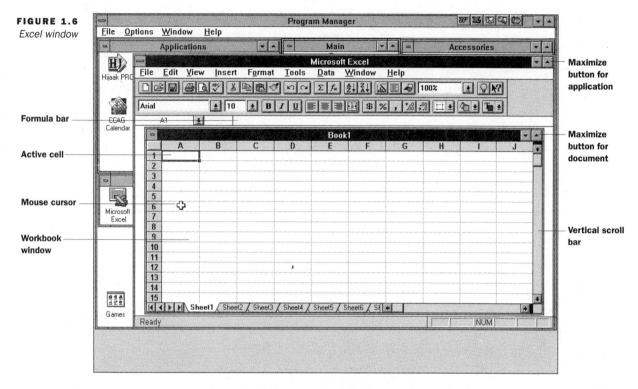

6. Press and hold [↓]. Notice that when the active cell moves below the lowest visible row, other rows scroll into view. Release the arrow key.

7. Click on the scroll bar beneath the scroll box. This should cause the display to jump down about 18 rows (in a maximized window).[4] (It has the same effect as pressing [PgDn].)

8. Press [End][→]. The active cell should remain in the same row but move all the way to column IV. Press [Ctrl][Home] to return to cell A1.

9. Press [Ctrl][→]. Press [Ctrl][↓]. The active cell should move to cell IV16384. You are at the extreme lower-right corner of the worksheet.

10. Press the arrow keys to move the active cell around the worksheet. Note that you cannot move down from row 16384 or right from column IV.

11. Move the active cell back to cell A1.

CHECKPOINT 1A What keys do you press to move quickly to cell A1?
The answers to checkpoint questions are contained in Appendix A.

12. Depending on how Excel has been configured, it may not fill the screen when it is first opened. If it does not fill the screen, there will be an arrow pointing upward in the upper-right corner of the application window. If the window is already maximized, the button will be a double arrow pointing up and down. In the

---

4 Some computer systems display more or fewer than 20 rows at a time. Clicking the scroll bar or pressing [PgDn] should take you down a full page.

FIGURE 1.7
Maximized Excel application and document windows

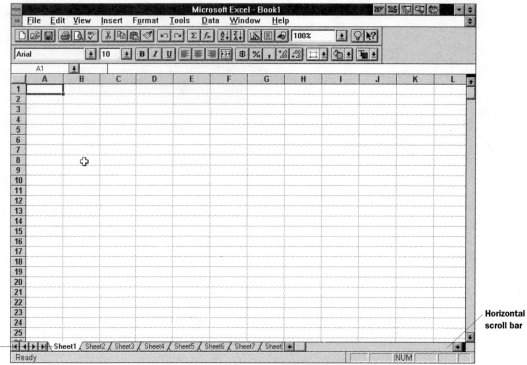

Sheet tabs

Horizontal scroll bar

latter case, it will not be necessary to perform this step. Click on the application Maximize button. Note that this is the button for the application, not the document window.

13. When Excel is opened, the document window (Book1) does not quite fill the application area. Click on the document Maximize button. This is the up-pointing arrow in the upper-right corner of Book1. However you do it, your screen should now look like Figure 1.7. Notice that the application title bar now includes the "Book1" designation, and that the document Maximize button has changed to a Restore button and is now positioned at the far right end of the menu bar.

14. Click on the document Restore button. This is the double arrow beneath the application sizing buttons.

CHECKPOINT 1B How does the size of the window compare to when Excel was first opened?

15. By default, there are 16 blank sheets in a new Excel workbook. (We discuss how to change this default in a later unit.) Click on various sheet tabs (located at the lower-left portion of the document window) to change to other sheets. To view tabs that are not visible, use the arrows left of the sheet tabs. The first arrow brings the tab for Sheet1 into view. The second arrow moves the tabs to one lower number (unless the tab for Sheet1 is already visible). The third arrow moves the tabs to one higher number (unless the last sheet tab is already visible). The fourth and last arrow brings the tab for the last sheet (usually Sheet16) into view.

16. We discuss how to use the workbook in the next unit. At this time, exit from Excel to Windows by choosing File | Exit with the mouse.

NOTE *You might have inadvertently made entries in the workbook. If Excel presents a dialog box asking whether you wish to save changes, click No.*

GUIDED ACTIVITY 1.5

Starting Excel Using the Keyboard

This Guided Activity introduces you to Microsoft Excel.

1. If you are not continuing from Guided Activity 1.3, open Windows as described in Guided Activity 1.1. Press [Ctrl][Tab] until the program group containing Excel is the active group, as shown in Figure 1.5. This group is usually Microsoft Office, but may be called Windows Applications, or sometimes Excel. If the group is minimized, press [Enter] to restore it. Use the arrow keys to highlight the Excel icon. Press [Enter].

2. As the program is loading, you will see the copyright screen.

3. Next, you see an empty Excel workbook, as shown in Figure 1.6—you are in a *workbook window*. Cell A1 is highlighted by a thick border. In Excel, there are three cursors: one in the formula bar that shows where you are making an entry, a mouse cursor that allows you to choose menu items and perform other navigation chores, and a third cursor in the workbook window that shows which cell is active. The latter cursor is also called the *active cell*.

4. Press the arrow keys to move the active cell around the workbook. Note that you cannot move up from row 1 or left from column A.

5. Press [Ctrl][Home]. The active cell should be cell A1.

6. Press and hold [↓]. Notice that when the active cell moves below row 20 (approximately), other rows scroll into view. Release the arrow key.

7. Press [PgDn]. This should cause the display to jump down about 20 rows.

8. Press [End][→]. The active cell should remain in the same row but move all the way to column IV. Press [Ctrl][Home] to return to cell A1.

9. Press [Ctrl][→]. Press [Ctrl][↓]. The active cell should move to cell IV16384. You are at the extreme lower-right corner of the worksheet.

10. Press the arrow keys to move the active cell around the worksheet. Note that you cannot move down from row 16,384 or right from column IV.

11. Move the active cell back to cell A1.

CHECKPOINT 1A What keys do you press to move quickly to cell A1?
The answers to checkpoint questions are contained in Appendix A.

12. Depending on how Excel has been configured, it may not fill the screen when it is first opened. If it does not fill the screen there will be an arrow pointing upward in the upper-right corner of the application window. If the window is already maximized, the button will be a double arrow pointing up and down. In the latter case, it will not be necessary to perform this step. Press [Alt][Spacebar], [X] to maximize the application window.

13. When Excel is opened, the document window (Book1) does not quite fill the application area. Press [Alt][-], [X] to maximize the document window. However you do it, your screen should now look like Figure 1.7. Notice that the application title bar now includes the "Book1" designation, and that the document Maximize button has changed to a Restore button and is now positioned at the far right end of the menu bar.

14. Press [Alt][-], [R] to restore the document window.

CHECKPOINT 1B How does the size of the window compare to when Excel was first opened?

15. We discuss how to use the workbook in the next unit. At this time, exit from Excel to Windows by pressing the following sequence of keys: [Alt][F], [X].

NOTE *You might have inadvertently made entries in the workbook. If Excel presents a dialog box asking whether you wish to save changes, press [N].*

File Manager

As the Program Manager provides a point-and-click interface for launching applications, the File Manager is another application within the Windows environment that provides a point-and-click interface for managing files. You will find the File Manager convenient for

- Finding files
- Renaming files
- Deleting files
- Copying files
- Determining file information, such as size and date
- Creating directories
- Formatting disks
- Copying disks
- Determining disk information, such as size and available space

When you start the File Manager by double-clicking on its icon in the Program Manager, you will see a window similar to the one in Figure 1.8. Your directory listing will be different and you may not have the Tools and Norton entries in the menu bar.

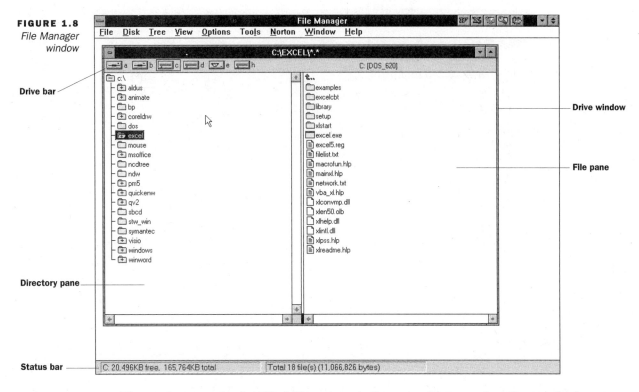

FIGURE 1.8 File Manager window

The main items in the File Manager window are the menu bar, from which you can select the various commands available; the drive window, which is divided into the drive bar, the directory pane, and the file pane; and the status bar, which provides information about the current drive. The drive window in Figure 1.8 shows six drives attached to the computer. The different drive icons represent different types of drives; drives A: and B: are floppy drives; drives C:, D:, and H: are hard drives (sometimes known as fixed disks); and drive E: is a CD-ROM drive.

The directory pane uses file folders to represent the various directories on a drive. File folders with plus signs indicate that subdirectories exist under that directory. If the plus signs do not appear in your copy of File Manager, click on the Tree | Indicate Expandable Branches command to make them visible. The File Manager uses an open file folder to represent the directory that is currently selected, such as the EXCEL directory in Figure 1.8.

The file pane also uses different icons to represent different types of files. Again, the file folder represents subdirectories. The icon for the file EXCEL.EXE represents an executable file, that is, a program file. The icon for the file EXCEL5.REG represents a document file. The icon for the file XLCONVMP.DLL represents a generic (unknown) file type. To view all the information available about the files on a certain disk, give the View | All File Details command, illustrated in Figure 1.9. The additional information includes the file size, the date and time the file was last modified, and any file attributes that apply to those files.

To access the various menu items in the File Manager, simply click on the item names with the mouse; or from the keyboard, press the [Alt] key, followed by the underlined letter of the item's name. To view a different drive in the same window, click on the drive's icon; or from the keyboard, press [Alt][D], [S] to open the Select

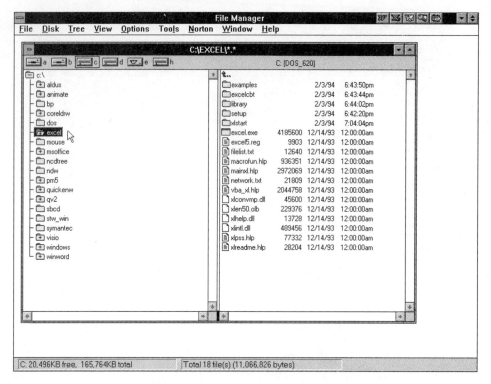

FIGURE 1.9
File Manager after selecting View | All File Details

Drive window, then use the arrow keys to select the desired drive and press [Enter]. To open a new drive window, double-click on the desired drive's icon; or from the keyboard, press [Alt][W], [N] to open a new window and use the Disk | Select Drive command to select the desired drive. To view both drive windows at once, click on the Window | Tile command with the mouse; or from the keyboard, press [Shift][F4].

GUIDED ACTIVITY 1.6

Using the File Manager

In this Guided Activity you will use the File Manager to accomplish common disk and file management tasks. You will need to perform many of these tasks in order to complete the assignments contained in this manual. For this activity, you need two *blank* (formatted or unformatted) disks that are compatible with your computer.

1. Start the File Manager by double-clicking on its icon, probably contained in the Main program group. Your screen should look similar to Figure 1.8, although you will have a different directory listing, and probably a different selected directory.

2. In this step, you format a blank disk.

   a. In the menu bar, click on Disk. The following menu will display.

b. Click on Format Disk. The following dialog box will display.

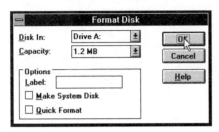

c. Your instructor will assist you in making the proper selections in the Disk In and Capacity drop-down list boxes.

d. Click in the Label box and type Data_Disk.

e. Click OK. The following dialog box will display.

f. Click Yes. The following dialog box will display.

g. When the formatting operation is complete, the following dialog box will display.

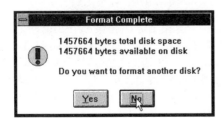

h. Click No. Click on the drive icon for the disk being formatted. The file pane should contain the phrase "No files found," and the status bar should show the capacity of the disk you formatted with the entire capacity as free space.

FIGURE 1.10
File Manager with tiled windows

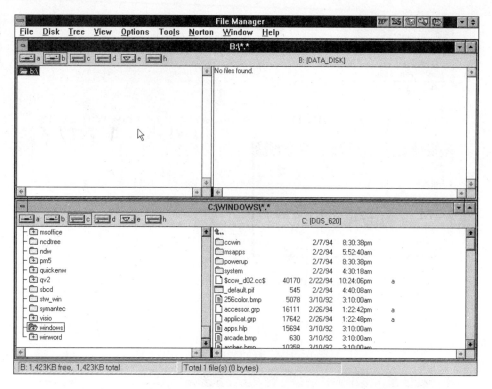

3. In this step, you copy files from the hard disk to the floppy disk you just formatted.

   a. Click on the icon for the drive where Windows is installed. Your instructor will inform you of the correct drive name. Click on the Windows directory. To see more information about the files in this directory, click on the View | All File Details command.

   b. Click in the center of the scroll bar several times until the CONTROL.EXE file is visible.

CHECKPOINT 1C What is the size (in bytes) of the CONTROL.EXE file?

   c. Open a new drive window for the disk you just formatted by clicking on its drive icon. Make both windows visible by clicking on the Window | Tile command. Your screen should look similar to Figure 1.10.

   d. Select the Windows drive by clicking in the directory pane of that window. If necessary, scroll back to the CONTROL.EXE file and select it by clicking on it. Extend the selection to include CONTROL.HLP and CONTROL.INI by holding down the [Shift] key and clicking on CONTROL.INI.[5] These three files are used by Windows to create the Control Panel program. Your drive window should look similar to this:

---

5 If the files are not located together, give the View | Sort command and select By Name.

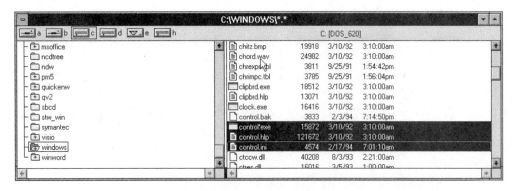

e. Copy the files to the newly formatted disk by clicking anywhere within the highlighted region, holding down the mouse button, dragging it to the directory pane of the drive window for the newly formatted disk, and releasing the button. This procedure is called drag-and-drop. The following dialog box will display.

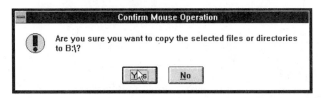

f. Click Yes. You will see a dialog box that shows you the progress of the copy operation. Once it is complete, your B: drive window should look like the following illustration. The files on the floppy disk are now identical to the files contained on the hard disk or the network drive where Windows is located.

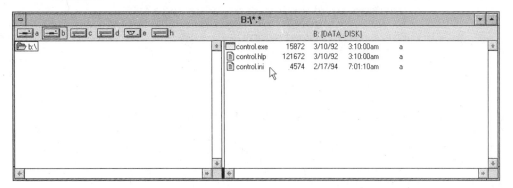

4. In this step, you make an exact duplicate of the floppy disk containing the Control Panel files.

   a. Click on the Disk | Copy Disk command. The following dialog box will display.

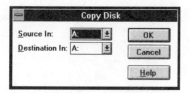

b. Choose either the A: or B: drive for both the Source In and Destination In drop-down list boxes, depending on the floppy disk drive that you have been using. Click OK. The following dialog box will display.

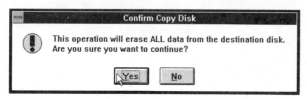

c. Click on Yes. The following dialog box will display.

d. Click OK. You will see a dialog box named "Copying Disk" informing you of the progress of the Copy command. When the source disk has been completely read, the Copying Disk dialog box will show approximately 50% complete, and a new dialog box will display requesting you to insert the destination disk. Change to the destination disk and click OK. The Copying Disk dialog box will then continue on to 100%.

e. You now have an exact duplicate of the floppy disk containing the Control Panel files.

5. Click File | Exit to close the File Manager and return to the Program Manager. Click File | Exit Windows to close the Program Manager and return to the operating system. Click OK when you see the dialog box confirming that you are exiting Windows.

Launching Excel from DOS

For those who are more familiar with DOS, it is possible to launch Excel from the DOS command line (C:>) by simply typing `excel`.[6] The effect is the same as loading Windows, selecting the Options | Minimize on Use command in the Program Manager, and then launching Excel from the Program Manager.

---

6 The instructions assume that a PATH statement is included in the AUTOEXEC.BAT file pointing to C:\EXCEL or other appropriate directory in both hard disk and network systems.

The next unit discusses how to enter data and perform calculations on the workbook.

Review Questions

The answers to questions marked with an asterisk are contained in Appendix A.

1. Describe how Excel uses the following keyboard keys:
   - a. [F1]
   - b. [F2]
   - *c. [F5]
   - d. [Home]
   - *e. [PgUp]
   - f. [Esc]
   - g. [Del]
   - *h. [Backspace]

2. Where is the mouse cursor located when it takes each of the following shapes?
   - a. Crosshairs
   - *b. Pointer
   - *c. Cross
   - d. I-beam
   - *e. Double arrow

3. Describe the function of each of the following parts of a window:
   - a. Title bar
   - *b. Scroll bar
   - c. Border
   - *d. Minimize button
   - *e. Maximize button

4. How can you bypass Windows and load Excel directly?

Key Terms

The following terms are introduced in this unit. Be sure you know what each of them means.

Active cell	Double-click	Restore button
Application window	Drag	Right-click
Border	Drop-down list box	Scroll bar
Cell mode	Edit mode	Scroll box
Check box	End mode	Selection mode
Click	Maximize button	Sizing mode
Clipboard	Minimize button	Text box
Command button	Mouse cursor	Title bar
Control Menu box	Paste	Workbook window
Dialog box	Program group	
Document window	Radio button	

Documentation Research

Documentation Research sections like this are at the end of most units. The Microsoft Excel Version 5 documentation is contained in one major book and several smaller books. The major book, titled *User's Guide,* contains explanations of all Excel commands. One of the most useful skills you can develop in this course is the ability to use the documentation supplied by the software manufacturer. If your school or organization makes that documentation available for your use, then use it to determine the answers to the following questions.

1. How much system memory do you need to run Excel?

2. Where would you find the sample files included with Excel?

3. How do you keep Help instructions visible while you carry them out?

The Excel Workbook

This unit takes you into the workbook, where the value of Excel is realized. The major topics include an introduction to the spreadsheet concept, a discussion of entering and editing information in the workbook, and an introduction to Excel commands. Also, the important concept of file backup is introduced.

Learning Objectives

At the completion of this unit you should know

1. the function of each component of the Excel window;
2. the function of the tools on the Standard and Formatting toolbars;
3. what a cell is;
4. the differences among text, formulas, and constant values;
5. how to determine a cell's reference;
6. the dimensions of the Excel workbook;
7. what the pointing method is.

At the completion of this unit you should be able to

1. determine whether or not any of the Lock keys are engaged,
2. enter text into a worksheet cell,
3. enter a constant value into a worksheet cell,
4. enter a formula into a worksheet cell,

5. edit the contents of a worksheet cell,
6. save a file to disk,
7. open a file from disk,
8. name a sheet,
9. back up the files on a data disk,
10. exit to Windows.

Important Commands

File | Exit

File | Open

File | Save

File | Save As

The Spreadsheet Concept

You might have heard the terms "spreadsheet" and "worksheet" and wondered if there is a difference between them. In most uses, there is no difference and the terms are interchangeable. To remain consistent with the terminology used by Microsoft and other publishers, however, we will use the term *worksheet* to refer to a row-and-column matrix and the term *spreadsheet* to refer to this type of computer application. We will use the term *workbook* to refer to the book of pages that is the standard Excel document. These pages can contain worksheets, charts, or macro modules. We discuss each of these page types in later units. *Workbook file* refers to the disk file that is used to save data and other information about the workbook.

Cells

The worksheet *cell* is the building block of Excel or any other spreadsheet program. There is a cell at the intersection of each row and column. A cell can contain a value, a formula, or a text entry.

Text entries are used to explain the contents of the workbook and are primarily for user information, although they can be used in some formulas.

Value entries can be one of two types, either constant values or formulas. The value of a formula changes when the *arguments* (components) of the formula change; by contrast, the value of a constant value does not change unless you put a new value into that cell. The great appeal of spreadsheet programs is the ability to change one value and watch all other values that depend on the first value (via formulas) automatically change when the spreadsheet is recalculated.

Rows, Columns, and Sheets

The Excel worksheet contains 16,384 *rows* that extend down the worksheet, numbered 1 through 16384.

The Excel worksheet contains 256 *columns* that extend across the worksheet, lettered A through Z, AA through AZ, BA through BZ, and so on, through IV.

The Excel workbook can contain as many as 256 *sheets*, labeled Sheet1 through Sheet256. The initial number of sheets in a workbook, which can be changed by the user, is 16. You can change the sheet label by double-clicking on the tab containing the sheet label and entering a new label.

Cell References

Cell references are the combination of column letter and row number. The upper-left cell is A1, while the extreme lower-right cell is IV16384. Notice how cell D5 is related to D4, D6, C5, and E5:

C4	D4	E4
C5	D5	E5
C6	D6	E6

Excel Window Tour

Most of the screen is devoted to the display of the workbook, shown in Figure 2.1. Twenty-five rows and twelve columns are displayed when the window is maximized on the author's Super VGA display; you might see more or less on your display.

Title Bar

At the top of the screen is the title bar. The title bar not only provides the name of the window but, as you learned in Unit 1, also provides a means of moving the window from one portion of the screen to another. To the left of the title bar is the application Control Menu box. On the far right are two buttons: the arrow pointing downward is the Minimize button (clicking the button will reduce the window to a small icon at the bottom of the screen); the shape and function of the other arrow depend on the current status of the window. If the window is currently maximized (as in Figure 2.1), two arrows point up and down and the button is referred to as the Restore button; clicking on the button will restore the window to its previous size (before maximizing). If the window is not already maximized, the arrow points upward only, and is the Maximize button.

The small icons displayed on the right half of the title bar are part of the Microsoft Office Manager. If your organization purchased Excel as part of the Microsoft Office package, you may have a similar group of icons on your display. You simply click on one of the icons to start (or switch to) each of these applications. In Figure 2.1, the icons represent, in order, Word for Windows, Excel, PowerPoint, Access, and Office Manager.

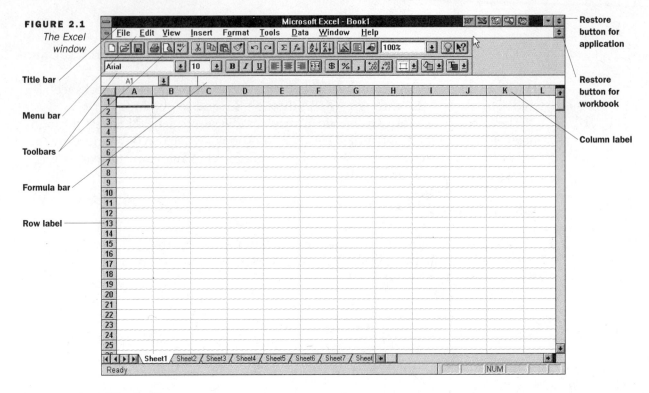

FIGURE 2.1 The Excel window

Menu Bar

The next line of the window contains the *menu bar*. The menu bar can be activated either by pressing [Alt] and a menu letter, or by clicking on any item on the menu. Either way, a drop-down menu will appear, offering the options under that menu item (if you press [Alt] while there is an open workbook, for example, the File menu will be highlighted). To get out of the menu bar without selecting a command, press the [Esc] key.

Toolbars

The third and fourth lines of the screen contain the Standard and Formatting *toolbars*. Let's examine these toolbars. Don't worry if you do not understand all of the functions discussed; we discuss each of these topics again in later units. If you forget the purpose of a particular tool, place the mouse cursor on the tool, let it rest for a second or two, and Excel will display a small label describing the tool's function. Microsoft, the publisher of Excel, refers to these labels as *ToolTips*.

STANDARD TOOLBAR

The Standard toolbar is a collection of 21 buttons and a drop-down list box that simplify many commonly used tasks to "point and click." The buttons are grouped according to similar functions.

The three buttons in this set deal with common file commands. The New Workbook tool opens a new blank workbook. It has the same effect as giving the File | New command.

The Open tool calls up the File | Open dialog box. It has the same effect as selecting File | Open from the menu.

The Save tool saves a previously saved file under the same name, or calls up the File | Save As dialog box if the file has not been previously saved. It has the same effect as selecting File | Save from the menu.

The three buttons in this set deal with printing. Although all the printing commands are contained in the File menu, they are detached into a separate group because printing is such a crucial function.

The Print tool sends one copy of the entire print area to the default printer. It is similar to the File | Print command.

The Print Preview tool opens the Print Preview window, where you can view a replica of your printout. It has the same effect as giving the File | Print Preview command.

The Spell Check tool checks the spelling of all words in the active worksheet. It has the same effect as selecting Spelling from the Tools menu, (or pressing [F7]).

The next set of four tools deals with the Clipboard. Windows applications use the Clipboard as a temporary holding location to copy and move data from one place to another. We discuss copying and moving in Unit 6.

The Cut tool clears the selected text or range of cells from the worksheet and copies them to the Clipboard. It has the same effect as giving the Edit | Cut command.

The next tool, the Copy tool, copies the selected text or range of cells to the Clipboard. It has the same effect as giving the Edit | Copy command. It differs from the Cut tool in that the selection is not removed from the worksheet.

The Paste tool copies whatever is contained in the Clipboard to the current selection. It has the same effect as giving the Edit | Paste command.

The Format Painter tool copies the formatting of the currently selected range to a new destination that you specify. It has the same effect as giving the Edit | Copy command and then choosing Formats from the Edit | Paste Special command.

These tools allow you to undo and repeat previous commands, respectively. Click on the Undo tool, and a drop-down list displays, allowing you to undo everything since the selected command. Likewise, click on the Repeat tool, and you can repeat everything since the command you select from the drop-down list.

The button labeled with the capital Greek letter sigma (Σ) is the AutoSum tool. Clicking on this tool will write a sum formula in the selected cell. Not only will this function write the sum formula, but it will make a guess at what range of cells you desire to sum, and will leave you in edit mode so that you can correct the sum range or press [Enter] to accept Excel's suggestion.

The second button in this set calls the Function Wizard. We fully discuss the Function Wizard in Unit 3.

The two buttons in this set sort the active selection. The first button sorts the selection in ascending alphabetic order, and the second button sorts in descending order.

The next group of three buttons deals with graphical items on the worksheet. One of the premier features of Excel is its ability to integrate graphics with traditional spreadsheet features.

The ChartWizard tool opens up a ChartWizard window. To use this tool, select the range to be charted, click the tool, then drag a range on the workbook where you want the chart to reside. Then follow the prompts of the ChartWizard. (We will discuss charting in detail in Unit 8.)

The second button allows you to place a text box on the worksheet. A text box is a graphical item that contains text. A text box is very different from entering text in a cell, as the text box does not reside on the worksheet, but on an invisible layer above the worksheet. We discuss graphical items fully in Unit 12.

The third button displays the Drawing toolbar. From this toolbar, you can select tools to draw many different types of graphical items on the worksheet. Again, we discuss this fully in Unit 12.

The Zoom drop-down list box allows you to change the displayed size of the worksheet. By selecting a number greater than 100%, you can see a smaller number of cells in more detail; by selecting a number smaller than 100%, you can see more cells, but in less detail. It has the same effect as selecting Zoom from the View menu.

The last two buttons in the Standard toolbar deal with Help. The first activates the TipWizard, a specialized toolbar containing suggestions to help you use Excel more efficiently. The TipWizard occupies the space below the toolbars, effectively reducing the space on your display allotted to any open workbooks.

The second button is the Context-Sensitive Help tool. Click on this tool and you are rewarded with a large question mark next to your mouse cursor. At this point, you can click on an Excel command or any object on the screen and a Help screen with information about that item will display.

FORMATTING TOOLBAR

The second toolbar that Excel displays by default is the Formatting toolbar, a collection of 12 buttons and 5 drop-down list boxes. Again, they are grouped by similar uses.

The first drop-down list box is the font list. Selecting a font name from this list will apply that font to the current selection.

The second drop-down list box is the font size list. Selecting a size from this list will apply that size to the current selection.

The **B**, *I* and U tools will **bold**, *italicize*, and underline the selected range, respectively.

The next four tools deal with alignment; clicking on the first three buttons will left-justify, center, and right-justify the selection, respectively.

The fourth tool in the group is the Center Across Columns tool. To use this tool, make an entry in a cell, select that cell plus several cells to the right by dragging with the mouse, then click on this tool. The entry in the left cell will be centered across the selected cells. This tool has the same effect as selecting Center across selection on the Format | Cells Alignment tab.

The next five buttons deal with number formats. Excel allows you to display numbers in many different ways. Clicking the first button, the Currency button, causes any numeric entries in the current selection to be displayed with a dollar sign ($). The second button causes numeric entries to be displayed with a percent sign (%). The third button selects a format with commas placed between the thousands, (as in 1,000,000). The last two buttons in this group increase and decrease the number of decimal places displayed, respectively.

 This drop-down list box allows you to apply a border to the selected range. Several buttons allow you many choices as to where the borders will be placed and whether they will be thin or thick, and single or double lines.

 The next drop-down list box allows you to change the interior color of a cell or graphic object. There are 56 different colors from which to choose.

 The last drop-down list box allows you to change the color of text in a selected cell or selected text in a cell or graphic object.

Formula Bar

The next line of the workbook window contains the *formula bar*. The formula bar is activated as soon as you begin typing in a cell. At the far left is the *reference section*, which will show the reference of the active cell. When you are selecting a range, the reference section does double duty, by showing you the size of the selected range. To the right of the reference section is an arrow for a drop-down list. This list allows you to move immediately to named ranges on the worksheet. We discuss named ranges in Unit 4.

 Next are the Cancel and Enter buttons, which are only visible while Excel is in edit mode. Excel is in edit mode anytime you begin typing an entry, click in the formula bar, or press [F2]. Edit mode looks like this:

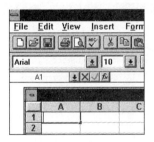

The X is the Cancel button (the effect of clicking this button is the same as pressing [Esc]), and the check mark is the Enter button (the effect is the same as pressing [Enter]). The right portion of the formula bar contains any text, numbers, or formulas that have been entered in the active cell. This is one of the two places where you can view any editing that is taking place. The other is in the cell itself. There are three ways to edit a formula in Excel:

- Click the I-beam cursor to the desired insertion point in the formula bar
- Double-click in the cell, then click the I-beam cursor to the desired insertion point
- Press [F2], then use the arrow keys to move the cursor in the formula bar

Once you have activated edit mode, use [Del] or [Backspace] as needed, enter or paste any new data, and press [Enter].

Status Bar

The bottom line of the screen contains the *status bar*. This shows any available explanatory text regarding any selected menu command or any button that is displaying a ToolTip (because you paused the mouse cursor on the button). The status bar includes indicators that light when the Lock keys [CapsLock], [ScrollLock], or [NumLock] are engaged: CAPS, SCRL, and NUM.

Excel Commands

Press [Alt], and Excel will highlight the File menu (the word File will appear in reverse type) if the document window is not maximized, or the document Control Menu box if the window is maximized. Remember that all Excel menus work in the same manner. You can select each item on the main menu by pressing [Alt] and then the underlined letter of the item; you can browse the menu by pressing the [←] or [→] key to bring down each of the drop-down boxes; or you can click the mouse on any item on the menu. As you move, the detailed description on the status bar changes to correspond with the highlighted option. For instance, in Figure 2.2, the highlighted cursor rests on the menu item File, the various options for File are listed in the drop-down menu, and the detailed description for File | New appears in the status bar.

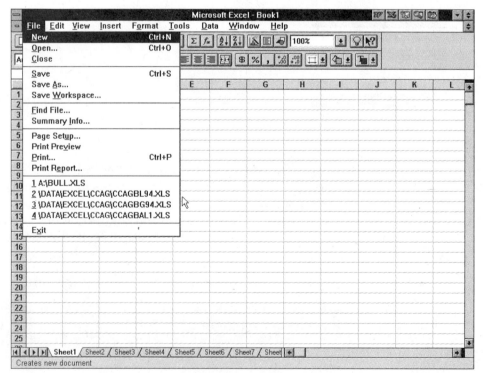

FIGURE 2.2
File menu

You can select an option from the drop-down menu by doing any of the following:

- Using [↓] to move to the desired option
- Pressing the underlined letter of the option
- Clicking on the option with the mouse

If you are selecting with the keyboard, choose the option you want and press [Enter]; Excel will execute that choice. To save time, you can press the first letter of your choice instead of using the arrow and [Enter] keys. At the main menu level, you can choose the following Excel menus.

FILE Operations that move files to and from disk storage, and others that control certain print options. The File menu also contains a list of the four most recently closed files.

EDIT Operations affecting the actual data of the workbook. These include cutting, copying, pasting, and filling cells with an entry. This menu item also includes find and replace functions.

VIEW Operations affecting what is displayed on the screen. This menu item also includes the View Manager, an easy way to create various views of your workbook with different display options.

INSERT Operations that insert various items in your workbook. These items include cells, rows, columns, worksheets, charts, macro modules, named ranges, functions, pictures, and objects.

FORMAT Operations that affect the appearance of the workbook. These include how a number is displayed, font selection, alignment, column width, and row height.

TOOLS Operations providing access to tools that are used in an Excel workbook. These tools include the spell checker, workbook auditing, goal seeking, scenario management, the solver, the macro recorder, and the add-in manager. This menu item also includes operations that affect the display preferences of the user, document protection, and workbook calculation.

DATA Operations that make it possible to use the workbook as a database. These include finding, sorting, filtering, and subtotaling records, as well as a database entry form and the Pivot Table Wizard.

WINDOW Operations that affect the way different windows share the display space.

HELP Options to open various Help windows, including comparisons to Lotus 1-2-3 and Multiplan, and two Excel tutorials.

We use two standard methods for referring to Excel commands in this text. One spells out the command words, while the other shows just the initial letters (the way you would type the command). For instance, File | Save and [Alt] [F], [S] are the same command. (Uppercase letters are used in this book for command instructions, but you can use lowercase letters as well; for instance, [Alt] f, s yields the same result as [Alt] F, S.)

Recall that [Esc] will cancel a menu call or an unwanted dialog box. For instance, if you wished to press [Alt][F], [S] but pressed [Alt][F], [A] instead, pressing [Esc] would close the menu. Then you can redo the command.

Heads-Up Computing

The Excel program is designed to provide hints and helpful information on the screen as you progress through menus and data entry. Learn to practice *heads-up computing*—watch the screen as you do your work.[1] Commands do not always work the way you think they will; if you watch the screen you will avoid many mistakes.

File Commands

The four commands discussed in this section are the first you should learn. They make it possible to save your workbook on a disk and retrieve it for later use. Before you use them, you need to know some basic file naming conventions.

File Names

Workbook files are saved on the disk with an eight-character name (usually called the *file name*) and an .XLS extension. The name can consist any of the characters A through Z, 0 through 9, _ (underscore), and - (hyphen). Alphabetic characters can be uppercase or lowercase. Excel tells you if you try to enter an illegal file name. If the file is not on the default disk drive, include the drive designation when naming the file (for example, B:\BALANCE). If you are using a tree-structured hard or floppy disk, you can also include a DOS subdirectory specification as part of the name of the file to be saved or retrieved (for example, C:\FINANCE\BALANCE).

The eight-character limitation for file names does not seem difficult at first, but in practice you will need to be creative. Ensure that the file name is as descriptive as possible; for example, BUDGET is much more descriptive than BWRKBK. If necessary, you can embed a date in the file name—for example, BUDGET96. If you will be sharing the workbook with others, consider including your initials; SRBUDG96 communicates that this is Steve Ross's budget for 1996.

File | Save As

Selecting File | Save As presents the dialog box shown in Figure 2.3. This dialog box gives you a number of options:

- You can give the file a name, or a different file name if you have already saved it, by typing a valid name in the File Name text box.

---

[1] The term heads-up comes from military fighter aircraft, which project information on pilots' windshields so that they do not have to continually watch their instruments.

UNIT 2 THE EXCEL WORKBOOK   41

FIGURE 2.3
File / Save As dialog box

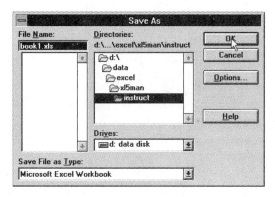

- You can save the file on a different drive by selecting a new drive in the Drives list box.

- You can save the file on a different directory by selecting a new directory in the Directories list box.

- You can save the file in a different format, such as Lotus 1-2-3, by making a selection in the Save File as Type list box. (This procedure is known as exporting and is discussed in more detail in Unit 13.)

- You can command Excel to save two versions of the file—the previous version on disk, with the extension .BAK, and the current version in memory with a standard extension—by clicking on the Options button and selecting Always Create Backup, as shown in Figure 2.4.

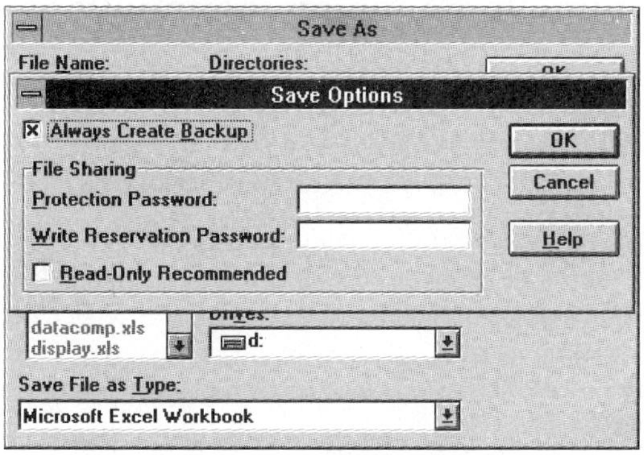

FIGURE 2.4
Save options dialog box

- You can assign a Protection Password to prevent unauthorized users from viewing the file. (This procedure is covered in detail in Unit 13.)

- You can assign a Write Reservation Password to the file, thus telling others, "Look, but don't touch!" (This procedure is covered in detail in Unit 13.)

- You can recommend that a file not be changed. This option calls a dialog box when the file is opened, informing the user that the file should be opened as read-only, but does not enforce the suggestion with a password.

NOTE *Unless you include an extension, Excel will append the extension .XLS to the end of the file name. (See the section above concerning legitimate file names.) While you can use an* extension other than .XLS, note that the default for opening an existing file is .XL*; therefore using an extension beginning with .XL will greatly simplify the opening of existing files.

File | Save

Selecting File | Save writes the entire workbook onto the disk in the disk drive. Excel will react differently depending on whether the file has been saved before. If the file has never been saved (the workbook title bar will show a name like Book1, Book2, and so on), Excel will present the File | Save As dialog box (see Figure 2.3), asking for the drive, directory, and file name for the new file. If the file has already been saved (a file with the same name as the one on the title bar already appears on the disk), Excel will automatically replace the file on the disk with the current version.

The File | Save command can be given by clicking the Save tool icon.

File | Open

Selecting File | Open loads a previously saved file from disk into the computer. A dialog box is presented, asking you to select the proper file. You can change directories by pressing [Alt][D], or drives by pressing [Alt][V], and then use the arrow keys to browse through the directory or drive list. Likewise, you can browse the file list by pressing [Alt][N], then [Tab], and using the arrow keys. Mouse users can use the scroll bars on the directory and file list boxes and select a file, drive, or directory by clicking on it. Once you have selected the desired file, Excel opens a new window and loads the new file into the window. If the file you are opening was saved with a write reservation or protection password, you will be prompted to enter the password before opening the file. Passwords are case-sensitive; capitals count! If you check the Read-Only button, you will open a version of the file that will not allow you to save changes. The only limitation on the number of windows you can open is the amount of memory in your computer.

The File | Open command can be given by clicking on the Open tool icon.

File | Exit

Selecting File | Exit closes the Excel program and returns to the Windows Program Manager, where File | Exit can be selected to return to the DOS command level. Before exiting, Excel will verify that no changes have been made to any open workbooks since the last File | Save. If there have been any changes, Excel will bring up a dialog box prompting you to save changes before exiting. *If you do not save at this time, any changes made since the last save will be lost when Excel closes.*

CAUTION *Do not simply shut off your computer with either Excel or Windows still running. Windows maintains several open files that can be damaged by turning off the computer while they are still open. Always exit completely before turning off the power to your computer.*

Shortcut Menus

FIGURE 2.5
Shortcut menu

One of the nicer innovations in Windows spreadsheet programs is the use of shortcut menus. If you right-click on a cell, chart, or graphical object, a list of menu commands that apply to that object will appear next to the object. This keeps the most-used commands just a mouse click away. We illustrate the shortcut menu for a cell in Figure 2.5. If the object were a chart or a graphical object, the list of commands on the shortcut menu would be different.

Entering Information into a Workbook

In a new workbook all the cells are empty. When you make a cell the active cell, its border is bolded on the display. If you enter information (text or value), that information is stored in the active cell.

Entering Text

If Excel cannot interpret an entry as a number, it assumes that the entry is text, and treats it as such. This will be the case if the entry contains any nonnumeric text (other than these special characters: / . , + - ( ) $ % E e). By default, all *text entries* will be left-justified (aligned with the left edge of the cell). (We will discuss how to modify the default alignment, along with other formatting changes, in Unit 4.)

Occasionally, it is desirable to enter a number as text, either to prevent it from being used in a calculation or to prevent it from being formatted as a number. To do this, simply surround the number with quotation marks and begin the entry with an equal sign (for example, ="123456"). You can also use the Lotus 1-2-3 method of converting a numeric entry to a text entry—begin the entry with a single quotation mark (for example, '123456). Excel will record the entry as a left-aligned text entry.

Text entries can be up to 255 characters in length. Even if the text is wider than the column, the remainder of the text is displayed across the row except where it would conflict with another entry in that row. When you have typed all the text, press [Enter] or one of the arrow keys to enter the text into the cell.

Entering Constant Values

Constant values in Excel can be either numeric, date, or time values (Excel stores date and time values as a number). All constant values are right-justified by default. (Again, we will discuss changing this default, along with other formatting changes, in Unit 4.)

Excel will try to duplicate the number format of the entry if it is close enough to one of the standard number formats. For example, if you enter 4 Jan, the cell entry will read 4-Jan (the nearest number format to your entry), even though the formula bar will read 1/4/1995 (Excel assumes the current year, unless you tell it otherwise). (We discuss the values of dates and times in the next unit.) Excel will also try to duplicate currency formats. For example, if you enter $495.63, the cell entry will read $495.63, even though the formula bar will read 495.63.

When you have typed the value, press [Enter] or one of the arrow keys to enter the value into the cell. If the value is too large to be displayed in the column, Excel displays pound signs across the cell or converts the result to scientific notation (for example, 999999999 is displayed as 1.0E+09, but 999,999,999 is displayed as ########). You must change the column width using the Format|Column Width command (discussed in Unit 4).

Entering Formulas

All formulas in Excel must begin with = (equal sign). When a formula is entered into a cell, the formula itself is displayed in the formula bar when that cell is highlighted, and the result of the formula is (usually) displayed in the cell in the workbook area. *Formulas* contain constant values, cell references, ranges, and functions (referred to as operands) connected by arithmetic and logical operators. (These elements of formulas are discussed in detail in Unit 3.) Formulas can be up to 255 characters in length. The simplest formula is =A5, which displays the value of cell A5 in the cell that contains this formula.

Formulas can be entered by typing or by using a combination of typing and pointing. Once you begin a formula by typing an equal sign, regardless of what you type or where you point, the formula is entered into the cell that was the active cell when you started typing. (*Remember*: a formula always begins with an equal sign.)

For example, assume that you want to sum the values in A2 and B2 and store the result in cell A1. Using the arrow keys, the mouse, or [F5], make A1 the active cell, then type =a2+b2 and press [Enter]. This would do the job quite nicely, but the preferred alternative is the *pointing method*. To achieve the same result, do the following:

Move to cell A1

Press [=]	*Excel is ready for a formula,*
[↓]	*makes A2 the active cell,*
[+]	*begin next reference; A1 becomes the active cell,*
[↓], [→]	*makes B2 the active cell,*
[Enter]	*enters formula and calculates result in A1.*

This is about as fast and has the advantage of displaying what you are including in your formula. Pointing is recommended, especially when your worksheet is larger than the visible area of the screen.

The pointing method can also be used with the mouse, as follows:

Click on cell A1

Press [=]	*Excel is ready for a formula,*
Click on A2	*makes A2 the active cell,*
Press [+]	*begin next reference; A1 becomes the active cell,*

	Click on B2	*makes B2 the active cell,*
✓	Click the Enter button	*enters formula and calculates result in A1.*

NOTE *Do not type spaces when you are entering formulas; spaces will be deleted by Excel.*

If the entry is not correct—for example, parentheses are mismatched—an error message appears and you are in edit mode (see the next section, "Editing Cell Entries"). If the formula is acceptable, a result is displayed. If the resulting value is too large to be displayed in the column, Excel displays ######## across the cell. You must then change the column width using the Format | Column Width command. (We will discuss this command in more detail in Unit 4.)

The result of the formula is calculated immediately and displayed in the cell. Whenever you make a change or enter a new value in the workbook, all formulas that are affected by that change are recalculated. (An exception to this statement is discussed in Part Two, but automatic recalculation is the normal state.) Excel displays one of the following error messages in the cell if the formula is correct but the result cannot be computed:

#DIV/0!	Attempted division by 0
#NA!	No value is available
#NAME?	Excel does not recognize a name in a formula
#NULL!	Intersection in formula does not exist
#NUM!	Indicates a problem with a number
#REF!	Reference to a cell that is not valid
#VALUE!	Wrong type of argument or operand in a formula

For example, the formula might be attempting to divide by 0 (zero) because the cell referred to in the denominator is currently empty. #DIV/0! means that the formula is correct, but the result is an error. The #DIV/0! is replaced by a result when whatever caused the incorrect result is changed (for example, placing a value in the cell that caused the division by zero error).

Formulas can also use text data. We discuss that feature of Excel in the next unit.

Editing Cell Entries

There are two ways to edit cell entries. If the text, constant, or formula is short, then the easiest method is to make the cell the active cell and retype the entire entry. When you press [Enter] the previous entry is replaced by what you have just typed.

The second method, edit mode, is better for correcting minor errors in long entries. Make the cell with the formula the active cell and then press [F2]. (If you enter a formula that it cannot accept, Excel automatically brings you to this point.) The cell contents are displayed in the formula bar and in the cell. Alternatively, you can click on the cell with the mouse, and then insert the I-beam cursor at the desired point in the formula bar. Finally, you can double-click on the cell with the mouse, and then insert the I-beam cursor at the desired point in the cell. Use [←] and [→] to move to the point to be corrected. The [Backspace] key deletes one character to the left of the cursor, and the [Del] key deletes the character to the right of the cursor. Any character typed is inserted into the line at the cursor. To replace several characters using the mouse, drag the I-beam over the characters to highlight them, then type the desired entry. Tell Excel that you are finished editing by pressing [Enter], or clicking on the Enter button.

GUIDED ACTIVITY 2.1

Entering Text and Constant Values

An old Spanish proverb proclaims that

*It is not the same to speak of bulls
as to be in the bull ring:*

Let us therefore speak no more, but proceed to the ring, or rather, the workbook.

1. Follow the startup procedure outlined in Unit 1 to load Windows and enter the Excel program.

   For your first workbook, you will count the bulls on your ranch. There are four kinds of bull:

Type	Count
Brahma	10
Hereford	5
Elephant	1
Chicago	12

2. The first task is to enter the headings in column A. (As you work, refer to Figure 2.6, which illustrates the finished workbook.)

   a. Make A1 the active cell.

CHECKPOINT 2A How do you make a cell the active cell?
The answers to checkpoint questions are contained in Appendix A.

   b. Type the word Type. Excel repeats what you type in the formula bar and on the workbook:

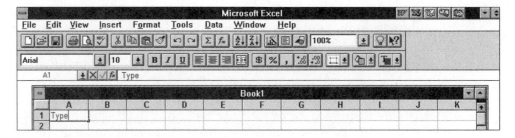

   c. Press [Enter] to enter the word into the cell. Excel automatically moves the cursor down one cell to cell A2.

   d. Enter the headings Brahma . . . Chicago down column A. (Remember to press [Enter] after typing each word.)

FIGURE 2.6
BULL.XLS worksheet, complete

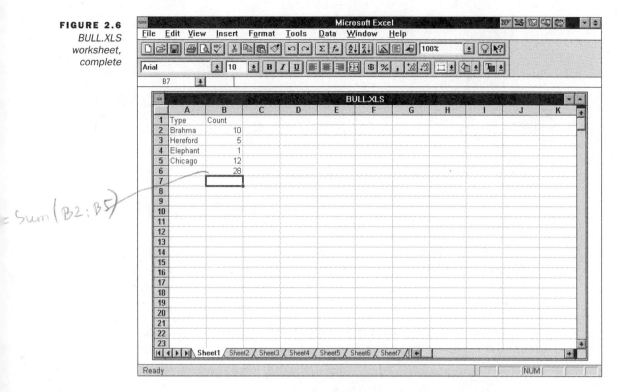

=Sum(B2:B5)

e. Notice that each heading is left-justified—that is, aligned with the left edge of the column:

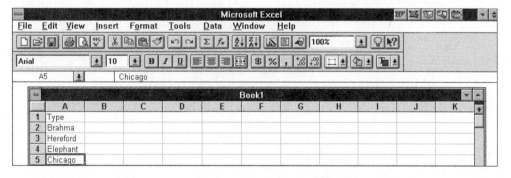

3. Use the arrow keys to move to cell B1 (or click on cell B1). Enter the heading Count in that cell.

4. Enter the counts in column B:

   a. Type 10. Excel repeats the entry in the formula bar:

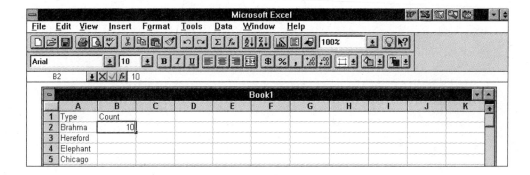

b. Press ⬇. Note that ⬇ enters the value into the cell (just like [Enter]) and then moves the active cell down one row, to cell B3.

5. Enter the remainder of the counts down column B. (*Remember*: Do not press [Spacebar] to align a number; Excel aligns it automatically.) Do not enter the value 28 in cell B6; you will create a formula in the next Guided Activity that computes the sum of the counts.

6. Before proceeding, save your work. Enter the following; notice how the menu bar changes with each character pressed.

   a. Press [Alt][F]. The menu bar will appear like this:

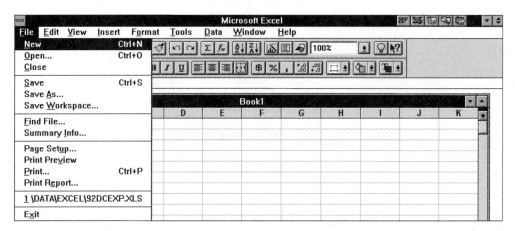

   b. Press [A].

UNIT 2 THE EXCEL WORKBOOK   49

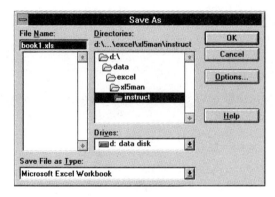

c. Excel suggests the file name BOOK1.XLS. If you start to type a different name, the suggested name will disappear. To save the file with the name BULL.XLS, type `bull` (do not press [Enter] yet). To save the file to your floppy disk, press [Alt][V] and use [↓] and [↑] to move to drive A:

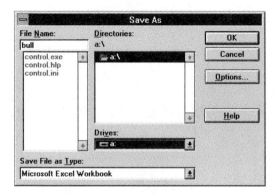

d. Press [Enter].

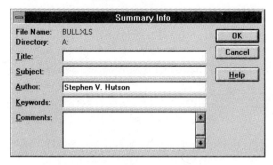

e. Excel displays a Summary Info dialog box where you can enter information that will enable you to find this file later. You do not need to include such information for this Guided Activity, so press [Enter]. You now have a workbook file named BULL.XLS on your disk. Notice that the title bar changes to display the name of the file:

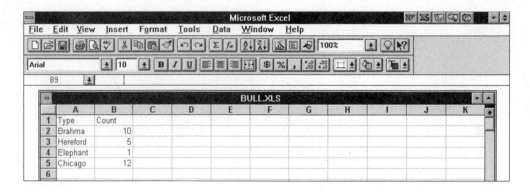

7. If you must leave the computer, choose File | Exit to exit to Windows. Exit to the operating system.

In the next Guided Activity you enter the formula that computes the sum of bulls.

GUIDED ACTIVITY 2.2

Entering Formulas

1. If you are not continuing from the previous Guided Activity, load Excel, select File | Open, and the file, BULL (the command is [Alt][F], [O], bull [Enter]). If you are opening a file from drive A:, select the drive by clicking on it, or by pressing [Alt][V] and using the arrow keys to select it, and then pressing [Enter].

NOTE *Mouse users can quickly open a file by double-clicking on the file name.*

2. Next, compute the sum of bulls (the formula is =B2+B3+B4+B5). Use the arrow keys or click on cell B6. Enter the following; notice how the formula bar and workbook change with each character pressed.

    a. Press [=].

    b. Press [↑] four times, highlighting cell B2, or click on B2:

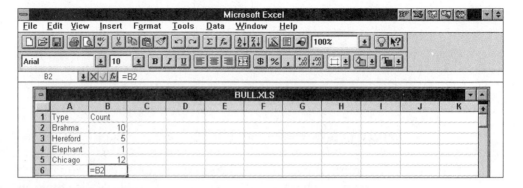

    c. Press [+].

    d. Press [↑] three times, or click on cell B3:

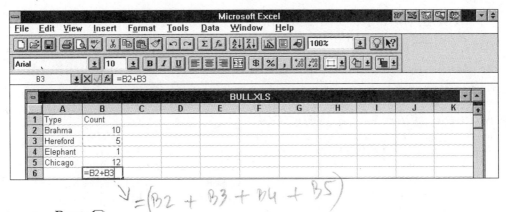

$= (B2 + B3 + B4 + B5)$

   e. Press [+].

   f. Press [↑] twice, or click on cell B4.

   g. Press [+].

   h. Press [↑] once, or click on cell B5.

   i. Press [Enter] or click on the [Enter] button.

3. Your workbook should now look like Figure 2.6.

4. If the number 28 does not appear in cell B6, you have made an error. Do the following to determine the cause of the error:

   a. Check the numbers in column B. If a number is incorrect, select that cell and reenter the number, being careful not to press any other key before entering the number.

   b. Move the cursor to cell B6. The formula in the formula bar should now read =B2+B3+B4+B5. If you have made an error, either reenter the formula or press [F2] to edit the entry.

5. The advantage of using a formula to calculate the total number of bulls is illustrated by the following example. Assume that one of the Chicago Bulls was sold to a Dallas ranch; change the number in cell B5 to 11 (eleven—use the number keys not the letter "l") and note that the total is immediately recalculated. If you had entered the constant 28 in cell B6, the total would no longer be correct.

6. Save your work again by using the File I Save command or the Save tool icon.

7. We will discuss printing workbooks in Unit 5. However, in order that you may have a printed copy of this workbook, do the following. *Follow these steps exactly.* (We will discuss the principles in Unit 5.)

   a. First, ensure that the printer is on, has paper, and is ready to print. Your instructor will assist you if necessary.

   b. Click the Print tool in the toolbar (illustrated at left). If you do not have a mouse, press [Alt][F], [P], [Enter].

52 PART ONE FUNDAMENTAL SPREADSHEET OPERATIONS

8. If you must leave the computer, give the File | Exit command to return to Windows. Exit from Windows to the operating system.

GUIDED ACTIVITY 2.3

Using Multiple Sheets in a Workbook

1. If you are not continuing from the previous Guided Activity, load Excel and select File | Open and the file, BULL (the command is [Alt][F], [O], bu11 [Enter]). If you are opening a file from drive A:, select the drive by clicking on it, or by pressing [Alt][V] and using the arrow keys to select it, and then pressing [Enter].

NOTE *Mouse users can quickly open a file by double-clicking on the file name.*

You have purchased a second ranch. The first ranch is in Wyoming; the second is in Colorado. In this Guided Activity, you use multiple sheets to track the bulls on the two ranches in the same workbook.

2. The first step is to name the sheet you have been working on. To do this, double-click on the sheet tab for Sheet1. The Rename Sheet dialog box will display:

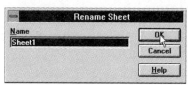

3. In the Name text box, type Wyoming and click OK.

4. Now copy the Wyoming sheet to a new sheet. To do this, press and hold [Ctrl] and use the mouse to drag the Wyoming sheet tab to the right (approximately to the center of the tab for Sheet2). Excel creates an exact duplicate of the Wyoming sheet and names it Wyoming (2). The result should look like this:

5. Next, repeat the procedure in step 2 to rename the new sheet Colorado. Now change the count of bulls to meet the Colorado inventory. The number of bulls for the Colorado ranch is illustrated below:

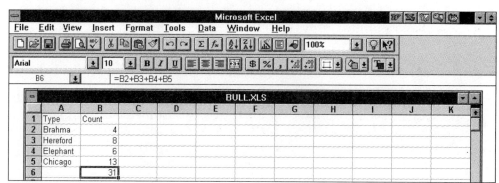

6. Save your work by using the File | Save command or the Save tool. Select File | Exit to return to Windows. Exit from Windows to the operating system.

Backup

Backup is one of those computer terms that can be used as a noun, an adjective, and a verb. A backup is a copy of the original file, usually stored in a safe place in case something happens to the original to render it unusable. Backup disks contain backups. To back up is to make backup copies.

There are a multitude of gremlins lurking out there that can ruin your day if you are not prepared. You might inadvertently ruin a file by making the wrong changes and saving it. Disks occasionally develop bad spots that make previously saved files unreadable. Spills (coffee, soda) and ashes can ruin a disk. Someone might steal your briefcase (or backpack) or you might misplace your box of disks. Unexpected electromagnetic radiation can erase disks. (Telephones, magnetic paper-clip holders, and library security systems all look innocent, but any of these might damage your disks.) Disks left in cars can be physically damaged by excessive heat or cold.

You should become obsessive about making backup copies of your work. We recommend that you make a backup every time you finish a session at the computer. There are several levels of backup:

- Same disk, different file name
- Different disk, same location
- Different disk, different location

SAME DISK, DIFFERENT FILE NAME

Save the file under two different names. If something goes wrong with one version of the file, the other might still be usable. To implement this method, select File | Save As and save the file with two different names. (Choosing the Backup option when saving the file saves an *earlier* version of the file under a different name, not the most recent version.)

This provides a minimal level of protection. It does protect you from random glitches that affect single data files, and might provide you a previous version if you later make unwanted changes. It does not help, however, if something (like a spilled cup of coffee) destroys the entire disk.

DIFFERENT DISK, SAME LOCATION

Save the file on two different disks, under the same file name. If one disk is destroyed, the other is available. To implement this method, either use File | Exit to exit the workbook and Windows, or use the application Control menu to switch to the Program Manager, and click on the File Manager icon. When you are in the File Manager, put the backup disk in drive B:, leaving your data disk in drive A:. (The backup disk must have been formatted previously, and can contain other files.) Open separate windows for the A: and B: drives and give the Window | Tile command to see both windows. Drag the files to be backed up from the A: window to the B: window.

CAUTION *If you drag the files in the wrong direction, or put the disks in the wrong drives, you can copy old versions of files over new versions. We recommend putting a tab over the write-protect notch of the 5.25-inch disk you wish to copy from (with new versions of the files) to prevent wrong-way copying. You can simply move the write-protect tab on a 3.5-inch disk to the "protect" (open) position.*[2]

To use this backup method on a hard disk or network system where you have been storing your data files on the hard disk, place your backup (floppy) disk in the disk drive, select the desired files by pressing and holding the [Shift] key when selecting all files subsequent to the first file, and drag the files from the hard disk to the backup (floppy) disk. Your instructor might suggest additional methods available in your particular school or organization.

This backup method provides additional protection. Keep the backup disk in the box except when you are using it, so that most local disasters (such as the spilled coffee) will not affect it. You are still at risk, however, for disasters such as theft of your backpack, fire, or electromagnetic fields.

DIFFERENT DISK, DIFFERENT LOCATION

Save the file on two different disks, under the same file name. Store the disks in separate locations, so that if the disk box is destroyed, the backup is available. This method is implemented in the same manner as the previous method, except that you have to find a place to store the backup. If you have a desk or locker at work/school, you could leave a copy there and take the other copy home. You might ask a friend to take your backup disk. Some computer areas have a place to store disks, and you could leave the backup there. This provides the greatest protection. It is very unlikely that the same disaster would destroy both of your disks.

GUIDED ACTIVITY 2.4

Retrieving and Backing Up Files

This Guided Activity is designed to explore the two most common methods of backing up your work. Your organization might have developed different procedures.

1. Before starting, you should have your data disk (the one with BULL.XLS on it) and two other formatted disks. If you are using a hard disk or network to store your data, then your "data disk" is the hard disk or network server.

2. Enter the Excel workbook.

---

[2] After completing the copying, remove the tab or close the slide so that you will be able to store files on the disk in the future.

3. Choose File | Open and the file, BULL. If you are opening a file from drive A:, change to drive A: by selecting it and pressing [Enter]. Notice that Excel presents a dialog box with a list of workbook files on the disk:

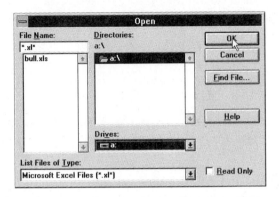

The easiest way to open a file is to highlight its name and then press [Enter]. Mouse users can double-click on the file name to open a file. (If you have several files on the disk, press [Ctrl][Tab] to move to the file list and use [↓] until the one you seek is highlighted.)

4. The first backup method is Same Disk, Different File Name. Save the file under the name BULL2.XLS with the command [Alt][F], [A], bull2 [Enter].

CHECKPOINT 2B What file names are on your disk now?

5. Press [Ctrl][Esc] to call up the Task List window. (This is a keyboard shortcut for double-clicking on the application Control menu and selecting the Switch to menu option.) Start the Program Manager by double-clicking on its name. From there, start the File Manager by double-clicking on its icon.

6. The next step is to back up all the files on your data disk, creating a backup data disk. The precise method depends on what you are using as your data disk and the type of computer system. Do one of the following:

   a. If you are keeping your data on a floppy disk and the computer you are using has two disk drives, place your data disk in drive A: and your backup data disk in drive B:. Open a window for the A: drive and another for the B: drive. Give the Window | Tile command. Drag the files to be backed up from A: to B:. Click Yes in the confirmation dialog box.

   b. If you are keeping your data on a floppy disk and the computer you are using has one disk drive, place your data disk in the disk drive. Open a window for the A: drive and another for the C: drive. With the C: drive active, give the command File | Create Directory. In the Create Directory dialog box, type AAA. [3] Drag the files to be backed up from the A: drive to the

---

[3] We use AAA for two reasons: it is unlikely that such a directory will already exist on your C: drive; and since the File Manager automatically alphabetizes directory names, this puts it at the top of the list.

AAA directory on the C: drive. Then place the backup data disk in the disk drive and drag the files from the C:\AAA directory to the A: drive.

c. If you are keeping your data on a hard disk or network file server, place your backup data disk in the disk drive. Open a window for the A: drive and another for the C: drive. Drag the files from the proper directory on the C: drive to the A: drive.

Your instructor might tell you to use a different drive or path for this command.

7. Remove your disks and put them in a secure place. A plastic disk box is best if you will be carrying your disks around. If possible, store your backup disks in a different location.

8. Your instructor might request that you prepare a disk for handing in your homework. Generally, the procedures followed in step 6 to make a backup disk are the same ones to be used to make a homework disk.

9. Use labels to clearly mark all your disks. At a minimum, you will have a working data disk and a backup data disk.

EXERCISE 2.1

Harold's G.P.A.

Besides the Guided Activities, which are step-by-step discussions of the techniques discussed in a unit, this manual also includes Exercises at the end of most units. These challenge your understanding of the material presented and do not include as many specific instructions as the Guided Activities.

1. Start with a clear workbook. (If you have another workbook on the screen, click the New Workbook tool for a clean workbook. If you do not have a mouse, issue the command File | New to open a new workbook window on the screen.) Start the workbook in cell A1. You need columns for the courses Harold has taken, the credit hours, and the grades received for the courses (in numeric form; for example, an A grade is recorded as a 4—do not enter the letters). Put each course on a different row and each type of information in a column.

Course	Hours	Grade
English	3	B
History	3	A
Psychology	3	A
Chemistry	4	C
Accounting	3	B
Statistics	4	B

NOTE *Convert letter grades to numbers before entering in the workbook.*

2. Note that some of the course names are cut off after you enter data in the Hours column (the actual number of characters in each cell will depend on the width of the characters). If you feel adventuresome, try using the Format | Column | Width command to change the width of the column containing the course names (put the active cell in that column before giving the command). If you do not feel adventuresome, leave things the way they are until after you have read Unit 4.

3. Next, put the product of hours times grades (this product is called Grade Points) in another column. For example, to compute the product of cells B2 and C2, place a formula such as the following in cell D2: =B2*C2 (the asterisk means multiply).

4. Finally, sum the Hours and Grade Points columns, putting the sums in the row below the last class (as you summed the bulls, putting the sum below Chicago). Then divide the sum of Grade Points by the sum of Hours to determine Harold's grade point average, putting this formula in the next row down. To divide cell D8 by cell B8, place the following formula in cell D9: =D8/B8 (the slash means divide). You should get 3.1 as the answer.

5. Save your work with the file name HAROLD.

EXERCISE 2.2

The Perfect Job (I)

In this Exercise you begin the development of a workbook that you use to keep track of numerous job offers. The workbook developed here is quite simple, but you will expand it in later units.

1. Start with a clear workbook. (If you have another workbook on the screen, use the command File | New to open a new workbook window on the screen.)

2. Starting in cell A1, build a table like the following. Put each column of data in a separate workbook column; for instance, put the salary data in column D. The entry in cell D3 should be right-justified. With the active cell in D3, click the proper icon on the toolbar.

```
My Job Prospects
Blank line
Company         City            Title           Salary
Blank line
Arthur's        Chicago         Manager         25000
Freddy's        Seattle         Buyer           26300
Mack's          Bangor          Associate       22135
Minnie's        L.A.            Partner         24900
Alice's         Memphis         Executive       21467
```

3. Save the workbook with the name JOBS.

EXERCISE 2.3

A Check Register (I)

In this Exercise you begin the development of a workbook that you use to record checks and deposits in a checking account. The workbook developed here is quite simple, but you will expand it in later units.

1. Start with a clear workbook. (If you have another workbook on the screen, use the command File | New to create a new workbook on the screen.)

2. Starting in cell A1, build a table like the following. Put each column of data in a separate workbook column. For the moment, do not make any entries in the Date or Balance columns (other than 200.00 as beginning balance). In the following units, you will learn how to enter dates and formulas, how to change the width of columns, and how to change the format of numbers (to properly display dates or dollars and cents). For the moment, some of the text entries will overlap and some of the text will not be visible.

Number	Date	Description	Payment Amount	Deposit Amount	Balance
		Beg. Balance			200.00
101		Bookstore	101.25		
102		Viking Apart.	263.50	500.00	
103		Charlie's Groc.	76.35		

3. Save the workbook with the name CHECKS.

EXERCISE 2.4

Business Mileage (I)

If you use a vehicle for both business and pleasure and want to claim business expenses on your taxes, the IRS requires that you keep a log of the miles driven for each use. In this Exercise you begin to develop such a log. Begin by entering the following data. Leave the Miles column empty for the moment. Notice that Excel automatically converts entries such as 1/1 to a date in the current year and that numbers such as 12459.0 are displayed without a decimal place. Enter all "notations" in one cell, even if they appear on two lines in this book.

Date	Reading	Use	Miles	Notation
1/1	12405.6	P		Reading at beginning of year, grocery shopping
1/3	12446.7	B		Call on Anderson account
1/3	12459.0	P		Take Sally skating
1/4	12477.3	B		Deliver Bertrand quotation

Save the file as MILES96. In subsequent units you will add data and formulas to the spreadsheet.

EXERCISE 2.5

Form 1040EZ (I)

In this Exercise you begin the development of a spreadsheet that contains the items and logic of IRS Form 1040EZ, the form used by many single Americans under the age of 65 whose taxable income is less than $55,500.[4] This Exercise uses the 1992 tax year version of Form 1040EZ. Your instructor might direct you to use a more recent version. In this Exercise, you enter only the line numbers and labels. In Unit 3 and later units, you enter the numbers and formulas that calculate the taxes. When you save the workbook, use the name 1040EZ.

Enter the following line numbers and labels. Each line of the following should be entered in a separate line (row) of the workbook. (The row numbers are listed to the left, in a different type style. If you make your entries on the rows we indicate, then you will be able to follow the instructions in later exercises more easily.) On lines with a number or a letter, put the number or letter in column A and the text in column B.

ROW

1 Form 1040EZ
2 Report your income
3 1 Total wages, salaries, and tips. This should be shown
4   in box 10 of your W-2 form(s). Attach your W-2 form(s).
5 2 Taxable interest income of $400 or less. If the total
6   is more than $400, you cannot use Form 1040EZ.
7 3 Add lines 1 and 2. This is your adjusted gross income.
8 4 Can your parents (or someone else) claim you on their return?
9   __Yes. Do worksheet on back; enter amount from line E here.
10   __No. Enter 5,900.00. This is the total of your
11   standard deduction and your personal deduction.
12 5 Subtract line 4 from line 3. If line 4 is larger than line 3,
13   enter 0. This is your taxable income.
14 Figure your tax
15 6 Enter your Federal income tax withheld from box 9 of
16   your W-2 form(s).
17 7 Tax. Look at line 5 above. Use the amount of line 5 to
18   find your tax in the tax table on pages 22-24 of
19   the booklet. Then, enter your tax from the table on this line.

---

[4] There are other restrictions, which might vary from year to year.

20 Refund or amount you owe
21 8   If line 6 is larger than line 7, subtract line 7 from line 6.
22   This is your refund.
23 9   If line 7 is larger than line 6, subtract line 6 from line 7.
24   This is the amount you owe. Attach your payment for full
25   amount payable to the "Internal Revenue Service."
26 Standard deduction workbook for dependents who checked "Yes" on line 4
27 A   Enter the amount from line 1 on the front.
28 B   Minimum amount.
29 C   Look at lines A and B above. Enter the
30   LARGER of the two amounts here.
31 D   Maximum amount.
32 E   Look at lines C and D above. Enter the SMALLER
33   of the two amounts here and on line 4 on the front.

EXERCISE 2.6

Things to Do (I)

Many people use computers to help them keep track of lists, and the "To Do" list is one popular subject. Excel is a nice program to keep the To Do list because it allows you to set up fancy formats. Then, if you don't feel like doing the things on your list, you can always fiddle around with the appearance of the list! In this Exercise, you create the list. In Exercise 4.6 in Unit 4, you make it pretty.

Create a list with column headings like the following. Enter your own tasks, not ours. If you make entries such as 2/9 in a cell, Excel will assume that you mean a date in the current year. To make an entry for a different year, enter it as 2/9/95.

Save the file with the name TO-DO.

```
Steve's list of things to do
Do/Due          What
2/14            Send flowers to sweetheart
3/17            St. Patrick's Day Festival
3/18            Term project due in Econ 101
4/15            Income taxes due
5/16/95         Mom and Dad's 25th Wedding Anniversary
```

Review Questions

The answers to questions marked with an asterisk are contained in Appendix A.

*1. What is a cell?
2. What is the difference between text and value cell entries?
*3. How do you determine a cell's reference?
4. What are the dimensions of the Excel workbook?
5. What is meant by the formula bar?
*6. What is the pointing method?
7. Look at Figure 2.1. Are any of the Lock keys engaged?
*8. How would you enter the text "General Generators" into a workbook cell?
9. How would you enter the constant value 98.6 into a workbook cell?
*10. How would you enter the formula =A6 - B7 into the workbook cell B6?
11. How would you save the file ASSETS to disk?
*12. How would you retrieve ASSETS from disk?
13. Why should you back up your data?
14. Develop a backup system that will work for you. Consider the most likely hazards to your data, organization policies about using data, and access to computers. Describe the system.
15. How do you exit to Windows?

Key Terms

The following terms are introduced in this unit. Be sure you know what each of them means.

Argument	Formula bar	Status bar
Backup	Heads-up computing	Text entry
Cell	Menu bar	Toolbar
Cell reference	Pointing method	ToolTip
Column	Reference section	Workbook
Constant value	Row	Workbook file
File name	Sheet	Worksheet
Formula	Spreadsheet	

Documentation Research

Using the Excel *User's Guide*, find and record the page number of each of the commands discussed in this unit. We recommend that you also write the page number in the margin next to the discussion of the command in the unit.

1. File | Save—If you select the Always Save Backup check box, in which directory is the backup file saved?
2. File | Save—If you open a workbook as read-only, what happens if you later try to save it?
3. File | Close—How would you close all open documents with one command?

Operators and Functions

Recall that formulas contain constant values, cell addresses, ranges, and functions connected by arithmetic and logical operators. You used constant values and simple addition of cells in the preceding unit. This unit introduces the remaining elements of formulas: arithmetic operators as well as mathematical, logical, special, financial, date, and statistical functions. In this unit we present those functions that are most useful to the business student and professional; we defer discussion of several of the functions to Part Three.

Do not try to memorize this material. Skim the unit to see how the material is arranged; look at the Index (at the end of the manual), which lists functions; glance at Appendix B; and work the review problems at the end of the unit. You will need to refer back to this unit often, but you do not need to memorize everything presented here.

Learning Objectives

At the completion of this unit you should know

1. what order of precedence means,
2. how each of the numeric operators is used in formulas,
3. what the various categories of functions are,
4. how the Help window is organized.

At the completion of this unit you should be able to

1. write formulas using arithmetic operators,
2. write formulas using functions,

3. annotate formulas,
4. access various portions of the Help window,
5. use the Help window to determine how to use a specific function.

Important Commands

Help | Contents

Help | Search for Help on

Insert | Function

Insert | Note

Arithmetic Operators

Operators are the glue that binds elements of formulas, the *operands*, together. All of us are familiar with operators such as the + (plus) sign:

2+2

In Excel, the operands can be constant values (such as 25), references to other cells (such as A8), or functions (for example, =MAX(17,A9), which determines the maximum [largest] of a list of values). Thus, you might enter the following in a cell:

=MAX(17,A9)-25*A8

You must know the order in which the expression will be calculated to ensure that you achieve the proper result. Will Excel determine the maximum of 17 or the value contained in cell A9, then subtract 25, then multiply the result by the value in cell A8? Or will Excel subtract the product of 25 and the value of cell A8 from the maximum of 17 and the value of cell A9?

Order of Precedence

Order of precedence refers to the sequence of calculation. (Another term for this concept is *hierarchy of operations*.) Formulas are evaluated from left to right, with expressions enclosed by parentheses ( ) evaluated first, and those operators with higher precedence evaluated before operators with lower precedence. For instance, from algebra you remember that

$$\frac{6^2}{12} = \frac{36}{12} = 3$$

and not

$$\frac{6^2}{12} = \left(\frac{1}{2}\right)^2 = \frac{1}{4}$$

The same situation occurs in Excel, where the cell entry
```
6^2/12
```
yields the result 3.

Arithmetic Operators in Order of Precedence

Expressions containing arithmetic operators are computed in the following order—that is, exponentiation is done before multiplication.

:	Range
Space	Intersection
,	Union
–	Negation (single operand)
%	Percent
^	Exponentiation
* /	Multiplication and division
+ –	Addition and subtraction
&	Text joining (also called "concatenation")
= < > <= >= <>	Comparison

Now you know how to evaluate the formula
```
=MAX(17,A9)-25*A8
```
Excel first will determine the product of 25 and the value of cell A8, then subtract that from the maximum of 17 and the value of cell A9. More examples are in the following section.

Using Arithmetic Operators in Formulas

Arithmetic operators are used to tie together constants, cell references, and functions into formulas. In the following examples, assume that cells A5 through A10 contain the following values:

A5: 3
A6: 4
A7: 2
A8: 2
A9: 7
A10: 5

The following are entered in various cells, yielding the indicated results.

=A5+A6	*Value of cell A5 is added to value of cell A6:* 7
=A5*A7	*The product of the values of cells A5 and A7:* 6
=A5^A8	*Value of cell A5 to the value of $A8^{th}$ power:* 9
=(A5+A6+A7)/A9	*Sum of cells A5, A6, and A7, divided by A9:* 1.285714
=A8/A9+A10	*Cell A8 divided by A9, plus A10:* 5.285714
=A8/(A9+A10)	*Cell A8 divided by sum of A9 and A10:* 0.166667

String Reference and Manipulation

Excel gives you the ability to refer to and manipulate text (or *strings*). The text contents of a cell can be referred to by another cell. Text can be entered as usual in cells, but text used in formulas must be enclosed in " " (double quotation marks). Text used in a formula is called a *literal string*. Text and literal strings can be combined in formulas using the & (*concatenation*) operator. For instance, if cell A1 contains the text United Consolidated Industries and cell F9 contains the text Overdrawn (with a space in front of the O), then

The cell entry =A1	displays the contents of cell A1—United Consolidated Industries—in the current cell.
The cell entry =A1&F9	yields United Consolidated Industries Overdrawn.
The entry =A1&" Ltd."	yields United Consolidated Industries Ltd.

The virtue of all this is that the same workbook can be used to analyze a different company by simply changing the contents of cell A1, which then changes the result displayed by all cells that reference A1.

Several functions are provided to further enhance use of string data. (These are discussed in Unit 14.)

Annotating Formulas

Excel allows you to add *comments* or *annotations* to explain the purpose or logic of a formula. All annotations on the sheet are displayed in the Cell Note window when you press [Shift][F2]; they are not visible in the workbook area. You can also view notes in the workbook by giving the Insert | Note command, or selecting Info Window from the View tab in the Tools | Options dialog box. The note is not printed when you print the workbook, unless you select Notes from the Sheet tab in the File | Page Setup dialog box. To enter a comment in a cell, make that cell the active cell, select Insert | Note, and then type the comment. Cells with comments have a small red mark, called a *note indicator*, in the upper-right corner of the cell.

GUIDED ACTIVITY 3.1

Using Operators

This Guided Activity provides experience in entering formulas that contain arithmetic and string operators. You will enter the formulas presented as examples in the preceding section.

1. Follow the startup procedure outlined in Unit 1 to load Excel. If you are continuing from a previous activity or exercise and already have a workbook on the screen, click on the New Workbook tool or give the command File | New to open a new workbook window.

TIP *Remember to save your old workbook if you decide to close it.*

2. Enter the following values and text in the cells indicated. Recall that to enter a value or text, you make the cell that is to contain the value or text the active cell, type the number (for a value) or words (for text), and then press [Enter] or one of the arrow keys. The completed workbook should look like Figure 3.1, shown later in this Guided Activity. Refer to that figure to see how the values and text are arranged.

Cell	Value or Text
A1	United Consolidated Industries
A5	3
A6	4
A7	2
A8	2
A9	7
A10	5
F9	Overdrawn *(There is a space before the word.)*

3. Make C5 the active cell. Enter the formula =A5+A6. You can use either pointing or typing methods. The result, 7, should appear. Notice that the result of the formula appears on the workbook. When the cell containing the formula is the active cell, the formula appears in the formula bar (this is illustrated in Figure 3.1).

4. Enter the following formulas in the indicated cells. Use either pointing or typing methods. As you enter the formulas, the results illustrated in Figure 3.1 should appear on the workbook.

Cell	Formula
C6	=A5*A7
C7	=A5^A8
C8	=(A5+A6+A7)/A9
C9	=A8/A9+A10
C10	=A8/(A9+A10)

5. Click on cell A13.

6. Enter =A1 in cell A13. Note that the contents of cell A1 are displayed in cell A13.

FIGURE 3.1
OPERATOR.XLS worksheet after all formulas have been entered

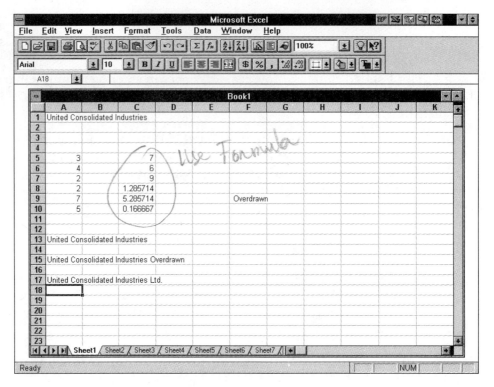

7. Enter =A1&F9 in cell A15. This formula concatenates the contents of two text cells.

8. Enter =A1&" Ltd." in cell A17. This formula concatenates the contents of a text cell and a literal string.

At this point the workbook should look like Figure 3.1.

9. Change the entry in cell A1 to General Industries. Note the effect in the cells that reference this text.

10. Change the entry in cell A5 to 2. Notice that the values displayed by several of the formulas change.

11. Annotate the formula in cell C10:

    a. Click on cell C10.

    b. Select Insert | Note.

    c. As illustrated below, type the text of the comment:

`This formula illustrates the effect of parentheses in formulas`

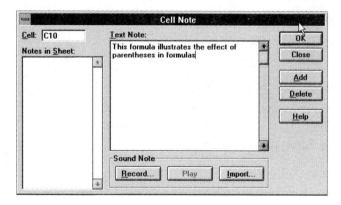

   d. Click OK to complete the process.

   Note that the comment is not visible in the workbook area, but there is a red note indicator in the upper-right corner of the cell.[1]

12. Use the File I Save command to save the file with the file name OPERATOR.

13. If you must leave the computer, click on File I Exit to exit to Windows. Exit to the operating system. Remember to back up your work.

   The next Guided Activity deals with functions.

Functions

Functions are used to form all or part of a formula. A partial list and discussion of mathematical, financial, date, time, and statistical functions follow. See the remainder of this book, the Excel Help window, and the Excel manual for discussions of the other functions. Appendix B provides a brief explanation of each function available in Excel 5. The Index lists all functions discussed in this book.

The terms in parentheses that follow a function are called *arguments* (components) of the function. In the examples below, x can be a cell, a constant value, a formula, or another function. For instance, ABS(x) could be either ABS(A10), ABS(5029), ABS(A10–B12), or ABS(MIN(G9,H9)). Some functions accept a range of cells as an argument. (The concept of a range of cells is discussed in the next unit.) If a function is the first entry in a formula, it must be preceded by = (equal sign).

Mathematical Functions

Excel provides two general types of mathematical functions: those that are of use in business applications and those that are more oriented to engineering and higher mathematics. The discussion that follows is limited to mathematical functions for

---

[1] If there is no red note indicator, someone has changed the default setting. Select Tools I Options and click the Note Indicator on the View card to the "on" position.

business applications. Additional mathematical functions are presented in Part Three as an advanced topic.

ABS(x) Absolute value of x. If cell J5 contains the value -2.95, the cell entry =ABS(J5) yields the result 2.95; a negative number is changed to a positive value.

INT(x) Rounds x down to an integer. If cell J5 contains the value -2.95 and cell K5 contains the value 2.95, the cell entry =INT(K5) yields the result 2, and the cell entry =INT(J5) yields the result -3.

MOD(x,y) Modular part (remainder) of x divided by y: x mod y. If cell J6 contains the value 6 and cell K6 contains the value 4, the cell entry =MOD(J6,K6) yields the result 2. (*Remember*: "Four goes into six one time, with a remainder of two.")

ROUND(x,n) Round number x to n decimal places. If cell J6 contains the value 6 and cell K6 contains the value 4, the cell entry =ROUND(K6/J6,2) yields the result 0.67.

SUM(number1,number2, ...) The sum of the items in the list. If the list contains NA( ), then the sum is #NA! The cell entry =SUM(A1,B5,C8) would display the sum of the current values of those three cells. The AutoSum button provides a shortcut method for entering this function.

The AutoSum Button

In Unit 2 we examined briefly the different buttons contained in the toolbar. One of these is the AutoSum button. Whenever you click the AutoSum button, Excel inserts a SUM( ) function in the active cell. Excel will take a guess at what arguments you desire to include in this function. It will examine the cells above and to the left of the active cell in making this guess. It will also look for text, other functions, or blank spaces to indicate the stopping point for the argument range. For instance, if you have a text entry in cell B1 with constant values in B2:B6, and you click the AutoSum button when B7 is the active cell, Excel will enter the formula =SUM(B2:B6) in cell B7.

Financial Functions

Financial functions are especially useful in finance and accounting applications. The financial function used most often in the remainder of this book is PMT( ); the others are listed for future reference. Where the argument is a percentage, it can be entered either as a decimal number (such as .139) or with a percent sign (such as 13.9%). Excel determines what you mean. Excel automatically sets the display format of the results of some functions, especially those that return dollar or percent results. Sometimes this is helpful, sometimes it is not. (In Unit 4, we discuss how to change the format of a number.)

CASH FLOWS

The following functions are used by financial analysts to determine how attractive an investment is over a period of time. In these functions, you must estimate either the interest rate you will receive or the amount of money you will receive, and

Excel computes the other. The first two functions, IRR( ) and NPV( ), deal with a series of numbers that must be put into a row or column of the workbook. This series of numbers is the anticipated net return (for example, revenue-cost) that an investment generates.

IRR(values,*guess*)[2] Internal rate of return of *values*, the series of cash flows in the range. Excel uses iteration to calculate the IRR. The guess is used to provide a starting point, since some income streams have more than one IRR. If *guess* is omitted, Excel will use 0.10 as *guess*. An example of the use of this function is contained in Exercise 3.2.

NPV(x,range) Net present value of the series of cash flows in *range*, discounted at *x* interest rate. An example of the use of this function is contained in Exercise 3.2.

ANNUITIES

The functions FV( ), PV( ), NPER( ), PMT( ), and RATE( ) deal with a fixed payment (an *annuity*) over a period of time. FV( ) is used to determine how much you will have in the future. PV( ) is used to determine the current value of a set of payments (for instance, "would you rather have $20,000 now or $100 a month for life?"). NPER( ) is used to determine how long (number of periods) you must make payments on a loan of a specific amount or save to accumulate a specific amount. PMT( ) is used to determine the periodic payment level necessary to pay back a loan. RATE( ) determines the interest rate on a loan.

FV(rate,nper,pmt,*pv*,*type*) Future value of an ordinary annuity with payments of *pmt* at a per-period interest rate of *rate* for *nper* periods. (See the next section concerning monthly and annual data.) *Pv* is the present value that a series of future payments is worth now; if omitted, it is assumed to be 0. *Type* is a code to indicate whether the payments are due at the end of the period (0) or the beginning of the period (1); the default is 0. For instance, if cell M1 contains .12 (the annual interest rate), M2 contains 5 (the number of years), and M3 contains -100 (the payment),[3] then the cell entry =FV(M1/12,M2*12,M3) would be used to determine how much would accumulate with monthly payments of $100, invested at 12% interest, over a period of five years. (The result is $8,166.97—Excel automatically formats the result as a dollar amount.)

PV(rate,nper,pmt,*fv*,*type*) Present value of an ordinary annuity at a per-period interest rate of *rate* with *nper* payments of *pmt* at the end of each period (*type* = 0) or the beginning of each period (*type* = 1). (See the next section concerning monthly and annual data.) For instance, if cell M1 contains .12 (the annual interest rate), M2 contains 5 (the number of years), and M3 contains -100 (the payment), then the cell entry =PV(M1/12,M2*12,M3) would be used to determine the current dollar

---

[2] *Italics* indicate that the argument is optional.

[3] Excel expects loan payments to be a negative number, since it represents cash outflow. If your function returns a value different than you expected, check to make sure that all arguments that represent cash outflow are negative.

equivalent of monthly receipts of $100, invested at 12% interest, over a period of five years. (The result is $4,495.50.)

NPER(rate,pmt,pv,fv,type) Number of periods, the number of payments necessary to achieve the present value *pv* (or the future value *fv*),[4] given the payment *pmt* and interest *rate*. (See the next section concerning monthly and annual data.) For instance, if cell M1 contains .12 (the annual interest rate), M6 contains -500 (the payment), and M4 contains 12000 (the present value), then the cell entry =NPER(M1/12,M6,M4) would be used to determine the number of months necessary for a $500 monthly payment to pay off a loan of $12,000 at 12% annual interest. (The result is rounded off to 27.6 months.)

PMT(rate,nper,pv,fv,type) Payment on a loan of principal *pv* at a per-period interest rate of *rate* for *nper* periods. (See the next section concerning monthly and annual data.) For instance, if cell M2 contains .12 (the annual interest rate), M3 contains 5 (the number of years to repay the loan), and M4 contains -10000 (the amount borrowed), then the cell entry =PMT(M2/12,M3*12,M4) would be used to determine the monthly payment on a $10,000 loan at 12% annual interest. (The result is 222.44.)

Recall that a payment should be a negative value, since it represents money to be paid out. Although this is good accounting, you wish in this case to see the payment represented as a positive value. To override the default, you enter the amount to be borrowed, *pv*, as a negative amount. This principle applies to all financial functions in Excel; amounts to be paid out will be in negative numbers.

RATE(nper,pmt,pv,fv,type,guess) The interest rate if a loan of principal *pv* is paid in payments of *pmt* for *nper* periods. (See the next section concerning monthly and annual data.) For instance, if cell K2 contains 2 (the number of years to repay the loan), K3 contains -200 (the monthly payment amount), and K4 contains 4000 (the amount borrowed), then the cell entry =RATE(K2*12,K3,K4) would be used to determine the interest rate on a $4,000 loan repaid in $200 payments for 24 months. (The result displays as 2%—multiplied by 12, it yields 18.16% annually.)

MONTHLY PAYMENTS BASED ON ANNUAL INTEREST AND TERM

Typically, interest rates and term are expressed in annual figures—for example, 11.9% annual interest and 3 years to repay. Because payments are usually made monthly, however, many of the formulas for annuities (above) and compounding (below) must be adjusted. To convert annual interest rates to monthly interest rates, divide by 12. To convert number of years to number of months, multiply by 12. For example, the monthly payment on $1,000 for 2 years at 18% is calculated by the cell entry =PMT(0.18/12,2*12,-1000).

---

[4] Use *pv* if you are calculating the number of periods for a loan; use *fv* if you are determining the number of periods to save a given future value.

COMPOUNDING

The annuity functions NPER( ) and RATE( ) also can be used to determine the amount of time or the necessary interest rate for a current amount to grow to some desired future amount with compound interest. Unlike annuities, there are no periodic payments, only the initial investment.

NPER(rate,pmt,pv,*fv,type*) To calculate the number of periods required for present value *pv* invested at a certain interest rate to increase to desired future value *fv*, set the *pmt* at 0 and proceed as above. (See the preceding section concerning monthly and annual data.) For instance, if cell N1 contains .12 (the annual interest rate), N2 contains 2000 (the future value), and N3 contains -1000 (the current value, or amount invested), then the cell entry =NPER(N1/12,0,N3,N2) would be used to determine how many months it would take for $1,000 to double in value if invested at 12%, compounded monthly. (The result is rounded off to 69.66 months; do not overlook the 0 [zero] in the *pmt* position.)

RATE(nper,pmt,pv,*fv,type,guess*) Periodic interest, the rate necessary for the present value *pv* to grow into the future value *fv* over the number of periods in *nper*. (See the preceding section concerning monthly and annual data.) For instance, if cell N4 contains 5 (the number of years), N2 contains 2000 (the future value), and N3 contains -1000 (the current value), then the cell entry =RATE(N4*12,0,N3,N2) would be used to determine the investment rate necessary for $1,000 to double in value over a period of 5 years, compounded monthly. (The result displays 1%, which, multiplied by 12, is 13.94% per annum.)

DEPRECIATION

The practice of reducing the value of an asset as it becomes older is called ***depreciation***. There are several methods for determining the amount of depreciation that can be charged in a given year, five of which are available in Excel 5. Each of the methods requires that you state the original cost of the item, the useful life of the item (how long it will last), and the salvage (resale or scrap) value at the end of that life.

DB(cost,salvage,life,period,*month*) Fixed-declining balance depreciation, the depreciation amount in a specific *period*, given the initial *cost*, *salvage* value, and *life* of the item. *Month* is the number of months in the first year; if omitted, Excel will assume it to be 12.

DDB(cost,salvage,life,period,*factor*) Double-declining balance depreciation, the depreciation amount in a specific *period*, given the initial *cost*, *salvage* value, and *life* of the item. *Factor* is the rate at which the balance declines; if omitted, Excel will assume it to be 2, thus using the double-declining balance method.

SLN(cost,salvage,life) Straight-line depreciation, which is the same amount for each period, given the initial *cost*, *salvage* value, and *life* of the item.

SYD(cost,salvage,life,period) Sum-of-the-years' digits depreciation, for a specified *period*, given the initial *cost*, *salvage* value, and *life* of the item.

VDB(cost,salvage,life,start_period,end_period,*factor,no_switch*) Variable declining balance depreciation, the depreciation amount in a specific period, given the initial *cost*, *salvage* value, and *life* of the item, a limited period during which to fully depreciate the asset, the option to use a factor other than double, and the option to switch to straight-line depreciation when that yields a higher write-off. This function offers more options in calculating the depreciation, but requires greater sophistication of the user.

Date and Time Functions

Excel date functions provide a method for doing arithmetic using dates (for instance, how many days have elapsed since July 4, 1976?) and for displaying those dates in an orderly manner. Excel calculates dates by counting the number of days that have elapsed between the date in question and January 1, 1900. To Excel, year 00 is 1900, year 95 is 1995, and year 150 is 2050. The following four functions yield a *serial date number*.

DATE(year,month,day) Serial number of a given date, where =DATE(00,01,01) (January 1, 1900) is number 1 and =DATE(178,12,31) (December 31, 2078) is number 65380.

SHORTCUT *To enter a date in the current year, type it as follows:* 23Jan [Enter]. *To enter a date in any other year, enter it as follows:* 23Jan96 [Enter]. *You may enter any years between 1920 and 2019 with just the last two digits of the year; all other years must be entered with all four digits. The year, regardless of how it is entered, must be between 1900 and 2078.*

NOW( ) Current date and time, assuming that you set the proper date when you started or reset the system. This returns both date (integer) and time (fractional) components. It is a good idea to include this in your workbooks so that you can see exactly when a given printout was produced. NOW( ) is updated whenever the worksheet is recalculated. *Note that the parentheses are empty, but they must be included to signal Excel that this is a function.*

TODAY( ) Current date, assuming that you set the proper date when you started or reset the system. This returns the date as an integer. TODAY( ) is updated whenever the workbook is recalculated. Use this function instead of NOW( ) when the date only, and not the time, is required.

DATEVALUE(date_text) String to date, converts a string to a serial date number; for example, =DATEVALUE("16-Feb-93") yields 34016.

Excel usually formats the results of DATE( ), NOW( ), and TODAY( ) so that they are meaningful. If a number is displayed, it must be formatted using the Format l Number command (see Unit 4). You can use these functions in formulas; for example, =TODAY( )+7 is one week from today.

Excel also enables you to calculate time as a fractional serial number, with midnight being 0 (zero) and noon being 0.5. One way to enter exact hours is to use fractions (=16/24 is 4:00 PM) and use the Format l Cells command to format the result as time. If the NOW( ) function is formatted to a time, then the current time is displayed. You can also use either of the following two functions:

TIME(hour,minute,second)   Serial time number. It computes the time number of the arguments.

TIMEVALUE(time_text)   String to time. It converts a string to a serial time number; for example, =TIMEVALUE("6:06 PM") yields 0.754167.

The other date and time functions yield a number:

DAY(serial_number)   Day of the month of the given date. *Serial_number* can be expressed as a function, a number, or a text string. If today is May 21, 1996, then =DAY(TODAY()) yields 21.

MONTH(serial_number)   Month number of the given date. *Serial_number* can be expressed as a function, a number, or a text string. If today is May 21, 1996, then =MONTH(TODAY()) yields 5.

YEAR(serial_number)   Year number of the given date. *Serial_number* can be expressed as a function, a number, or a text string. If today is May 21, 1996, then =YEAR(TODAY()) yields 1996.

HOUR(serial_number)   Hour value of the time number. *Serial_number* can be expressed as a function, a number, or a text string. If the time is now 8:10:25, then =HOUR(NOW()) yields 8.

MINUTE(serial_number)   Minute value of the time number. *Serial_number* can be expressed as a function, a number, or a text string. If the time is now 8:10:25, then =MINUTE(NOW()) yields 10.

SECOND(serial_number)   Second value of the time number. *Serial_number* can be expressed as a function, a number, or a text string. If the time is now 8:10:25, then =SECOND(NOW()) yields 25.

WEEKDAY(serial_number)   Day of the week of *serial_number*. *Serial_number* can be expressed as a function, a number, or a text string. If today is Aug. 22, 1992, then =WEEKDAY(TODAY()) yields 7 (Saturday). You can use the TEXT() function to convert the number to a specified format; so =TEXT(WEEKDAY(TODAY()), "dddd") yields Saturday.

DAYS360(start_date,end_date)   Difference in dates using a 360-day year (that is, 12 months, each with 30 days). This function is used when interest paid or earned is calculated on a 360-day year instead of a 365-day year.

Statistical Functions

Statistical functions are very useful for business calculations. For instance, you can use MIN( ) to discover the minimum value in a list of sales figures and AVERAGE( ) to determine the average sales. In the examples below, the list can be any number of arguments (up to the 255-character limit), separated by commas. The arguments can be any combination of numbers, formulas, cell addresses, range specifications, or range names. For example, AVERAGE(number1,number2, …) could be

AVERAGE(A1:A25) or a more complex list, such as AVERAGE(A1,A9,25,B6:B32, SUM(D3:D18)).

AVERAGE(number1,number2, ...) The average value of the items in the list. If any cell in the list contains NA( ), then the average is #NA! The NA( ) function is a special function discussed with Excel logic in Part Three.

The cell entry =AVERAGE(-5,8,3/12,(-6-2)) yields the result -1.1875, which is the average of the values. The cell entry =AVERAGE(A1,B5,C8) would compute the average of the current values of those three cells.

COUNT(value,value2, ...) The number of cells that contain numeric entries in the list.

MIN(number1,number2, ...) The minimum value in the list. The cell entry =MIN(-5,8,3/12,(-6-2)) yields the result -8, which is the smallest of the values. MIN(A1,B5,C8) would display the smallest of the current values of those three cells.

MAX(number1,number2, ...) The maximum value in the list. The cell entry =MAX(-5,8,3/12,(-6-2)) yields the result 8, which is the largest of the values. MAX(A1,B5,C8) would display the largest of the current values of those three cells.

SUMPRODUCT(array1,array2, ...) The sum of the products of the items in the two arrays. This is sometimes called the *sum of the crossproducts* and is used in some statistical procedures.

There are also database statistical functions that operate on a subset of the data in a range. See Part Three for more details.

Using the Function Wizard

Excel provides two alternatives for entering function names. You can type the name of the function—for example, you could type =SUM( ).[5] You can also use the Function Wizard, called by clicking the Function Wizard button (on the formula bar when in edit mode) or by giving the Insert | Function command (the keyboard shortcut for this command is [Shift][F3]). To use the latter method, press [Alt][I], [F], or just press [Shift][F3]. Excel will present the Function Wizard dialog box:

---

[5] If the function is the first entry in a cell, type = (equal sign) before the function name.

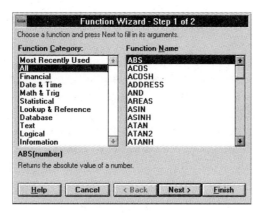

Highlight the name of the function you want (press ↓ or PgDn, or click on the scroll bar to bring more of the list into view). After highlighting the function name, click on Next or press Enter. The next window of the Function Wizard looks like this:

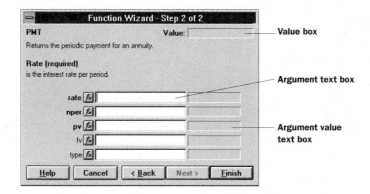

Notice that this window contains a brief description of the function you selected. The Value box contains the value of the function based on the currently entered arguments. As you select each argument list box, there is also a brief description of that argument. To enter an argument, first click in the text box for that argument. Then click on the cell that contains the value of the argument or enter the argument directly. The cell on which you click will display in the text box. Its value will appear in the box next to the text box. Move through the arguments, using this technique to enter each in turn. If there are optional arguments that you are not using, bypass them. Using the Function Wizard requires more keystrokes but is handy when you forget the exact spelling of a function name (and also provides you with the required and optional arguments, in the correct order).[6] Click the Back button if you need to select a different function. Click the Cancel button to exit the dialog box without entering a function.

---

6 When you are typing function names, it is a good idea to type them in lowercase letters. If you correctly type the name of the function, Excel will convert the function name to capitals. If Excel does *not* convert the function name to capitals, you probably misspelled the function name. This practice will eliminate one possible problem if your function does not work as expected.

Using the Help Window

We touched on the subject of the Help window in Unit 1, while discussing the various function keys and their effects. Here, we provide a thorough introduction into the use of the Help window, with specific reference to getting Help on the different functions that are available in Excel.

While the Function Wizard is very useful in simplifying the entry of functions, it is of limited use in determining which function you need. Excel's Help system provides a wealth of information about what different functions accomplish and their limitations, arguments, and so on.

If you already know the name of the function you want to use, click on Help, then Search for Help on. You will see the following window (after scrolling):

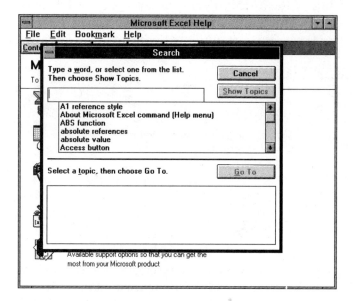

Type the name of the function in the text box; as you type, the drop-down list will change to show topics that begin with the letters you are typing. When you see the desired subject in the list box, double-click on the topic to select it, then click on the Go To action button to see the Help on that function (or another topic). For instance, if you double-click on the ABS function in the above window, you see the following Help window:

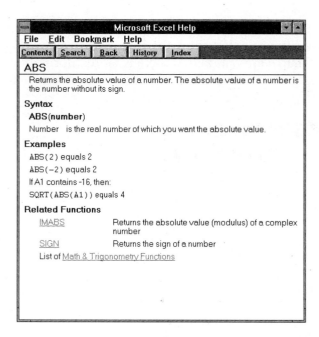

However, more often than not, you will probably be unsure as to which is the best function to use. For purposes of example, suppose you are looking for a function that will show the interest portion of a car payment, but are unsure as to what function will best meet your need. Since you do not know what function name to type in the Search text box, that is not the best way to proceed. Instead of using Help | Search for Help on, use the Help | Contents command. When you issue this command, you see the following window:

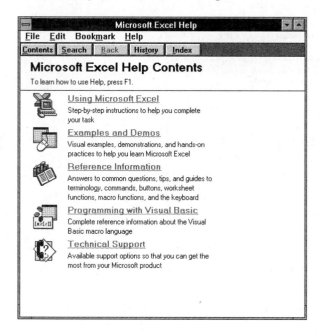

The explanation of the Reference Information item includes worksheet functions. As you place the mouse cursor on that entry, the cursor changes to a hand with a pointing finger. This is Help's indication that there is more information connected to that entry. If you do not have a mouse, press [Tab] to move from one to the other. When you click on the entry, you see this next window:

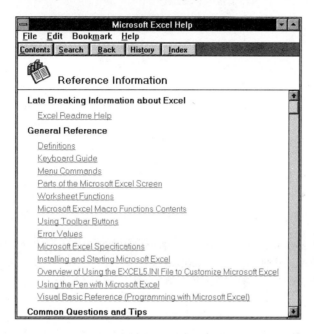

Since you are looking for information about worksheet functions, click on that item to see this window:

Since you know at least the type of function you are looking for, it is logical to move to Worksheet Functions Listed by Category. Click that item to see this window:

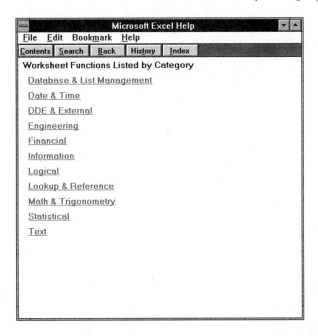

You can readily see that you are progressing more deeply into the Help system. Now you are confronted with a listing of Excel's function categories. Since you are looking for a financial function, place the mouse cursor on the Financial entry. You are again rewarded with a pointing finger cursor, informing you that there is yet another level to check. Click on the Financial category. For purposes of this example, we have clicked twice on the scroll bar before creating the next illustration:

In the above illustration you will notice an entry, IPMT, with an explanation, "Returns the interest payment for an investment for a given period". Once more, you click on this entry to gain further information. You see the following window:

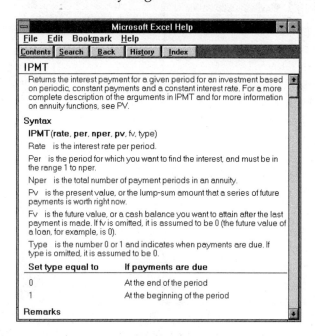

Finally, you see what you have been looking for! This window provides detailed information about what the function does, lists the mandatory and optional arguments, explains the arguments, gives an example of how to use the function, and lists related functions.

There is one other aspect of the Help window that is of interest: the bar of action buttons just below the menu bar. The Contents and Search buttons have the same effect as giving the Help|Contents and Help|Search for Help on commands, respectively. The Back button backs the user up to the last viewed window. The History button calls up this window:

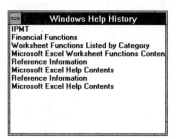

By using the History window, you can move back through a very long series of steps to any point in the Help process and take a different path. This is very useful if you discover that you did not find what you were looking for, or if you have more than one search to make.

The Help facility is extremely valuable in many circumstances; it is especially useful when looking for one specific function among the 320 workbook functions that are a part of Excel 5.

GUIDED ACTIVITY 3.2

Using Functions

This activity requires you to use formulas in a workbook.

1. If you are not continuing from the previous Guided Activity, follow the startup procedure outlined in Unit 1 to load Windows and enter Excel. If you are continuing from a previous activity or exercise and already have a workbook on the screen, use the command File | New to open a new workbook.

2. In cells D5 and D6, enter the numbers 18 and 7, as shown in Figure 3.2.

3. Make D7 the active cell. In cell D7, use the AutoSum button to compute the sum of the numbers in cells D5 and D6. After you press the AutoSum button, the range D5:D6 will be highlighted. Press [Enter] to accept the formula.

4. In cell D8, compute the absolute value of the difference (that is, D6–D5) as follows:

    a. Select cell D8. Type =abs(. The formula bar will look like this:

    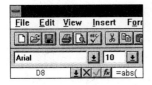

    b. Click on cell D6.

    c. Press [-] (hyphen), then click on cell D5.

    d. Press [)] (a right parenthesis).

    e. Press [Enter].

    When the formula is entered properly, the result appears as illustrated in cell D8 of Figure 3.2.

5. In cell D9, compute the integer part of D5 divided by D6 (that is, D5/D6). This requires the INT( ) function.

6. In cell D10, compute the remainder of D5 divided by D6. This requires the MOD( ) function.

NOTE *When using the MOD( ) function, separate the dividend and the divisor by a comma, not a slash.*

FIGURE 3.2
FUNCTION.XLS
workbook

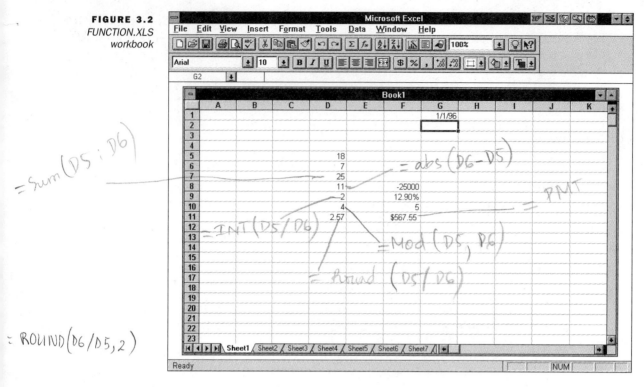

7. In cell D11, compute the quotient of D5 divided by D6, rounded to two decimal places. This requires the ROUND( ) function.

8. In cell F8, enter the amount -25000 (the amount you need to borrow to buy your BMW).[7] In cell F9 enter the annual interest rate: 12.9%. You plan to pay back the amount in five years (payments will be made monthly); put 5 in F10. In cell F11 you will write a formula that computes the monthly payment. This requires the PMT( ) function.

NOTE *Did you forget the order of the arguments? Use the Function Wizard; it will give you the correct argument names in order and separated by commas. All you have to do is fill in the correct arguments (and, of course, adjust annual figures to monthly figures).*

   a. The *rate* argument is selected; click on cell F9. Type /12 to convert the annual interest rate to a monthly rate.

   b. Select the *nper* argument by clicking in the text box, and click on cell F10. Type *12 to convert the number of years to the number of months.

   c. Select the *pv* argument by clicking in the text box, and click on cell F8. Then press Enter.

9. In cell G1, enter the formula to calculate the serial number of the date January 14, 1996. This requires the DATE( ) function, or the shortcut method discussed with the DATE( ) function. Do not be concerned if you fail to see a serial date number.

---

[7] This amount is negative in order to make the payment amount positive. See the earlier discussion of the PMT( ) function.

By default, Excel converts serial date numbers to a standard date format. (You learn how to change the number format in Unit 4.) The result may be too wide to fit in the cell. (You also learn how to adjust the column width so that you can see the date, in Unit 4.)

10. The completed workbook should look like Figure 3.2. Save your work with the file name FUNCTION.

CHECKPOINT 3A What command do you use to save the file?

11. If you must leave the computer, select File | Exit to return to Windows. Exit to the operating system. Remember to back up your work.

GUIDED ACTIVITY 3.3

Using the Help System

In this Guided Activity you gain experience manipulating Excel's Help system.

1. If you are not continuing from the previous Guided Activity, follow the startup procedure outlined in Unit 1 to load Windows and enter Excel. If you are continuing from a previous activity or exercise and already have a workbook on the screen, use the command File | New to open a new workbook window.

2. In this step, follow the instructions in the earlier section, "Using the Help Window," to call up the Help screen for the IPMT( ) function.

   a. Give the Help | Contents command.
   b. Click on Reference Information.
   c. Click on Worksheet Functions.
   d. Click on Worksheet Functions Listed by Category.
   e. Click on Financial.
   f. Scroll down, then click on IPMT.

3. Next, you need to locate a function that will count the number of arguments (cells) that contain entries, numeric or otherwise. As a starting point, recall that there is a statistical function named COUNT( ) that counts all arguments (cells) containing values, but ignores those containing text entries.

   a. Click on the History button. You are not looking for a financial function, so you must go back one step further than that. Double-click on Worksheet Functions Listed by Category.
   b. Since you are relatively sure that you are looking for a statistical function, click on Statistical.
   c. Although the list of statistical functions is long, it appears that COUNTA( ) may do what you need. Click on that entry.

d. Reading through the explanation of COUNTA( ), you are assured that it will meet the requirements.

4. Click on File | Exit to close the Help window. Give the File | Exit command to return to Windows. Exit to the operating system.

EXERCISE 3.1

More Fun with Functions

1. If you are not continuing from the previous Guided Activity, follow the startup procedure outlined in Unit 1 to load Windows and enter Excel. If you are continuing from a previous activity or exercise and already have a workbook on the screen, use the command File | New to open a new workbook window.

2. Put your name in cell A1. Put the name of your boy/girl/dog/cat/hamster friend in A2. In cell A3, enter =A1&" loves "&A2 (put a space on each side of the word "loves"). Cute. Now, change the name in cell A2 and notice the result in cell A3.

3. In cell A5, put the number 123.456789. In cell A6, round the number in A5 to three decimal places. In cell A7, place a formula that computes the integer (A5 multiplied by 1,000) divided by 1,000. You should see 123.457 in A6 and 123.456 in A7. Why are the numbers different?

4. You want to accumulate a million dollars. Put 1000000 in cell D1. You have a thousand dollars. Put -1000 in cell D2 (the amount is negative, because it is paid into an investment account). Put 15% in cell D3 and 50 in D4. Use formulas in cells D5 through D7 to determine the following. If you can earn 15% per year on your money, how long will it take to have a million dollars? (49.4 years). What rate would you have to earn to have a million dollars after 50 years? (15%). If you invest a thousand dollars each year at 15% per year (ignoring the thousand dollars you already have), how long will it take to accumulate a million dollars? (35.9 years).

5. With cell A12 as the upper-left corner, build the following table:

```
Cost        23450
Salvage       950
Life           10
Period          1
```

In cells C12 through C14, compute the depreciation for each of the following methods: double-declining balance, straight-line, and sum-of-the-years' digits. Note which yields a higher depreciation in period 1, then change the period to 2, 3,...10, and notice how the amount of depreciation changes. (For period 1, you should obtain these results: DDB yields 4690, SLN yields 2250, and SYD yields 4090.91.)

6. Save your work with the file name MOREFUNC.

7. Select File | Exit to return to Windows. Exit to the operating system. Remember to back up your work.

EXERCISE 3.2

The Lottery Winner

1. If you are not continuing from the previous Guided Activity or Exercise, follow the startup procedure outlined in Unit 1 to load Windows and enter Excel. If you are continuing from a previous activity or exercise and already have a workbook on the screen, use the command File | New to open a new workbook.

2. Your friend Troy has just won the state lottery. He has been given the choice of receiving his $1,000,000 prize immediately, or $80,000 per year for the next 20 years. Since $80,000 for 20 years is $1,600,000, he thinks that he should take the money over time. He would like you to use your Excel expertise to determine the internal rate of return implied in this choice—that is, by spreading the receipt of $1.6 million over 20 years, what rate of interest is he earning?

3. To analyze this problem, start by putting the text `Prize` in cell A1. Enter the amount of money that Troy is giving up, `-1000000` (negative one million) in cell B1. Enter his receipts in the cells below B1—that is, enter `80000` in every cell in the range B2 through B21.

4. In cell C1, enter the text `IRR`. In D1, enter the formula `=IRR(B1:B21,10%)`. You should get the result `5%`, which means that Troy is earning about 5% per year on his prize.

5. Another way to analyze this problem is to determine the net present value: how much the stream of income is worth if it were to be paid today, assuming that you could earn a certain percentage (called the discount rate) on the money. Troy figures he could earn 10% on the money if he had it available now. To determine the net present value, enter the text `NPV` in cell C2 and the formula `=NPV(10%,B2:B21)` in cell D2. You should get the answer `$681,085.10`, which means that the $1,000,000 prize is really worth less than $700,000 if paid at $80,000 for each of 20 years, and that he could earn 10% on the money if he had it available now.

NOTE *On some screens, the result will not fit in the cell width and Excel will display a string of pound signs ########. To see the result, give the command Format | Column and click the AutoFit Selection option.*

6. Save this workbook with the name LOTTERY. If you would like to know more about how IRR( ) and PV( ) formulas are used to analyze the time value of money, consult with a finance or accounting professor.

EXERCISE 3.3

A Check Register (II)

This exercise continues the development of a workbook that you use to record checks and deposits in a checking account.

1. Open the file CHECKS.

2. Use the shortcut method (for example, `1jan95`) to enter dates. These will appear as numbers (not as words and numbers as you see below) until you learn how to format them in the following unit.

   ```
   Number    Date
             January 1, 1995
   101       January 5, 1995
   102       January 6, 1995
   103       January 7, 1995
   ```

3. Enter a formula in the Balance column, on the row with check 101. This formula should compute the balance as balance from the row above minus the payment amount plus the deposit amount. Even though some rows in your check register will not include both payments and deposits, the formula should be complete. Enter a similar formula for the other checks. Compute the balance by hand and compare it with the results you obtain on the workbook.

4. Save the file.

EXERCISE 3.4

Business Mileage (II)

Open the MILES96 workbook. Enter a formula in the Miles column that subtracts the reading of the current row from the reading of the row below. Thus, for the first entry you should obtain `41.1`, which is the number of miles you drove on January 1 and 2 for your grocery shopping. Enter this formula in each row of the spreadsheet. You will get a negative number on January 4, but that will change when you add an entry for the following day (which you do in a later unit). Save the file.

EXERCISE 3.5

Form 1040EZ (II)

In this exercise you continue the development of a spreadsheet for Form 1040EZ. Open the 1040EZ workbook. These instructions assume that you made the entries in the rows as noted in Exercise 2.5 in Unit 2. When we say "*row* 3" or "*cell* C3," we are referring to spreadsheet row 3. When we say "*line* 1," we are referring to line 1 of the tax form (which is in row 3). Enter the following numbers and formulas in *column* C. When you make an entry in column C, you will cut off the text of an entry in column

B. (In Unit 4 you will learn how to correct this problem by making column B wider. For the moment, ignore the problem.)

1. On line 1, enter $15,000.00. (This entry should be in cell C3.) This is your wage for last year. You find this amount on the W-2 form your employer supplies.

2. On line 2, enter $325, the interest you earned last year.

3. On line 3, enter a formula that adds lines 1 and 2. C1 + C2

4. On line 4, enter the formula =C32. Here, we are assuming the answer to the question is yes—this formula points to the cell that contains the result of line E from the workbook.

5. On line 5, enter a formula that subtracts line 4 from line 3. = C3 - C4

6. On line 6, enter $2,500.00. This is the amount withheld for federal taxes last year. You find this amount on the W-2 form your employer supplies.

7. On line 7, enter the number 1759. (We determined this number by looking in the tax tables on pages 22–24 of the 1992 Form 1040EZ book. In a later unit, we will develop a formula that computes the tax.)

8. On line 8, enter the formula =MAX(C15-C17,0). If line 6 is larger than line 7, then the difference between the two will be a positive number, which will be displayed by the function since it is larger than zero. If line 6 is not larger than line 7, then the difference between the two will be a negative number, and zero will be displayed by the function.

9. Enter a formula that will accomplish the desired result on line 9.

10. On line A, enter a formula that points to the entry for line 1.

11. On line B, enter the number 600.00. This is the minimum amount specified by the IRS.

12. Enter a formula that will accomplish the desired result on line C.

13. On line D, enter the number 3,600.00. This is the maximum amount specified by the IRS.

14. Enter a formula that will accomplish the desired result on line E.

Remember to save your work.

EXERCISE 3.6

Buford Fencing Company (I)

Sara Buford, your best friend's mother, has asked you to develop a simple spreadsheet for her business. She installs fences on residential property and needs a quick method to estimate the price of a job. She has given you a copy of the form she now uses, illustrated below. Build a spreadsheet that looks like the following. Put Buford Fencing Company in cell A1, labels in column A and rows 4 and 10, and the numbers listed here in columns B and C. Leave the cells with an *f* blank; you will enter a formula in them. When you save this spreadsheet, use the name BUFORD.

```
Buford Fencing Company
Blank line
Details
                        Length      Width
    Area                  25          20
    Gates                  2
    Prep. Labor            4
Blank line
Calculations
    Item                Price    Quantity    Extension
    Fence                 5         f            f
    Gates                15         f            f
    Prep. Labor          10         f            f
    Inst. Labor          20         f            f
    TOTAL                                        f
```

= 2 * (B5 + C5) * (3 * C12)   [handwritten annotation pointing to Fence quantity]

Enter formulas in columns C and D to compute the following:

- Fence quantity is twice the sum of the length and width, minus 3 for each gate.
- Gates quantity is the same as the entry in B6 (enter =B6 in cell C12).
- Prep. Labor quantity is the same as the entry in cell B7.
- Inst. Labor quantity is determined as follows: the installers install 20 feet of fence per hour and it takes one-half hour to install each gate.
- Extension is computed by multiplying price times quantity.
- TOTAL is the sum of the extensions. If you've done everything correctly, the total for this job will be 594.

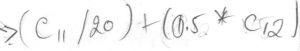
(C11/20) + (0.5 * C12)   [handwritten annotation]

Review Questions

*1. What is meant by the order of precedence?

2. Say that cells D5 and D6 each contain a number. Give the formula to compute the following:
   a. The sum of the two numbers
   *b. The absolute value of the difference between the two numbers
   c. The integer part of D5 divided by D6
   d. The remainder of D5 divided by D6

e. The quotient of D5 divided by D6, rounded to 2 decimal places

*3. Suppose that cell F8 contains the amount you need to borrow to buy your BMW. Cell F9 contains the annual interest rate. You plan to pay back the amount in 60 equal monthly payments. Write the formula that computes the monthly payment.

4. What formula calculates the serial number of the date January 14, 1995?

Key Terms

Annotation	Depreciation	Operator
Annuity	Hierarchy of operations	Order of precedence
Argument	Literal string	Serial date number
Comment	Note indicator	String
Concatenation	Operand	Sum of the crossproducts

Documentation Research

Using the Excel *User's Guide*, find and record the page number of each of the functions discussed in this unit. Write the page number in the margin next to the discussion of the function in the unit.

1. What is the effect of a % sign in a formula?

2. How can you enter the fraction 1/2 so that it does not get interpreted as a date (Jan. 2)?

APPLICATION A

Poor Richard's (I)

In this exercise you build a simple workbook, using a good sample of the material presented in the previous units. You start an Excel session; enter text, constant values, and formulas; use a function; and save your work. *Read the following instructions carefully: every word is important.*

1. Follow the startup procedure outlined in Unit 1 to load Windows and enter Excel.

2. Use the following information to create a workbook that looks like Figure A.1.

   a. Enter the text shown into column A and column E. Note that most of the text in column A extends into column B, and also from column E into column F.

   b. Enter the numbers shown into cells C4, C5, C6, C8, C9, G4, G5, and G6. List Price and Trade-in Value are negative numbers because they represent cash paid by the purchaser to Poor Richard. Likewise, Percent Profit and Net Price are negative numbers from the purchaser's point of view.

   c. In cell C12, enter the formula for Net Cost, which is Dealer Cost plus Trade-in Value (that is, =C5+C8).

   d. The formula for Net Price is List Price plus Trade-in Allowance. Note that this is a formula: do not enter the value 10100.

   e. The formula for Percent Profit is

   $$\frac{\text{Net Price} + \text{Net Cost}}{\text{Net Cost}}$$

   Remember the rules for order of precedence as you compose this formula.

FIGURE A.1
AUTO.XLS
worksheet

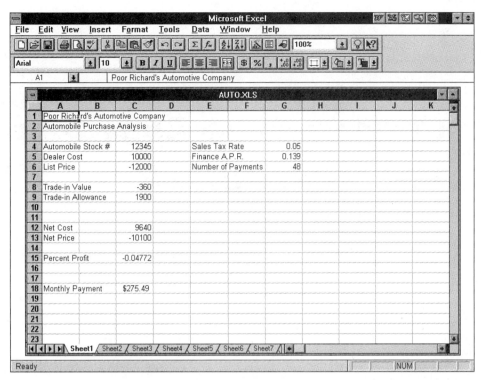

f. In cell C18, enter the function that computes payments based on principal, interest, and term: =PMT(G5/12,G6,C13). Recall the discussion in Unit 3 concerning the conversion of annual data for monthly payments. Why is the interest rate divided by 12, but the term not multiplied by 12?

3. Periodically, save your work under the name AUTO.

4. Now enter the number 2500 as the Trade-in Allowance. Notice what happens to the Net Price, Percent Profit, and Monthly Payment. If these numbers did not change, you probably entered constant values instead of formulas into cells C13, C15, and/or C18. If you made a mistake, correct it.

5. When you are finished, save your work one last time, then exit to Windows. Exit to the operating system. Remember to back up your work.

Changing the Appearance of the Workbook

In this unit we introduce the menu that affects the appearance of the workbook: the Format menu. Here we discuss only a subset of the commands; we describe other options in later units. We also examine the concept of ranges and various options under the Edit and Insert menus.

Learning Objectives

At the completion of this unit you should know

1. what a range is;
2. the proper procedures for formatting numbers, alignment, fonts, and borders;
3. how to use these formatting tools to create a style.

At the completion of this unit you should be able to

1. change the default number format to any desired format;
2. insert and delete rows and columns in a worksheet;
3. insert, delete, and rename sheets in a workbook;
4. specify a range;
5. erase a specific area of the worksheet;
6. reformat numeric values within a specified range;
7. realign cell entries, whether numeric or alphabetic;
8. insert borders around cells as desired;

9. change the font in a specified range;
10. use the formatting tools to create a style;
11. change the column widths or row heights for a specified range or for the entire worksheet;
12. create a template consisting of boilerplate text and predefined styles.

Important Commands

Edit | Clear

Edit | Delete

Format | AutoFormat

Format | Cells

Format | Column

Format | Row

Format | Sheet

Format | Style

Insert | Cells

Insert | Columns

Insert | Rows

Insert | Worksheet

Ranges as a Concept

A *range* is a rectangular block of cells. It can be any of the following:

- One row by one column: a single cell
- One row by many columns: a partial row
- One row by all columns: a complete row
- Many rows by one column: a partial column
- All rows by one column: a complete column
- Many rows by many columns: a block
- An entire worksheet

Ranges are specified by listing the upper-left and lower-right corners, separated by a colon. The following are legitimate range specifications, illustrated in Figure 4.1:

- A1 (in the case of a single cell range the colon and ending cell address are not needed)
- 3:3—a complete row
- B5:F5—a partial row
- A9:A14—a partial column
- C8:E10—a block
- H:H—a complete column
- A1:IV16384—the entire worksheet

A single cell can be selected by pointing the mouse cursor at the cell and clicking. A block, partial row, or partial column can be selected by placing the mouse cursor in the upper-left cell, pressing the button and dragging to the lower-right cell, and then releasing the mouse button. A complete row can be selected by placing the mouse cursor on the number identifying the row and clicking. A complete column can be selected by placing the mouse cursor on the letter identifying the column and clicking. The entire worksheet can be selected by clicking on the blank button between column label "A" and row label "1." This button is called the *Select All button*.

A single cell can be selected by using the arrow keys to move the selection cursor to the desired cell. A block, partial row, or partial column can be selected by moving the selection cursor to the upper-left cell, holding down [Shift], and moving the

FIGURE 4.1
Range selection

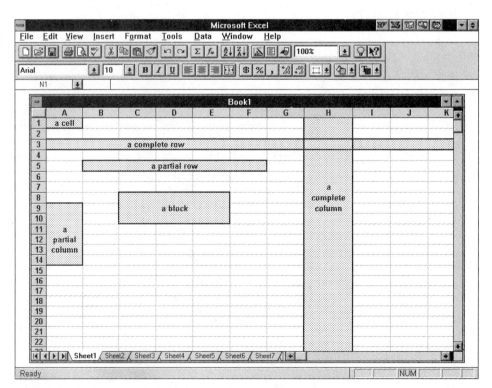

selection cursor to the lower-right cell. A complete row can be selected by placing the selection cursor in any cell in the row and pressing [Shift][Spacebar]. A complete column can be selected by placing the selection cursor in any cell in the column and pressing [Ctrl][Spacebar]. The entire workbook can be selected by pressing [Shift][Ctrl][Spacebar]. All occupied cells are selected by placing the selection cursor on the first occupied cell and pressing [Shift][Ctrl][End].

Excel also allows the selection of *discontinuous ranges*, as illustrated in Figure 4.2. For example, to use the keyboard to select A1:D4 and E6:F12 as one range, place the selection cursor in cell A1, press and hold [Shift], and move the selection cursor to cell D4. Press [Shift][F8] (the status bar at the bottom of the screen should read ADD). Move the selection cursor to cell E6, press and hold [Shift], and move the selection cursor to cell F12. To select discontinuous ranges with the mouse, drag through the first range, release the mouse button, then move the selection cursor to cell E6 and hold [Ctrl] while dragging through subsequent ranges.[1]

Many things are accomplished using ranges. For instance, the format used to display values can be changed for an entire range. All the values in a range can be referred to when writing a formula. A range of cells can be protected, which means that the contents of those cells cannot be altered. Data input can be simplified and set to proceed through a specific sequence.

Ranges can have permanent names assigned, or they can be indicated as required by commands or in formulas. *Named ranges* are created using the Insert | Name command. Once named, the range can be referred to either by entering the range name,

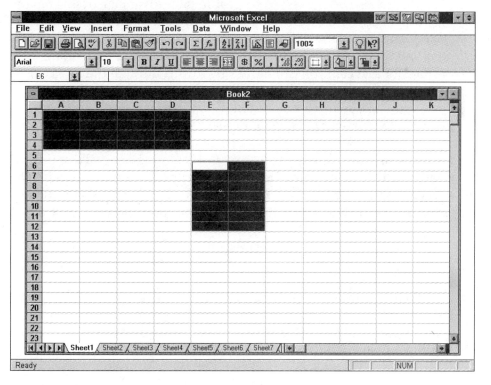

FIGURE 4.2
Discontinuous ranges

---

1 Do not hold [Ctrl] while selecting the first range. This causes Excel to select the first range twice, and could produce unpredictable results if the range is referred to in formulas.

by using the Apply selection from the Insert I Name command, or by pressing [F3] and responding to the dialog box. (Named ranges are discussed in detail in Unit 13.)

Ranges can be used to simplify input of data from other workbooks. You can also go to a named range using the Edit I Go To command or using [F5] and responding to the dialog box.

We discuss advanced range topics in later units. This unit is devoted to the most common uses of ranges.

Three-Dimensional Ranges

Each of the range types just discussed can also be selected on multiple sheets in a workbook. You can use the ability to select ranges on multiple sheets to format several sheets identically, or in formulas. Suppose, for example, that you have a budget workbook with one sheet for each month and a total sheet for the end of the year. You need to be able to sum the monthly entries for the annual sheet. To select a range of sheets, click on the tab of the first sheet, then press the [Shift] key and click on the tab of the last sheet. To select discontinuous sheets, select the first sheet by clicking on its tab and press the [Ctrl] key as you click on the subsequent sheets. You must have a mouse to select a group of sheets.

Entering Data in Ranges

Data can also be entered in ranges. To take advantage of this time-saver, first select a range. This can be done by either pressing the arrow keys while holding [Shift], or dragging the mouse through the range. All the selected cells will be in reverse type, and the active cell will be in the upper-left corner of the range. After entering the data for that cell, you can move downward through the range by pressing [Enter], or move to the right by pressing [Tab].

If you make an error, you can move upward by pressing [Shift][Enter], and you can move left by pressing [Shift][Tab]. To deselect the range, simply press any one of the arrow keys, or click the mouse on any cell. Entering data in ranges is substantially faster for large amounts of data entry than entering one cell at a time. The advantage is increased when the data is mostly numeric; use the number pad at the right of the keyboard and the [Enter] key that is part of that number pad. This makes data entry the same as using an adding machine; watch for opportunities to use this feature.

Edit Commands

To edit a range in Excel, first select the range you wish to change and then select the command to perform. The Edit menu generally affects the content of the workbook. Two of the Edit commands that we discuss in this unit affect that content by erasing or deleting cells.

Edit | Clear is the workbook equivalent of an eraser. Selecting this command allows you to remove unwanted elements from the selected range. The options in the Edit | Clear dialog box are shown here:

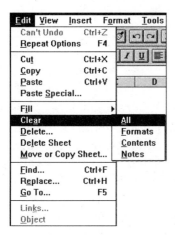

The default is All, which erases all keyboard entries, formulas, formula results, and formatting. Selecting Formats returns the cell formatting to the Normal style. (We discuss styles later in this unit.) Remember our discussion of cell annotation in Unit 3. Selecting Contents erases all keyboard entries, formulas, and formula results. The Clear Contents command is available on the shortcut menu. Right-click after selecting a cell or range of cells, then select Clear Contents from the shortcut menu. Selecting Notes removes any notes attached to the cells in the range.

Edit | Delete is similar to Edit | Clear, with one major exception. While Edit | Clear removes the contents of the cells in the range, Edit | Delete also removes the cells themselves. The Edit | Delete dialog box has the following options:

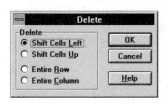

It appears anytime the range is not a complete column or a complete row and asks the user to specify whether the remaining cells should move up or to the left to fill the gap left by the deleted cells. If the range is a complete row (or group of rows), the cells move up without prompting the user. Likewise, if the selected range is a complete column (or group of columns), the cells move to the left without bringing up the dialog box. Note that the column and row labels adjust after an Edit | Delete, leaving no indication that the deletion has occurred. The Edit | Delete command is available on the cell shortcut menu. Right-click after selecting a cell or range of cells and select Delete from the shortcut menu.

Insert Commands

The Insert menu contains several commands that perform the opposite of Edit | Delete. The commands on the Insert menu that are of interest to us right now are Insert | Cells, Insert | Rows, Insert | Columns, and Insert | Worksheet. The

Insert | Cells command calls a dialog box similar to the one used by the Edit | Delete command:

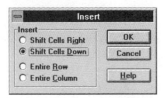

If you wish to insert cells to the left of existing cells, click the Shift Cells Right check box. If you wish to insert cells above existing cells, click the Shift Cells Down check box. If you wish to insert entire columns or rows, click the appropriate check box. Alternatively, you can insert rows by selecting a row or rows and giving the Insert | Cells command, or by simply giving the Insert | Rows command. Likewise, you can insert columns either by selecting a column or columns before giving the Insert | Cells command, or by giving the Insert | Columns command. You can also insert a new sheet in a workbook by giving the Insert | Worksheet command; the new sheet will be placed in front of the currently active sheet.

The Insert command is also available on the cell shortcut menu. Right-click after selecting a cell or range of cells and select Insert from the shortcut menu. You will see the dialog box illustrated above.

Format Commands

The Format menu primarily contains those commands that affect the *appearance* of the workbook, rather than its *content*. The Format | Cells command displays the dialog box shown in Figure 4.3.

FIGURE 4.3
Format | Cells, Number tab

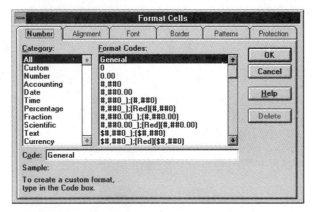

Numeric Format

The Number tab allows you to change the display format for all numeric entries in the specified range. As shown in Figure 4.3, these include **number, accounting,** *date, time, percentage, fraction, scientific, text,* and *currency* formats, for a total of 35 predefined number formats. In addition, Excel allows the user to define up to 221 *custom formats*. *General format* is a number format with no thousands separator and 0 (zero) mandatory decimal places. (Decimals are displayed if they are entered as part of the number.) General format changes the number to scientific format, if necessary, to allow it to fit in the column width.

To apply an existing format to a selected (highlighted) range, simply select the format desired in the Category list box. To make it easier to select a format, they are divided into the categories named above. To create a custom format, type the characters representing the new format in the Code text box at the bottom of the dialog box. The characters used in the number format codes are shown in Table 4.1. The following illustrates a percentage format with one decimal place:

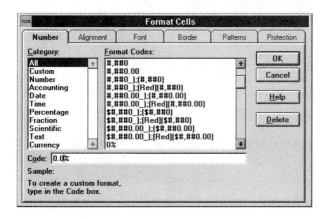

TABLE 4.1
Custom format characters

CHARACTER	EFFECT
$. ( ) : + – / space	These characters all print as themselves. To display a character other than these, either enclose the character in double quotation marks ("...") or precede it with a backslash (\).
0	Displays a required numeric entry. For instance, if two zeros are placed after the decimal, every number is formatted to two decimal places.
#	Displays an optional numeric entry. The # sign is used as a placeholder to reserve that place, if needed.
?	Displays an unknown numeric entry. It is used for fractional formats that must be calculated.
, (comma)	Acts as a thousands separator when surrounded by 0s or #s.
%	Excel multiplies by 100 and inserts the % sign.
\	Displays the next character; similar to enclosing the next character in quotation marks.

TABLE 4.1 (Continued)

CHARACTER	EFFECT
;	Separates formatting between conditional values. The default is that formatting before the semicolon is applied to numbers greater than or equal to zero; the formatting after the semicolon is applied to negative numbers.
[Red]	Any of the eight standard colors may be inserted in the brackets. This is usually used in conjunction with the semicolon to change negative numbers to red. However, it can be used to change any numeric entry to any of the eight standard colors—black, white, red, green, blue, yellow, magenta, and cyan.
[Color n]	Displays the corresponding color in the color palette, where n is a number from 1 to 56.
E+ E– e+ e–	Forces the number to scientific notation. The number of placeholders (0s and #s) to the right determines the number of digits in the exponent. The minus sign inserts a minus sign in front of negative exponents; the plus sign inserts a plus sign in front of positive exponents and a minus sign in front of negative exponents.
*	Repeats the next character in the format to the end of the cell width.
_ (underscore)	Inserts a space the width of the next character in the format. (Use this feature to allow different types of formats, especially those with parentheses, to align properly.)
" "	Displays the text string contained in the quotation marks.
@	Text placeholder. Inserts any text entered in the cell where the @ sign appears.
m	Displays a numeric month entry, for example, 4 for April. If m or mm is used immediately following an h or hh, Excel provides the minute rather than the month.
mm	Displays a two-digit numeric month entry, for example, 04 for April.
mmm	Displays a month abbreviation, for example, Apr for April.
mmmm	Displays a month name, for example, April for April.
d	Displays a numeric day entry.
dd	Inserts a leading 0 in a numeric day entry.
ddd	Displays a day abbreviation, for example, Mon for Monday.
dddd	Displays a day name, for example, Monday for Monday.
yy	Displays a two-digit year entry, for example, 91 for 1991.
yyyy	Displays a complete four-digit year entry.
h	Displays an hour entry.
hh	Displays a two-digit hour entry.
m	Displays a minute entry, if it follows an h or hh.

TABLE 4.1 (Continued)

CHARACTER	EFFECT
mm	Displays a two-digit minute entry.
s	Displays a second entry.
ss	Displays a two-digit second entry.
[ ]	Displays hours greater than 24, or minutes or seconds greater than 60. Use this feature if you need to work with more than 24 hours or more than 60 minutes or seconds.
AM/PM	Forces hours and minutes to be formatted to a 12-hour clock with an AM or PM designation. If omitted, times are formatted to a 24-hour clock. Excel also recognizes a/p, A/P, and am/pm.

It is extremely important to realize that changing the numeric format only changes the *display* of the numeric entry, not its *value*. Table 4.2 shows some examples of numeric entries, number formats, and their resulting appearance. Note that in all cases the underlying number remains the same, regardless of how different it is in appearance. The Format | Cells command is available on the shortcut menu. Right-click after selecting a cell or range of cells and select Format | Cells from the shortcut menu.

TABLE 4.2 Numeric format examples

NUMERIC ENTRY	FORMAT	RESULT
1.23456	0	1
1.2356	0.00	1.24
123456.78	#,##0.00	123,456.78
123456.78	$#,##0.00_);($#,##0.00)	$123,456.78
-123456.78	$#,##0.00_);($#,##0.00)	($123,456.78)
.25	0%	25%
123456.78	0.00E+00	1.23E+05
1.25	# ?/?	1 1/4
123456.78	# ??/??	123456 39/50

Alignment

The Alignment tab of the Format | Cells dialog box allows you to change the alignment for all entries in the specified range. There are several options, as illustrated in Figure 4.4.

Left, Center, and Right are self-explanatory. General alignment provides right alignment for numeric entries and left alignment for text entries. Fill alignment fills the cell with repetitions of any entry in the cell. The Alignment tab also includes a check box named Wrap Text; when this option is checked, the row height automatically increases to allow multiple lines in that cell, and new lines are added as needed to cause all text typed in a cell to fit in that cell. The Justify selection is similar to the

FIGURE 4.4
Format / Cells,
Alignment tab

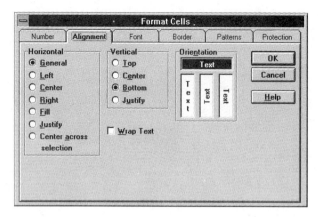

Wrap Text option, but Justify also widens the spaces between words so that both the left and right sides of the cell are aligned.

 NOTE *Left-, center-, and right-aligned text, as well as Center Across Selection, may be achieved by clicking on the appropriate buttons on the Formatting toolbar.*

Center Across Selection allows you to center a heading above a selected number of columns.

The Vertical section in the Alignment tab allows you to align an entry vertically in a cell. This allows for a much neater alignment when you are using the Wrap Text option and you observe that some headings are long enough to wrap while others are not.

The Orientation section is self-explanatory. Figure 4.5 illustrates the various alignment options.

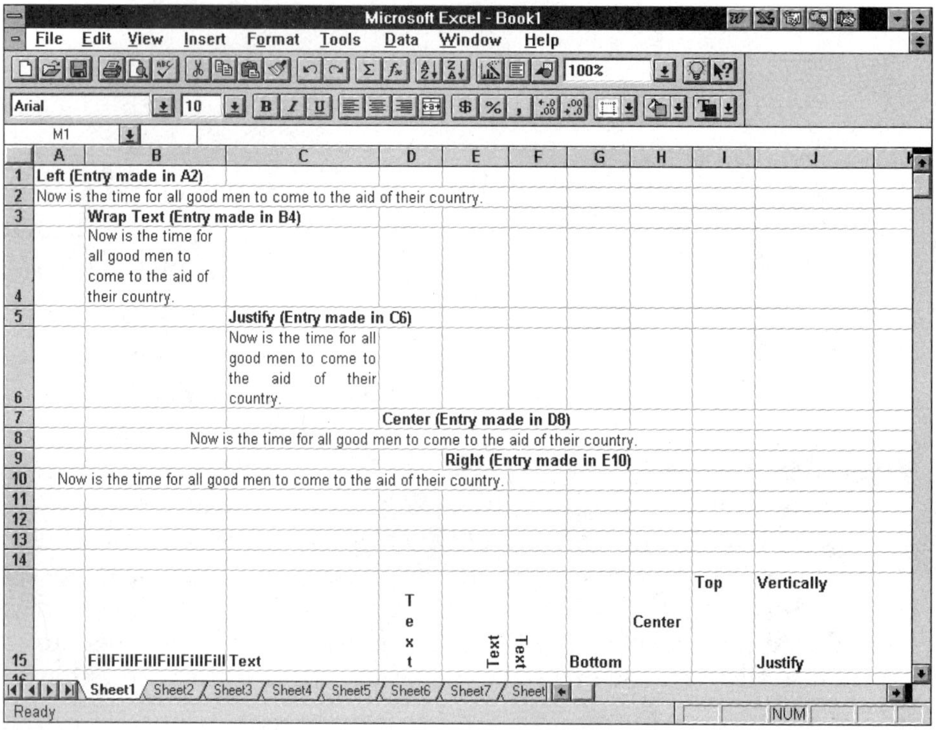

FIGURE 4.5
Alignment options

Fonts

The Font tab allows you to change the font for all entries in the selected range. The Font tab is different from the other tabs in the Format | Cells dialog box in that you can have multiple font settings in one cell. For example, if the cell contains a text entry with three words, you can change the font size, style, and color of the middle word without affecting the other two words. Double-click on the cell to enter edit mode (remember from Unit 2) and then select the desired portion of the cell entry by dragging with the mouse. There are seven option groups in the Font tab. As shown in Figure 4.6, these include Font, Font Style, Size, Underline, Color, Normal Font, and Effects.

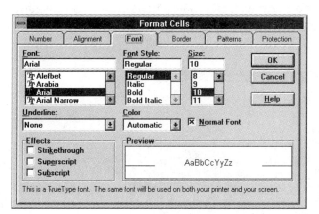

FIGURE 4.6 Format | Cells, Font tab

The Font list box refers to the specific typeface. The font options depend on what fonts are installed on your computer. Note that these are the Windows system fonts and may or may not be available on a particular printer. Other fonts may be available to you. If you select a font that is not available on your printer, Windows substitutes the nearest available font, based on font family and size.

NOTE *Different fonts can be selected from the Formatting toolbar by using the drop-down list.*

The Font Style list box allows the user to change the appearance of any font selected. The normally available choices are Regular, Italic, Bold, and Bold Italic.

The Size list box refers to the size of the font desired. Font sizes are listed in "points." A point is $1/72$ inch. A capital letter in a 12-point font prints approximately $1/6$-inch tall. The sizes available depend on what fonts are installed in your computer.

NOTE *Font size can be changed from the Formatting toolbar by using the drop-down list.*

The Underline section includes four options: Single, Double, Single Accounting, and Double Accounting. Accounting underlining extends the width of the column while standard underlining (single or double) extends the width of the entry. Note that underlining is a property of the font and is unrelated to cell borders, which we discuss in the next section.

NOTE *Bold, italic, and single standard underlined text can be selected or deselected from the Formatting toolbar by clicking on the appropriate buttons.*

The Effects section includes three check boxes: Strikethrough, Superscript, and Subscript. You can select any of these settings; however Superscript and Subscript are mutually exclusive.

The Normal Font check box automatically turns off all changes in the Font tab and returns the cell entry to the default font.

The Color list box changes the color of text in the selected range. The colors that are available depend on the choices made in the Tools | Options | Color menu option.

NOTE *Text color can be changed from the Formatting toolbar by clicking on the text color button and selecting from the drop-down list.*

The Preview window allows you to preview the result of your choices.

Borders

The Border tab in the Format | Cells dialog box allows you to change the border characteristics for all cells in the selected range. The three areas within the tab, illustrated in Figure 4.7, are Border, Style, and Color.

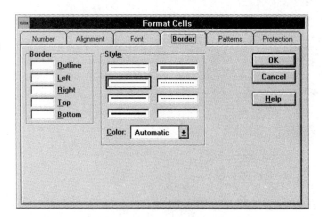

FIGURE 4.7
Format | Cells, Border tab

The Border options include Outline, Left, Right, Top, and Bottom. Left, Right, Top, and Bottom place borders on the designated sides of every cell in the selected range. Outline places borders only on the outside edges of the range. For instance, to put a double-line border below every cell in a range:

1. Highlight the range.
2. Select the Border tab from the Format | Cells dialog box.
3. Choose the double-line box under Style.
4. Choose the Bottom box under Border.
5. Click OK.

The Style box shows eight different patterns available for border lines. The Color list box changes the color of the borders selected.

Patterns

The Patterns tab in the Format | Cells dialog box, when selected for a workbook cell, provides options for shading cells. As illustrated in Figure 4.8, the dialog box allows the user to select from a number of different shading patterns and then change both the foreground and the background colors. The Color list box displays the color options for the cell's background. Click on the Pattern list box, and the drop-down list contains both pattern and color options for the foreground.

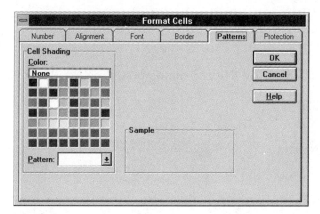

FIGURE 4.8
Format | Cells, Patterns tab

Protection

Shown in Figure 4.9, the Protection tab of the Format | Cells dialog box allows you to determine whether a cell's contents can be changed and whether a cell's underlying formula will be displayed in the formula bar. We discuss this concept and its usage in Unit 11.

FIGURE 4.9
Format | Cells, Protection tab

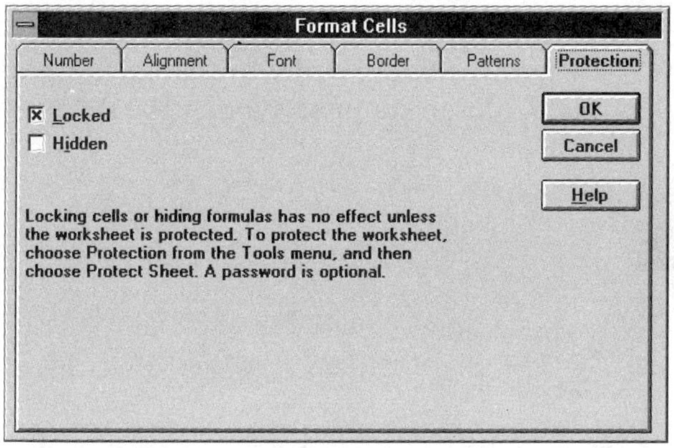

Row Heights

Format | Row provides the option of changing the height of all rows within the selected range. The Format | Row command looks like this:

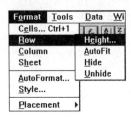

Selecting Height calls the Row Height dialog box, illustrated below.

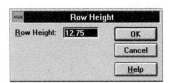

This dialog box allows the user to key in the desired height of the row in points.

The AutoFit option automatically calculates the best row height for the font sizes in the selected range. The Hide and Unhide options reduce the row height to 0 or return the row height to its last measurement, respectively.

Row height can be changed with the mouse by placing the mouse cursor in the row label numbers on the left side of the screen, moving between two numbers until the mouse cursor becomes a two-headed arrow, and dragging the top row up or down to the desired height.

Column Widths

Format | Column gives the user the opportunity to change the widths of all columns in the range. The Format | Column command looks like this:

Selecting the Width option calls the Column Width dialog box illustrated below.

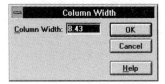

Choosing AutoFit Selection causes Excel to measure the width of the displayed value or text of each cell in a column and adjust the column width to accommodate the widest cell. As in Format I Row, the Hide and Unhide options set the column width to 0 and restore it to its original width, respectively.

Column widths can be changed with the mouse by placing the mouse cursor in the column label letters on the top of the screen, moving between two letters until the mouse cursor becomes a two-headed arrow, and dragging the left column to the desired width.

Changing the entry in the Standard Width entry box changes all columns in the workbook that do not have a specific width set.

Styles

One of the most powerful features of Excel is the ability to combine the various elements of the Format menu that we have already discussed into a *style*, and apply that style to a range, thus accomplishing many formatting steps in a very few keystrokes. The dialog box for Format I Style (illustrated in Figure 4.10) contains a command button marked Modify....

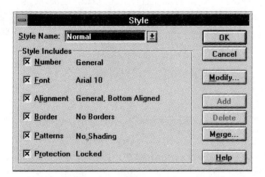

FIGURE 4.10
Format I Style dialog box

Clicking on the Modify button calls up the now familiar Format I Cells dialog box. Now, instead of being applied to the currently selected cells, the settings made in the dialog box are applied to the style.

To use Format I Style to define a new style, simply type the name of the new style in the Style Name box (or select a style in the list box to modify an existing style). Uncheck any items that you do not want the style to affect. For example, if you are creating a heading style, and you do not want the heading style to determine the numeric format, uncheck the Number option in the Format I Style dialog box. Then click the Modify button and make the appropriate selections in the Format I Cells dialog box. Click OK to verify the setting and then click on Add to add this new style to the Style Name list box in the Format I Style dialog box. Click on OK to verify the changes and close the dialog box.

Creating Styles by Example

Styles can also be defined by example. Simply select a cell containing the formatting you want for the new style and type the new style name in the Style Name box in the Format | Style dialog box.

Applying Styles

Applying your new styles is as easy as (1) selecting a range, (2) clicking on the down-pointing arrow next to the Style Name list box in the Format | Style dialog box, and (3) selecting the desired style name. All formatting defined for that style name is applied to the range. Simply select the range, select Format | Style, click on the desired style name in the list box, and click on OK to confirm your choice.

Merging Styles

The Format | Style dialog box can also be used to merge styles from other workbooks or templates into the current workbook. Suppose you wish to merge styles from SOURCE.XLS to OBJECT.XLS. Open both files, make OBJECT.XLS the active workbook, and select Format | Style. Select Merge in the dialog box, and Excel displays a list of all files currently open in the workspace. Select SOURCE.XLS and click on OK twice to confirm the selection. Excel copies the styles from SOURCE.XLS into OBJECT.XLS.

Using Templates to Preserve Styles

As useful as styles are, they are limited by the fact that they only apply to the current workbook. To make styles even more useful, create the styles that are needed for a particular use, say monthly status reports, and save the workbook as a *template*. Then, the next time you need to use those styles, open the template and begin working.

To create a template, use the File | Save As command, choose Template from the Save File as Type list box, enter the name of your template, and click OK. As a bonus, you can also include boilerplate text as a part of your template. *Boilerplate* is text that you want to use in every file based on your template. It might be as simple as a company logo or report title, or as complex as an entire form for a report with only the specific data missing.

While it may take a few minutes to define a template the first time it is used, this new feature is a tremendous time-saver over the long haul. Because the template and the styles in it can be used over and over again, you can define a style like "Header" and use it in every workbook or report you create based on that template. Besides the time saved, you will achieve a uniformity of appearance from one report to the next that is very much appreciated in today's business world.

AutoFormat

One of the strengths of Excel as a spreadsheet program is its formatting abilities. You can access all of its formatting commands directly from the menu bar and see the exact results without changing to a different display mode. Still, formatting can be as time-consuming as creating a workbook. Excel's answer to this problem is the Format l AutoFormat command. Select a range of cells, give this command, and Excel will present you with a list of 16 predefined table formats, as illustrated in Figure 4.11.

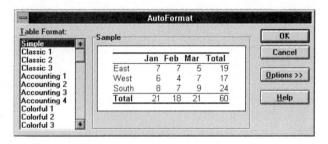

FIGURE 4.11
Format l
AutoFormat
dialog box

While it is essentially an advanced application of the style concept, AutoFormat is a tremendous time-saver. Excel looks at the type of information in the selected range, along with any outlining information (we will discuss outlining in Unit 6) to apply the most accurate formatting possible. By clicking on the Options button, you can retain portions of the existing formatting, or you may change portions of the AutoFormat by using the Format commands discussed in this unit.

GUIDED ACTIVITY 4.1

Using Numeric and Date Formats

This activity requires you to use several of the formatting commands in a worksheet.

1. Follow the startup procedure outlined in Unit 1 to load Windows and enter Excel.
2. Enter formulas, numbers, and text in the cells indicated:

Cell	Formula or Number	Cell	Text
A1	186000	B1	speed of light
A2	=1/3	B2	one third
A3	.0525	B3	interest
A4	21000	B4	salary
A5	=NOW( )	B5	today
A6	=NOW( )	B6	this minute

   After you enter these data, your workbook should look like Figure 4.12.

3. For the entire worksheet, set the default number format to 0 (zero) decimal places, using the following procedure. Watch how the worksheet changes as you follow each step of the procedure.

FIGURE 4.12
FORMATS.XLS worksheet, before formatting

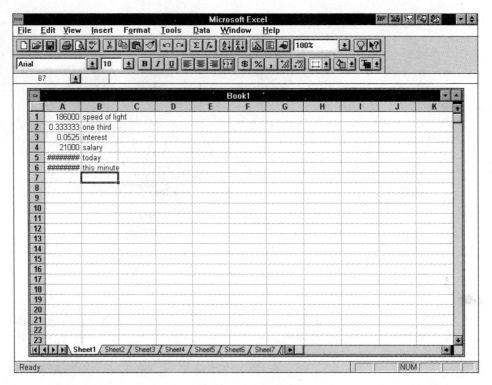

a. Select the entire worksheet by clicking on the Select All button (the blank button between column label "A" and row label "1"). From the keyboard, press [Ctrl][Shift][Spacebar].

b. Click on the Format | Cells command.

c. Click on the Number tab.

d. The second selection in the Format Codes box is 0. Use [↓] or the mouse to select it, and press [Enter] or click OK to accept it.

After you give this command, some of your entries will change to 0 (zero). Do not be concerned. The entries in cells A2 and A3 round to zero, but the original values are still in the cells, as you will see when you format those cells in the next step.

4. Using the Number tab of the Format | Cells command, format the following cells as indicated. Specific instructions follow this table.

Cell	Format
A1	Include thousands separator, 0 decimal places
A2	0 before decimal, 3 decimal places
A3	Percentage, 2 decimal places
A4	Currency, 0 decimal places
A5	Date (d-mmm-yy)
A6	Time (h:mm AM/PM)

a. To format cell A1, make it the active cell.

b. Give the Format|Cells command and select Number.

c. Use ⬇ or the mouse to highlight #,##0.

d. Press Enter or click OK to accept.

e. Use the same sequence to format the other cells. You will need to create a custom format for cell A2. After selecting the Number tab, press Alt+O to edit the Code box, or click in the code area and type 0.000. As you format the other cells, you might see that cell A5 appears as a row of ######## if the date format is too wide for the column. You change the column width in step 6.

5. Change the alignment of cells B2:B6 to centered.

    a. Select the range B2:B6.

    b. Click on the Center Alignment button.

CHECKPOINT 4A Can you name two ways to access the Format|Cells command so that you can use the Alignment tab?

6. Next, change the width of column A to 12.

    a. Click on any cell in column A.

    b. Give the Format|Column command and select Width. Excel presents the following dialog box:

    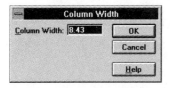

    c. Type 12 for the column width.

    d. Press Enter or click OK to accept.

7. Move to any cell in column B, then give the Format|Column command again and change the width of column B to 15.

8. Next, insert new data between A2:B2 and A3:B3.

    a. Select A3:B3 by dragging.

    b. Right-click A3:B3. Select Insert from the shortcut menu.

    c. Select Shift Cells Down and click OK.

    d. Enter .25 in cell A3 and type one fourth in cell B3.

    e. Select cell A3, give the Format|Cells command, select the Number tab, and select the Fraction category with the format, # ?/?.

FIGURE 4.13
FORMATS.XLS worksheet, after formatting

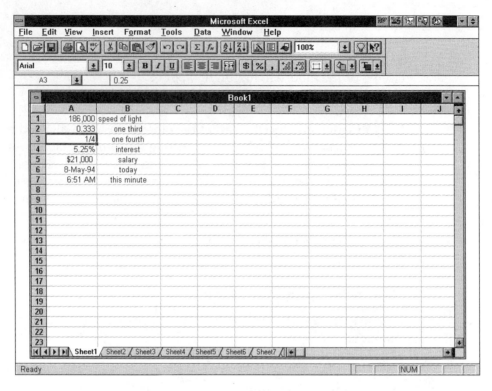

9. Your workbook should now look like Figure 4.13, except that the date and time in cells A6 and A7 are different.

CHECKPOINT 4B Why is the date different?

10. Save your work with the file name FORMATS. If you are not continuing on to the next Guided Activity, exit to Windows. Exit to the operating system. Remember to back up your work.

GUIDED ACTIVITY 4.2

Using Styles and Templates

Your manager has asked you, in your new position as Customer Service Supervisor, to turn in a weekly report showing each Customer Service agent's time available, on incoming calls, on outgoing calls, and unavailable. You would like to create this report on a template in order to minimize the amount of time you spend each week creating the report.

1. If you are not continuing from the previous Guided Activity, follow the startup procedure outlined in Unit 1 to load Windows and enter Excel. If you are continuing from a previous activity or exercise and already have a workbook on the screen, use the command File I New to open a new workbook window.

2. Change the font in cell A1 to Arial 12-point bold. Add a border around all sides of the cell and select vertical centering, horizontal centering, and wrapped text.

To define this formatting as a style, choose the Style command from the Format menu and type `Heading` in the Style Name box.

3. Select the range A1:E1, give the Format|Style command, and select Heading. Set the column width for A:D at 12, and column E at 14. Enter the following headings:

   ```
   Agent's Name
   Available
   Incoming Calls
   Outgoing Calls
   Unavailable
   ```

4. In cell A2, select bold text and add borders to all four sides of the cell. Define a style based on cell A2 and name it Agent.

5. Select the range A2:A7 and apply the Agent style. Enter the following names:

   ```
   J. Smith
   B. White
   T. Jones
   P. Brynen
   C. Walker
   A. Long
   ```

6. Next, you need to define a style for the data area. These entries will all be times, and since it is a weekly report, there is the possibility that the times will exceed 24 hours. You need to use a time format that will allow the hours entry to exceed 24.

   a. Make cell B2 the active cell and press [Ctrl][Shift][End]. You should have selected the range B2:E7.

CHECKPOINT 4C Why was this range selected?

   b. Choose the Cells command from the Format menu and select the Number tab. Select the Time category and set the number format to `[h]:mm:ss`.

   c. Give the Format|Style command and type `Data` in the Style Name box.

7. Now that you have created all of the styles for your report, you need to save it as a template to make it easy to retrieve. Choose Save As from the File menu, select Template in the Save File as Type box, and name the file REPORT.XLT. Your worksheet should look like Figure 4.14.

8. Close REPORT.XLT. Open the file REPORT.XLT; instead of opening the template, you should open a new worksheet based on the template. To verify this, the title bar of your document should read REPORT1. Because you left it selected when you saved REPORT.XLT, the data area is already selected and ready for data entry. You can now create as many copies of REPORT as you need.

9. Close REPORT1 without saving it. Exit to Windows. Exit to the operating system. Remember to back up your work.

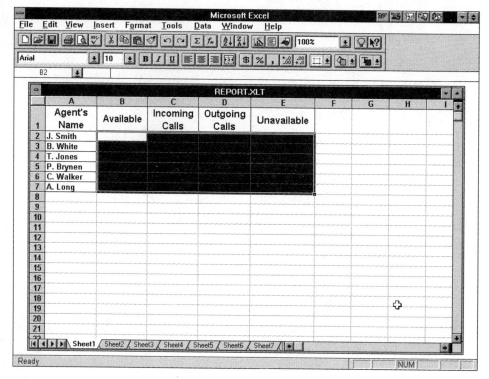

FIGURE 4.14
REPORT.XLT
template

EXERCISE 4.1

Date and Currency Formats

1. If you are not continuing from the previous Guided Activity, follow the startup procedure outlined in Unit 1 to load Windows and enter Excel. If you are continuing from a previous activity or exercise and already have a workbook on the screen, use the command File | New to open a new workbook window.

2. Use the TODAY( ) function to enter today's date into cell A1. Enter your birth date into cell A2 using either the DATE( ) function (for example, DATE(76,5,14)) or the shortcut method (for example, 14-May-76). Format both of these to date formats and change the column width, if necessary, so that they are displayed properly. In cell A3, enter the difference, which is how many days old you are. Format A3 to #,##0.

3. Use the Insert menu to insert a row at row 1, which should cause your work in step 2 to move down into cells A2, A3, and A4. (Highlight row 1 before using this command.) Insert two columns at column A, which moves the previous work into column C. (Highlight columns A and B before giving this command.) Move the cell pointer to C4 and notice that the formula changed to reflect the new cell positions. Also note that the width set for column A is now the width of column C.

4. Enter the following data in columns E and F of your workbook, starting in cell E1. You can (and should) type the $ sign and comma in these entries.

```
Revenue    $45,000.18
Expenses   $38,905.33
Income
```

Change the width of column F, if necessary. If everything is working correctly, F1 and F2 are formatted to $#,##0.00_);[Red]($#,##0.00). (Check the format by giving the Format|Cells command.)

5. In cell F3 put the formula that computes income as the difference between revenue and expenses. If necessary, format cell F3 to the following: $#,##0.00_); [Red]($#.##0.00). Finally, change the value of revenue to $35,000.55 and note what happens to the value and the format of income.

6. Put a single-line border under cell F2 and a double-line border under cell F3.

7. Save your workbook with the name MOREFORM.

EXERCISE 4.2

The Perfect Job (II)

1. If you are not continuing from the previous Exercise or Guided Activity, follow the startup procedure outlined in Unit 1 to load Windows and enter Excel.

2. Open the JOBS workbook created in Exercise 2.2 at the end of Unit 2.

3. Format the dollar amounts to $#,##0.00_);($#,##0.00). These cells show ######## because the formatted numbers are too wide for the columns.

4. Change the width of column D to accommodate the formatted numbers. Use the command that changes only one column. Set the width so that there is space between the $ and the text entries in column C.

5. Put a single-line border under text entries in row 3.

6. Put a double-line border under cells A1:B1.

7. Make the font of the entry in cell A1 one point larger.

8. Save the workbook.

EXERCISE 4.3

A Check Register (III)

1. If you are not continuing from the previous Exercise or Guided Activity, follow the startup procedure outlined in Unit 1 to load Windows and enter Excel.

2. Open the CHECKS workbook.

3. Format the dollar amounts to $#,##0.00.

4. Format the dates to d-mmm.

5. Change the width of the columns to accommodate the formatted numbers and the descriptions.

6. Put a single-line border under headings in row 1.

7. Using the Patterns tab, put a light-gray shading on headings in row 1.

8. Save the workbook.

EXERCISE 4.4

Business Mileage (III)

Open the MILES96 workbook. Format the Reading column so that all numbers have commas and one decimal place. Center the data in the Use column. Save your work.

EXERCISE 4.5

Form 1040EZ (III)

In this exercise you continue the development of a spreadsheet for Form 1040EZ. Open the 1040EZ workbook. Adjust the width of column B so that all labels are visible. Set the numeric format of column C so that two decimal places are displayed and all numbers greater than 1,000 have commas. Boldface entries in cells A2, A14, A20, and A26. Save your work.

EXERCISE 4.6

Things to Do (II)

Retrieve your TO-DO spreadsheet. Experiment with character formats; for instance, you can boldface headings and use italics for the fun things on your list. Use shading to mark those things you've accomplished. Save your work.

EXERCISE 4.7

Buford Fencing Company (II)

Open BUFORD. Format all monetary entries to show the dollar sign and two decimals. Format all other numbers to show only one decimal place. Right-justify labels that appear over numeric columns (for instance, "Price"). Change the format of cell A1 to a larger, different font. Boldface "Details" and "Calculations." Save your work.

Review Questions

1. What is the effect of each of the following in a number format?
   a. _ (underscore)
   *b. d
   c. 0
   *d. a
   *e. @
2. What is a range?
*3. How do you change the numeric display format of the entire workbook?
4. What procedure changes the numeric display of a specific portion of the workbook?
*5. What procedure inserts a row into the workbook?
6. What procedure deletes a workbook column?
7. What procedure erases a specific area of the workbook?
*8. What procedure realigns entries within a specified range?
9. What procedure combines formatting choices into a style?
*10. How do you apply this style to a range?

Key Terms

Accounting format
Boilerplate
Currency format
Custom format
Date format
Discontinuous range

Fraction format
General format
Named range
Number format
Percentage format
Range

Scientific format
Select All button
Style
Template
Text format
Time format

Documentation Research

Using the Excel *User's Guide*, find and record the page number of each of the commands discussed in this unit. We recommend that you also write the page number in the margin next to the discussion of the command in the unit.

1. How do you delete a style?
2. What happens if you select a range with conflicting cell formatting and attempt to define a style by example?

3. If you change the column width after wrapping text in a cell, the row height will not automatically readjust to the new column width. What is the fastest way to readjust the row height after you change the column width?

4. What is the result of the formula =A1*B1 ...

   a. if you clear cell B1?

   b. if you delete cell B1?

5. How would you change the color of a cell entry that is less than 0? (*Hint:* Examine the discussion of the semicolon and custom number formats.)

6. How would you change the color of a cell entry that is over 1,000? (*Hint:* Examine the discussion of conditional custom number formats.)

5 Printing the Workbook

In this unit we discuss the various printing commands. These commands allow you to print all or a part of the workbook. You will observe that such Excel features as Page Setup and Print Preview help you to fit exactly the right amount of information on a given page, and also enable you to check its final appearance before printing.

Learning Objectives

At the completion of this unit you should know

1. what a print area is,
2. what the various printing items in the File menu do,
3. how the Windows Control Panel affects printing.

At the completion of this unit you should be able to

1. print all or a portion of a workbook;
2. change the appearance of a printout with the File | Page Setup command;
3. use print areas, print titles, and page breaks to control the printout;
4. select and set up a printer using File | Print;
5. use the Print Preview command to see exactly what the printout will look like, without first having to print it.

Important Commands

> File | Page Setup
>
> File | Print
>
> File | Print Preview
>
> Insert | Page Break

Page Setup

The File | Page Setup command provides the basic mechanism for controlling the appearance of the printed output of Excel. The resulting dialog box contains several options that we examine individually.

Using the Sheet Tab

If you invoke the File | Print command without making any preparations by setting the print options, you will be rewarded with a printout that includes dotted gridlines and all cells that contain an entry or formatting. While this is better than nothing, it is likely that this is not what you want. The Sheet tab of the File | Page Setup dialog box includes items that deal with printing from the perspective of the worksheet.

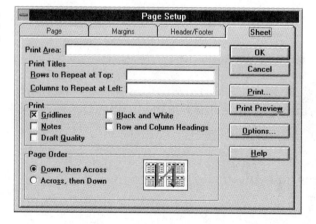

FIGURE 5.1 *File | Page Setup, Sheet tab*

SETTING THE PRINT AREA

The first thing to do before printing the workbook is to determine how much of it will actually print. To do this, give the File | Page Setup command, click on the Sheet tab (illustrated in Figure 5.1), click in the Print Area text box, and select the desired range. Once you have done this, Excel assigns the name Print Area to that range and will only print what is in the ***print area***. You may change the print area, or delete it by invoking Insert | Name, selecting Print Area in the Names in Workbook section of the dialog box, and either editing the description in the Refers to box or clicking on Delete.

SETTING PRINT TITLES

Another feature that can affect the appearance of your printed output is to have a range of cells print as a title or header on every page. To set *print titles*, give the File | Page Setup command, click on the Sheet tab, click in either the Rows to Repeat at Top or Columns to Repeat at Left section, and select a cell or cells in the desired range.

AVOIDING THE MOST COMMON ERROR

It is very important not to include the print titles in the print area. If you do not correctly set your print area (or if you set no print area at all), the print titles will print twice on page 1 of your output.

SETTING PRINT ITEMS

The Print section of the Sheet tab contains five check boxes. The first of these check boxes give you the option of printing gridlines. You will usually leave this box unchecked. If checked, gridlines print in dashed lines for the entire print area. If you want to emphasize the spreadsheet structure this way, you can use the Border tab of the Format | Cells command; the borders look better and give you control of where they appear and do not appear.

The next check box allows you to print notes. These are the annotations that you can enter to include additional information about cells. If selected, Notes will print on a separate page from the worksheet.

Draft Quality uses a lower resolution, if available on your printer, to provide a lesser quality printout in less time.

The next check box prints all cell entries and text boxes in black and white. (We will discuss text boxes in Unit 12.) This is very convenient if you have used color in your formatting (perhaps for screen presentations or because you used one of the Format | AutoFormat settings) and you have a black-and-white printer. This option prevents your printer from trying to convert all the colors to shades of gray.

Row and column headings, which you can add by selecting the last check box, are useful for developmental work but are seldom printed in final output.

PAGE ORDER

Generally, Excel prints multipage documents in a down, then over, order. The Page Order option allows you to instruct Excel to print multipage documents in an over, then down, order. This option changes both the page number and the collation (integration) order.

Using the Page Tab

The Page tab, illustrated in Figure 5.2, includes those items that deal with the printed page itself.

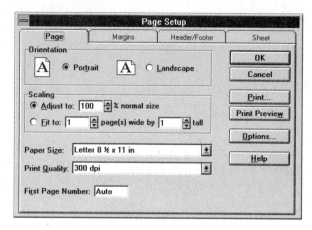

FIGURE 5.2
File | Page
Setup, Page tab

SELECTING PAPER ORIENTATION

Portrait is a vertical *paper orientation* (8½ by 11 inches), while landscape is a horizontal orientation (11 by 8½ inches). The choice you make in this option overrides the default specified in the Printer Setup dialog box (discussed later in this unit). Using this feature is much easier and faster than changing the Printer Setup setting and makes the choice a part of the workbook file.[1] Some printer drivers may not allow you to change the orientation.

SCALING OPTIONS

The first radio button in the Scaling section of the Page tab allows you to scale the workbook to a certain percentage of its standard size. The *default* setting that the program uses unless you change it is 100%. With this option, you can reduce the workbook to as little as 10% of the standard size, and enlarge the workbook to as much as 400% of the standard size.

The second radio button in this section allows you to instruct Excel to print the workbook on a specified number of pages (both across and down). Excel will then calculate the percentage of reduction needed to print to the specification. The percentage of reduction may not be less than 10%; this option will not enlarge your workbook.

---

[1] Printer Setup changes the Windows Control Panel setting and is not saved when you save a document. Each change remains in effect until it is changed again using the Windows Control Panel or Excel's Printer Setup. Since File | Page Setup is strictly an Excel command, any settings are saved as part of the workbook file and only need to be set once for the life of the file.

PAPER SIZE

The Paper Size option overrides the default specified in the Printer Setup dialog box. As in Orientation, this becomes part of the workbook file and simplifies future print jobs.

PRINT QUALITY

The Print Quality option is similar to the Draft Quality check box on the Sheet tab. Depending on your printer, it allows you to set a lower resolution in order to reduce printing time.

FIRST PAGE NUMBER

First Page Number is a text entry box that determines the starting page number. Occasionally, you may wish to print several different workbooks that will become part of one presentation and therefore need consecutive page numbering. This option allows you to start the page numbering at a number other than one (1).

Using the Margins Tab

The next tab of the File | Page Setup dialog box, illustrated in Figure 5.3, allows you to enter the desired margin settings (in inches) for each edge of the paper. There is also a provision for centering the document horizontally or vertically. We find it very effective to center documents horizontally and set the margins at 0. As long as the document fits horizontally on one page, this provides the best-looking output with the least work. This technique is not quite as effective vertically, however, because the worksheet is likely to print over headers and footers, and because the last page of multipage documents usually needs to be vertically aligned from the top of the page. The Margins tab also allows you to set the distance from the page that headers and footers print. Be careful with this tab—most laser printers will not print within .25 inch of any edge of the page.

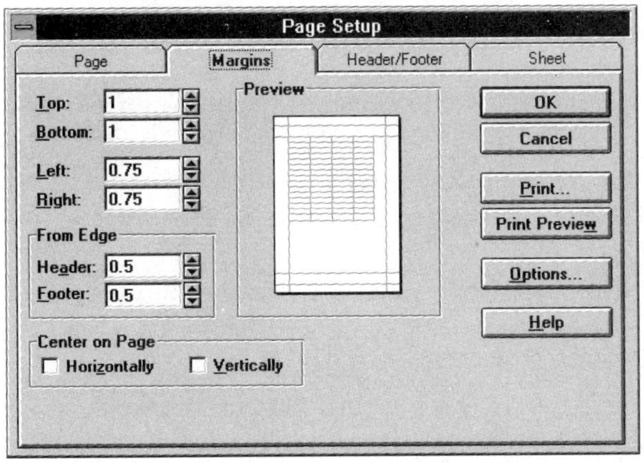

FIGURE 5.3
File | Page Setup, Margins tab

Using the Header/Footer Tab

The Header/Footer tab presents the dialog box illustrated in Figure 5.4. A *header* is text that prints at the top of every page; a *footer* prints at the bottom of every page. Excel deals with headers and footers identically; the only difference is the location.

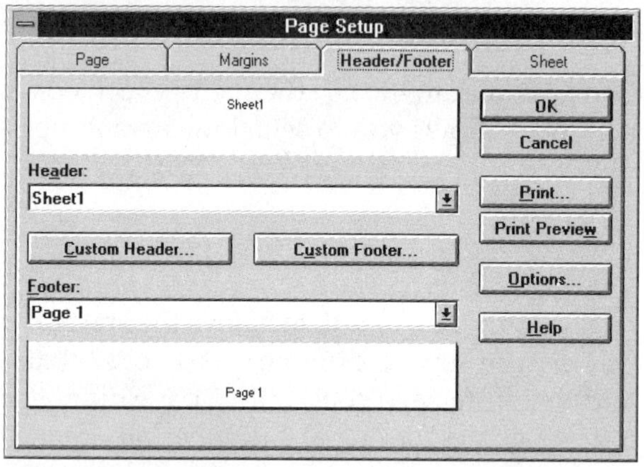

FIGURE 5.4
File | Page Setup, Header/Footer tab

Click on either the Header or the Footer drop-down list box to see 18 different predefined headers and footers (including none). These include various combinations of the worksheet name, workbook name, date, time, creator's name, page number, and other assorted text. To use a predefined header or footer, simply select it and click OK.

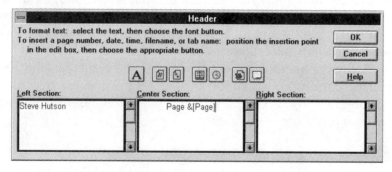

FIGURE 5.5
Header dialog box

If you wish to design your own header or footer, click on the Custom Header or Custom Footer button to see the dialog box illustrated in Figure 5.5. The text boxes in the Header dialog box are divided into the Left Section, Center Section, and Right Section. The text entered in each of these boxes will print in the corresponding part of the header or footer. There are seven tools available in the dialog box: the first allows you to change the font formatting; the others allow you to enter the codes for page number (&[Page]), total number of pages (&[Pages]), date (&[Date]), time (&[Time]), file name (&[File]), and worksheet name (&[Tab]).

The Header and Footer boxes use the & (ampersand) character to control formatting. If you wish to include an actual ampersand in a header or footer, enter a double ampersand (&&) to inform Excel that it is not a formatting control character. The default for typeface and size is determined by the Normal style.

In the example in Figure 5.5, `Steve Hutson` will print at the left margin and `Page 1` will be centered in the heading.

Setting and Removing Page Breaks

Excel sets *automatic page breaks* when it reaches the end of the printable area of any page. This is affected by the size and orientation of the paper and the sizes of the margins.[2]

Frequently, you will want to set the page breaks at other places in the workbook. Perhaps you will want to break a budget worksheet between major categories or an efficiency report between departments. You can set both vertical and horizontal *manual page breaks* with the Insert | Page Break command. The breaks are set above and to the left of the active cell.[3]

If you look carefully, you can tell the difference between automatic and manual page breaks; the dashed line of a manual page break has larger dashes and larger spaces between the dashes than the automatic page break line. If the active cell is below or to the right of a manual page break, the Insert menu contains the command Remove Page Break, rather than Page Break. Select this command to remove manual page breaks and return to the automatic page breaks set by Excel. You can remove all manual page breaks in the workbook by clicking on the Select All icon and invoking Insert | Remove Page Break.

Printer Setup

The Printer Setup command button in the File | Print dialog box calls the Printer Setup dialog box from the Windows Control Panel, as shown in Figure 5.6. The exact options available in the Printer Setup dialog box depend on the individual printer driver. A dot-matrix driver may give you the option to decide whether or not to use the tractor feed; the driver for the HP LaserJet Series IIID printer asks which paper source to use, and so on. For our purposes, we examine four options that are fairly universal.

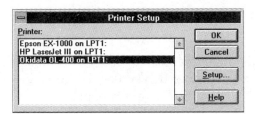

FIGURE 5.6
Printer Setup dialog box

---

2 You can tell Excel whether to show these automatic page breaks in the Tools | Options dialog box. This dialog box gives you several other choices regarding how the workbook appears on your monitor, including whether or not gridlines and row and column labels are displayed. These Tools | Options choices have nothing to do with the appearance of your printout; they only affect your monitor display.

3 It is easy to inadvertently set manual vertical page breaks where they are not wanted by placing the cell pointer in a column other than column A. It is a good practice always to press [Home] before setting manual page breaks.

Selecting a Printer

Printer drivers are files telling the program how to print your work on a specific model of printer; they can be from the original Windows installation disks or after-market drivers written for Windows.[4] This may have nothing whatever to do with the printers that are actually connected to your computer; you can install drivers without a printer. You may wish to create a workbook on one computer and then print it out on another computer with a LaserJet or a PostScript printer. Click on a printer name, then click the Setup button, and Excel presents the dialog box specific to that printer, as shown in Figure 5.7.

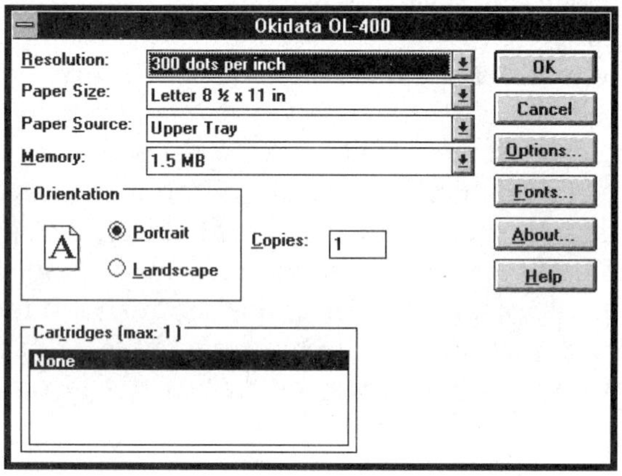

FIGURE 5.7
Printer Setup dialog box for Okidata OL-400

This dialog box may present options other than the ones discussed in this book. You may wish to experiment with the others. Since most drivers are written to serve several printers, there is frequently a list box containing the printer models that this driver supports. Setting this is usually a one-time exercise. Simply ensure that the model selected is the same as the printer you will use for printing your workbook.

Selecting a Paper Size

The next step is to select the default paper size to be used for this printer. The options available again depend on the printer driver. Legal- and letter-sized paper are universal; others may include A4 and B5 (European paper sizes) and 14 by 11 inches (standard computer paper). Simply select the most frequently used paper size.

Selecting Default Paper Orientation

Now you select the default paper orientation. Portrait (vertical orientation) refers to 8½ by 11 inches; landscape (horizontal orientation) refers to 11 by 8½ inches. Note that landscape is the default orientation; you have the opportunity to override this decision in the File | Page Setup dialog box, as you learned earlier.

---

4 Many of the drivers in Windows have been rewritten by the printer manufacturers and give you access to more features than the original Windows drivers. Contact the printer manufacturer for more information regarding drivers.

Selecting Printer Resolutions

Almost all printer drivers give you the opportunity to select a *printer resolution* for graphics and large fonts. Sometimes they are labeled in dots per inch (300 dpi, 240 by 144, 120 by 144, or 120 by 72); other times they are labeled by their common use (draft, quality). Low resolutions print faster and give you immediate feedback for necessary changes; higher resolutions give you the best quality the printer is capable of for presentation purposes, but take longer to print.

Print Preview

While the normal workbook window gives you a very close approximation of what your printout will look like, the File | Print Preview command will give you a *WYSIWYG* (what you see is what you get) look at your document. You can access this command either through the menu or by choosing the Print Preview button in the File | Print dialog box (see the next section). Once in the Print Preview window, you can perform the functions discussed in Table 5.1.

TABLE 5.1 *Print Preview functions*

OPTION	EFFECT
Next	Looks at the next page of a multipage document
Previous	Looks at the previous page of a multipage document
Zoom	Zooms in for a close look or out for an overview
Print	Invokes the File|Print command
Setup	Calls the File|Page Setup dialog box
Margins	Displays margin markers and moves them with the mouse
Close	Closes the print preview and returns to the worksheet window
Help	Opens a Help window for the Print Preview screen

The Print Command

The dialog box for the File | Print command, illustrated in Figure 5.8, gives you the options listed in Table 5.2.

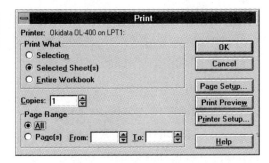

FIGURE 5.8 *File | Print dialog box*

TABLE 5.2
Print options

OPTION	EFFECT
Print What	Prints the current selection, the current worksheet, or the entire workbook
Copies	Prints the number of copies desired (from 1 to 9999)
Print Range	Prints all pages or a range of page numbers
Page Setup	Opens the File|Page Setup dialog box
Print Preview	Opens the Print Preview window before printing
Printer Setup	Opens the Printer Setup dialog box

Using the Tools | Options Command with Printing

The View tab on the Tools | Options command allows the user to decide how the worksheet is displayed on the monitor. The View tab is illustrated in Figure 5.9. With only a couple of exceptions, these selections do not change the appearance of the printout, only the monitor. The Window Options are listed in Table 5.3; two of these options affect printing.

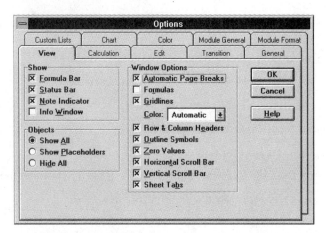

FIGURE 5.9
Tools | Options, View tab

TABLE 5.3
Window Options in the Tools | Options View tab

OPTION	EFFECT
Automatic Page Breaks	Causes automatic page break symbols to display
Formulas	Causes formulas, rather than results, to display in the cell (this item affects the printout)
Gridlines	Causes gridlines to display in the worksheet window
Row & Column Headers	Causes labels to display for row and column headings
Outline Symbols	Causes outline symbols to display
Zero Values	Causes zero values to display 0 (this item affects the printout)
Horizontal Scroll Bar	Causes horizontal scroll bar to display
Vertical Scroll Bar	Causes vertical scroll bar to display
Sheet Tabs	Causes worksheet name tabs to display

GUIDED ACTIVITY 5.1

Printing the Workbook

This activity provides practice in using the printing commands.

1. Before starting this activity, determine what steps are necessary to use the printer. (Your instructor or lab supervisor will provide the answers.)

    a. How do you turn on the power?

    b. If the printer is shared by more than one computer, how do you get it to select your computer?

    c. Who is responsible for loading paper into the printer? If you are, how is paper loaded?

    d. What do the switches on the printer do?

    e. Is there anything else that you must do before printing?

2. Follow the startup procedure outlined in Unit 1 to load Windows and enter Excel. Use the data disk that has the BULL.XLS file from Unit 2.

3. Select File | Open and the file, BULL.

4. Prepare the printer for operation.

5. Do the following to print the workbook. Watch the effect on the screen.

    a. Give the command File | Print.

    b. Click on the Printer Setup command button.

    c. Select (highlight) the printer prepared in step 4. Press [Enter] or click OK.

    d. Make the following selections in the File | Page Setup dialog box:

       - *Header:* Center the current date.

       - *Footer:* Place the file name on the left, leave the page number in the center, and enter your name on the right.

       - Center the print area horizontally.

       - Use portrait orientation.

       - Make the range A1:B6 the print area.

       - Click on OK to leave Page Setup.

    e. Use File | Print Preview to view the results.

    f. Click the Print button in the Print Preview window to call the Print dialog box.

    g. Press [Enter] or click OK to print one copy.

6. Click on the Print button, illustrated at left, to print the workbook again. Notice that the previous range has printed. (Excel has named A1:B6 `Print_Area`; it

remains until you change it, so you do not need to respecify the range each time you print.)

7. Change the display to show formulas rather than results:

    a. Give the Tools | Options command and click on the View tab.

    b. Click on Formulas.

    c. Click on OK.

    d. Now print the document again.

CHECKPOINT 5A How did the printout differ?

8. Use Tools | Options to return values to cell display; remove the X next to Formulas.

9. Save the workbook. Because the most recent print settings are saved with the file, the next time you open the file you do not need to specify the options you set in this Guided Activity.

10. Exit to Windows. Exit to the operating system. Remember to back up your work.

EXERCISE 5.1

Printing a Header

This exercise requires you to add a header to the file HAROLD, then print the workbook. Not all necessary keystrokes are listed in the following instructions. Practice heads-up computing as you accomplish this exercise, and you will see how to get from one instruction to the next.

1. If you are not continuing from the previous Guided Activity, follow the startup procedure outlined in Unit 1 to load Windows and enter Excel.

2. Open the file HAROLD. If you have not already done so, change the width of column A so that the entire text is visible.

3. Select File | Page Setup and click on the Header/Footer tab. Delete the Footer text. In the Header box, enter the necessary keystrokes to print (use the correct codes for data within the angle brackets < >):

    ```
    Harold's G.P.A. as of <today's date> in the left header
    Page <page number> in the right header.
    ```

4. Instruct Excel that the print area is the occupied portion of the worksheet.

5. Print the worksheet.

6. Save the file.

EXERCISE 5.2

A Check Register (IV)

1. If you are not continuing from the previous Exercise or Guided Activity, follow the startup procedure outlined in Unit 1 to load Windows and enter Excel.

2. Open the CHECKS workbook.

3. Select options that will produce an attractive printout:

    a. Ensure that the left and right margins are sufficient for the width of the register.

    b. If the last columns do not fit on paper of normal width, change the font size or typeface to fit the register on the paper. Remember, use the WYSIWYG feature of Print Preview to keep track as you make changes.

    c. Create a header that includes your name and the words `Checking Account at Student's State Bank`. The text will wrap when you type it in the header box, but it will print on one line.

    d. Create a footer that includes the date and page number.

    e. Add any other options that you would like.

4. Print a copy of the worksheet.

5. Save the workbook.

EXERCISE 5.3

Business Mileage (IV)

Print the MILES96 workbook with the file name as the header and with the date, time, and page number as the footer. Save your work.

EXERCISE 5.4

Form 1040EZ (IV)

Print the 1040EZ workbook with no header and with the date, time, and page number as the footer. Save your work.

EXERCISE 5.5

Things to Do (III)

Print your TO-DO spreadsheet. The footer should contain the date, time, and page number. Save your work.

EXERCISE 5.6

Buford Fencing Company (III)

Print BUFORD. The footer should contain the date, time, and page number. The header should be blank. Save your work.

Review Questions

*1. What is a print area?

2. What is the difference between changing orientation in File | Page Setup and in the Printer Setup dialog box?

Key Terms

Automatic page break	Manual page break	Printer driver
Default	Paper orientation	Printer resolution
Footer	Print area	WYSIWYG
Header	Print title	

Documentation Research

Using the Excel *User's Guide*, find and record the page number of each of the commands discussed in this unit. We recommend that you also write the page number in the margin next to the discussion of the command in the unit.

1. What happens to the mouse pointer in Print Preview?
2. How do you begin page numbering at a specified page number?
3. How do you adjust column widths in Print Preview?

APPLICATION

Poor Richard's (II)

In this Application, you make modifications to the workbook you created in Application A. Then you are introduced to one of the most useful facets of Excel: the ability to seek a desired result by changing an input variable.

1. Follow the startup procedure outlined in Unit 1 to load Windows and enter Excel.
2. Open the AUTO workbook you created in Application A.
3. Change Trade-in Allowance to 1900.
4. Your accountant has pointed out two errors in AUTO. Correct your workbook.

   a. The correct formula for Percent Profit is

   $$\frac{(Net\ Price + Net\ Cost)}{(Net\ Price)} \quad (Net\ Price\ is\ a\ negative\ number)$$

   b. In cell C18, the function that computes payments based on principal, interest, and term was incorrect because it did not consider sales tax. Change the formula so that the principal amount is Net Price + (Sales Tax Rate × Net Price).

NOTE *You must still use the PMT( ) function; the arguments for interest and term do not change.*

5. Use the Format | Cells command to format all dollar amounts in a currency format with two decimal places and all percent figures in a percentage format with one decimal place. You must use the Format | Column command to change the width of column C to accommodate the reformatted numbers. Your final workbook should look like Figure B.1.
6. Print a copy of the entire workbook.

One of the selling points of spreadsheet programs is that they facilitate what-if calculations. The user is able to see the effect that changing one number has on all other results in the spreadsheet. This facility is especially useful when a certain

FIGURE B.1
AUTO.XLS workbook

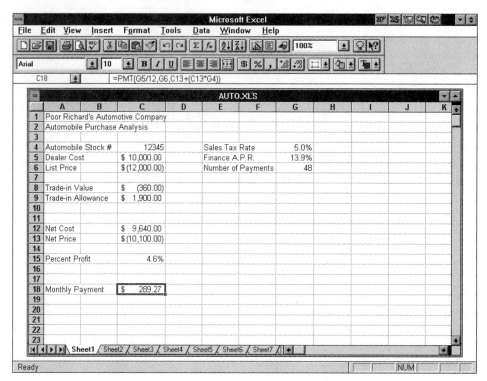

goal (such as minimum profit of 10%) is sought. Step 7 asks you to perform a simple what-if procedure.

7. Now enter the number 2500 as the Trade-in Allowance. Notice what happens to the Percent Profit. Keep changing the Trade-in Allowance number in steps of 100 until you discover the maximum Trade-in Allowance that gives Poor Richard a 10.0% or greater profit. Assume that the other three variables contributing to the function are fixed.

8. Print your workbook again.

9. When you are finished, save your work one last time.

10. Exit to Windows. Exit to the operating system. Remember to back up your work.

Intermediate Worksheet Operations and Graphics

UNIT SIX   Clipboard Commands and Outline Operations
UNIT SEVEN   Cell Reference and Calculation
UNIT EIGHT   Charts
UNIT NINE   Workbook Tools

■ **PART TWO** In this part, we continue our discussion of worksheet operations. Unit 6 is dedicated to the Windows Clipboard and outlining. Two important concepts are presented in Unit 7: cell references and recalculation. It is necessary to understand these concepts before you progress from the simple worksheets created in Part I. Excel's charting capabilities are presented in Unit 8. Finally, Unit 9 examines the different tools provided by Excel to simplify the process of analyzing and presenting data.

The application exercises in this part require you to develop a worksheet with sophisticated formulas and to develop and print charts. When you complete this part, you will have been exposed to almost all the Excel worksheet operations.

Clipboard Commands and Outline Operations

In this unit we complete the basic set of workbook commands. These commands enable you to build workbooks quickly with multiple similar formulas and to rearrange cell entries.

Learning Objectives

At the completion of this unit you should know

1. how the Edit | Copy command affects cell addresses,
2. how the Edit | Cut command affects cell addresses,
3. the difference between Cut and Copy and when to choose one or the other,
4. the variations of the Edit | Paste command,
5. the variations of the Edit | Fill command,
6. why and how to outline a workbook.

At the completion of this unit you should be able to

1. copy a portion of the worksheet to another place on the worksheet or to another sheet in the workbook,
2. move a portion of the worksheet to another place on the worksheet or to another sheet in the workbook,
3. fill a range with either values or formulas to speed data entry,
4. outline a worksheet.

Important Commands

Data | Group and Outline
Edit | Copy
Edit | Cut
Edit | Fill
Edit | Paste
Edit | Paste Special
Insert | Copied Cells
Insert | Cut Cells

Copy and Paste

The Edit | Copy command is used to place a copy of the selected range on the *Windows Clipboard* (a temporary holding location for data). The Clipboard contents can then either be pasted to another area of the workbook, thus creating new cell entries that are copies of existing entries, or pasted to another Windows application. Be careful using the Edit | Paste command, since whatever existed in the paste area prior to pasting is erased. The Edit | Copy command automatically adjusts most cell formulas to reflect new positions on the workbook. See Unit 7 for a discussion of this feature and how to control it.

To use the Edit | Copy command, simply select the *copy area* and execute the command. A *marquee* (a rectangular area bounded by dotted lines) surrounds the copied range. At this point, the contents of the copied range exist in their original location on the workbook as well as on the Windows Clipboard. To paste the data in another location on the workbook, select the *paste area* and give the Edit | Paste command.

There are four variations of the Copy and Paste operation:

- From one cell to another cell
- From one cell to several other cells
- From one range to one cell
- From one range to another range

The manner in which the copy area (from) and paste area (to) ranges are specified determines which variation you are using. Each of these variations is illustrated in the Guided Activities that follow.

FIGURE 6.1
RB96PROJ.XLS worksheet, step 1

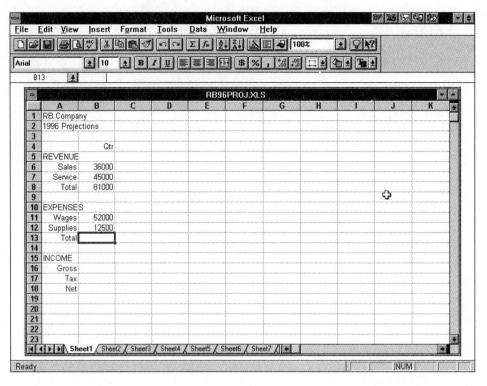

GUIDED ACTIVITY 6.1

Making Preliminary Entries in the Workbook

Our discussion of the Edit | Copy command will center on the steps necessary to build a simple income statement. Look ahead to Figure 6.9 for the end product.

1. Follow the startup procedure outlined in Unit 1 to load Windows and enter Excel.

2. Make the entries displayed in Figure 6.1.

   a. The text in the following cells is right-justified: B4, A6:A8, A11:A13, A16:A18. Use the toolbar to align these cells.

   b. Numbers are entered in cells B6, B7, B11, and B12.

   c. Enter the formula that sums Sales and Service in cell B8.

3. Save the workbook with the name RB96PROJ.

GUIDED ACTIVITY 6.2

Copying from One Cell to Another Cell

In cell B8, Total Revenue is calculated with the formula =B6+B7 or =SUM(B6:B7). Since the same basic formula is used to compute Total Expenses in cell B13, you can use the Edit | Copy command to copy from one cell to another cell.

UNIT 6 CLIPBOARD COMMANDS AND OUTLINE OPERATIONS   141

1. If you are not continuing from the previous Guided Activity, load Excel and open RB96PROJ.

2. Click on cell B8.

3. Give the Edit|Copy command. Excel places a marquee around the cell, as shown here:

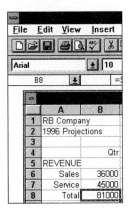

4. Click on cell B13:

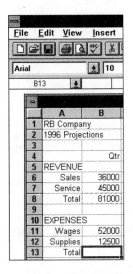

You have moved to the paste area.

5. Give the Edit|Paste command (or use the shortcut: press `Enter`) to paste the range to the paste area. If you used Edit|Paste rather than `Enter`, you need to press `Esc` to cancel the marquee.

6. Look at the entry in cell B13. The formula in B13 is =SUM(B11:B12) (or =B11+B12). Note that the cells referenced in the formula have adjusted relative to the formula's new position. The workbook should now look like Figure 6.2.

CHECKPOINT 6A How does the formula in cell B13 differ from the original formula in cell B8? In what ways is it similar?

FIGURE 6.2
RB96PROJ.XLS worksheet, step 2

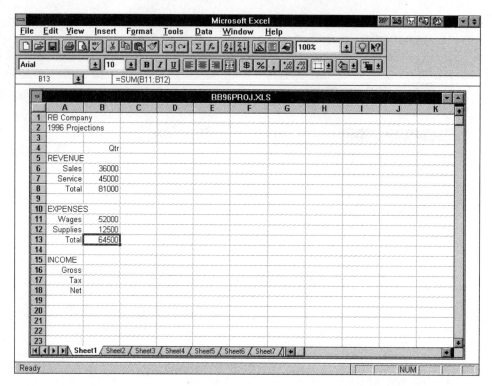

7. Save your work before proceeding.

GUIDED ACTIVITY 6.3

Copying from One Cell to Several Other Cells (I)

Next, in order to duplicate the Qtr heading across columns C through E, you will make a copy from one cell to several other cells.

1. If you are not continuing from the previous Guided Activity, load Excel and open RB96PROJ.

2. Right-click on cell B4. Give the Copy command. Excel responds by placing a marquee around the single cell as the copy area.

3. Highlight the paste area. Point to cell C4. Click and drag to cell E4, as shown below:

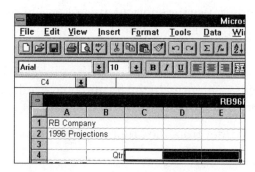

FIGURE 6.3
RB96PROJ.XLS
worksheet,
step 3

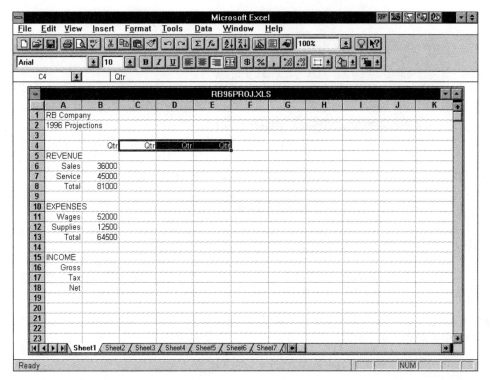

4. Right-click on the selected area and choose Paste to paste the Clipboard contents to the paste area. Press [Esc] to clear the marquee. The workbook should now look like Figure 6.3.

5. Save your work before proceeding.

GUIDED ACTIVITY 6.4

Copying from One Cell to Several Other Cells (II)

The next step is to fill in the range cell C6:E7 with projected revenues. The formula =B6*1.05 is entered in cell C6. (The company expects each quarter's revenue to be 5% higher than the previous quarter's revenue.) This same formula can be copied to the entire range. Again, this is a situation where you copy from one cell to several other cells.

1. If you are not continuing from the previous Guided Activity, load Excel and open RB96PROJ.

2. Make C6 the active cell.

3. Enter the formula =B6*1.05 in cell C6.

 4. Click the Copy button. Excel responds by placing a marquee around the current cell.

5. Drag the area from cell C6 to cell E7, as shown below:

6. Click the Paste button to paste to the paste area.
7. Use the arrow keys to move around in the range C6:E7 and observe the cells' formulas. At this point the workbook should look like Figure 6.4.

CHECKPOINT 6B How are the formulas in C6:E7 different from the original formula in cell C6? How are they similar?

8. Save your work before proceeding.

In this example you have duplicated a single cell throughout a block. The cell itself is one corner of the block. If you look at any of the entries in the range you have just created, you will note that each formula multiplies the cell to the left (that is, the previous quarter) by 1.05. For instance, the formula in cell E7 is =D7*1.05.

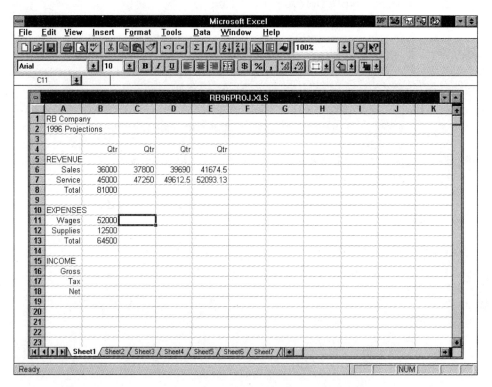

FIGURE 6.4
RB96PROJ.XLS worksheet, step 4

The last three Guided Activities have demonstrated three different ways to execute an Edit | Copy command—by executing the command from the menu, by using the command on the shortcut menu, and by using the Copy button on the toolbar. (You can also use the keyboard shortcut [Ctrl][C].) The very fact that there are so many available methods to execute one function highlights the importance of copying when creating a workbook.

Fill Command

The Edit | Fill command provides another means of copying data and formulas from one location on the workbook to another. Edit | Fill | Down copies the data or formula in the top cell(s) of a range to all the cells below, while Edit | Fill | Right copies the data or formula in the left cell(s) of a range to all the cells to the right. Edit | Fill | Left and Edit | Fill | Up work in the same manner as Fill | Right and Fill | Down. The advantage of these commands is that they are each a one-step process; you do not need to copy and then paste—you only need to select the range and invoke one command. References are adjusted relative to the initial cell, identically to the Copy and Paste operation.

A Keyboard Shortcut

Excel has an additional way to copy an entry to more than one cell—the [Ctrl][Enter] key combination. It is most powerful when used together with the range entry discussed in Unit 4 (see "Entering Data in Ranges"). To use this feature, select the range that will contain the same entry or formula. Type the entry or formula and press [Ctrl][Enter]. Excel will fill the range as if you had used the Edit | Fill command.

GUIDED ACTIVITY 6.5

Adding Formulas

In this Guided Activity, you add more formulas to the workbook.

1. If you are not continuing from the previous Guided Activity, load Excel and open RB96PROJ.

2. Projected Expenses in the range C11:E12 are computed as 1.03 times the value of the previous quarter. Enter the formula =B11*1.03 in cell C11. Copy this to C11:E12 using one of the methods discussed previously.

3. Select B8:E8. Give the Edit | Fill command and choose Right.

4. Select B13:E13. Press [F2] to enter edit mode. Press [Ctrl][Enter].

5. Enter these formulas in the INCOME section:

   Gross Income (B16) is Total Revenue less Total Expenses: =B8-B13
   Tax (B17) is 33% of Gross Income: =B16*.33

FIGURE 6.5
RB96PROJ.XLS worksheet, step 5

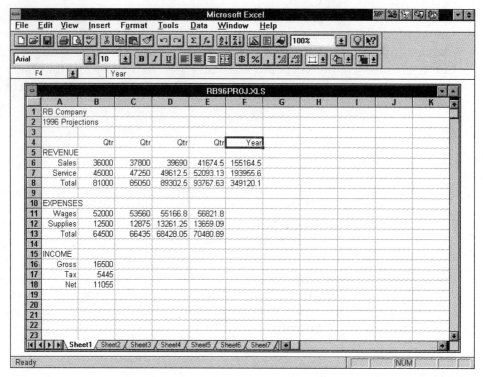

Net Income (B18) is Gross Income less Tax: =B16-B17

6. Enter the formula =SUM(B6:E6) in cell F6. Select F6:F8. Give the Edit | Fill command and select Down.

7. Enter the text Year in cell F4. Right-align this text. The workbook should now look like Figure 6.5.

8. Save your work before proceeding.

GUIDED ACTIVITY 6.6

Copying from a Range to a Cell

The formulas in F6:F8 can be duplicated in the area F11:F13. This requires that you copy from one range to one cell.

1. If you are not continuing from the previous Guided Activity, load Excel and open RB96PROJ.

2. Click and drag to highlight the range F6:F8, as shown below:

UNIT 6 CLIPBOARD COMMANDS AND OUTLINE OPERATIONS   147

3. Give the Edit | Copy command. Excel responds by placing a marquee around the range F6:F8.

4. Click on cell F11, then issue the Edit | Paste command (or press Enter). Excel pastes the Clipboard contents to F11:F13. The workbook should now look like Figure 6.6.

5. Save your work before proceeding.

Even though you specified only one cell (F11) in the paste area, the entire copy area was copied, yielding a three-cell paste area, the same size as the copy area.

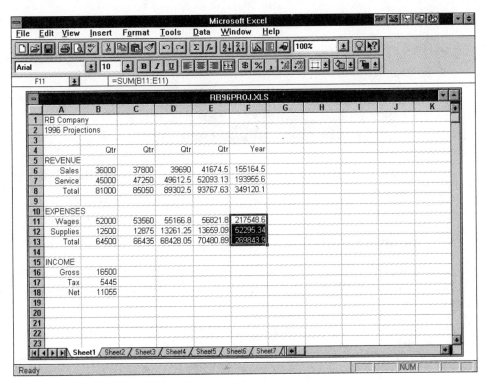

FIGURE 6.6
RB96PROJ.XLS worksheet, step 6

GUIDED ACTIVITY 6.7

Copying from a Range to a Range

The final copy operation is to duplicate the Income formulas across columns C through F. This requires you to copy from one range to another range.

1. If you are not continuing from the previous Guided Activity, load Excel and open RB96PROJ.

2. Select the range B16:B18. Give the Edit | Copy command. Excel responds by placing a marquee around B16:B18.

3. Drag to highlight the range C16:F16.

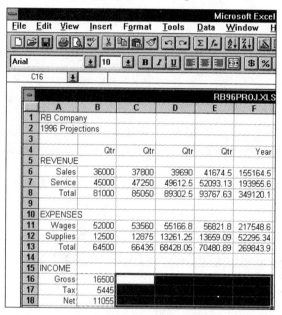

4. Give the Edit | Paste command (or press [Enter]) to paste the Clipboard contents to the new range.

5. Move to cell A1. The workbook should now look like Figure 6.7.

6. Save your work before proceeding.

In this Guided Activity, a column range has been copied into a row range. Four copies of the column are made—as many copies as there are columns in the paste area.

FIGURE 6.7
RB96PROJ.XLS worksheet, step 7

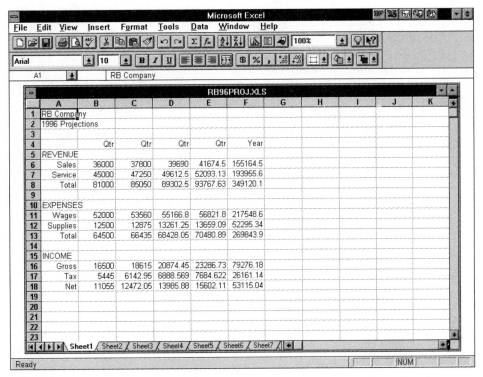

General Rules for Copying

Together, these examples illustrate a general rule of copying: starting at each cell of the paste area, Excel attempts to place a copy of the entire copy area.

Where there was one copy area cell and one paste area cell, one copy was made because there is only one cell in the paste area. In Guided Activity 6.3, there were one copy area cell and three paste area cells; therefore, three copies of the copy area were made. Next, a single-cell copy area was copied six times into the paste area. Whenever the copy area is a single cell, the number of copies is the number of cells in the paste area.

Where the copy area was a range of cells but the paste area was one cell, the copy area was copied once into the paste area. Finally, in Guided Activity 6.7, the copy area was copied four times because the paste area held four columns. Table 6.1 presents the general rules for copying.

TABLE 6.1 Summary of effects of Edit | Copy and Edit | Paste Commands

COPY AREA	PASTE AREA	RESULT
Single cell	Single cell	One copy of cell
Single cell	Row of r cells	r copies of cell
Single cell	Column of c cells	c copies of cell
Single cell	Block $r \times c$ cells	$r \times c$ copies of cell
Row of r cells	Single cell	One copy of row, r cells across
Row of r cells	Row of n cells	Error message[1]

TABLE 6.1
(Continued)

COPY AREA	PASTE AREA	RESULT
Row of r cells	Column of c cells	c copies of row, r cells across
Row of r cells	Block $n \times c$ cells	Error message[1]
Column of c cells	Single cell	One copy of column, c cells down
Column of c cells	Column of m cells	Error message[1]
Column of c cells	Row of r cells	r copies of column, c cells down
Column of c cells	Block $r \times m$ cells	Error message[1]
Block $r \times c$ cells	Single cell	One copy of block, $r \times c$
Block $r \times c$ cells	Row of n cells	Error message[1]
Block $r \times c$ cells	Column of m cells	Error message[1]
Block $r \times c$ cells	Block $n \times m$ cells	Error message[1]

NOTE: c and m refer to the number of cells down the column; r and n refer to the number of cells across the row.

1. "Copy and Paste areas are different shapes." If n is an exact multiple of r, or m is an exact multiple of c, Excel will paste multiple copies of the copy area, rather than display the error message.

Cut and Paste

The Edit | Cut command operates the same way as the Edit | Copy command. There are, however, two major differences in effect. First, the copy area is cleared. Second, some cell references in a Cut and Paste operation are treated as if they were absolute: if the formula =A2+B2 is moved from cell A1 to cell F25, the result in F25 is =A2+B2. The cell reference is changed, however, if the referenced cell is part of the block being moved. For instance, if the formula =A2+B2 is in cell A1, and both cells A1 and A2 (but not B2) are moved to cell F25, then the result in cell F25 is =F26+B2. The effect is that you have the same number of cell entries referencing the same information after the move.

Dragging

Excel provides yet another means of accessing the Cut and Paste and Copy and Paste operations. Until now, we have looked at various ways of accessing the Edit | Copy or Edit | Cut commands. *Dragging*, also referred to as **drag and drop**, is different; it does not use the menu structure, but directly affects the workbook using the mouse.[1]

---

1 Before you can move cells by dragging, the Allow Cell Drag and Drop check box must be selected in the Edit tab of the Tools | Options dialog box. This box is checked when Excel is installed, but may have been deselected since the initial setup.

To move a cell or range of cells, as a Cut and Paste operation would, select the range of cells to be moved, then drag the border of the selected range to its new location (the mouse cursor will change to a pointing arrow when you selecte the cell border). Excel will provide a moving border (also called a crawling border) to help you place the range in the correct place. When clicking on the border, be sure to avoid the small square in the lower-right corner. This is the AutoFill handle (we discuss its use in Unit 11).

To copy a cell or range of cells, as a Copy and Paste operation would, select the range of cells to be moved, then hold the [Ctrl] key while dragging the border of the selected range to its new location. Again, Excel will provide a moving border to help you place the range in the correct place. Once more, be sure to avoid the AutoFill handle when clicking on the border.

GUIDED ACTIVITY 6.8

Moving a Range with Cut and Paste

Continuing with the income statement workbook, let's move cells A1 and A2 to cells C1 and C2 so that they are centered over the data.

1. If you are not continuing from the previous Guided Activity, load Excel and open RB96PROJ.

2. Click and drag to highlight A1:A2.

3. Give the Edit | Cut command. Excel responds by placing a marquee around A1:A2, as shown here:

4. Click on B1:

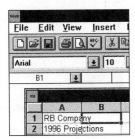

5. Finally, give the Edit | Paste command or press [Enter]. Excel pastes the Clipboard contents to the new location. Notice that A1:A2 are now empty.

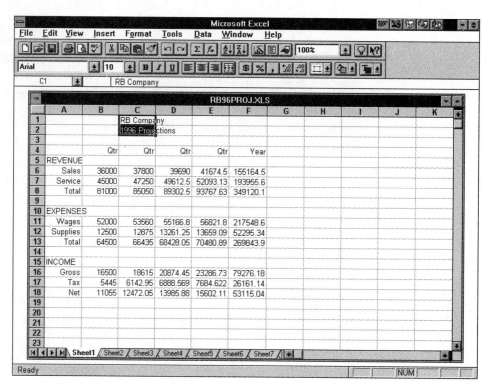

FIGURE 6.8
RB96PROJ.XLS worksheet, step 8

6. Cells B1:B2 are still selected. Point to the border of this range (the mouse cursor will change to an arrow pointer when it is over the border). Press and hold the left mouse button, then drag the selected range to C1:C2. The workbook will now look like Figure 6.8.

7. Save your work.

GUIDED ACTIVITY 6.9

Performing a Sensitivity Analysis

Finally, let's check the income statement workbook to see how sensitive it is to fluctuations in the wage expense. This workbook shows steadily rising income because initial revenues are higher than initial expenses, and revenues grow at 5% per quarter while expenses grow at only 3% per quarter. In this Guided Activity, you determine what happens if the initial estimate of wages is too low. In the first Guided Activity in Unit 7, you determine what happens if the rates of change are not correct.

1. If you are not continuing from the previous Guided Activity, load Excel and open RB96PROJ.

2. Format all numbers by clicking the Currency button on the toolbar, and adjust column widths, if necessary.

3. Make B11 the active cell.

4. Enter 70000 in cell B11.

5. Notice that the Gross Income for the first quarter changes to -1500, the Tax is -495 (that is, a tax credit), and Net Income is -1005 (a loss).

6. Notice, further, that the company still makes a profit: net income for the year (cell F18) is 2660.50.

7. Increase the wage expense in B11 in increments of 100 until Net Income for the year changes from positive to negative. This demonstrates the effect of varying wage levels on profitability for the company.

8. Save the workbook with this latest change. You will do further sensitivity analysis in Unit 7.

9. Remember to back up your work.

Copy and Paste vs. Cut and Paste

Copy and Paste is normally used to replicate the same formula to several places in the workbook. It is most useful when building a workbook. By contrast, Cut and Paste is often done purely for visual reasons: cells are moved because they fit better in one place than another.

Edit | Paste Special

Occasionally, you will want to copy only some of the attributes of a range to another range in the workbook. The Edit | Paste Special command gives you this flexibility plus other useful features. Note that Edit | Paste Special is only available after a Copy command, not after a Cut command.

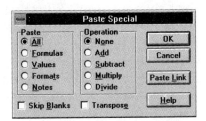

The options for Edit | Paste Special are as follows:

ALL Copies all attributes of the copy area (identical to Edit | Paste).

FORMULAS Copies only the formulas from the copy area to the paste area (text and numerical values are also considered a formula).

VALUES Copies only the results of formulas; the formulas cease to exist in the paste area.

FORMATS Copies the formatting from one range to another; this can also be done with style definition.

NOTES Copies annotations from one range to another.

OPERATION The options in this section combine the copy area values and the paste area values by using the arithmetic operation selected.

SKIP BLANKS Causes the paste area not to include any cells from the copy area that did not contain an entry (0 is an entry).

TRANSPOSE Copies rows as columns and columns as rows.

PASTE LINK This command button executes a *linked paste*. If you are copying information that you expect will change in the future, and you want that change to be automatically reflected in the paste area, use a linked paste instead of Edit | Paste. This creates a link between the copy area and the paste area. Anytime the data in the copy area is changed, the data in the paste area will be updated automatically. Use this option with care, since it will make changes to your workbook without consulting you first.

Inserting Copied (or Cut) Cells

You will not be designing workbooks for long before you realize that you have omitted an important item. In previous versions of Excel, you could only add data by first inserting a range of cells to make room for the new data, and then copying the new information into the newly inserted range. Now you may simply use the Insert | Copied Cells command; it moves the current cells down or to the right (as you specify) and pastes the new information in one step.

Pasting Multiple Copies

By now you have probably used [Enter] as a shortcut for the Edit | Paste command, as suggested in the Guided Activities. If you use Edit | Paste, you are aware that you have to press [Esc] to cancel the marquee. If you do not press [Esc] (or issue another command), the data from the copy area stays on the Clipboard and may be pasted as often as you wish. If you are copying from one range to several other ranges, you will find that this ability to paste multiple copies of a single copy area is a real time-saver.

GUIDED ACTIVITY 6.10

Special Pasting Procedures (I)

The accountant for the RB Company has just seen your 1996 Projections workbook and has approached you, asking where you included the income and expenses from the company's West Coast subsidiary. Since the accountant failed to provide you with that information, it is not included. You will correct that now. Your investigation reveals that income is projected at $16,000 for the first quarter, expenses are projected at $13,000, and both should increase at the same rate as that of the parent

RB Company. At this time, the accountant is not interested in separating the income or expenses into categories.

1. If you are not continuing from the previous Guided Activity, load Excel and open RB96PROJ.
2. First, change cell B11 back to 52000.
3. Select A6:F6. Issue the Edit | Copy command.
4. Click to make A8 the active cell.
5. Issue the Insert | Copied Cells command. Check Shift Cells Down (if not already selected) and click OK. Press [Esc] to cancel the marquee.

   Row 8 is now an exact copy of row 6. Notice that row 8 did not replace anything already existing on the workbook, but moved the rows downward as you requested in the dialog box.

6. Edit cell A8 to read West Coast and cell B8 to read 16000. Change the column width of column A, if necessary.
7. Repeat the above procedure to insert West Coast in cell A14, expenses of 13000 in cell B14, and the proper formulas in C14:F14.

CHECKPOINT 6C Select cell B9. What is wrong with the formula?

8. Move the cell pointer to B9. Press the AutoSum button on the toolbar. Press [Enter] to accept Excel's suggested formula, =SUM(B6:B8).
9. Select B9:F9. Give the Edit | Fill command and choose Right to fill the correct formula through the entire row.
10. Repeat the above procedure for row 15. How did that change the company's total profitability for the year? The workbook should now look like Figure 6.9.
11. Remember to save your work.

GUIDED ACTIVITY 6.11

Special Pasting Procedures (II)

It is now July 1996, and the RB Company has completed all the financial reports for the first two quarters. The figures have come in exactly as projected. The next task is to substitute the results of the formulas in the first and second quarters for the formulas themselves.

1. If you are not continuing from the previous Guided Activity, load Excel and open RB96PROJ.
2. Select columns B and C. Issue the Edit | Copy command.

CHECKPOINT 6D How do you select an entire column with the mouse? with the keyboard?

FIGURE 6.9
RB96PROJ.XLS worksheet, complete

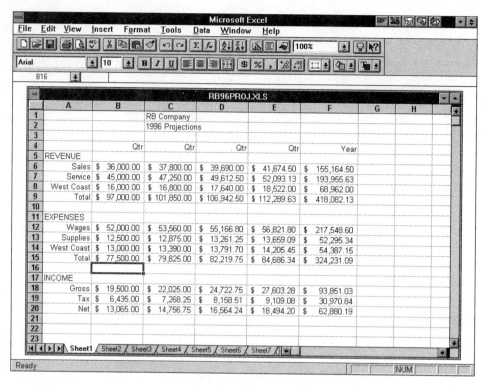

3. Issue the Edit | Paste Special command and click Values. Then click OK. This removes the formulas and replaces them with the actual values or results of the formulas.

4. Press [Esc] to cancel the marquee. Look at the formula bar as you browse through the cells in column C. What has changed?

5. Note that nothing has changed in the workbook window, except that the entries are now constants. When you changed cell B12 in Guided Activity 6.9, cell C12 was changed as a result. Cell C12 is no longer dependent on the value of cell B12.

6. Give the File | Save As command to save your work with the name RB96MID. It is important that you change the name of the file; you will be using the old version of RB96PROJ in the next unit.

Outlining a Workbook

One common use of a spreadsheet program is to create a budget similar to the simple financial projection you have been working on in this unit's Guided Activities. Such a budget can quickly become complex, showing forecasts on a monthly or even a weekly basis, and breaking income and expenses down to very detailed levels. This is a great help to the person who needs to track revenues and expenditures and justify discrepancies. However, upper management will usually only want to look at "The Big Picture" and skip all the minutiae.

Before outlining was available, an overall view was provided by linking the columns and rows that represent totals to a second workbook, which would only show the major categories. However, by creating an *outline* of a workbook, you can keep the details and the totals on one worksheet, and present either the totals only or all the detail, or something between.

Excel allows you to create up to eight levels of detail. Look ahead to Figure 6.10 to see an example of an outlined worksheet showing the outline symbols. You can

- Click on the Expand buttons to show more detail
- Click on the Collapse buttons to show less detail

- Click on a Level button to see a specific level of detail

Clicking on the Expand button displays collapsed levels of the outline.

Clicking on the Collapse button hides the rows or columns indicated by the level bar.

Clicking on the Level button hides all levels of the outline with a lower priority than that button.

The easiest way to create an outline is to use the Data | Group and Outline command and select Auto Outline. If you organize your worksheets so that summary rows are placed below detail rows and summary columns are placed to the right of detail columns, Excel will usually come very close to defining the outline the way you wish.

Unfortunately, it is inevitable that computers and users will eventually disagree on how something should be done. In this case, there are several ways to manually fine-tune an automatic outline:

- Select smaller ranges and choose Auto Outline from the Data | Group and Outline command. This lessens Excel's analytical capability and increases your control over the outlining process.

- Select ranges and choose Group from the Data | Group and Outline command. This puts you in complete control and allows you to create a manual outline.

- Select ranges and use the shortcut key combinations [Alt][Shift][→] and [Alt][Shift][←] to manually demote or promote rows and/or columns. You can use this to edit an existing automatic outline or to create a manual outline.

The choices available from the Data | Group and Outline command are as follows:

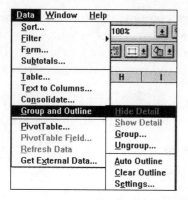

HIDE DETAIL Hides detail information in an outline; similar to clicking on a Collapse button.

SHOW DETAIL Displays detail information in an outline; similar to clicking on an Expand button.

GROUP Demotes selection to a lower level of the outline. If the selection does not comprise complete rows or columns, a dialog box displays inquiring whether to demote selected rows or columns.

UNGROUP Promotes selection to a higher level of the outline. If the selection does not comprise complete rows or columns, a dialog box displays inquiring whether to promote selected rows or columns.

AUTO OUTLINE Excel analyzes the selection based on position and presence of formulas and creates an automatic outline.

CLEAR OUTLINE Removes all outline styles and returns the selection to normal.

SETTINGS Displays a dialog box in which the user can determine where Excel should look for summary information when creating an automatic outline. It also allows the user to manually define outline styles.

GUIDED ACTIVITY 6.12

Outlining a Worksheet

The vice president of finance for the RB Company has seen your 1996 Projections and needs a brief worksheet showing only the annual totals for Revenue, Expenses, and Net Income to include in a memo to the president.

1. If you are not continuing from the previous Guided Activity, load Excel. Open RB96PROJ.

2. Select B4:E20. Give the Data | Group and Outline command and choose Group. Select Columns in the dialog box and press [Enter]. A column level bar appears above the workbook. (See Figure 6.10.)

FIGURE 6.10
An expanded, outlined worksheet

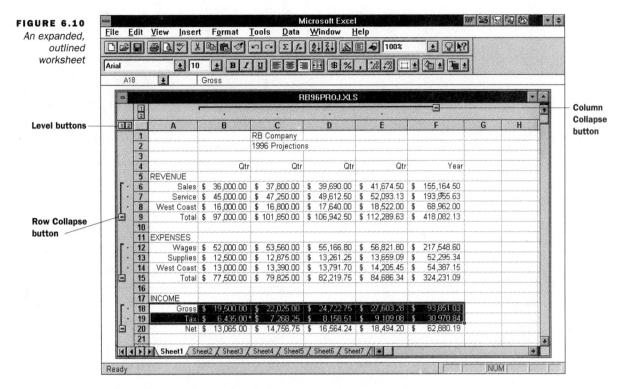

3. Select A6:F9. Give the Data | Group and Outline command and choose Auto Outline. Excel presents this dialog box:

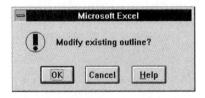

Click OK in the dialog box and press Enter. A row level bar appears to the left of the workbook. (See Figure 6.10.)

4. Select A12:F14, give the Data | Group and Outline command, and select Group. Ensure that Rows is selected in the dialog box and click OK.

5. Select A18:F19 and press Alt Shift →. Ensure that Rows is selected in the dialog box and click OK.

6. Save your work. The workbook should now look like Figure 6.10.

7. Click on the Collapse buttons located above column F and to the left of rows 9, 15, and 20. Your workbook should now look like Figure 6.11.

8. The remaining nonhidden cells show the annual figures for total Revenue, Expenses, and Income. (See Figure 6.11.) Note that the detail cells are still a part of the workbook; they are simply hidden and can be restored at any time.

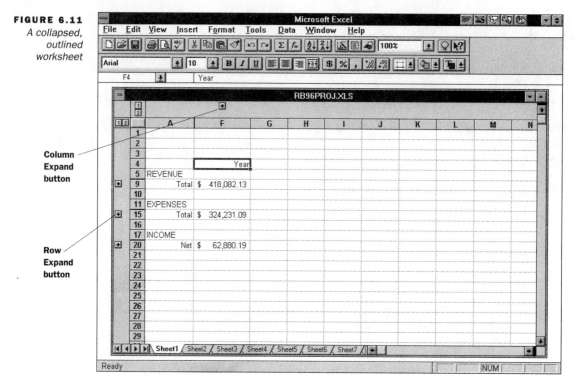

FIGURE 6.11
A collapsed, outlined worksheet

9. Click on the Expand buttons to return the workbook to a nonhidden state, and save your work.

10. This completes the Guided Activities for this unit. Exit to Windows. Exit to the operating system. Back up your files.

EXERCISE 6.1

A Sales Workbook (I)

1. If you are not continuing from the previous Guided Activity, follow the startup procedure outlined in Unit 1 to load Windows and enter Excel. If you are continuing from a previous activity or exercise and already have a workbook on the screen, use the command File | New to open a new workbook window.

2. Enter the following information into your workbook, starting in cell A1. (Enter the column headings in A1:D1 and the items and costs down columns A and B.)

    ```
    Item        Price       Tax         Total
    Computer    895
    Monitor     278
    Printer     449
    Desk        199
    TOTAL
    ```

3. Sales tax is 5% of the price. In cell C2, enter the formula for sales tax on the computer: =B2*.05.

4. In cell D2, place the formula that adds the price and the sales tax.

5. Use Edit | Fill or Copy and Paste to copy the formulas from C2:D2 to C3:C5. Mentally check the results. For instance, the tax on the desk should be about $10, and the total for the desk should be about $209.

6. In the row labeled TOTAL, enter a function that sums the price column, then use either Edit | Fill or Copy and Paste to copy that formula to the other two columns. Again, mentally check the results.

7. Format the dollar amounts with the Currency button on the toolbar. Change column widths as necessary. Use the correct button to right-justify the text in columns B, C, and D.

8. Next, use the Edit | Cut command to reposition the entire table to cell B11. (B11 is the upper-left corner.) Look at the formulas (which are now in columns D and E): did they change to reflect the new cell locations? If necessary, change column widths.

9. Give the File | Save As command and save the file as COMPCOST.

EXERCISE 6.2

The Perfect Job (III)

1. If you are not continuing from the previous Exercise or Guided Activity, follow the startup procedure outlined in Unit 1 to load Windows and enter Excel.

2. Open the JOBS workbook created in the Exercises at the end of Units 2 and 4.

3. You would like to adjust the salaries by some factor of the cost of living in the different cities. You decide to use data from the *Places Rated Almanac*.[2] The first step is to add the following to your workbook:

My Job Prospects

Company	City	Title	Salary	Adj. Sal.	Index	Housing	Food	Other
Arthur's	Chicago	Manager	$25,000.00			131	100	106
Freddy's	Seattle	Buyer	$26,300.00			122	103	112
Mack's	Bangor	Assoc.	$22,135.00			87	94	97
Minnie's	L.A.	Partner	$24,900.00			166	95	105
Alice's	Memphis	Exec.	$21,467.00			84	103	97

4. In the Index column, Chicago row, create a formula that computes the index as

$$\frac{2 \times Housing + 2 \times Food + Other}{5}$$

---

[2] Richard Boyer and David Savageau, *Places Rated Almanac*, 2d ed. (Chicago: Rand McNally, 1985). A newer edition of this book is now available.

You should obtain the answer 113.6. Copy this formula to the other cities. If you have done this correctly, you should obtain the result 94.2 for Memphis.

5. Next, compute adjusted salaries. The adjusted salary is 100 times salary divided by the index. For Seattle, you should obtain the result $23,398.58.

6. Format the Adj. Sal. (adjusted salary) column with the Currency button on the toolbar and adjust the column width as necessary.

7. Save the workbook.

EXERCISE 6.3

A Check Register (V)

1. If you are not continuing from the previous Exercise or Guided Activity, follow the startup procedure outlined in Unit 1 to load Windows and enter Excel.

2. Open the CHECKS workbook.

3. Add the following data. Look for chances to use the Copy or Fill commands: copy the name of the grocery store from check 103 to 105. Copy the date from 104 to 105. Copy the formula for balance from 103 to 104 and 105.

Number	Date	Description	Payment Amount
104	10-Jan-96	Cosmic Records	32.30
105	10-Jan-96	Charlie's Groc	16.75

4. Format the new entries as necessary.

5. Save the workbook.

EXERCISE 6.4

League Standings (I)

In this Exercise you are to make a copy of the team standings in a sports league as of a particular date. Your instructor will tell you which league (such as National Football League or Pac-10 Conference Basketball) and which date. A typical set of standings is printed here (Pac-10 Basketball as of January 26, 1993). Note that the "percentage" is really a three-decimal number—use a formula to calculate the percentages because later you will enter updated data. Save the file with the name LEAGUE. You will use this file in an Exercise in Unit 8.

Team	Conference			Overall		
	W	L	PCT.	W	L	PCT.
Arizona	5	0	1.000	11	2	.846
Oregon St.	5	1	.833	9	6	.600
USC	4	2	.667	11	4	.733
California	3	2	.600	9	4	.692
UCLA	3	3	.500	12	5	.706
Arizona St.	2	3	.400	8	5	.615
Washington	2	3	.400	8	6	.571
Washington St.	2	3	.400	8	6	.571
Stanford	1	4	.200	6	11	.353
Oregon	0	6	.000	7	11	.389

EXERCISE 6.5

Business Mileage (V)

Open the MILES96 workbook. Add the following data. Copy the formula in the Miles column that subtracts the reading of the current row from the reading of the row below.

Date	Reading	Use	Miles	Notation
1/5	12509.2	B		Visit site of Charlestowne Mall
1/6	12575.0	B		Call on Anderson account
1/7	12588.3	B		Pick up blueprints for Devonwood Clubhouse
1/8	12632.8	P		Drive to Vista Park, other family use
1/10	12775.1	B		Deliver Devonwood Clubhouse plans to Bertrand

EXERCISE 6.6

Gas Mileage (I)

Many of us drive compact and subcompact cars to get fuel efficiency, and we never tire of boasting about our gas mileage. Excel provides a very good platform for maintaining this type of record. In this Exercise you create a workbook that can be carried in the car. The driver need only record the date, odometer reading, price per gallon, and amount spent on gasoline.

1. In the range A4:G4, enter the following headings:

Date   Odometer   Unit Cost   Total Cost   Gallons   MPG   Cumulative MPG

2. Format A4:G4 as bold, vertically and horizontally centered, and wrapped text. Add borders left, right, top, and bottom. Adjust the column widths as necessary. Change the numeric format of columns B, F, and G to 0.0 and that of column C to 0.000 (these are custom formats). Change the numeric format of columns D and E to 0.00.

3. Enter the new car odometer reading, 11, in cell B5.

4. Beginning in cell A6, enter the information for the first fill-up—1/5/95 as the Date, 325 miles, 1.399 as the Unit Cost, and 11.00 as the Total Cost.

5. The formula for Gallons is Total Cost / Unit Cost. Enter the correct Excel formula.

6. The formula for MPG is (Current Odometer − Previous Odometer) / Gallons. Enter the correct Excel formula. You should get the value 39.9.

7. For now, the formula for Cumulative MPG is (Current Odometer − Beginning Odometer) / SUM(Gallons). Enter the correct Excel formula. You should get the value 39.9.

8. Save the file as GASMILE. In subsequent units you will add data and formulas to the workbook.

Review Questions

1. What are the four variations of the Copy and Paste operation?

*2. How does the Edit|Copy command affect cell addresses in formulas in the paste area?

*3. How does the Edit|Cut command affect cell addresses of cells external to the range being moved?

4. How does the Edit|Cut command affect cell addresses of cells internal to the range being moved?

5. What is the difference between Edit|Copy and Edit|Cut?

*6. When would you choose the Edit|Copy command?

7. When would you choose the Edit|Cut command?

*8. What options are available under Edit|Paste Special?

9. When would you outline a workbook?

Key Terms

Copy area
Drag and drop
Dragging

Linked paste
Marquee
Outline

Paste area
Windows Clipboard

Documentation Research

Using the Excel *User's Guide*, find and record the page number of each of the commands discussed in this unit. We recommend that you also write the page number in the margin next to the discussion of the command in the unit.

1. Copy and Paste—how would you combine the contents of the copy and paste areas?
2. How do you fill a selected range with the entry in the formula bar?
3. How many times can you repeat Insert | Copied Cells after an Edit | Copy command?
4. Excel includes built-in cell styles for the levels of an outline. What are the names of these styles?

7 Cell Reference and Calculation

Excel is an extremely well designed spreadsheet program. In many earlier spreadsheet programs, the user had to carefully arrange values that would be used in formulas in other cells of the spreadsheet. Excel uses a natural order of recalculation, which means that the user need not worry about the relative placement of values that are used in later formulas.

Excel also provides the ability to replicate formulas and values from one cell to one or more other cells, as demonstrated in previous units. This allows the user to build the formula once, then copy that formula to many cells, greatly expediting the workbook development process.

This elegance is not without its cost, however. To take full advantage of the powers of Excel, the user must understand the methods of calculation and cell reference used by the program.

Learning Objectives

At the completion of this unit you should know

1. the distinctions between the three types of cell references,
2. when to use mixed or absolute references instead of relative references,
3. when to use manual instead of automatic recalculation,
4. what natural order of recalculation is,
5. what a circular reference is.

At the completion of this unit you should be able to

1. enter a formula containing relative, absolute, and mixed references using the pointing method;
2. change the recalculation method from manual to automatic, and vice versa;
3. change the recalculation method to a specific number of iterations.

Important Commands

Tools | Options

Cell References

A cell reference included in a formula can be one of three types:

- Relative cell reference (normal)
- Absolute cell reference
- Mixed cell reference

You use relative and absolute addressing every day, perhaps without realizing it. If you ask for the directions to my house, I may say something like, *Go two blocks north; then turn left and go three blocks to the corner.* I have just given you a relative address to my house. If you start in the right place and follow the directions, you will arrive at my house. On the other hand, I might say something like, *I live at 234 Main Street, Anytown, Ohio, in the USA.* This is an absolute address. There is only one place on the planet that fits that description, and you can get there regardless of where you start.

Coming back to the worksheet, normal addresses are stored as relative addresses; that is, they are a set of directions starting at the current cell and arriving at the target cell. Sometimes you want to use absolute addresses; these addresses refer to the same cell regardless of where you start. A mixed address has either an absolute column address or an absolute row address; the other portion of the address is relative.

Recall the example from Unit 2, where you put the sum of cells A2 and B2 into cell A1. Using the pointing method, you enter the formula:

Move to cell A1

Press [=]   *Excel is ready for a formula,*
      [↓]   *move to A2,*
      [+]   *begin next reference; active cell returns to A1,*
      [↓], [→]   *move to B2,*
      [Enter]   *enters formula and calculates result in A1.*

The result in A1 is =A2+B2.

Excel does not remember this as = *A2 + B2*, however, but rather as = *down-1 & same column + down-1 & right-1*. If you copy the formula from cell A1 to another place on the workbook, say cell F25, then Excel still remembers the formula as = *down-1 & same column + down-1 & right-1*. In cell F25, the formula reads =F26+G26.

Relative Cell References

The example above illustrates how Excel normally handles cell references in formulas: as relative movements from the cell in which the formula resides. Relative referencing occurs irrespective of the method used to input the formula. Both pointing and typing methods yield a *relative cell reference*.

If you do not intend to copy the formula, then relative references are fine. On many occasions, however, you build a set of formulas that you want to duplicate elsewhere in the workbook. In some cases, relative references are acceptable, but in other cases they are not.

Absolute Cell References

When an *absolute cell reference* appears in a formula, that reference does not change as the formula is copied to other places in the workbook. For instance, you might put a percentage value in cell A2 that is used in several places in your workbook. As you copy formulas from one place to another, you do not want the reference to cell A2 to change.

To indicate to Excel that cell A2 is an absolute rather than a relative reference, it must be entered into the formula as $A$2. The $ tells Excel that this is an absolute reference, not to be changed in a Copy procedure.

Following the earlier example, if cell A1 contains the formula =$A$2+B2 and you copy that formula to cell F25, then the result is =$A$2+G26. Notice that the relative component of the formula (B2) changes (to G26), but the absolute component ($A$2) does not change.

Mixed Cell References

A third possibility is that you wish to hold the row (or column) absolute while allowing the column (or row) to vary relative to the reference. This is called a *mixed cell reference*, and it is obtained by putting the $ prior to the item that does not vary:

$A2   *Column A is constant, row varies.*
A$2   *Row 2 is constant, column varies.*

Continuing with the example, if cell A1 contains the formula =$A2+B2 and you copy that formula to cell F25, then the result is =$A26+G26. Notice that the relative component of the first reference (row 2) changes (to row 26), but the absolute component (column A) does not change.

What would be the result if cell A1 contains the formula =A$2+B2 and you copy that formula to cell F25?

Example

If you put money into a savings account paying compound interest, compounded yearly, the ending balance (principal + interest) is expressed by the algebraic formula

$$bal = inv \times (1 + int)^n$$

where *bal* is ending balance, *inv* is initial investment, *int* is periodic interest rate, and *n* is number of periods. Your boss would like you to build a table that shows the effect of leaving various amounts of money, from $10 to $100, in a savings account for 1 to 5 years. She tells you to assume a 5.25% interest rate and yearly compounding.

You put the interest rate in cell A1 (see Figure 7.1). Then you put the amounts in column A, from cell A3 to A12, and the years in row 2, from cell B2 to F2. The formula for $10 invested for 1 year is to be put into cell B3. If you were to use relative references, the formula would be:

```
=A3*(1+A1)^B2
```

That formula could not be copied to the other cells in the table, however, because the references of the cells would then point to the wrong cells for investment, interest, and number of periods. Therefore, you decide to try to use mixed and absolute references.

First, identify the reference(s) in the formula that should remain constant wherever the formula appears. In this case, you want cell A1 to remain constant because the same interest rate is used for all calculations. Make a note that you want $A$1 in

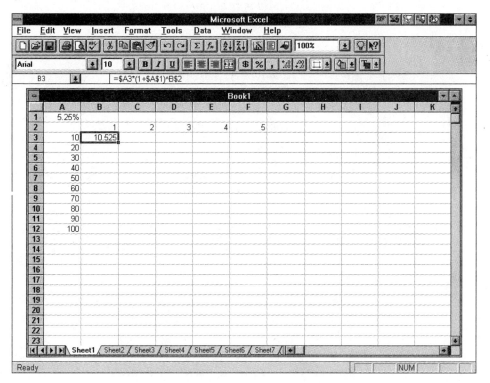

FIGURE 7.1
COMPOUND.XLS worksheet, step 1

the final formula. Neither cell A3 nor cell B2 should be absolute references, however, because the investment and the term vary.

Second, look for references that must refer to the same row as they are copied down a column. In this case, row 2 contains the number of years, and each of the numbers in row 2 applies to all entries in the column below that number. Therefore, the term (B2) must always refer to row 2 as you copy the formula from row 3 to row 12. Thus, the formula must include the term B$2.

Finally, look for references that must refer to the same column as they are copied across a row. Here, the investment (A3) must always refer to column A (the amount invested) as you copy the formula from column B to column F. Thus, the formula must include the term $A3.

The final formula is:

=$A3*(1+$A$1)^B$2

You build this worksheet with mixed and absolute references in Application C, which follows this unit.

Entering References into Formulas

The pointing method is the preferred method for entering references—relative, absolute, or mixed—into formulas. The type of reference can be changed by pressing [F4] while pointing at the cell. Assume that you want the formula =$A3*(1+$A$1)^B$2 in cell B3. The method is as follows:

Move to cell B3

Press	
[=]	*Excel is ready for a formula.*
[←]	*Cell pointer moves to A3,*
[F4]	*changes A3 to $A$3,*
[F4]	*changes $A$3 to A$3,*
[F4]	*changes A$3 to $A3.*
*(1+	*Begin next reference,*
[↑],[↑],[←]	*moves to A1,*
[F4]	*changes A1 to $A$1.*
)^	*Begin next reference,*
[↑]	*moves to B2,*
[F4]	*changes B2 to $B$2,*
[F4]	*changes $B$2 to B$2.*
[Enter]	*Enters formula into B3.*

The formula in cell B3 is =$A3*(1+$A$1)^B$2, with the result 10.525.

GUIDED ACTIVITY 7.1

Cell References

In this Guided Activity you employ absolute and mixed cell references in a revision of the RB96PROJ workbook developed in Unit 6.

1. Follow the startup procedure outlined in Unit 1 to load Windows and enter Excel.
2. Open RB96PROJ.
3. If the outline symbols are showing, choose the View tab from the Tools | Options command and deselect the Outline Symbols check box to hide them.
4. Check the net income for the year (cell F20). If the value is not $62,880.19, check all entries against Figure 6.9 and reenter the values (or formulas) shown in that figure.
5. Type the text `Projected Growth` in cell G4. Change the alignment format of G4 to wrap text.
6. Enter 5% (or .05) in cell G5 and 3% in cell G11. These are projected growth figures for revenues and expenses, respectively. Format these two cells to 0%.
7. Change the formula in cell C6 to `=B6*(1+$G$5)`. The value displayed in the cell should remain $37,800.00.
8. Give the Edit | Fill command to copy the formula from cell C6 to the range C6:E6. Use Edit | Fill again to copy the formula from C6:E6 to C6:E8.

CHECKPOINT 7A What should the formula in cell E8 be?

9. Change the formulas in C12:E14 so that they refer to cell G11. The workbook should now look like Figure 7.2.
10. Save the workbook. Continue to use the name RB96PROJ.
11. These modifications allow you to change the projected growth value in one cell (either G5 or G11) and see the impact on the "bottom line." For instance, notice what happens if the projected growth rate for expenses is 10% (enter 10% in cell G11).
12. You can modify the values in six cells and test a wide variety of situations. Under which of the following sets of values for the first quarter will RB Company have a positive net income for the year? After you enter each set of values, print the workbook.

FIGURE 7.2
RB96PROJ.XLS worksheet

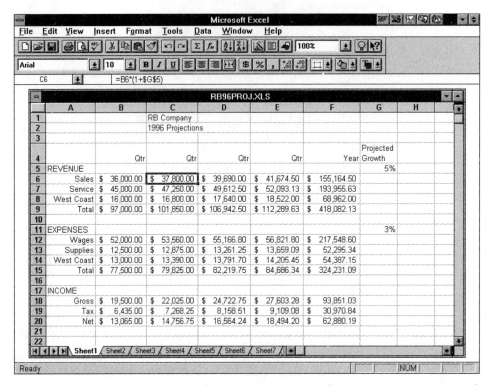

	REVENUE	Sales	36000	Services	45000	West Coast	16000	Growth	5%
a.	EXPENSES	Wages	52000	Supplies	12500	West Coast	13000	Growth	6%
b.	REVENUE	Sales	36000	Services	45000	West Coast	16000	Growth	5%
	EXPENSES	Wages	52000	Supplies	32500	West Coast	15500	Growth	6%
c.	REVENUE	Sales	36000	Services	35000	West Coast	12000	Growth	7%
	EXPENSES	Wages	52000	Supplies	22500	West Coast	11000	Growth	3%
d.	REVENUE	Sales	36000	Services	45000	West Coast	16000	Growth	5%
	EXPENSES	Wages	52000	Supplies	12500	West Coast	14000	Growth	10%

13. Reset the workbook to the original figures and save it again.

Recalculation

There are two primary aspects of recalculation: method and iterations. Normally the workbook is recalculated every time an entry is made or edited, with each cell recalculated only once. This can be changed, however. You can set the method to Manual or Automatic, and Maximum Iterations (the number of recalculations) from 1 to 32,767.

Different spreadsheet programs handle calculation order differently. Some use a *rowwise* or a *columnwise order of recalculation*. This means that the program progresses across one row after another, or down one column after another, calculating each cell with a formula. Excel uses a *natural order of recalculation*, meaning that if cell B2 contains the formula =5+5, and cell A1 contains the formula =B2, Excel determines that it must calculate cell B2 before it can calculate the value of cell A1. If you import a file from a spreadsheet program that uses a rowwise or columnwise order of recalculation, Excel converts the order of recalculation to natural.

Manual vs. Automatic Recalculation

Each time a cell is input or edited, Excel recalculates all the entries in the workbook that are dependent on that cell. Generally, you want Excel to do this, but *automatic recalculation* after every change can become noticeably slow if the workbook is large or has complicated formulas. You can use the Tools | Options command to establish *manual recalculation* (see the dialog box illustrated at left). A Calculate indicator appears in the status bar when changes have been made that require recalculation. The workbook is recalculated only when the Calc Now button is pressed on the Calculation tab of the Tools | Options dialog box (or when F9 is pressed).

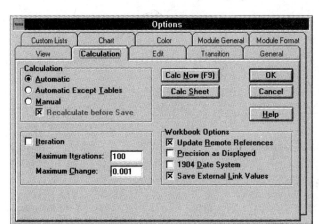

Circular References

Problems arise when a *circular reference* exists. For instance, you might have the following situation:

Cell	Contents
A1	=A2
A2	=A1

Here, the value of cell A1 depends on the value of cell A2. But the value of cell A2 depends on the value of cell A1. Which comes first, the chicken (A1) or the egg (A2)?

The following is a more complex and less obvious situation:

Cell	Contents
A1	=A2+B2
A2	.0525
A9	=A1*2
B2	=C2*A9
C2	1.29

When Excel tries to recalculate this, the following happens. First it goes to cell A1, but finds that it must go to cells A2 and B2 first. A2 is no problem, because it contains a constant value, but Excel must go to cells C2 and A9 before it can calculate B2. C2 also contains a constant value, but A9 contains a formula that requires Excel to evaluate A1 first. Excel then goes to cell A1, but finds that it must go to cells A2 and B2 first. A2 is no problem, because it contains a constant value, but Excel must go to cells C2 and A9 before it can calculate B2. C2 also contains a constant value, but A9 contains a formula that requires Excel to evaluate A1 first. Excel then goes to cell A1....

Actually, Excel is too smart to spend its time running around in circles without complaint. Given the situations described, Excel displays a dialog box with the message shown here:

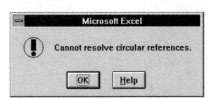

Usually, circular references are unintentional and indicate that there is an error in the workbook. When Excel tries to calculate a formula containing a circular reference, a Circular indicator appears in the status bar, followed by the cell where the circular reference starts.

Unless you have intentionally constructed a system of *simultaneous equations* (which *do* require a circular reference), you should search through your workbook for the culprit. Often, the circular reference is created by a Copy and Paste procedure.

TIP *Always save your workbook immediately prior to copying; then you can open a previous version if you cannot discover the problem.*

Simultaneous Equations

If the system of simultaneous equations is intentional, you must use the Tools | Options command to ensure that Excel does things the way you wish. You can specify the number of Maximum Iterations and the desired level of Maximum Change on the Calculation tab.

If you set the Maximum Change value near 0, Excel continues to recalculate until either the Maximum Change value is reached, or the maximum number of iterations have been performed.

CAUTION *Take care with these two options—setting Maximum Iterations to a high number and Maximum Change to a very low number can cause Excel to calculate for hours before reaching a solution.*

The Calculation tab of the Tools | Options dialog box has four other check boxes in the Workbook Options group:

- You can choose whether Excel will automatically update references from other applications.

- You can set the precision of calculation to equal the display precision (see the Format | Cells command) instead of the default 15-digit precision.

- You can change the serial number of dates to be based on Jan. 1, 1904 (the default for the Apple Macintosh, if you will be exporting the file to a Macintosh) instead of Jan. 1, 1900.

- You can choose whether Excel will save copies of external linked documents when it saves the current workbook.

For more information on the implications of these last two options, see Unit 13.

Example

There are occasions when simultaneous equations are necessary. Consider the situation in which a company must have a certain amount of money to operate for a period of time and must borrow to achieve this level of operating capital. Interest must be paid on the borrowed amount, however, and the amount of the interest payment must be added to the amount of operating capital needed. A portion of the workbook might look like this:

Cell	Contents	Explanation
A1	1000000	Operating capital needs excluding interest
A2	50000	Cash on hand
A3	=A1-A2+A4	Amount to borrow
A4	=A3*0.10	Interest on amount borrowed

For an intellectual exercise, ponder the following: Where is the circular reference? Why does the formula in cell A3 include a reference to cell A4? Try working this problem by hand, then put it into a workbook (see the following Guided Activity).

GUIDED ACTIVITY 7.2

Recalculating

In this Guided Activity you to use the Calculation tab of the Tools | Options command.

1. If you are continuing from the previous Guided Activity, save RB96PROJ, then use the command File | New to obtain a clear workbook. If you are not continuing from the previous Guided Activity, follow the startup procedure outlined in Unit 1 to load Windows and enter Excel.

2. Use the Currency button to set the default value format. Using the Format | Column command, set the width of column A to 20 characters.

3. Recall the example of a simultaneous equation just presented, in which a company must have a certain amount of money to operate for a period of time and must borrow to achieve this level of operating capital. Interest must be paid on the borrowed amount, however, and the amount of the interest payment must be added to the amount of operating capital needed.

4. Build a worksheet with the following entries:

Cell	Contents
A1	`1000000.00`
B1	`Operating Capital Needs Excl. Interest`
A2	`50000.00`
B2	`Cash on Hand`
A3	`=A1-A2+A4`
B3	`Amount to Borrow`
A4	`=A3*0.10`
B4	`Interest on Amount Borrowed`

5. Note the Circular indicator in the center of the status bar (see Figure 7.3). If you entered the entries in the order A1, B1, A2 … A4, B4, the Circular indicator and the "Cannot resolve circular references" error message appeared immediately after you made the entry in cell A4. At that point, the value of cell A3 is $950,000.00, and the value of A4 is 0 (zero).

CHECKPOINT 7B Where is the circular reference?

6. Give the Tools | Options command and select the Calculation tab. Check Iteration and set the maximum number of iterations to 10. Observe cell A3 now. The amount to borrow should be $1,055,555.56.

7. Save your work with the file name RECALC. Print a copy of the worksheet.

FIGURE 7.3
Simultaneous equations

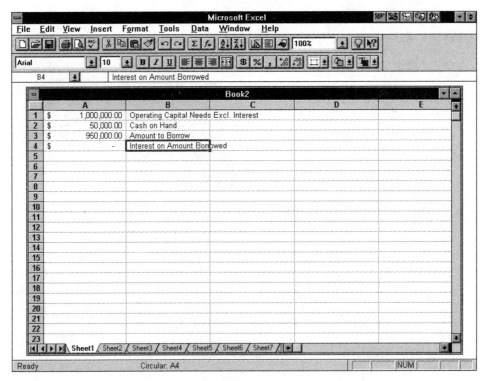

8. Now, change your operating capital needs (cell A1) to $100,000.00. The workbook should quickly calculate a new amount to borrow: $55,555.56.

9. Save your work again. Print a copy of the workbook.

Calculating with Displayed Values

A common difficulty for spreadsheet users is resolving the apparent discrepancies caused by the precision used for calculations being greater than the precision used for display. For example, when two numbers are formatted to two decimal places and added together, the result is based on the complete number, rather than the displayed number. If each of these numbers has a 4 in the third decimal place, they will both be rounded down. However, the sum of the two numbers will place an 8 in the third decimal place and cause the sum to be rounded up. The sum will appear to be incorrect on the spreadsheet and cause some people to question the accuracy of the spreadsheet.

Excel has a simple solution to this problem, however. When you select Precision as Displayed in the Calculation tab of the Tools | Options dialog box, Excel will use the displayed values in the calculation rather than the actual values. Before making this change, Excel issues the following warning message:

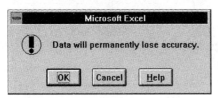

Once you click OK on the dialog box, Excel will change the method of calculation. Note that this change is effective for the entire workbook, not for a selected range. Note, further, that the new value of the cell permanently equals the formatted value.

GUIDED ACTIVITY 7.3

Calculating with Displayed Values

Say you are a finance officer at a car dealership. One of the salespersons has just sold two automobiles to a couple. They will be financing both of them through your dealership at 11% interest for 48 months. The amount to be financed for his car is $11,735; the financed amount for hers is $13,030. It is your job to prepare a workbook that shows the monthly payment for each car and the total of the two payments.

1. If you are not continuing from the previous Guided Activity, follow the startup procedure outlined in Unit 1 to load Windows and enter Excel, or use the File | New command to access a new workbook.

2. Enter the text entries shown in Figure 7.4 in A1:A8. Set the width of columns A:C to 15. Make the entries in cells B5:B8.

FIGURE 7.4
DISPLAY.XLS
worksheet,
step 1

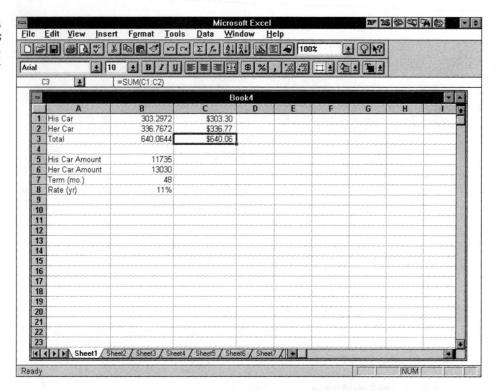

3. Enter the appropriate payment formula for his car in cell B1. Enter the appropriate payment formula for her car in cell B2. Be sure to use absolute references so you can copy the formulas.

4. Copy the formulas from B1:B2 to C1:C2. Format B1:B3 to 0.0000.

5. Use the AutoSum button to enter the Total formulas in B3:C3. Format cell C3 to Currency with two decimal places. The workbook should now look like Figure 7.4. There is an apparent error in the Total formula in cell C3. The explanation for this error is shown by the formatting of the cells in column B.

6. Give the Tools | Options command and select the Calculation tab. Check the Precision as Displayed box. Click on OK after receiving the warning message.

7. The workbook should now look like Figure 7.5. Save your work with the name DISPLAY.

8. Exit to Windows. Exit to the operating system. Remember to back up your work.

EXERCISE 7.1

Sales by State

In this Exercise you develop a workbook that compares sales by state.

1. If you are not continuing from the previous Guided Activity, follow the startup procedure outlined in Unit 1 to load Windows and enter Excel. Or, after you have saved DISPLAY, use the File | New command to access a new workbook.

FIGURE 7.5
DISPLAY.XLS
worksheet,
complete

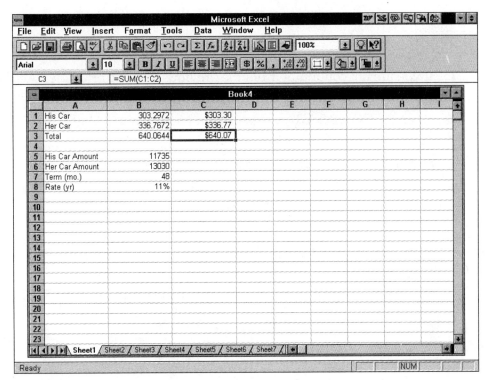

2. Make the following entries in cells A1..B8 (Sales by...Region all goes in cell A1).

   ```
   Sales by State, Western Region
   Alaska          198
   California     2593
   Hawaii          231
   Idaho           165
   Oregon          508
   Washington      552
   TOTAL
   ```

3. Adjust the width of column A to accommodate the state names.

4. In cell B8, enter a formula that sums the state figures.

5. In cell C2, enter a formula that computes the percentage of sales in Alaska. As you enter the formula, think about relative and absolute referencing, and consider how to create a formula that can be copied to the rest of the states.

6. Format cell C2 to 0.00%.

7. Use Edit | Fill to copy cell C2 to C3:C8. Note that the format is copied also. You should have 100.00% in cell C8.

8. Save your workbook with the name WESTREG.

EXERCISE 7.2

A Sales Workbook (II)

1. If you are not continuing from the previous Exercise or Guided Activity, follow the startup procedure outlined in Unit 1 to load Windows and enter Excel.

2. Open the COMPCOST workbook that you created in Unit 6.

3. Modify COMPCOST so that the sales tax percentage is in a separate cell (D10) and all formulas in the Tax column refer to that cell.

4. Save the workbook.

EXERCISE 7.3

Gas Mileage (II)

In this Exercise you add data and correct a formula in the GASMILE workbook.

1. Enter the following data, beginning in cell A7:

1/12/95	540.3	1.399	7.00
1/18/95	825.8	1.379	9.25
1/25/95	1110.0	1.389	9.50

2. Copy the formulas in E6:F6 to E7:F9. If your formulas are correct, the result in cell F9 should be 41.6.

3. Edit the formula in cell G6 so that the beginning mileage entry and the initial cell of the Gallons SUM( ) formula are absolute references. Copy the formula to G7:G9. If your formulas are correct, the result in cell G9 should be 41.6. Once you have the correct formulas, save your work.

$$= (B6 - \$B\$5) / \text{Sum}(\$E\$6:\$E6)$$

Review Questions

1. What are the three types of cell references, and what are the distinctions between them?

*2. When do you use mixed or absolute references instead of relative references?

3. How does the Copy and Paste procedure affect relative cell references?

*4. How does the Copy and Paste procedure affect absolute cell references?

5. How does the Copy and Paste procedure affect mixed cell references?

6. When do you use manual instead of automatic recalculation?

*7. What is the natural order of recalculation?

8. What is a circular reference?

9. Assume that cell C8 contains the formula =C9+B8.

*a. Express the formula in terms of relative movements from cell C8.

b. If the formula is copied to cell D8, what is the formula in cell D8?

10. Assume that cell C8 contains the formula =C9+$B$8.

a. Express the formula in terms of relative movements from cell C8.

b. If the formula is copied to cell D8, what is the formula in cell D8?

11. Assume that cell C8 contains the formula =C9+$B8.

a. Express the formula in terms of relative movements from cell C8.

b. If the formula is copied to cell D8, what is the formula in cell D8?

*12. What command is used to allow iteration of circular references?

Key Terms

Absolute cell reference
Automatic recalculation
Circular reference
Columnwise order of recalculation
Manual recalculation
Mixed cell reference
Natural order of recalculation
Relative cell reference
Rowwise order of recalculation
Simultaneous equations

Documentation Research

Using the Excel *User's Guide*, find the discussion of circular references and the Calculation tab of the Tools | Options command. Write the page numbers in the margin next to the appropriate text sections in this unit.

1. What is the order in which the F4 key changes cell reference types?

APPLICATION

Compound Interest (I)

In this Application you build a new workbook using many of the commands and concepts discussed in Units 6 and 7. You enter a formula containing absolute and mixed references, copy that formula, and print the resulting workbook.

1. Follow the startup procedure outlined in Unit 1 to load Windows and enter Excel.

2. For this Application, you complete the first example discussed in Unit 7. You might wish to review the COMPOUND.XLS worksheet presented there before proceeding.

3. In cell A1, enter .0525 (or 5.25%).

4. In cells A3:A12, enter the figures 10, 20, 30 ... 100.

5. In cells B2:F2, enter the figures 1, 2 ... 5.

6. In cell B3, enter the formula =$A3*(1+$A$1)^B$2, using the arrow keys to point to the cells and [F4] to create the absolute and mixed references. Check the formula carefully. Your workbook should now look like Figure 7.1.

7. Copy from cell B3 to B4:B12.

8. Copy from cells B3:B12 to C3:F12.

9. Look at the formula in cell F12. It should be =$A12*(1+$A$1)^F$2.

   If not, repeat steps 6, 7, and 8.

10. Format cell A1 to 0.000%. Format range B3:F12 to $#,##0.00.

11. When your workbook looks like Figure C.1, save it as COMPOUND and print a copy.

12. Exit to Windows. Exit to the operating system. Remember to back up your work.

FIGURE C.1
COMPOUND.XLS worksheet, complete

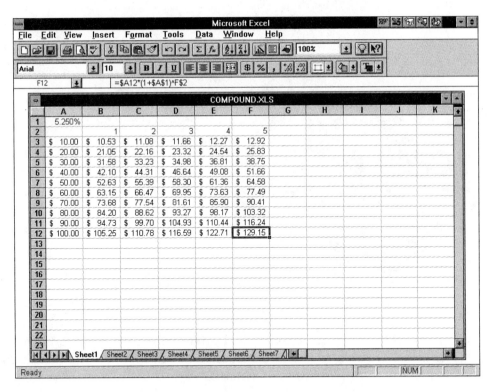

Charts

One of the major features of Excel, after worksheets, is its ability to produce charts that illustrate the numbers on the worksheet. In this unit, we discuss the creation, formatting, and printing of charts.

Learning Objectives

At the completion of this unit you should know

1. the major types of charts and the appropriate uses of each.

At the completion of this unit you should be able to

1. define any of the types of chart,
2. add titles and legends to the chart,
3. save the chart on its own sheet,
4. embed the chart as part of a worksheet,
5. print the chart.

Important Commands

Format | 3-D View

Format | AutoFormat

Format | Chart Type

Format | Selected Object

Insert | Axes

Insert | Chart

Insert | Data Labels

Insert | Gridlines

Insert | Legends

Insert | New Data

Insert | Picture

Insert | Titles

Window | Arrange

Window | New Window

Steps in Creating a Chart

Before Excel can draw a chart, the numbers that compose the chart must be entered in a worksheet. There are five general steps in defining or preparing a chart:

1. Enter the numbers (or formulas) into the workbook, such as that shown in Figure 8.1.
2. Select the data to be charted.
3. Invoke the command Insert | Chart.
4. Use either the Format | Chart Type command or the ChartWizard to tell Excel the type of chart you wish to draw—for example, a line or a column chart (these types are explained later in this unit). Excel draws a column chart if you do not instruct it otherwise.
5. (*Optional*) Define parameters such as titles, scaling, color, patterns, and legend.

These five steps should be performed in this order; however, because the chart is linked to the workbook data, any subsequent changes made to the workbook are automatically reflected in the chart.

To illustrate the operation of the Insert | Chart command, assume that you operate a hotel that has three classes of guests: the general public (who pay full rate), business customers (who pay a lower rate), and convention customers (who pay the lowest rate). You have data that show how many of each group stayed in your hotel last year.

FIGURE 8.1
HOTEL.XLS worksheet

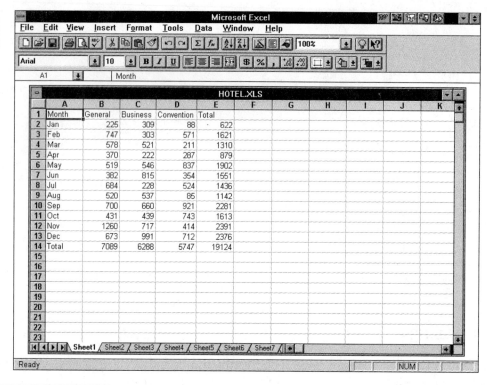

Worksheet Preparations

The data to be charted generally lie in a row, in a column, or in parallel rows or columns. You might build a worksheet such as that illustrated in Figure 8.1. There are several ways of looking at these data. For instance, you might want to compare the three types of customers for each month, or for the year. You might want total registration per month, regardless of type. You might want total registration per year, by type. Note that sometimes you look across a row (for example, who gave the most business in January?), sometimes down a column (for example, which month has the highest business registration?). And sometimes you need numbers that are not yet computed (for example, which month has the highest total registration?).

Automatic Charts

Excel offers a shortcut method for defining a chart called the ***automatic chart***. If data are in a set of adjacent columns, then you simply select the cells to be charted and press [F11]. This is the same as invoking Insert | Chart | As New Sheet and choosing all the defaults in the ChartWizard; it provides a "quick and dirty" column chart that treats each column of data as a separate data series. If the first column in the range contains text or dates, such as the month names in Figure 8.1, then these labels appear across the bottom of the chart. The chart in Figure 8.2 was created by selecting A1:D13 and pressing [F11]. This feature allows a quick look at your data, but you will normally want to use the power of Excel to provide a more professional chart, as discussed in the remainder of this unit.

FIGURE 8.2
Automatic chart

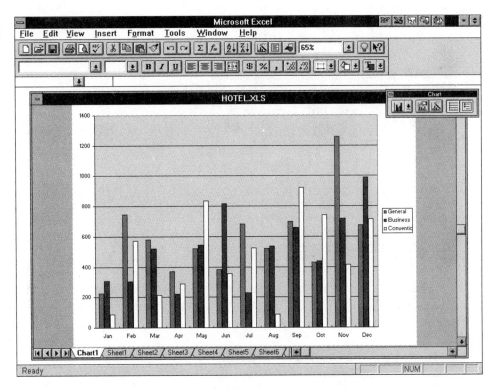

 Another type of automatic chart that can be created by Excel is the *embedded chart* (a chart that is part of a workbook). To create an embedded chart, simply select the data to be charted, click on the ChartWizard button on the toolbar (shown left), drag an area on the workbook for the chart to reside in, and follow the ChartWizard prompts. The first dialog box, illustrated below, allows you to verify your selection of data. When the reference is correct, click Next.

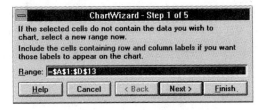

The second dialog box, illustrated below, is similar to the Format | Chart Type command. Select one of the 15 basic chart types and click Next.

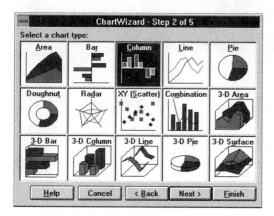

The third dialog box, illustrated below, allows you to select the chart specifics. Selections will vary depending on the chart type you selected. Once you have made a selection, click Next.

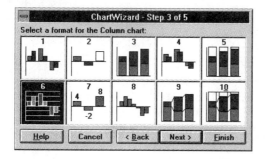

The fourth dialog box, illustrated below, presents you with a sample chart based on your selections thus far. It also gives you an opportunity to instruct Excel to treat your data differently. We discuss data series and axis labels later in this unit. When your chart is correct, click Next.

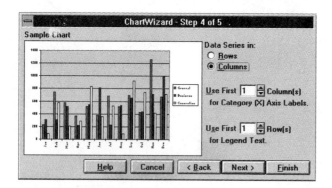

The fifth, and final, dialog box allows you to add optional items, such as a legend, a title, and axis labels to your chart. When you click Finish in the dialog box shown below, Excel will embed your newly created chart in the area you selected.

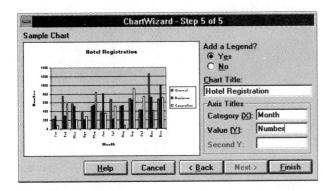

The chart in Figure 8.3 is an example of an embedded chart. To format a chart of this type, select it by placing the mouse cursor anywhere inside the chart area (the mouse cursor becomes a pointer) and double-click. Once the chart is selected, the chart menu bar replaces the worksheet menu bar and allows all the formatting techniques of a chart on a separate sheet. These techniques are discussed in the remainder of this unit.

FIGURE 8.3
Embedded chart

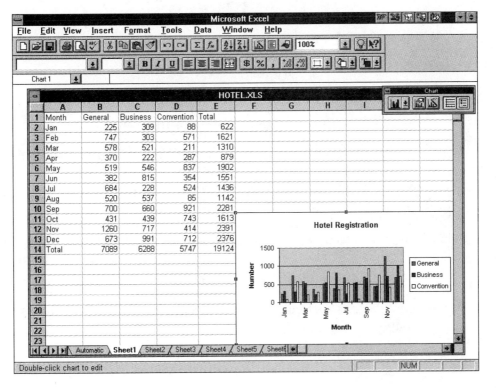

Insert | Chart Command

Give the Insert | Chart | As New Sheet command, and Excel presents the ChartWizard explained previously. Once you complete the ChartWizard, Excel displays the new chart sheet, the Chart toolbar, and the chart menu bar. Data selected on the worksheet are graphed in the chart. The chart menu bar is similar to the worksheet menu bar, except the Insert and Format menus have some different commands.

Format | Chart Type

Once the initial chart has been created, you usually start the chart definition process by specifying the type of chart desired in the Format | Chart Type command. The Format | Chart Type dialog box presents eight 2-D chart types and six 3-D chart types.

Clicking on the Options button allows you to fine-tune the chart type. While the specific options available depend on the chart type, what follows serves to illustrate the possibilities in defining a chart type.

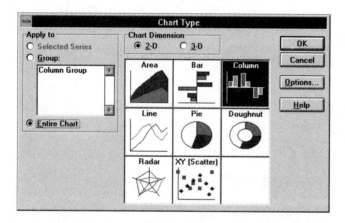

The Subtype tab of the Format | Column Group dialog box, illustrated below, allows three variations of the basic column chart. The first choice is a standard column chart, in which all values are charted against the same scale and the data points for the various series are grouped by common X-axis values. This subtype highlights each individual data point. The second choice is a stacked column chart, in which the data points with common X-axis values are stacked atop one another. This subtype highlights the total of the various series at each X-axis value. The third choice is a 100% stacked column chart, in which the data points with common X-axis values are stacked, but each column is the same height, representing 100% of the total. This subtype highlights not the total, but the difference between the different series at each X-axis value.

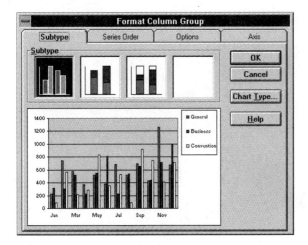

The Series Order tab, illustrated below, allows you to rearrange the order of the data series on the chart. Before this option was available, the only way to rearrange the order of the data series on the chart was to rearrange their order on the worksheet. Simply select a data series name and click on the Move Up or Move Down button to relocate it.

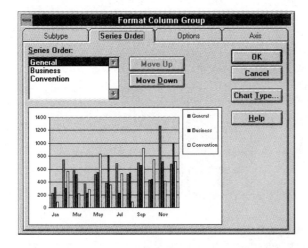

The Options tab, illustrated below, allows you to modify the appearance of the chart. Overlap is the percentage of bar width (from 0% to 100%) that the bars in a cluster will overlap. Gap Width is the percentage of a bar width (from 0% to 500%) that defines the gap between clusters. Series Lines instructs Excel to draw lines between the data points on stacked column charts. Vary Colors by Point allows you to change the color of each data point if your chart has only one data series.

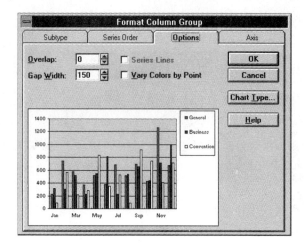

The Axis tab, illustrated below, allows you to choose to plot a specific data series against either the primary axis (the left side of the chart) or a secondary axis (the right side of the chart).

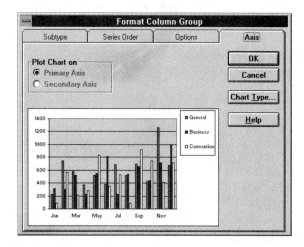

Each type of chart has its virtues, constraints, and limitations. Figures 8.4 through 8.18 illustrate the various types of charts, using data from the hotel guests worksheet. All of the charts shown in those figures can be requested directly from the commands in the Insert and Format menus. By the time you finish this unit, you will be able to duplicate any of the charts illustrated.

FIGURE 8.4
Area chart

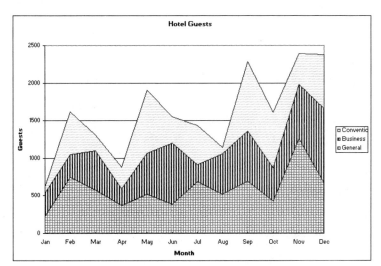

Area charts, sometimes called *stacked line charts*, show trends like a line chart, but the trend is the total of the component parts. When the focus is on the individual parts, a line chart is better, but when the focus is on the total, an area chart is preferable. In Figure 8.4, you see that January and April have the lowest total customers at the hotel.

Bar charts use bars of varying lengths to indicate amount. Note that 255 sets of data can be plotted; the bars are of different colors or patterns to indicate the different types of data, and they are run horizontally across the chart. In Figure 8.5, you see the same data that are in Figure 8.4; it is easy to pick out months where there is a preponderance of one type of guest—for instance, Business guests in June and December.

FIGURE 8.5
Bar chart

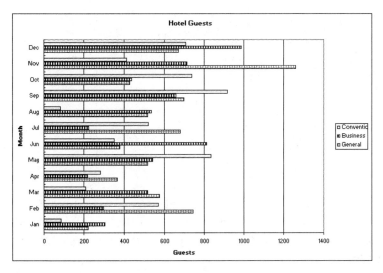

Column charts are similar to bar charts, except that the data bars are vertical rather than horizontal. (See Figure 8.6.)

FIGURE 8.6
Column chart

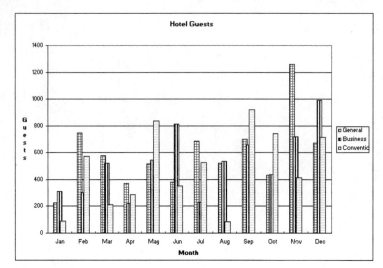

Line charts are good for showing trends, such as the profit-line chart shown in many business cartoons. Up to 255 lines can be drawn, representing 255 types of data (for example, type of hotel guest).

In Figure 8.7, you see that the number of Convention guests is quite low in January and August, but high in May and September. There do not appear to be clear trends—the number of each type of guest zigzags up and down.

FIGURE 8.7
Line chart

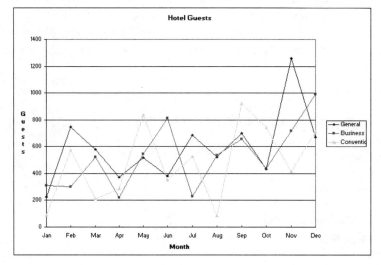

Pie charts are used to show relative proportions of the whole, for one data series only. For instance, the pie chart in Figure 8.8 shows the relative proportion of guests in each category for the month of July. Almost half of the guests for that month are in the General category.

FIGURE 8.8
Pie chart

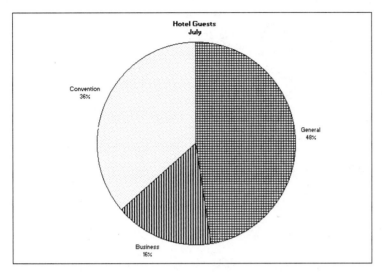

Doughnut charts are very similar to pie charts and are also used to show relative proportions of the whole. The major difference between doughnut and pie charts (other than the hole in the middle) is that the doughnut chart can display more than one data series. For instance, the doughnut chart in Figure 8.9 shows the relative proportion of guests in each category for the months of August and September.

FIGURE 8.9
Doughnut chart

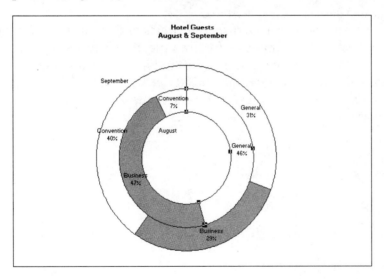

Radar charts are used to illustrate changes within a set of data or to compare small sets of data with one another. Each set of data (in Figure 8.10, each row) is plotted as a "ring" around the center point; each group of matching data points (in Figure 8.10, each column) is plotted on the same axis away from the center.

FIGURE 8.10
Radar chart

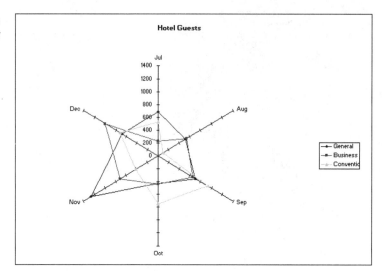

XY charts are used to plot numeric functions and other data in which the horizontal axis (the X-axis) is numeric rather than text. Each point on the chart (which is usually a marker or label) represents a pair of numbers, one from the **X-axis** (reading across the bottom; General in the example in Figure 8.11) and the other from the **Y-axis** (the data range reading up the left side; Business in this example). Up to 255 different lines (data series) can be included.

XY charts are sometimes called *scatter charts* and are used to show the relationship between two sets of numbers—for example, the relationship between numbers of Business and General guests. In the chart in Figure 8.11 the point labeled "Sep" indicates that there were approximately 700 General and 700 Business guests in September. Notice that the number of Business guests tends to rise as the number of General guests rises.

FIGURE 8.11
XY (scatter) chart

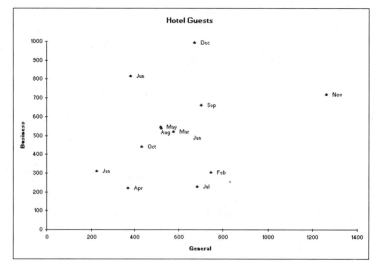

Combination charts are used when you want to combine two types of display. In Figure 8.12, for instance, we have plotted each type of guest in a column chart format and the total number of guests in a line chart format. Data series 4 (the Total column) is overlaid onto a standard column chart (data series 1, 2, and 3) and formatted as a line chart. Excel allows you to have up to 255 data series divided into multiple groups.

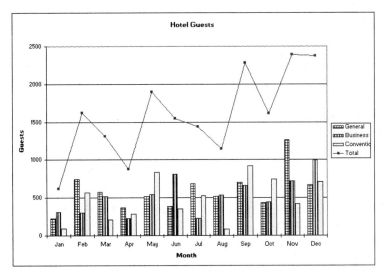

FIGURE 8.12 Combination chart

3-D area charts, like 2-D area charts, emphasize the total of the values in a data series more than the individual points. One use of the 3-D chart can be simply to give the impression of depth to a standard area chart. Its better use by far, however, is to give you the ability to put separate data series in individual rows; in effect allowing you to have two category axes. The example in Figure 8.13 is a true 3-D chart; the X-axis (bottom tick marks) is the category axis, the *Z-axis* (left tick marks) is the value axis, and the Y-axis (right tick marks) contains separate areas for the individual data series.

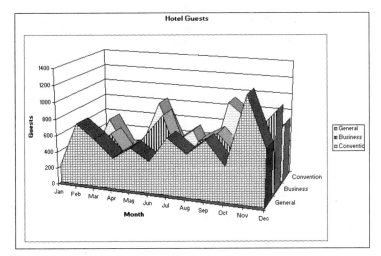

FIGURE 8.13 3-D area chart

3-D bar charts are appearance charts only. The bars in the chart are given the illusion of depth. Figure 8.14 is an example of a 3-D bar chart.

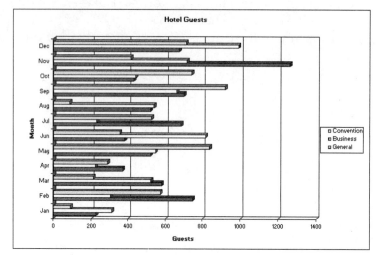

FIGURE 8.14
3-D bar chart

3-D column charts, like 3-D area charts, provide the option of either giving the appearance of depth to a standard column chart, or being a true 3-D chart. The illustration in Figure 8.15 is a true 3-D chart.

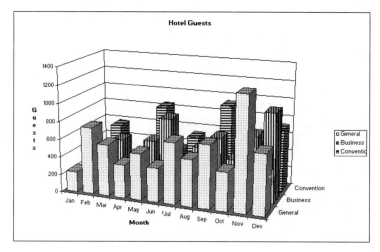

FIGURE 8.15
3-D column chart

3-D line charts turn a standard line chart into a ribbon chart. If a line chart has two or more lines, the 3-D line chart separates the different data series across the Y-axis. (See Figure 8.16.)

FIGURE 8.16
3-D line
(ribbon) chart

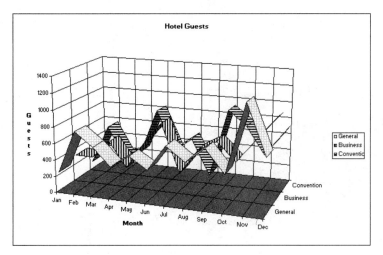

3-D pie charts give the illusion of height to a standard pie chart. Because of the angle of view, it draws attention to the slice(s) that are placed to the front of the pie chart. (See Figure 8.17.)

FIGURE 8.17
3-D pie chart

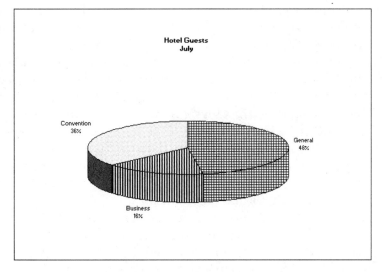

3-D surface charts are true 3-D plots. The Help window for this chart type suggests imagining a rubber sheet stretched over a 3-D column chart. The first two selections in the ChartWizard are 3-D views of the chart; the last two selections are overhead 2-D views of the plot. 3-D surface charts are good for examining the interrelationships between two sets of data. While you cannot easily see the actual numbers, you can see whether or not they are the same general height. These charts require at least two, and preferably only two, sets of data. (See Figure 8.18.)

FIGURE 8.18
3-D surface chart

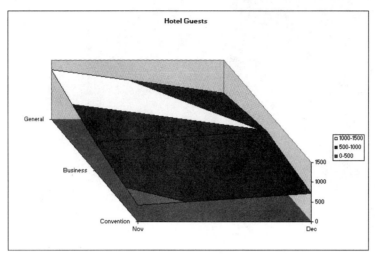

Data Series

Every chart is composed of one or more series of data. The appearance of your chart depends on which direction (row or column) of your workbook Excel interprets as the *data series*. The other direction contains *categories*. In the example workbook, the *category names* are found in column A. Each row (2:13) contains a different category (month). The data series are located in columns B, C, and D; each column contains a different series (General, Business, Convention). The first cells in the data series, here B1:D1, contain the *data series names*, which are the labels for the *legend*. Each value in the worksheet is a *data point*. Each data point is represented by a *data marker*. The data marker in a column chart is the top of the column; in a line chart, the data marker is the symbol used along the line; in a pie chart, it is the individual slice; and in a scatter chart, it is the symbol placed on the grid. All the data markers in a specific series are usually formatted identically.

In 2-D charts, one of the axes is called the *category axis* and the other is the *value axis*. In line, area, and column charts the horizontal axis is the category axis and contains the category names (Jan, Feb, and so on), while the vertical (value) axis contains a numeric scale that indicates the values of the data points. The axes are reversed in a bar chart. In an XY chart, the horizontal axis contains values of the X data range. If you attach a legend to these charts, it contains the data series names.

In some 3-D charts, for example Figure 8.14, the third dimension is purely for visual effect and there are only two axes, as described above. In other 3-D charts, as in Figures 8.13 and 8.15, the third dimension contains data series names, duplicating information found in the legend.

One of the most difficult tasks in creating a chart is understanding how Excel interprets the columns and rows of a workbook into data series and categories. Actually, Excel follows several steps in making this determination:

1. The first step is to check whether the upper-left cell of the range is blank. If so, Excel uses the first row and the first column as data series names and category

names. Note that no decision has been made yet as to which contains the category names and which contains the data series names.

2. If the upper-left cell is not blank, then Excel checks to see if the first row and the first column contain either text or dates. If they do, then again Excel uses the first row and the first column as data series names and category names.

3. Next, Excel checks the dimensions of the selected range. Excel always assumes that you want fewer data series than categories. So, if there are more rows than columns, the rows are the categories and the columns are the data series (the case illustrated by the hotel data). If there are more columns than rows, the columns are the categories and the rows are the data series.

4. If the workbook is square (that is, it has the same number of rows and columns), Excel interprets the rows as the categories and the columns as the data series.

Controlling Assignment of Series

Now that you understand the steps Excel uses in determining how to plot a chart, you need to know how to force the type of chart you want. For example, what if the chart you need has more data series than categories? Or what if you have a square data range, and you want the columns to represent the categories? For instance, the chart in Figure 8.19 contains the months as the data series and the types of guest as the categories. To create a chart like this, do the following:

1. Select the range, including as usual the data series names and the category names (in this example, select A1:D13).

2. Create a new chart by giving the Insert | Chart command.

3. Follow the ChartWizard; on the fourth step, select Data Series in Rows.

4. Click on OK. Excel will create a chart arranged like that in Figure 8.19.

FIGURE 8.19
A chart with more data series than categories

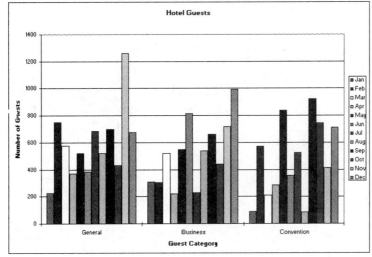

Displaying Workbook and Chart Windows

You will frequently want to have several windows open at once when you are charting data from a worksheet. You may, in fact, have several different charts as you decide which type of chart you want, which data you want charted, and how you want to format the chart. Frequently, you will want to be able to view more than one window at a time in order to see the effect that a change in the worksheet has on a particular chart. The workbook model used by Excel 5 makes it convenient to store the different charts as sheets in a workbook, but it does not make it easy to view the different sheets at the same time.

To accomplish this goal, you will use two new commands. The first is Window | New Window, which will open multiple windows viewing the same workbook. Each window can view a different sheet in the workbook, or a different part of the same sheet. The second new command is Window | Arrange. Invoking this command and selecting the Tiled option and the Windows of Active Workbook check box tiles all the currently open windows in the available workspace. (See Figure 8.20.) While the exact arrangement depends on the number of open windows, the active window is always in the upper-left corner. If you later change the size of the Excel application window, you may want to reissue this command, as the resizing only happens once. The windows do not automatically resize to fit a larger or smaller space. Likewise, if you later open or close another workbook or chart window, you will need to reissue the Window | Arrange command to be able to see all open windows.

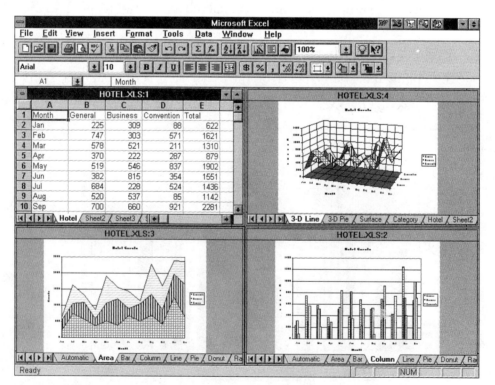

FIGURE 8.20
Tiled windows

NOTE *To make all the charts resize within the windows, as in Figure 8.20, select each chart in turn, click on the Zoom drop-down list on the Standard toolbar (illustrated at left) and select Selection.*

Moving Between Windows

Whether the windows are tiled in the Excel application window or not, you want to be able to move between them when you are editing and formatting the chart. If the window is visible and you are using a mouse, this is as simple as placing the mouse cursor anywhere in the window and clicking. If you cannot see the window, or if you are not using a mouse, the Window menu contains a list of all open windows. You may move to any window by pressing the number next to the window title in the Window drop-down menu box. There is a shortcut key for this procedure: pressing [Ctrl][F6] toggles the active window through all open windows.

GUIDED ACTIVITY 8.1 *diskette (3 sheet in one file)*

Making Your First Charts

In this Guided Activity you build a workbook and create a few simple charts. In subsequent Guided Activities you learn how to create more sophisticated charts.

1. Follow the startup procedure outlined in Unit 1 to load Windows and enter Excel.

2. Create a workbook that looks like Figure 8.1. This workbook will be used in this unit and in Application D. Once the workbook looks like Figure 8.1, double-click on the sheet tab and type `Hotel` as the name. Save the workbook as HOTEL.

NOTE *If you do not enter the correct numbers, or if you do not capitalize the text exactly as in Figure 8.1, you will obtain results different from the illustrations in this unit.*

3. Select A1:D13.

4. Press [F11]. You should obtain a chart that looks like Figure 8.2, but variations in display screens and printing might cause your chart to be proportioned slightly differently from the figure. This is an automatic chart—Excel analyzed the range and plotted a column chart. If your chart is a line or pie chart instead of a column chart, the person who set up the software probably changed the default settings. Double-click on the sheet tab and type `Automatic` as the name.

You use the chart menu bar in the following steps to gain control over the process.

5. In this step you duplicate the steps that Excel used to create the automatic chart. (If your chart did not look like Figure 8.2, it will when you finish this step.)

   a. Click on the Hotel tab to return to the worksheet.

   b. Select A1:D13.

   c. Give the command Insert | Chart | As New Sheet. Click the Finish button on the ChartWizard. A chart, like that obtained in step 4, will appear.

d. Give the command Format | Chart Type and select the column chart.

 e. Click on the Options command button and choose the first subtype on the Options tab. Click OK.

 f. Double-click on the chart tab and type `Column` as the name.

6. Create a line chart: Make a copy of the chart by holding the `Ctrl` key and dragging the Column tab one-half tab width to the right. You should now have a chart labeled Column (2). Give the command Format | Chart Type; select the line chart, click the Options button, then select the first line chart type. Your chart should look like Figure 8.7.

7. Double-click on the chart tab and type `Line` as the name. If you like, experiment with other chart types, always naming the tab according to the type of chart. Save your work.

8. If you are not continuing to the next Guided Activity, exit from Excel and Windows. Return to the operating system. Remember to back up your work.

Selecting Items in a Chart

Before we can discuss the details of how to edit and format a chart, you need to be able to select the different parts of a chart. Like almost everything else in Excel, this is very easy if you are using a mouse: you simply click on the desired item. If you do not have a mouse, press the `↓` key and then use the arrow keys to move through the possible selection items. The `↑` and `↓` keys move you through the major items; `←` and `→` move you through the specific items within a major item (for example, the data points in a data series). As you toggle through the selections, you see *handles* (small squares that mark the corners and midpoints of the perimeter of the selected item), and the reference area of the formula bar states the name of the selected item. The possible major items in a chart are:

- Plot area
- 3-D floor
- 3-D walls
- Legend
- Axes
- Text
- Arrows
- Gridlines
- Data series (each one is a separate major item)
- Drop lines
- Hi-lo lines

Editing the Data Series Formulas in a Chart

From your experience with Excel thus far, you are probably not surprised to learn that the charts you have been studying and creating are made up of *series formulas*. The formula appears in the formula bar anytime the data series is selected. The function that defines the data series takes the form =SERIES(series name,category names,values,plot order). Each of these arguments is in the form of an *external reference* (that is, a link to another document—in this case the worksheet). An external reference always begins with the external document name, followed by an ! (exclamation) symbol. By default, external references are absolute references. (We discuss external references in greater detail in Unit 13 and see the effect of changing the reference type.)

For now, you are learning how to edit this particular type of external reference. Suppose you are the hotel manager using the workbook from the previous Guided Activity. This gives you a lot of good information on what happened last year, but you need information far more frequently than once a year. You decide to maintain the workbook on a monthly basis. Each month, as you add the data from the previous month to the workbook, you will want to update and reprint the chart. By using the Window I Arrange command, you can view the worksheet and the chart at the same time. When you select each data series, you are able to view the range that is being plotted for that data series. By editing the range reference for the category name and the values arguments for each of the three data series, you can redraw the chart with the new information for that month.

Now that you have seen the difficult way to accomplish this, let's learn to do it the easy way! While the chart is the active sheet, give the Insert I New Data command to see this dialog box:

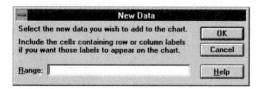

Select the range containing the new data by selecting the worksheet, pointing to the data range, and clicking OK. Excel will redraw the chart, including the new data. Note that, whichever method you use to accomplish it, the SERIES( ) formula now contains the new data.

Enhancing the Chart

The purpose of a chart is to make raw data more informative. This requires more than just a pretty picture; the user of your charts will need more information to readily understand the import of the data. Excel allows you to add this information by means of graphic items, text items, and formats.

Using the Insert Menu

The Insert menu allows you to add many items to the chart to make it more useful and/or more attractive. The Insert | Titles command displays this dialog box:

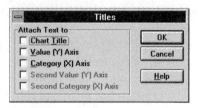

From this dialog box, you can add a title to the chart, or a label to any of the possible axes of the chart.

Give the Insert | Data Labels command and you will see this dialog box:

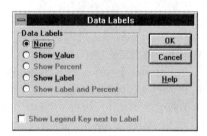

This dialog box allows you to add data labels to each of the data points in the chart. These labels can consist of the value charted, the category (X-axis) label of the data point, a percentage of the whole (for pie and doughnut charts), a legend key for the data point, or a combination of the above.

The Insert | Legend command does not present a dialog box. It automatically adds a legend to the chart based on the series name arguments of the SERIES( ) functions in the chart.

Give the Insert | Axes command, and Excel will present this dialog box, (or one similar to it):

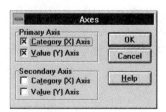

With this command, you can add a secondary axis to your chart. This is most useful when you are charting related series that are on completely different scales, such as units sold during a particular period and dollar sales during the same period. The dollars can frequently be several orders of magnitude larger than the units. By adding a secondary Y-axis, you can include both in the same chart and still be able to see definitive movement in each series.

The Insert | Gridlines command displays this dialog box:

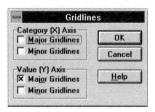

From this dialog box, you can insert either vertical (Category (X) axis) or horizontal (Value (Y) axis) gridlines in the chart. The major and minor settings correspond to the settings in the Scale tab of the Format | Selected Axis command.

The Insert | Picture command displays this dialog box:

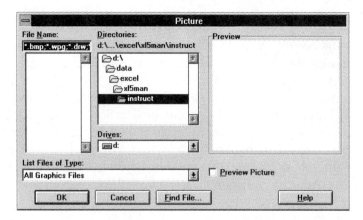

From this dialog box, you can select a picture file from any disk on your system, in any of the installed graphic formats. To see the file before inserting it in your chart, check the Preview Picture box. Select a file name and click OK, and the graphic will be inserted in your chart. You can then move and size it as you need.

Using Format | Selected Object

The Format | Selected Object command changes its name based on the item selected. For example, if you have selected the plot area, it will become Format | Selected Plot Area. There are many variations of this command and its associated dialog boxes, so we will discuss only the most common of these.

CHANGING SOLID AREA CHARACTERISTICS

You can use the Format | Selected Object command to change fill patterns on objects with solid areas, such as pie, column, bar, and area charts. Simply select the object to be changed (a data series or data point in a pie, column, bar, area, or 3-D chart; the plot area; the chart area; and so on) and give the Format | Selected Object command. (As a shortcut, double-click on the object.) You will see a dialog box with a Patterns tab similar to the following:

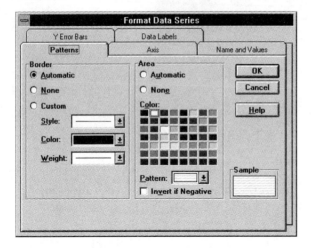

Solid areas have both a border and an area fill. The Border options allow you to choose the automatic border, no border, or a custom border. If you select a custom border, you can change the line style, color, and weight of the border.

The Area options allow you to choose the automatic fill, no fill, or a custom fill. If you select a custom fill, you can change the fill pattern, the foreground color, and the background color. The color grid shown in the illustration above is for the background color; the foregound color is included in the grid with the pattern selections. To select a custom pattern with a white background, you need to change the background color to white, then use the Pattern drop-down list to change the pattern, then use the Pattern drop-down list again to change the foreground color. If you select the Invert if Negative check box, the foregound and background colors will be reversed for all negative numbers.

CHANGING LINE CHARACTERISTICS

You can also use the Format | Selected Object command to change the characteristics of lines in your chart. Select the object (a data series or data point in a line, radar, or XY chart; an axis; a gridline; and so on) and give the Format | Selected Object command. Excel displays a dialog box similar to the following:

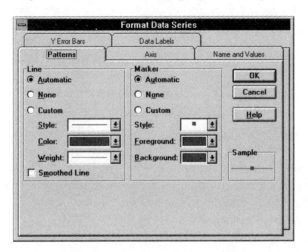

Lines have a line definition and, frequently, a marker definition. The Line options allow you to select the automatic line, no line, or a custom line. If you select the custom line, you can specify its style, color, and weight. You can also choose a smoothed line, which will cause the line's changes in direction to curve, rather than cusp.

Likewise, the Marker options allow you to choose the automatic marker, no marker, or a custom marker. If you select the custom marker, you can specify its style, foreground color, and background color.

CHANGING THE SCALE OF A CHART

Another major use of the Format | Selected Object command is to change the scale of a chart. Excel uses a complicated rounding algorithm to automatically decide on a *scale* for the values axis of a chart. Occasionally, you will want to change that *automatic scale*. Perhaps you are going to be charting sales on a monthly basis for an entire year, and you want each chart to have the same scale. The automatic scale for the month of January is not sufficient to include sales later in the year. Select the Y-axis and give the Format | Selected Axis command to see this dialog box:

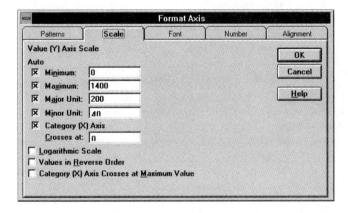

There are several items to consider when deciding on a scale (each item has an Auto check box if you want to accept Excel's suggestion):

MINIMUM Unless the data include a negative number, the Auto check box defaults to 0. Perhaps you will want to start at a higher minimum number, to make your chart more responsive to small changes in the data, or you might wish to allow for the possibility of negative numbers.

MAXIMUM The Auto check box defaults to a number large enough to include the largest number in the plot area. You might wish to set it higher to allow for later entries, or set it lower so that certain values go "off the scale."

MAJOR UNIT This determines where the major tick marks occur. The Auto check box calculates this, based on the difference between the minimum and maximum values and the current size of the chart. The Auto check box also recalculates anytime the data changes or when the chart is resized.

MINOR UNIT This determines where the minor tick marks occur. This is also the smallest change in value to which the chart will respond.

CATEGORY (X) AXIS CROSSES AT The Auto check box causes the X- and Y-axes to intersect at 0, or as close as possible. You may wish to change this.

LOGARITHMIC SCALE If checked, the Y-axis (Minimum, Maximum, Major Unit, Minor Unit) is recalculated as powers of 10.

VALUES IN REVERSE ORDER If checked, inverts the chart, placing the Minimum value and the X-axis at the top of the chart and the Maximum value at the bottom.

CATEGORY (X) AXIS CROSSES AT MAXIMUM VALUE If checked, places the X-axis at the top of the chart at the Maximum value. Use this with discretion; a column chart will read exactly opposite as the column *descends* to the value of the data point.

CHANGING THE CATEGORY AXIS OF A CHART

By selecting the X-axis before giving the Format | Selected Axis command, you can modify the Category axis. Excel displays the dialog box illustrated below:

Normally, the Y-axis intersects the X-axis at the first category. Enter a number in the first box to move that intersection point.

The default for Number of Categories between Tick Mark Labels depends on the length of the labels and the number of tick marks. When feasible, it is nice to have a label for each category. If it is not feasible, enter a number larger than 1 to skip labels. For example, in the hotel charts, entering the number 2 would cause only the odd-numbered months to be labeled.

If you do not wish to have a tick mark between each category, enter a number larger than 1 in the Number of Categories between Tick Marks box to skip tick marks between categories.

The default for the next check box depends on the type of chart. Generally, the line types of charts have the Y-axis intersect at the categories (the Value (Y) Axis Crosses between Categories box is cleared). Column and bar type charts, on the other hand, have the Y-axis intersect between the categories.

Checking the next box would display the categories in reverse order. For example, in the hotel charts, December would be the first category, and January would be the last.

Checking the last box in this dialog box would place the Y-axis near the Maximum value rather than the Minimum value. In a line or column chart, this would place the Y-axis at the right of the chart, rather than the left, where you might expect to see it.

Using Graphic Items

One type of graphic item that adds to the effectiveness of a chart is an arrow. You can add arrows by using the Arrow tool on the Drawing toolbar. Click the Drawing tool on the Standard toolbar to view the Drawing toolbar. Click on the Arrow tool, then drag the arrow on the chart, from the tail to the arrowhead. To change an arrow's position or size, click on it with the mouse. You can then drag the shaft of the arrow to move it, or drag each end of it to resize it and change the angle of the arrow.

To change the format of the arrow, double-click on it, or select the arrow as described in the earlier section, "Selecting Items in a Chart," and then use Format | Selected Object to change the line and arrowhead characteristics.

Now that you have added an arrow, it is time to add some explanatory text to the chart. To add a free-floating comment, referred to as *unattached text*, which you will then place at the tail end of the arrow, simply select the chart or plot area by clicking in the middle of the chart, away from any data points; then start typing. Once you press [Enter] you are able to select the text entry and drag it to place it where you wish. You have probably guessed by now that you can use [Alt][Enter] to place line breaks in the text.

Exporting a Chart

Because of the open architecture of the Windows environment, you do not need to save the chart in a special format in order to use the chart in another format. The Windows Clipboard is available to any Windows application, so if you want to export a chart to a memo in Word for Windows, for example, simply select the chart and invoke the Edit | Copy command. Then, from Word for Windows, select the location for the chart and invoke Edit | Paste. Note that the Word for Windows command is identical to the one you would use in Excel; this similarity in the interface of the two applications is one of the greatest strengths of the Windows environment.

Printing a Chart

Printing a chart is as simple and straightforward as printing a workbook. There is, however, one difference in the File | Page Setup dialog box. The Chart tab allows you to print the chart in the size shown on the monitor, to fill the page while maintaining the height/width ratio on the monitor, or to fill the page regardless of the height/width ratio. You also have the option of informing Excel that you are printing to a black-and-white printer; Excel will then automatically convert the chart's colors to various fill patterns when the chart is printed. Any of the graphics-capable printers supported by Windows will print charts.

GUIDED ACTIVITY 8.2

Charting RB Company Data

In this Guided Activity you explore Excel's chart commands.

1. If you are not continuing from the previous Guided Activity, follow the startup procedure outlined in Unit 1 to load Windows and enter Excel.

2. Open the RB96PROJ workbook used in Units 6 and 7. Check to ensure that the projected growth numbers are 5% and 3%.

3. To draw a line chart of the data:

    a. Select A4:E4, A9:E9, A15:E15, and A18:E18. Remember to hold [Ctrl] while dragging the mouse through the second and subsequent ranges.

CHECKPOINT 8A Why did we choose these ranges?

    b. Press [F11].

    c. Give the Format | Chart Type command; select Line and click OK. The chart should look like Figure 8.21 except that you must still refine the legend and change some formatting.

    d. Look at your chart. There should be three lines. The line marked with blue boxes is the data from row 9, the line marked with magenta boxes is the data from row 15, and the line marked with yellow boxes is the data from row 18.

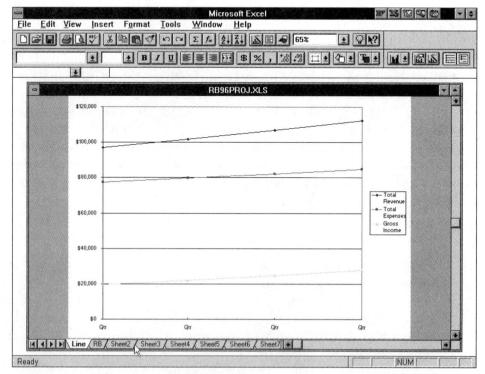

FIGURE 8.21 Line chart with side legend

e. Look at the legend. Unfortunately, the legend Total, Total, Gross is not very illuminating. It's time to discover an undocumented feature of Excel. Click on the Sheet1 tab to return to the workbook.

f. In cell A9, type `Total`; then press [Alt][Enter]; then type `Revenue`. Press [Enter]. Pressing [Alt][Enter] places a symbol (the symbol varies depending on your display) in the workbook cell and forces a line break in the legend entry.

g. Use [Alt][Enter] to enter `Total Expenses` in cell A15 and `Gross Income` in cell A18. Click the chart tab to look at the chart now.

h. Select the Y-axis and give the Format | Selected Axis command. Click on the Number tab of the Format Axis dialog box and change the number format to Currency, no decimals.

i. Select the plot area and give the Format | Selected Plot Area command. In the Area group, select Automatic.

4. Rename the chart tab Line, the sheet tab RB, and save the workbook (File | Save command).

5. To draw a column chart of the data:

   a. Return to the Line sheet. Copy the sheet to a new sheet.

CHECKPOINT 8B How do you copy an existing sheet to a new sheet?

   b. Select the Line (2) sheet. Give the Format | Chart Type command; choose Column.

   c. Look at the chart. There should be four sets of three columns. In each set, the column on the left is the data from row 9: Total Revenue; the center column is the data from row 14: Total Expenses; and the right column is the data from row 18: Gross Income.

   d. Select the legend, then use Format | Selected Legend to move it to the bottom of the chart, which should now look like Figure 8.22.

   e. Change the tab label to Column and save the workbook.

6. For a stacked column chart, you use the three components of Revenue: Sales, Service, and West Coast. Return to the RB sheet and select A4:E4 and A6:E8. Give the Insert | Chart command. Give the Format | Chart Type command. Select the Options command button. Select the stacked column option. Format the Y-axis and plot area as you did for the line chart. The chart should now look like Figure 8.23.

7. Rename the sheet Stack and save the workbook.

8. Our next chart is a pie chart illustrating the relative proportions of Total Revenue devoted to Wages, Supplies, West Coast Expenses, Tax, and Net Income for the year. Select A12:A14, A19:A20, F12:F14, and F19:F20.

   The rest of the task is easy. First, give the command Insert | Chart and select As New Sheet. This will invoke the ChartWizard. In step 1, click on Next. In step 2,

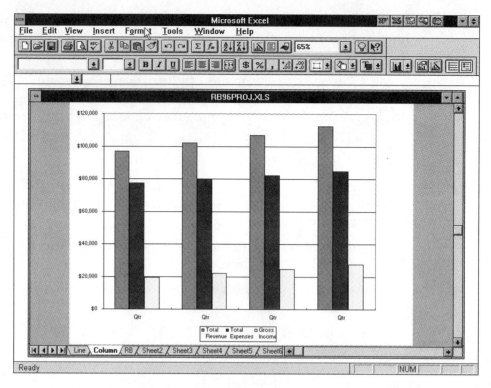

FIGURE 8.22
Column chart with bottom legend

click on the pie chart. In step 3, select option 7 (with percentages and labels). In step 4, select Data Series in Columns. Then enter 1 in Use First ? Columns For Pie Slice Labels. Then enter 0 in Use First ? Rows For Chart Title. In step 5, click

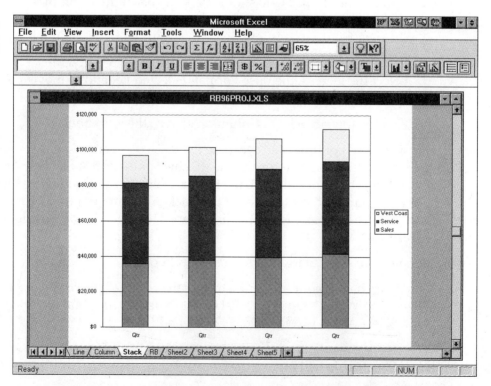

FIGURE 8.23
Stacked column chart

FIGURE 8.24
Pie chart with labels and percentages

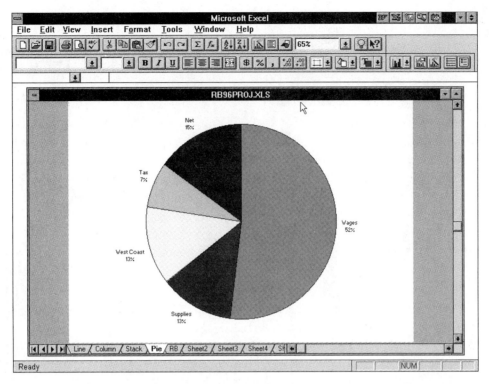

on Finish. The chart should look like Figure 8.24. This chart illustrates the relative proportions of the five factors. Option 7 also calculates the percentage of each factor and labels it, eliminating the need for a legend. Rename the chart tab as Pie and save the workbook.

9. Next, let's create an XY chart showing the relationship between the five uses of Revenue and Total Revenue.

   a. Select A9:E9, A12:E14, and A19:E20, give the Insert | Chart command, and select As New Sheet.

   b. In step 1 of the ChartWizard, click Next. In step 2, select the XY chart. In step 3, select option 2 (without gridlines, with lines and markers). In step 4, make sure that the data series are in rows, that the first (1) row is used as X data, and that the first (1) column is used as legend text.

   c. In step 5, enter Revenues as the X-axis label, and Expenses as the Y-axis label. Click Finish.

   d. Reformat the plot area and Y-axis as you did for the line chart.

   e. Select the X-axis and give the Format | Selected Axis command. Select the Number tab and set the Number format to Currency, no decimals. Select the Scale tab and enter 4000 for the Major Unit. Your chart should now look like Figure 8.25.

   f. Rename the chart tab as XY.

10. Save the workbook.

FIGURE 8.25
XY chart

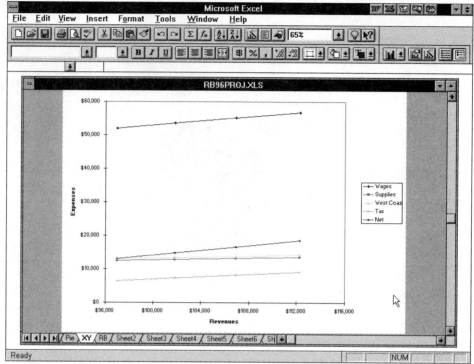

GUIDED ACTIVITY 8.3 *print out (3 graphs) (header & footer).*

Adding Optional Features to the Charts

In this Guided Activity you add titles and other features to some of the charts.

1. If you are not continuing from the previous Guided Activity, load Excel and open RB96PROJ.

2. Select the Pie tab. Excel should display the pie chart you created in the previous Guided Activity.

3. You would like each segment of the pie to have a different pattern, and you want the Net [Income] segment to be *exploded* (pulled out from the remainder of the pie). To accomplish this:

    a. Select one segment of the chart.

    b. Use Format | Selected Data Point to select a custom pattern. (You will need to select both a pattern and a background color in order to see the pattern.)

    c. Repeat the above procedure with each segment of the chart (using a different pattern for each).

    d. Select the segment of the chart representing net income.

    e. Using a dragging motion with the mouse, pull the segment away from the rest of the chart.

FIGURE 8.26
Pie chart with exploded segment

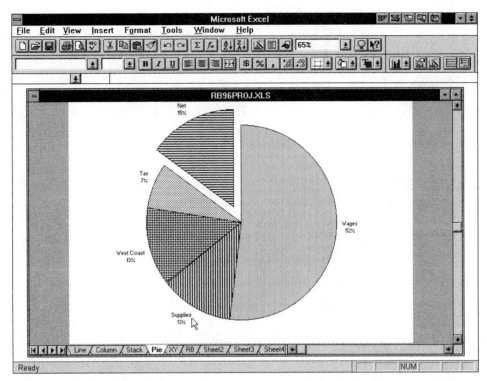

4. The chart should look similar to Figure 8.26. Save the workbook before proceeding.

5. Select the Column tab. Excel displays the column chart you created in the previous Guided Activity.

6. To add titles to the column chart:

   a. Invoke Insert | Titles. Select Chart Title and click OK.

   b. The word `Title` is selected; type `RB Company`. (The text from the old title will be erased automatically.)

   c. Press [Alt][Enter].

   d. Type `1996 Projections`.

   e. Press [Enter].

   f. Invoke Format | Selected Title. Select the Patterns tab. Place a shadow box with a medium heavy line around the title.

   g. Invoke File | Page Setup and select the Header/Footer tab.

   h. Enter `Created by your name` in the left section footer box and delete the default entry in the center section footer box. Select (none) for the header.

   i. Give the File | Print Preview command and preview the chart. The note should appear in the lower-left corner. When the printout looks correct, click Close.

FIGURE 8.27
Annotated column chart

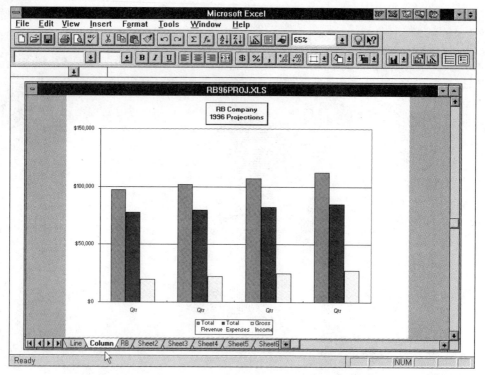

7. To change the format of the Y scale:

   a. Select the Y-axis.

   b. Invoke Format | Selected Axis and select the Scale tab.

   c. Enter 150000 in the Maximum box.

   d. Enter 50000 in the Major Unit box.

   e. Press Enter.

   f. The chart should look like Figure 8.27; notice that the format of the numbers on the vertical axis has changed.

8. Save the workbook before proceeding.

9. Exit to Windows, then return to the operating system. Remember to back up your work.

EXERCISE 8.1

Charting State Sales Data

In this Exercise you create charts illustrating the differences among the state-by-state sales data you entered in the workbook in Unit 7.

1. Open the WESTREG file you created in Unit 7.

UNIT 8 CHARTS   219

2. Create a pie chart that shows the relative proportion of sales for each state. Do not include the TOTAL row when you define the ranges. The California segment should be exploded. Name this chart sheet Pie.

3. Create a column chart that compares California to all other states combined. You must create new ranges of data to accomplish this. Name this chart sheet Column.

4. Remember to save the workbook.

EXERCISE 8.2

The Perfect Job (IV)

Create a chart that illustrates the levels of salary and adjusted salary for the five jobs in the JOBS workbook. It is up to you to determine the chart type, the data ranges, and which options are needed. For "extra credit," make your chart a combination chart with a second Y-axis that has the Index values on a line.

EXERCISE 8.3

A Sales Workbook (III)

Create a chart that shows the relative proportion of the cost (before tax) of each of the components of the computer system in the workbook COMPCOST. Name the chart sheet Proportion. Create a second chart that includes one additional segment: the total amount of sales tax paid on the purchase. Name the chart sheet With Tax.

EXERCISE 8.4 *[handwritten: print out (Gasmiles 4 data points) (header & footer).]*

Gas Mileage (III)

Open GASMILE. Create a chart that compares over time the current MPG with the cumulative MPG. Embed the chart in the workbook in the range I4:P20. Save your work as GASMILE.

EXERCISE 8.5

League Standings (II)

Create a graph illustrating the win and loss data in the LEAGUE file created in Unit 6. If you have both conference and overall records, as in the example, create the graph based on conference wins and losses. Name your chart sheet Win-Loss.

Review Questions

*1. What are the 15 types of charts listed in the ChartWizard?

2. Which type of chart would you use to illustrate each of the following? (There are no single correct answers to most of these, although there are arguably preferable answers.)

   a. Relative proportion of tax revenue from individuals, partnerships, corporations, and other sources

   *b. Growth and decline of college-age population

   c. Revenues of three different divisions over a five-year period

   *d. Total revenue from all divisions over a five-year period

   *e. Relationship between unemployment level and welfare expenditures

Key Terms

Area chart	Doughnut chart	3-D area chart
Automatic chart	Embedded chart	3-D bar chart
Automatic scale	Exploded segment	3-D column chart
Bar chart	External reference	3-D line chart
Category	Handle	3-D pie chart
Category axis	Legend	3-D surface chart
Category name	Line chart	Unattached text
Column chart	Pie chart	Value axis
Combination chart	Radar chart	X-axis
Data marker	Scale	XY chart
Data point	Scatter chart	Y-axis
Data series	Series formula	Z-axis
Data series name	Stacked line chart	

Documentation Research

Using the Excel *User's Guide*, find and record the page number of the commands and the types of charts discussed in this unit. We recommend that you also write the page number in the margin next to the discussion of each command and chart in the unit.

1. How does Excel respond to multiple selections as the plot range?

2. How do you select a specific data point with the mouse?

3. How do you combine chart types using 3-D charts?

4. Area—what is the fundamental difference between an area chart and a line chart?

5. Pie—how many data series should be displayed?

6. Surface—how do you format the levels in a surface chart, since you cannot select them?

APPLICATION D
The Hotel Manager

This Application requires you to draw five charts.

1. Follow the startup procedure outlined in Unit 1 to load Windows and enter Excel.

2. Refer to the hotel customer data that were presented in Figure 8.1. In Unit 8 you should have created a workbook with the file name HOTEL with that data. If not, do so before proceeding.

3. Create the following charts. Some of your charts will look like those in Unit 8, but others will look different.

    - A column chart depicting guests by type by month
    - A stacked column chart depicting the total patronage for each month
    - A line chart showing guests by type, as well as total patronage, by month
    - A pie chart showing the relative proportion of each type of guest for the total year
    - An XY chart comparing General and Business registrations for each month of the year

    For each chart, make liberal use of titles, legends, and any other appropriate options.

4. Make printed copies of the charts.

Workbook Tools

Spreadsheet programs have long been powerful tools for analyzing numbers and assisting in the decision-making process. In recent years, however, they have also become easier to use as they have acquired tools to assist the user in creating common types of reports and analyses. Excel is no exception; it now has a toolkit that includes tools to correct spelling, solve complex goal-seeking problems (how many units of each of our four product lines should we manufacture to maximize profit? to maximize sales?), perform sensitivity analyses (what happens to profits if sales slump 10%? if labor costs increase 5%?), and analyze spreadsheet structures. In this unit, we examine several of the most valuable components of that toolkit.

Learning Objectives

At the completion of this unit you should know

1. how Excel uses the various spelling dictionaries,
2. when to use the Goal Seek versus the Solver command,
3. the advantages of using Scenario Manager in performing sensitivity analyses,
4. the various auditing tools available in Excel.

At the completion of this unit you should be able to

1. spell check a worksheet,
2. set up a worksheet to achieve a desired value,
3. manage multiple scenarios in a worksheet,
4. audit a worksheet.

Important Commands

Tools | Auditing

Tools | Goal Seek

Tools | Scenarios

Tools | Solver

Tools | Spelling

Spell Checker

Management types can be a demanding lot. While it is true they will have no mercy if a workbook does not contain correct data, or if it contains incorrect formulas, they also expect the little things to be correct. Nothing is more frustrating than to have a manager return a project for further work because the word "actual" is spelled "acutal." (Try it; it's easy to do.) But do not lose hope; here comes the spell checker to the rescue.

The spell checker works in an admirably simple fashion: give the Tools | Spelling command and it compares each word in your workbook to a dictionary installed by Excel on your hard disk. If it finds a word that is not included in that standard dictionary, it then compares the word to a personal dictionary that you create in the spell checking process. By default, this personal dictionary is named CUSTOM.DIC.[1] This is valuable for names and technical words that apply to your industry or company that are not included in a standard dictionary. If the spell checker does not find the word in the standard or the personal dictionary, it then displays a dialog box, illustrated in Figure 9.1, explaining that the word was not found and offering you several choices as to how to proceed.

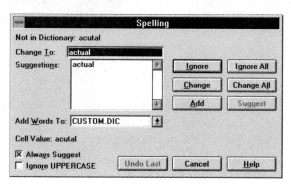

FIGURE 9.1
Spelling checker dialog box

---

1 If you have other Microsoft Office products installed on your computer, they share both the standard dictionary and the personal dictionary.

Your main choices are as follows:

- Ignore this occurrence of this word. This is useful if it is a valid word, but not one that you will be using often enough to include it in your personal dictionary.

- Ignore all occurrences of this word. This is useful if it is a valid word that you have used several times in this document, but you are unlikely to use in the future.

- Change this word. If the word is spelled incorrectly, you would decide to change it to make it correct.

- Change all occurrences of this word. This would be your choice for "acutal." You have already recognized this error, and you know it might be repeated. Changing all occurrences saves you the embarrassment of looking at every occurrence of the error.

- Add this word to the personal dictionary. You might choose this option for your boss's name. You can expect to type it frequently in the future.

- Suggest alternatives from the dictionary for the correct spelling. This item is grayed out in the dialog box in Figure 9.1 because it is already the default setting.

- Set the default to Always Suggest (or not to suggest unless requested). You will usually find the suggestions to be helpful.

- Set the default to Ignore (or not to ignore) words in uppercase.

Solving for a Desired Result

Frequently, you know the results you wish to obtain, and you know that you can adjust one variable of the equation in order to obtain that desired result. To do this, you start plugging in approximate values for that one variable until you get close to the desired result. Excel makes this process much simpler with the Tools | Goal Seek command.

Example

Suppose, for instance, that you have decided to purchase a house. You have $20,000 to use as a down payment on a house; you can get a loan at 9.9% interest for 30 years; and you know that you cannot afford more than $1,200 per month for a house payment. You originally planned to purchase a house selling for $175,000, but you used the PMT( ) function in Excel and discovered that =PMT(0.099/12,30 *12,-155000) yields $1348.80. The only part of this equation that you can vary is the principal. To use Tools | Goal Seek, place the *pv* (or principal) in cell B1, the *rate* in cell B2, the *nper* in cell B3, and the formula in cell B4. Leave the active cell at cell B4. Give the Tools | Goal Seek command. Excel will present this dialog box:

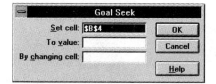

In the dialog box, cell $B$4 is already specified as the Set cell; in the To value field, enter 1200; in the By changing cell field, specify cell B1. When you click on OK, Excel will edit the variable cell to show the correct principal to achieve your desired monthly payment. Figure 9.2 illustrates the solution to this problem.

GUIDED ACTIVITY 9.1

Using the Goal Seek Tool

In this Guided Activity, you complete the example presented in the previous section.

1. Start Excel and open a new workbook.
2. Enter the following data, beginning in cell A1:

   ```
   Principal      155000
   Rate             9.9%
   Years             30
   Payment
   ```

   Use the format commands to properly represent your cell entries.

3. In cell B4, enter the formula that will calculate the monthly payment. Be sure that the *pv* argument is a negative number.
4. Give the Tools | Goal Seek command.
5. Fill in the dialog box to set cell B4 to a value of $1,200 by changing cell B1. The dialog box should look like this:

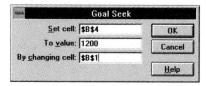

6. Click OK. The solution screen should look like Figure 9.2. After reading the Goal Seek dialog box, click on OK and save your work as GOAL.

Solving Complex Problems

All too often, the goal-seeking problems you need to solve in the real world are not as simple as the previous example. Consider the case of the T-shirt manufacturer

FIGURE 9.2
Goal-seeking solution

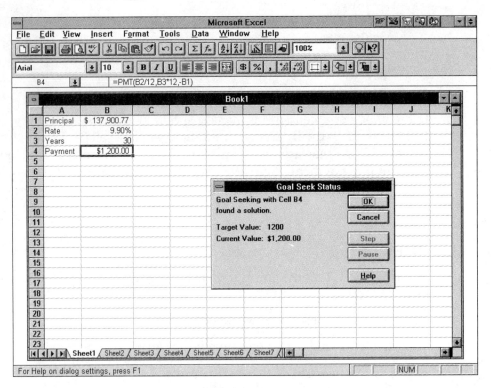

who has four lines of shirts and needs to determine the best product mix to manufacture. The plain line consists of simple colored T-shirts. The current top seller in the survival line contains the slogan, "I survived the 1994 Northridge earthquake," but they can change to a new disaster in under four hours by replacing the photo and the bottom line of the slogan. The deco line has beads, rhinestones, and other baubles attached to the shirt. Finally, the cartoon line has different cartoons and is a popular seller.

The managment has decided that, in order to maximize the use of equipment, they need to manufacture at least 500 units of each line daily. The production limits for each line are:

Plain	2,000
Deco	1,200
Survival	2,000
Cartoon	1,500

There is a further limit for the entire facility of 5,000 shirts daily. The cost and price of each shirt is reflected in Figure 9.3. The Cost per Unit figure refers to variable costs such as materials and direct labor. The Fixed Cost per Line figure refers to fixed costs such as indirect labor (administration, finance, M.I.S., and so on) and overhead (rent, utilities, equipment depreciation, and so on).

What product mix will provide the highest profit for the company, assuming all shirts manufactured are actually sold? Excel provides the Tools | Solver command to answer this sort of question. Like the Goal Seek command used earlier, it works by changing a cell or cells to reach a stated goal. However, it is much more powerful in that it offers more latitude in defining the goal and in setting constraints. A

FIGURE 9.3
T-shirt problem

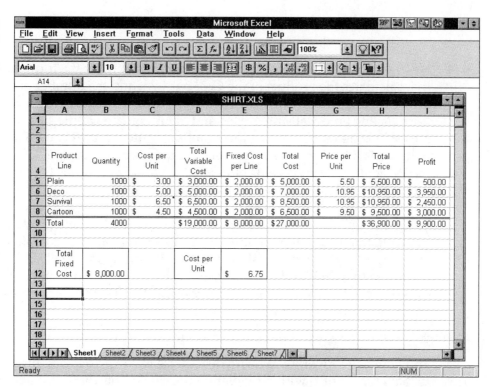

constraint is any limitation that the solution must meet. (For example, it is not practical to reduce costs by reducing the number of units produced below the minimum of 500 units per day.) The goal is a formula contained in the *target cell* and is referred to as the *objective*. The Solver reaches the objective by changing the content of the *changing cell*, also known as the *decision variable*. Guided Activity 9.2 illustrates the details of using this tool.

GUIDED ACTIVITY 9.2

Using the Solver

This Guided Activity illustrates the use of Excel's Solver.

1. If you are not continuing from the previous Guided Activity, start Excel and give the File | New command to open a new workbook.

2. Begin by entering the labels in row 4, column A, and cell D12. Create a style named Header that has borders on all four sides of the cell and is center-aligned both horizontally and vertically with wrapped text; then apply it to all of these entries.

3. Now add some constant values and perform some more formatting.

   a. Select the range C5:I9, and click the Currency button. Select the range B5:I5 and set the column width to 11. The entries in B5:C8, G5:G8, and B12 are constant values. Format cells B12 and F12 as currency and place borders around both cells. Place a double-line border at the bottom of the range A8:I8.

b. Select cell C7 and add a cell note: `Includes $2.00 donation to American Red Cross`.

4. Next, you need to add formulas to the workbook. Enter the formula in D5:D8 that calculates the product of the Cost per Unit and the number of units (=B5*C5, and so on). Use the [Ctrl][Enter] shortcut so that you only have to type the formula one time. Cells B9, D9:F9, and H9:I9 contain simple sum formulas and are easily entered by clicking the AutoSum button. (Since you do not have entries in the cells B9, D9:F9, and H9:I9 yet, you may need to edit the default entry to correctly identify the arguments of the SUM( ) functions.) Cells E5:E8 contain formulas that multiply the Fixed Cost by the percentage of the total production, =$B$12*(B5/$B$9), and so on. Cells F5:F8 contain the sum of cell D5 and cell E5, and so on. H5:H8 contain the formula that calculates the product of the Price per Unit and the number of units, =B5*G5, and so on. I5:I8 contain the difference between Total Price and Total Cost, =H5-F5, and so on. Finally, cell E12 contains a formula that divides the Total Cost in cell F9 by the total number of units produced in cell B9, =F9/B9. Save your work as SHIRT. Your workbook should now look very much like Figure 9.3.

CHECKPOINT 9A Why does the entry in cell E5 contain absolute references?

5. You now have a workbook that you can use to solve your first problem, which is to maximize profits without violating the constraints discussed above.

    a. Select cell I9 and give the Tools | Solver command. The following dialog box will display:

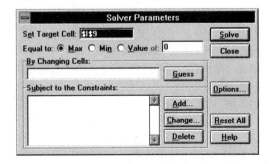

    b. Click on the Max radio button to maximize profit.

    c. Click in the By Changing Cells box and select the range B5:B8.

    d. Click on the Add button to add the constraints. Click the Add button after each one until you have entered the last constraint and then click OK. The constraints are:

        $B$5 <= 2000
        $B$6 <= 1200
        $B$7 <= 2000
        $B$8 <= 1500
        $B$9 <= 5000

```
$B$5:$B$8 >= 500
$B$5:$B$8 integer
```

    e. Click on the Solve button. The following solution box will display:

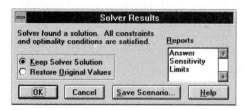

    f. Double-click on Answer in the Reports box. Excel will create a new sheet named Answer Report 1 and save the new entries in the workbook. Your company should now show a profit of $15,900. Answer Report 1 lists all of the parameters of your problem, shows a listing of the constraints, and shows which constraints were binding; that is, which ones reached the limit.

6. You have now been asked if you can rerun the problem to minimize the cost per unit. (This is an example of the very important business principle that whatever you have done will never be quite enough.) Desiring to remain gainfully employed, you have cheerfully agreed.

    a. Being the cynic that you are, you don't want to lose the work you have done, so you create a copy of the sheet and work with it. Hold the [Ctrl] key and drag the sheet tab to the right until it is in the center of the Sheet2 tab and release it. Double-click on the first sheet tab and enter the name `Profit`. Double-click on the second sheet tab and enter the name `Cost`. The Cost sheet should now be the active sheet.

    b. Give the Tools | Solver command. The following dialog box will display:

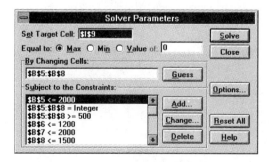

    c. Notice that all the entries from the last problem remain. This saves you from having to reenter all the constraints. Move the dialog box if necessary by dragging its title bar, and click on cell E12 (Cost per Unit). Click on the Min radio button, since you are trying to minimize cost per unit. Click the Solve button and the Solver solution box will again display.

d. Again, select the Answer report and click OK. Not surprisingly, the Answer report reveals that different constraints were binding this time. Move over to the Cost sheet and note that Cost per Unit was reduced from $6.79 to $5.80, Total Cost was reduced from $33,950 to $29,000, and Profit was reduced from $15,900 to $12,675.

7. Save your work.

Managing Scenarios

Most of what we call analysis in the business world consists of attempting to predict the future. Will interest rates go up or down or remain steady? Will next year's inflation rate be 3% or 13%? Will sales fall at the 13,000,000 units predicted by Sally or the 16,000,000 predicted by Bill? One common method for dealing with this type of conundrum is to create a prediction based on the worst case assumptions, another based on the best case assumptions, and a third based on the most likely assumptions, thus creating a range of possible solutions.

All of the above questions deal with managing scenarios. It is such a common problem that Excel contains a tool called the Scenario Manager. To access this tool, give the Tools | Scenarios command. There are several facets to the Scenario Manager, but we will examine two of them. The first is the ability to enter multiple values in a single cell, controlled by the scenario name. The second is the ability to generate a report showing the various possible values and how the result cell is affected by the different scenarios.

Let us return to the RB Company's 1996 Projections workbook that you have used in previous units. In Unit 7, you saw how to perform a sensitivity analysis by manually changing the data on this worksheet. Now, you will use the Scenario Manager to perform the same function. You gain several advantages by performing the analysis using the Scenario Manager. First, the data entry is more straightforward, since you set up the changing cells one time, and then just key the new data and the scenario name into the dialog box created by the Scenario Manager. Second, you can maintain all versions of the analysis at the same time, rather than replacing the data in the changing cells each time. Third, you can use the Scenario Manager reporting function to see the results of all entered scenarios on one worksheet. You perform this analysis in Guided Activity 9.3.

GUIDED ACTIVITY 9.3

Using the Scenario Manager

In this Guided Activity, you perform the sensitivity analysis from Guided Activity 7.1 using the Scenario Manager.

1. Open RB96PROJ. If the RB sheet is not already the active sheet, click on its sheet tab to select it.

2. From the Tools menu, select Scenarios. Excel will display the following dialog box:

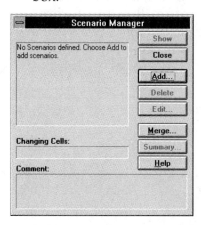

3. Click the Add button. Excel will display the following dialog box:

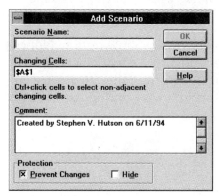

4. As in Guided Activity 7.1, you will use the letters a, b, c, and d for the scenario names. In the Scenario Name box, enter Scenario A. Press Tab to move to the Changing Cells box. Select the following ranges by dragging on the worksheet (in this order): B6:B8, G5, B12:B14, and G11. Remember to hold Ctrl when selecting the second and subsequent ranges. Click OK. Excel displays the following dialog box:

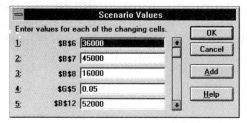

5. Enter the data from the following table in the dialog box. Press Tab to move between fields in the dialog box. Press Enter when you have entered all the data for each scenario. Excel will return you to the Scenario Manager dialog box, where you can add new scenarios. Click on Add and type the new scenario name in the

Scenario Name box. Notice that you can either maintain the changing cells from the last scenario or have different changing cells for different scenarios. Since you are maintaining the same changing cells for all scenarios, click OK and enter each scenario in turn. When you have completed scenarios a through d, enter the scenario name `Original` and enter the data from point e. of the table below. (This allows you to maintain the integrity of the original worksheet.)

a.	REVENUE	Sales	36000	Service	45000	West Coast	16000	Growth	5%
	EXPENSES	Wages	52000	Supplies	12500	West Coast	13000	Growth	6%
b.	REVENUE	Sales	36000	Service	45000	West Coast	16000	Growth	5%
	EXPENSES	Wages	52000	Supplies	32500	West Coast	15500	Growth	6%
c.	REVENUE	Sales	36000	Service	35000	West Coast	12000	Growth	7%
	EXPENSES	Wages	52000	Supplies	22500	West Coast	11000	Growth	3%
d.	REVENUE	Sales	36000	Service	45000	West Coast	16000	Growth	5%
	EXPENSES	Wages	52000	Supplies	12500	West Coast	14000	Growth	10%
e.	REVENUE	Sales	36000	Service	45000	West Coast	16000	Growth	5%
	EXPENSES	Wages	52000	Supplies	12500	West Coast	13000	Growth	3%

6. Select the different scenarios and click on the Show button. Notice that Excel "plugs in" the values from the scenario into the worksheet. (You may have to move the Scenario Manager dialog box by dragging its title bar to see different parts of the worksheet.) Click on the Summary button. Excel displays this dialog box:

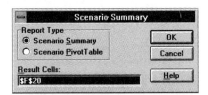

7. Notice that Scenario Summary is already selected and that Excel has correctly deduced that cell F20 is the result cell in which you are most interested (the bottom line). Click OK to generate a new sheet containing the Scenario Summary report.

8. You should see a report like the one illustrated in Figure 9.4. The figures in row 15 provide a concise comparison of the results of the different scenarios you created. Click on the RB sheet tab to make it the active sheet and save your work. If you are not continuing on, exit Excel, then exit Windows to return to the operating system.

Auditing Worksheets

The Tools | Auditing commands provide a visual method of determining the structure of a worksheet. These commands draw arrows (called *tracing arrows*) on your worksheet to illustrate which cells depend on which other cells. The

FIGURE 9.4
Scenario Summary report

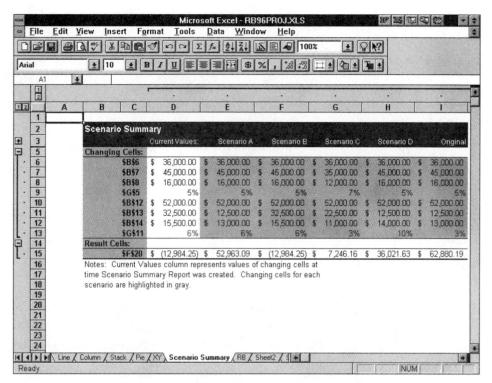

Tools | Auditing | Trace Precedents command highlights the *precedents* of the current cell (that is, cells that are referenced by the current cell). The Tools | Auditing | Trace Dependents command highlights the *dependents* of the current cell (that is, cells that refer to the current cell). If the current cell returns an error value, the Tools | Auditing | Trace Error command highlights the source of that error value. The Tools | Auditing | Remove All Arrows command removes all tracing arrows from your worksheet. The Tools | Auditing | Show Auditing Toolbar command displays the Auditing toolbar. (You can also display this with the View | Toolbars command.)

Suppose your manager presents you with a worksheet file and asks you to evaluate its conclusions. If it is complicated, it could take a very long time just to determine which cells contain formulas and which cells are referred to by those formulas. The Tools | Auditing commands allow you to quickly determine the worksheet structure, so that you can then concentrate on checking the validity of the formulas, assumptions, data, and so forth. Alternatively, suppose you open a worksheet you have used in the past and find several dozen cells that contain the #VALUE! error. Since you have used the worksheet successfully in the past, you are relatively certain that only one cell has been changed. While there is nothing to prevent you from laboriously tracing the error one cell at a time, the Tools | Auditing | Trace Error command will instantly draw an arrow or a series of arrows leading back to the cell that is the culprit.

The Auditing toolbar, illustrated in Figure 9.5, has eight tools. The first pair trace precedents and remove precedent arrows, respectively. The second pair trace dependents and remove dependent arrows, respectively. The fifth tool removes all tracing arrows. The sixth tool traces errors. The seventh inserts a cell

FIGURE 9.5
Auditing toolbar

note, and the last tool opens the Info window, where you can view detailed information about the current cell.

GUIDED ACTIVITY 9.4

Auditing a Worksheet

This Guided Activity illustrates the use of the Tools | Auditing commands.

1. Open RB96PROJ. If the RB sheet is not already the active sheet, click on its sheet tab to select it.

2. First, let's introduce an error to the worksheet. Click on cell G5, press [Spacebar], then [Enter]. Cell G5 now contains a text value (a space) that Excel cannot convert to a number. All cells that contain formulas that refer to the number in cell G5 (C6:F9 and C18:F20) should display the #VALUE! error.

3. Since this is a relatively simple worksheet, it would not take a lot of time to discover the source of the error. However, it still provides an excellent means of illustrating the error tracing capability of Excel. Select cell F20 and give the Tools | Auditing | Trace Error command. Your screen should look like Figure 9.6.

4. Let's take a moment to analyze this screen. The red arrows going back to cell C6 indicate that it is the first cell (logically speaking) that contains an error. The blue arrows pointing at cell C6 show the cells (not containing error values) that are precedents of cell C6. Now you can quickly check cells B6 and G5, determine that cell G5 should contain a number value, and correct the problem. Replace the

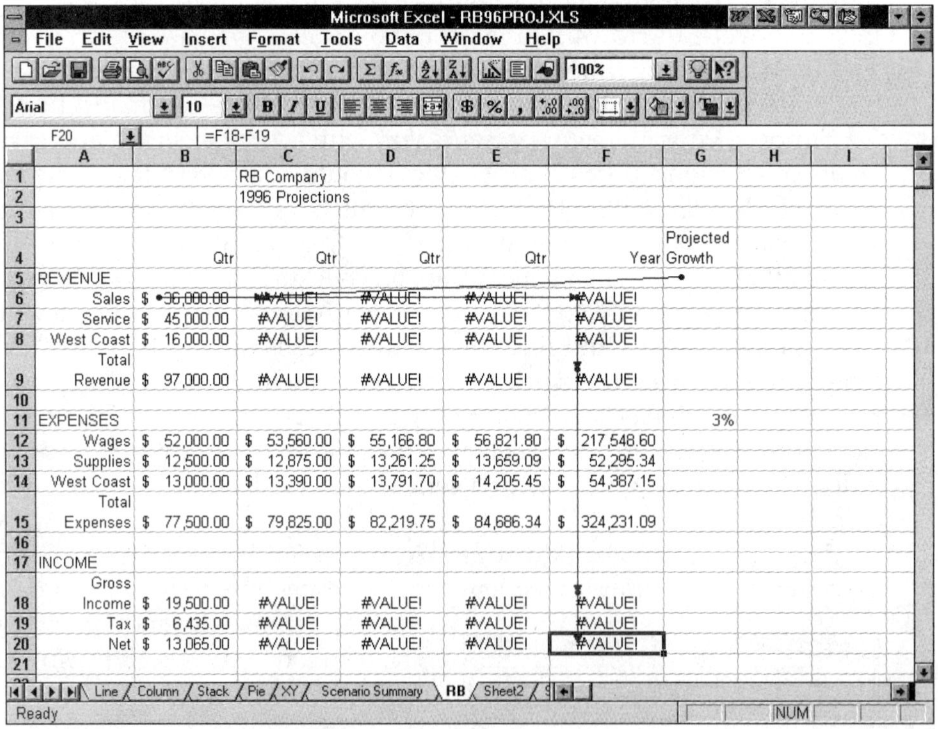

FIGURE 9.6
Worksheet with error tracing arrows

FIGURE 9.7
Worksheet with dependent tracing arrows

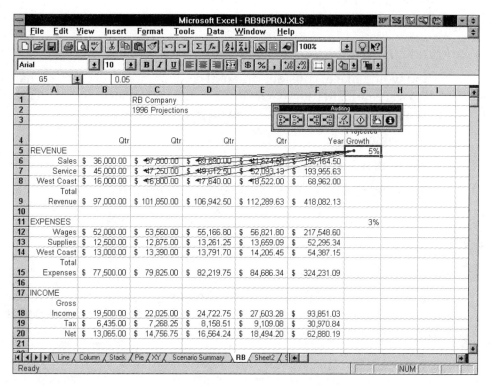

correct value (5%) in cell G5. Notice that all arrows change to blue, indicating that the error is resolved.

5. Give the Tools | Audit | Show Auditing Toolbar command.

CHECKPOINT 9B What other command will accomplish the same thing?

6. Click the Remove All Arrows tool.

7. You can already see that cell G5 is relatively important to the structure of this worksheet. To illustrate how important, select cell G5 and click the Trace Dependents tool. Your worksheet should look like Figure 9.7.

8. Clear the arrows and the toolbar and save your work. If you are not continuing on to the Exercises, exit Excel. Then exit Windows to the operating system before turning off the computer.

EXERCISE 9.1

Finding an Interest Rate

You have decided that you really must have the $155,000 house (see Guided Activity 9.1). Since the term of the loan cannot be more than 30 years, you need to find a lower interest rate so you can afford the house with $1,200 per month payments. Use Goal Seek to determine what interest rate you must obtain.

EXERCISE 9.2

A Sales Workbook (IV)

You would like to consider different combinations of computer hardware, saving each as a scenario. Retrieve COMPCOST, the spreadsheet first developed in Unit 6 and refined in subsequent units. Develop three scenarios:

- The original data
- One with no desk but a $200 more expensive monitor
- One with no desk but a $300 more expensive printer

EXERCISE 9.3

Pleasant Cove Marina (I)

Your friend "Cap" has obtained a shoreline permit to develop a marina in Pleasant Cove on Chesapeake Bay.[2] The following data have been obtained from various engineering, governmental, and marketing sources.

SLIP CONSTRUCTION

Length of Boat	Area	Total Cost	Debt Service - Annual Payment		
30	832.5	$9,300	($947)	rate	8%
40	1,119.3	$9,450	($963)	years	20
50	1,779.8	$11,400	($1,161)		
60	1,512.0	$13,350	($1,360)		
80	2,628.3	$16,800	($1,711)		
100	3,948.3	$19,800	($2,017)		

MOORAGE REVENUE & (COST) - ANNUAL

Length of Boat	Fee per Foot $36	Administration $300	Debt Service Annual PMT	NET
30	$1,808	($300)	($947)	($167)
40	$1,440	($300)	($963)	$177
50	$1,800	($300)	($1,161)	$339
60	$2,160	($300)	($1,360)	$500
80	$2,880	($300)	($1,711)	$869
100	$3,600	($300)		$1,283

---

2 This example is fictitious, although reasonably close to a real situation.

DECISION

Length of Boat	Minimum	Maximum*	Quantity Built	Total NET	Total Area	Area Available
30	24	96	24	($4,013)	19,980.0	
40	24	72	24	$4,260	26,863.2	
50	24	48	24	$8,133	42,715.2	
60	1	1	1	$500	1,512.0	
80	1	2	1	$869	2,628.3	
100	1	2	1	$1,283	3,948.3	
			75	$11,032	97,647.0	200,000.0

* Maximum number of 60' slips is the integer part of the quantity built of 30' slips divided by 24; max(80')=int[n(40')/24]; max(100')=int[n(50')/24]

The entries in normal type are constants. Area and Total Cost are engineering estimates based on length, average ratio of length to width, room necessary to maneuver, and construction costs. Minimum number of slips of a given size is determined by the agency granting the shoreline permit—they want your friend to build a mixture of sizes to serve a variety of boaters. Maximum number of 30-, 40-, and 50-foot slips was determined by a marketing survey. The area available is the maximum amount of square footage that the marina can occupy.

The entries in *bold-italic* in the tables are formulas:

- Under Slip Construction, Debt Service - Annual Payment is computed based on the cost of the slip, using the interest rate and number of years displayed.

- Under Moorage Revenue & (Cost) - Annual, fees are calculated by multiplying Fee per Foot times the boat length. Administration is a fixed cost, constant regardless of boat length. Debt Service - Annual PMT is a formula that refers to the corresponding number in the Slip Construction table. NET is the sum of the three.

- Under Decision, the maximum number of 60-, 80-, and 100-foot slips is determined by the number of smaller slips—you can put one 60-foot slip at the end of two rows of twelve 30-foot slips—thus the equation $N_{60} = INT(N_{30}/24)$. Total NET is the product of Quantity Built times NET from the Moorage Revenue & (Cost) - Annual table. Total Area is the product of Quantity Built times Area from the Slip Construction table. The three formulas at the bottom of the table are simple sums.

Build a worksheet modeling this problem. Then use Solver to determine the optimal mix of slip sizes (represented in the Quantity Built column), maximizing Total NET, constrained by maxima and minima for each size and the total area available. Also, constrain each quantity built to be an integer value. Save the file, with your solution, as MARINA.

EXERCISE 9.4

Pleasant Cove Marina (II)

Cap is impressed by your analytical skills. He would like you to develop other scenarios and determine if the optimal solution changes:

- Moorage fee at $48 per foot, with no administration fee
- Original fees, debt service at 12% for 30 years
- Moorage fee at $48 per foot, with no administration fee, debt service at 12% for 30 years

Save each scenario.

Review Questions

1. What is the file name for the default personal dictionary used by the spell checker?
*2. What is the relationship between the target cell and the changing cell(s) in a Solver problem?
3. Name three advantages of using the Scenario Manager for sensitivity analysis, rather than manually changing cell values.

Key Terms

Changing cell	Dependent	Target cell
Constraint	Objective	Tracing arrow
Decision variable	Precedent	

Documentation Research

Using the Excel *User's Guide*, find and record the page number of each of the commands discussed in this unit. We recommend that you also write the page number in the margin next to the discussion of the command in the unit.

1. What are the three types of problems Solver can analyze?
2. How do you restore a deleted scenario?
3. How many characters are allowed in a scenario name?

Advanced Workbook and Database Operations

UNIT TEN *Data Computation Operations*
UNIT ELEVEN *Data Selection Operations*
UNIT TWELVE *Advanced Windowing and Preference Operations*
UNIT THIRTEEN *Advanced File Operations and Data Interchange*
UNIT FOURTEEN *Advanced Functions*
UNIT FIFTEEN *Macro Commands and Customization*
UNIT SIXTEEN *Programming with Macros*

■ **PART THREE** covers the third main application of Excel: database management. Although the database capabilities of Excel are modest, they are a convenient addition to the workbook and graphics components. In this part we discuss the Data commands.

This part also deals with advanced techniques that enhance your ability to create sophisticated workbooks. These techniques—advanced Excel functions, macros, and advanced Window and File commands—allow you to work faster and achieve more impressive results.

Before you start doing the Guided Activities, Exercises, and Applications in this part, you must copy data files to your data disk. You perform this task in Guided Activity 10.1.

Data Computation Operations 10

This unit deals with those commands (from the Edit and Data menus) that are more related to computation than to selection. These commands allow you to fill a range with a series of numbers and to compute the values of a formula over a range of variables. Two related Paste Special options are also reviewed.

Learning Objectives

At the completion of this unit you should know

1. how to write a formula with one or two variables.

At the completion of this unit you should be able to

1. fill a range with a series of numbers,
2. compute a one-variable data table,
3. compute a two-variable data table,
4. convert a series of formulas to their values.

Important Commands

Data | Table

Edit | Fill

Edit | Paste Special

Tools | Options

Creating a Range of Values

You use the Series option from the Edit | Fill command to fill a row or column range with a series of ascending or descending numbers.

The Edit | Fill | Series command is used when the difference between each value in the series is constant. Before giving the Edit | Fill | Series command, you select a range that contains at least one number. This number (or numbers) is the *start value* of the series. After you choose Series from the Edit | Fill command, Excel will present the dialog box shown here:

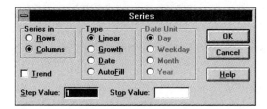

This dialog box gives you the opportunity to specify a Step Value, a Type, a Stop Value, a series direction, and whether to use a Trend calculation to determine the series. The *step value* can be either positive or negative. If the series type is Date, you will also be able to control how the date changes in the series. If the series type is AutoFill, Excel follows the rules of the AutoFill handle in creating the series; we save this discussion for later in this unit.

If the Trend check box is selected, Excel ignores the entered step value. If Type is Linear, Excel uses the TREND( ) function to calculate values for a best-fit line and returns those values in the series range. If Type is Growth, Excel uses the GROWTH( ) function to calculate values for a best-fit exponential curve and returns those values in the series range.

The start value is determined by the value(s) entered in the worksheet. The step value must be precise, but either the range need not be specified or the *stop value* can be left blank. Excel erases the range, then fills the range, beginning with the start value and incrementing by the step value, until the stop value is reached or the end of the range is reached, whichever happens first. A *linear series* adds the step value to each cell in the series; a *growth series* multiplies each succeeding cell by the step value.

For instance, say you wanted to build a series of numbers from 0 (zero) to 100,000 with an increment of 400, starting at cell B5 and continuing down column B. In this

FIGURE 10.1
A linear data series

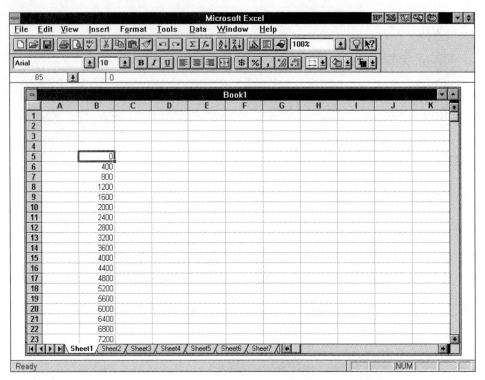

case you know the start, step, and stop values, so you do not need to determine the end of the range. You merely tell Excel that the series is in a column, as shown in Figure 10.1. This operation is illustrated in Guided Activity 10.2.

Alternatively, you might wish to build a series of 11 dates starting with January 15 and having increments of one month. The sequence is to start in cell C2 and continue to cell M2. In this case, you know the start and step values and the number of values (therefore the range). Excel provides a shortcut for entering dates in an Edit I Fill I Series command. Enter the start value as `15-jan` (for the current year) or `15-jan-92` (for a specific year). For the type, select Date; for the Date Unit, select Month; for the step value, enter `1`. You may leave the stop value blank. This operation is also illustrated in Guided Activity 10.2. Because you formatted the entry in the start cell, Excel will follow that formatting through the entire series, as shown in Figure 10.2.

You might use a growth series to see the value of interest to a savings account. Suppose you put $10,000 in a certificate of deposit for 10 months, at an interest rate of 9%. You can use the *date series* created in the previous paragraph. In cell C3, enter the start value of `$10,000`. Select C3:M3 as the series range. For the type, select Growth, and for the step value, enter `1.0075` (100% + 9%/12). You should receive $10,775.83 on November 15, as shown in Figure 10.3.

You might use a *trend series* to predict next month's sales based on the sales volume figures for the last six months. Enter the known sales figures in a range of the worksheet and give the Edit I Fill I Series command. This is illustrated in Figure 10.4. If you are unsure of whether the change in sales figures is linear or exponential, plot all three sets of data on the same chart and compare them visually. We complete this example in Guided Activity 10.3.

FIGURE 10.2
A date series

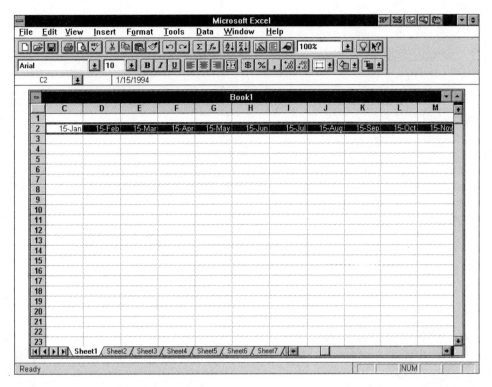

When the interval between numbers in the series is not constant, you might be able to build a series of formulas that yield the desired sequence. Then you can use the Copy and Paste Special Values procedure to copy the values of formulas to a

FIGURE 10.3
A growth data series

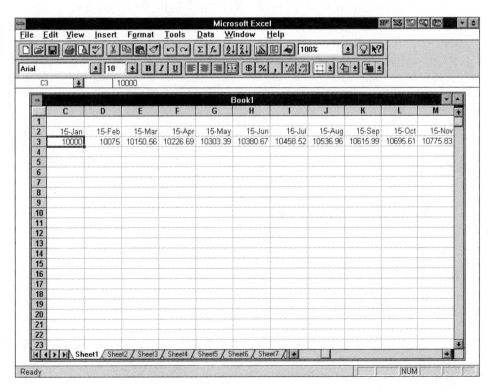

FIGURE 10.4
Linear and growth trend data series

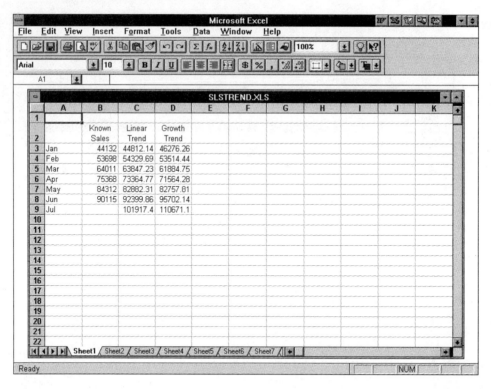

separate place on the workbook, leaving the formulas intact. Or you can copy the range over itself, replacing the formulas with their values and eliminating the original formulas.

For instance, you might wish to create a list containing every Monday, Wednesday, and Friday in 1996, starting in cell A1 and proceeding down column A. In cell A1, put the function for the first relevant date in 1996 (Monday, January 1), =DATE(96,1,1). In cell A2, put the formula =A1+2, which computes the serial number of Wednesday, January 3. The formula =A2+2 occupies cell A3. In cell A4 you can enter a formula that adds 7 to the value 3 cells above—that is, =A1+7. Format A1:A4 to (ddd, mmm d, yyyy). The formula in cell A4 can be copied as far as necessary, in this example from cell A4 to A5:A157. Now, start the Copy and Paste Special Values procedure. The range to Edit | Copy is A1:A157. The range to Edit | Paste Special is A1:A157. Before clicking OK, check the Values box, as illustrated here:

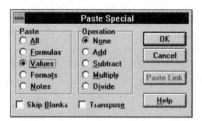

The result is that the formulas are replaced by their values. Although this procedure is slightly more complex than Edit | Fill, the result is the same: a series of constant values, as shown in Figure 10.5.

FIGURE 10.5
A variable data series

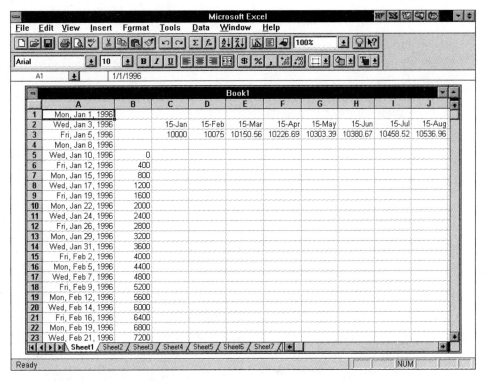

Edit | Fill | Series and the Copy and Paste Special Values procedures are especially useful for building a series of numbers for the Data | Table command discussed later in this unit.

GUIDED ACTIVITY 10.1

Copying the Data Disk

1. Before we proceed to the matter of creating ranges, you need to copy the files from the Student Data Disk (available from your instructor) to your data disk (or hard disk directory). Make sure the Student Data Disk is copy protected. Then exit to the DOS prompt and do one of the following:

    a. If you are keeping your data on a floppy disk and the computer you are using has two disk drives, place your data disk in drive A: and the Student Data Disk in drive B:. Issue the command:

       xcopy b:*.* a: [Enter] [1]

    b. If you are keeping your data on a floppy disk and the computer you are using has one disk drive, place the Student Data Disk in the disk drive and issue the command:

       xcopy a:*.* b: [Enter]

---

[1] The XCOPY command is not available in all versions of DOS. If the command does not work on your system, use the COPY command instead.

The computer will instruct you to change disks as necessary.

c. If you are keeping your data on a hard disk or network file server, place the Student Data Disk in the disk drive and issue the command:

    xcopy a:*.* c: [Enter]

Your instructor might tell you to use a different drive or path for this command.

The effect of the previous step is to copy files to your data disk, just as if you had created them yourself. You can now return the Student Data Disk to your instructor.

GUIDED ACTIVITY 10.2

Creating a Range of Values

In this Guided Activity you use Edit | Fill and the Copy and Paste Special Values procedure to create several ranges of values.

1. Follow the startup procedure outlined in Unit 1 to load Windows and enter Excel. If you are continuing from a previous Guided Activity or Exercise and already have a workbook on the screen, use the command File | New (or click on the New Workbook tool) to open a new workbook.

2. Now you build a series of numbers from 0 (zero) to 100,000 with an increment of 400, starting at cell B5 and continuing down column B.

   a. Click on cell B5. Enter the value 0 (zero).

   b. Give the command Edit | Fill and choose Series.

   c. Click Columns under Series in.

   d. In the Step Value text box, enter 400.

   e. In the Stop Value text box, enter 100000.

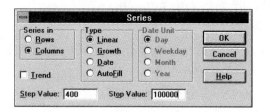

   f. When the dialog box looks like the one shown above, click on OK or press [Enter]. Excel then fills the range from cell B5 to cell B255 with values from 0 to 100,000 in increments of 400. (See Figure 10.1.)

3. Press [Ctrl][↓] to move to the bottom of the data column. You should end up in cell B255, which has a value of 100,000. Press [↑] several times to move up the column, assuring yourself that each cell contains a constant value that differs by 400

from the cells immediately above and below it. When you are convinced, press
[Ctrl][Home] to return to the top of the worksheet.

4. Save your work with the name DATACOMP.XLS.

5. Now build a series of 11 dates, starting with January 15 and having increments of one month. The sequence is to start in cell C2 and continue to cell M2.

   a. Enter 15-jan in cell C2. Select C2:M2.

   b. Give the Edit | Fill | Series command.

   c. As shown in the following dialog box, in the Step Value text box, enter 1; in the Type list box, select Date; in the Date Unit list box, select Month.

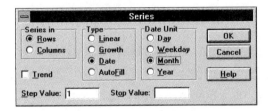

   d. Click on OK or press [Enter].

   Excel will then compute the results. (See Figure 10.2.) Note that the dates created by this command are constant values, not formulas.

6. Save your work before proceeding.

7. Now build a growth series to show accumulated interest during the time period displayed in C2:M2.

   a. Enter 10000 in cell C3. Select C3:M3.

   b. Give the Edit | Fill command and choose Series.

   c. As shown in the following dialog box, in the Step Value text box, enter 1.0075; in the Type list box, select Growth.

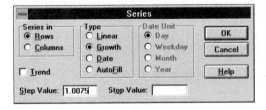

   d. Select OK.

8. Save your work before proceeding.

9. In column A, starting in cell A1, build a list of dates that includes every Monday, Wednesday, and Friday in 1996. The first date is Monday, January 1.

a. Click on cell A1. Enter the function =DATE(96,1,1) in that cell. This computes the serial number of the date January 1, 1996 (which is a Monday).

b. Move to cell A2. Enter =A1+2 in that cell. This calculates the serial number of the day two days later than the date in cell A1.

c. Enter the formula =A2+2 in cell A3.

d. Move to cell A4. Enter =A1+7 in that cell. This calculates the serial number of the day one week later than the date in cell A1.

e. Use the Format | Cells command to format the range A1:A4 to (ddd, mmm d, yyyy). You must type this into the Code text box since it is not a predefined choice. Use the Format | Column | Width command to change the width of column A to 16.

f. The next step is to copy the formula in cell A4 to a range that will include all dates in 1996. Unless you are very smart, you probably do not know how many cells it will take. Here is how to figure out how far to copy the formula:

- There are 52 weeks, plus a few extra days, in a year.
- You need three dates for every week.
- If you multiply 53 times 3, you should have more than enough rows.

Therefore, copy from cell A4 to the range A5:A159. (*Hint*: Highlight A4:A159 and give the Edit | Fill | Down command.)

g. After copying, press [Ctrl][↓] to go to the bottom of the column. Since the copy operation copies both formula and format, it is easy to see that you have copied two cells too many. Use Edit | Clear to erase them.

h. Press [Ctrl][Home] to return to cell A1. At this point, you have formulas that give the desired dates. Next, you want to turn those formulas into constant values. (This will make the worksheet recalculate faster since Excel will have 157 fewer formulas to calculate.)

i. Select A1:A157. The fastest way to do this from cell A1 is to press [Shift][Ctrl][↓]. Give the Edit | Copy command.

j. Give the Edit | Paste Special command. In the dialog box, shown below, select Values.

k. Click on OK or press [Enter]; then press [Esc] to cancel the copy marquee. Excel converts each formula in the original range to its current value, then places that value in the corresponding cell in the destination range. Since the source and destination ranges are the same, the formulas are replaced by their values (and the formulas no longer exist).

10. The worksheet should now look like that shown in Figure 10.5. Use the arrow keys to move down the range, convincing yourself that the formulas have been replaced by values. Press [Ctrl][Home] to return to cell A1.

11. Save your work again.

GUIDED ACTIVITY 10.3

Creating a Trend Series

In this Guided Activity you explore the results of selecting the Trend box in the Edit | Fill | Series dialog box.

1. If you are not continuing from the previous Guided Activity, load Excel. If you are continuing from the last Guided Activity, click on the New Workbook tool to open a blank workbook.

2. Select the range A3:A9 and enter the labels Jan, Feb,...Jul in those cells. Select the range B2:D2 and enter the labels Known Sales, Linear Trend, and Growth Trend in those cells. Give the Format | Cells command, choose the Alignment tab, and select Horizontal Center, Vertical Center, and Wrap Text.

3. Select the range B3:B8 and enter the following list of values:

   44132
   53698
   64011
   75368
   84312
   90115

4. Copy B3:B8 to C3:D8. You should now have three columns of identical numbers.

5. Select C3:C9 and choose Series from the Edit | Fill command. In the dialog box, shown below, select Linear and Trend. Leave the Step Value as is; Excel ignores it. Click OK or press [Enter].

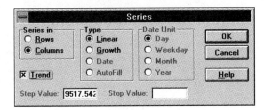

6. Select D3:D9 and choose Series from the Edit | Fill command. In the dialog box, shown below, select Growth and Trend. Leave the Step Value as is; Excel ignores it. Click OK or press [Enter].

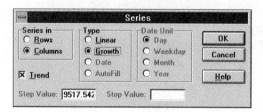

7. Your worksheet should now look like Figure 10.4. You have created two projections for July sales based on the trend over the first two quarters of the year. Unfortunately, there is almost a $10,000 difference between them. You will use a chart to determine which is the more accurate indicator.

8. Select A2:D9 and press [F11]. Give the Format | Chart Type command and select Line. To get the clearest picture, select the Y-axis (by clicking on it) and give the Format | Selected Axis command. On the Scale tab, change the Minimum to 40000. This has the effect of amplifying any differences between the lines on the chart. Your chart should now look like Figure 10.6.

9. It appears that the line representing the linear trend series better matches the original numbers and is therefore the more accurate forecaster of July's sales. Save the workbook as SLSTREND.XLS.

FIGURE 10.6
A trend series chart

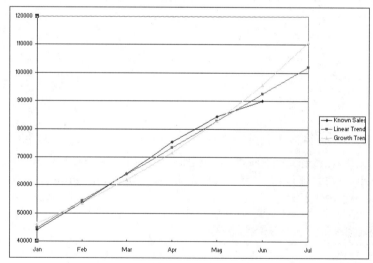

The AutoFill Handle

The lower-right corner of the border of the active cell contains a small black square similar to the handles you observed when selecting chart items. This is known as the ***AutoFill handle*** (or ***fill handle***). When you place the mouse cursor on the AutoFill handle, it changes to black crosshairs. The fill handle provides a shortcut method of copying cells and creating data series. To use the fill handle, place the mouse cursor on it and drag either down or to the right.

How the fill handle fills the destination range depends on the data contained in the source range. If the source range contains text, a single numeric value, or a formula, the fill handle will copy those data to the destination range, using the same criteria as the Edit | Fill commands. If the source range contains a date, the fill handle will create a date series with a step value of one day. If the source range contains a time, the fill handle will create a date series with a step value of one hour. If the source range contains a linear series of numbers (that is, the difference between succeeding numbers is a constant), the fill handle will create a linear data series. If the source range contains a nonlinear series of numbers (that is, the difference between succeeding numbers varies), the fill handle will use the TREND( ) function to create a linear trend data series. The fill handle is also programmed to understand ordinals, such as 1st and 2nd, and certain special terms, such as quarter, qtr, and the names (Monday/January) and abbreviations (Mon/Jan) of days of the week or months.

The fill handle also has other uses. By dragging up or to the left outside of the source range, you can create a series in those directions (like the Edit | Fill | Up and Edit | Fill | Left commands). By dragging up or to the left within the source range, you can clear a range (Edit | Clear). By dragging up or to the left while holding the Shift key, you can delete a range (Edit | Delete). By dragging down or to the right while holding the Shift key, you can insert a range (Insert | Cells).

Admittedly, this may all be rather overwhelming, but when you consider that you can perform all of these functions without accessing a single menu, and you can do much of it without touching the keyboard, the fill handle becomes a very powerful tool for quickly creating a workbook. A vast majority of the workbooks that you design will require that you create a series of month names, days of the week, or dates. Learn to use this powerful tool and you are well on your way to becoming a proficient Excel user.

Creating Custom Lists

The AutoFill handle's ability to recognize many commonly used words and abbreviations, such as the days of the week and the months of the year, is a great convenience. However, it is not limited to those predefined lists. Suppose your company has a list of departments that you need to use often, in budgets, employee reports, and so on. Excel allows you to create *custom lists*, which the AutoFill handle will repeat as easily as it does the days of the week.

To create a new list, give the Tools | Options command and choose the Custom Lists tab. From there, you can either define a new list by entering it directly in the dialog box, or import it from a range of cells in the worksheet. When you click OK, the AutoFill handle will now recognize your new list as one that it will re-create.

GUIDED ACTIVITY 10.4

Using the AutoFill Handle

This Guided Activity gives you experience in using the AutoFill handle and observing how it treats different types of source ranges.

1. If you are not continuing from the previous Guided Activity, load Excel. If you are continuing from the last Guided Activity, click on the New Workbook tool to open a blank workbook.

2. Select the range A1:I3, and enter the following data:

A	B	C	D	E	F	G	H	I
234	Text	Jan	1-Jan	1st Qtr	1:00	1	1	Mon
						3	3	
							4	

3. Select cell A1 and drag the fill handle to cell A10. The source range does not contain series information, so the effect is the same as using Edit|Fill|Down.

4. Select cell B1 and drag the fill handle to cell B10. The source range contains text, so the effect is the same as using Edit|Fill|Down.

5. Select cell C1 and drag the fill handle to cell C14. The fill handle is programmed to recognize month abbreviations, so it creates a date series with a step value of one month.

6. Select cell D1 and drag the fill handle to cell D34. As you drag past the bottom border of the window, the screen will scroll to give you access to lower rows. The fill handle is designed to recognize dates, so it creates a date series with a step value of one day.

7. Select cell E1 and drag the fill handle to cell E12. This range demonstrates the fill handle's recognition both of the special term "Qtr" and of ordinal number endings (1st, 2nd, and so on).

8. Select cell F1 and drag the fill handle to cell F26. The fill handle recognizes times and creates a date series with a step value of one hour.

9. Select G1:G2 and drag the fill handle to cell G14. The fill handle recognizes a linear series and creates a series of odd numbers.

10. Select H1:H3 and drag the fill handle to cell H14. The fill handle recognizes a nonlinear series and creates a linear trend series. The only difference between using the fill handle and the Edit|Fill command is that the fill handle does not erase the source range.

11. Select cell I1 and drag the fill handle to cell I14. The fill handle recognizes the abbreviation for Monday and creates a date series with a step value of one day.

12. Your workbook should now look like Figure 10.7. Save it as AUTOFILL.XLS.

FIGURE 10.7
Effects of the AutoFill handle

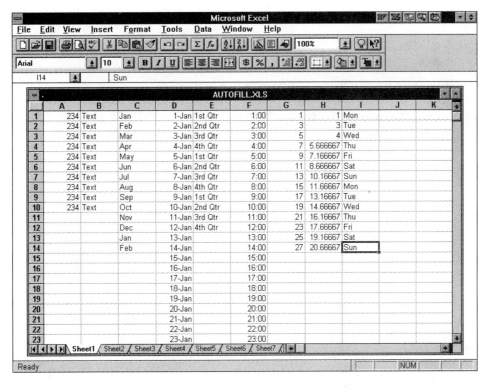

GUIDED ACTIVITY 10.5

Adding a Custom List

This Guided Activity gives you experience in using the AutoFill handle to re-create a custom list.

1. If you are not continuing from the previous Guided Activity, load Excel. If you are continuing from the last Guided Activity, open the AUTOFILL.XLS workbook.

2. Click the scroll bar to move columns J and K toward the center of the worksheet. Select both columns and change the column width to 22.

3. Enter the following list of departments in J1:J10:

    ```
    Administration
    Information Services
    Human Resources
    Finance
    Sales
    Marketing
    Research & Development
    Engineering
    Production
    Quality Assurance
    ```

4. Give the Tools | Options command. Click on the Custom Lists tab. Excel displays this dialog box:

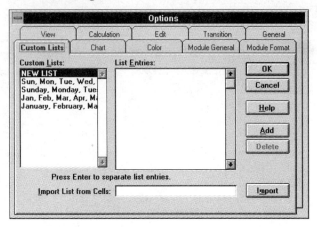

5. Click in the Import List from Cells box, then drag the range J1:J10. (You will need to drag the dialog box out of the way first.) Click the Import button; then click OK.

6. In cell K1, type Administration. Drag the fill handle to cell K10. Your worksheet should look something like Figure 10.8. Save your work.

FIGURE 10.8
A custom list

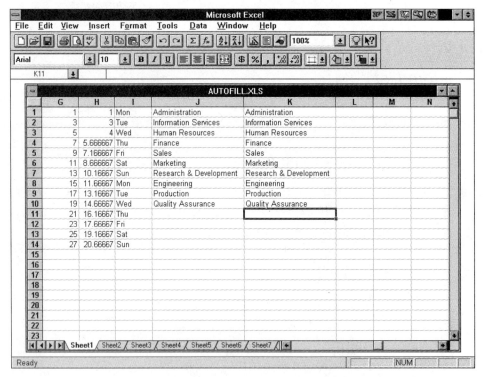

One-Variable Table

The data table is a powerful tool for performing what-if analyses. You can see how results change as the value of one (or two) variables change.

The Data I Table command is used to evaluate the impact of one or more values of one variable in one or more formulas. In the language of mathematics, these are equations with one unknown. When complete, the table is structured as follows:

blank	formula$_a$	formula$_b$	etc.
value$_1$	result$_{a1}$	result$_{b1}$	
value$_2$	result$_{a2}$	result$_{b2}$	
value$_3$	result$_{a3}$	result$_{b3}$	
etc.			

The top row of the table contains formulas. You want to determine the results of these formulas as one of the variables in the formulas changes. For instance, you might want to see how cost and revenue change as the level of sales changes (see the example that follows). The left column of the table contains a set of values for the variable. The results area will contain the result of the formulas when the variable has the various values. Thus, result$_{a1}$ is the value of formula$_a$ when the variable has value$_1$.

When you construct a one-variable data table, you need enter only the formulas and the values. The Data I Table command computes the results.

EXAMPLE

Assume that you want to build a table with columns that contain the cost and revenue of differing levels of sales, from 0 (zero) to 100,000 units, at intervals of 400. The cost to produce each item is $125, and the selling price is $200. If x is the number of units sold, the algebraic formulas would be:

$125x$ for total cost
$200x$ for total revenue

Excel does not allow you to use x as part of a formula, however. Instead, a cell name must be used. Assuming that cell X1 is vacant, you can use that cell in the formula. The Excel formulas would then be:

```
=125*X1
=200*X1
```

In this example, cell X1 is called the ***input cell***.

Now, choose an empty area of the worksheet. The area must be 3 columns wide (2 formulas plus 1) and 252 rows deep (251 values plus 1). This area is called the table range. For this example, use B4:D255 as the table range. Cell B4 remains blank. You have already used Edit I Fill to fill the range B5:B255 with numbers 0, 400,...100000. Place the formulas into cells C4 and D4. Return the cursor to cell B4. Select B4:D255. Now (finally!) you can give the Data I Table command. In the input cell dialog box (shown after step 6.b. in Guided Activity 10.6), type X1 in the Column box (since the values are in a column). Excel calculates the results and places them in cells C5:D255. This operation is illustrated in the following Guided Activity.

You probably recall that Excel will recalculate a result any time a value that affects that result is changed. Note that Excel will recalculate the table when you change the value of any cell that would affect the table's results. You may decide to turn off automatic calculation in the Tools | Options dialog box if you will be doing a lot of work with tables, because the number of calculations, and hence the time to perform the calculations, can be quite large.

GUIDED ACTIVITY 10.6

Creating a One-Variable Table

In this Guided Activity you create a one-variable data table.

1. If you are not continuing from the previous Guided Activity, load Excel and open DATACOMP.

2. Build a table with columns that contain the total cost and revenue of differing levels of sales, from 0 (zero) to 100,000 units, at intervals of 400. Use B4:D255 as the table range. The cost to produce each item is $125, and the selling price is $200. If x is the number of units sold, the formulas would be:

    $125x$
    $200x$

CHECKPOINT 10A What are the Excel formulas?

3. Use the previously entered range of values as one part of the table. Recall that the range B5:B255 contains a series of numbers ranging from 0 (zero) to 100,000 in increments of 400.

4. The next step is to enter the Excel formulas one row above and one column to the right of the lowest value. Therefore, enter =125*X1 in cell C4 and =200*X1 in cell D4.

5. Make cell B4 the active cell. Drag to extend the selection to B4:D255.

6. To compute the table:

    a. Give the Data | Table command. Excel presents the input cell dialog box.

    b. Type X1 in the Column Input Cell box, as shown here:

    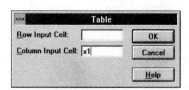

    c. Click on OK or press [Enter].

FIGURE 10.9
A one-variable data table

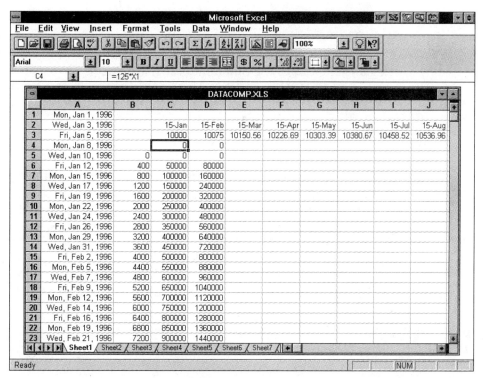

d. Excel completes the table, with the result illustrated in Figure 10.9. Move around in the results area, using the arrow keys.

7. Save your work before proceeding to the next step.

8. You decide to raise the price to $210. Change the formula in cell D4 to =210*X1. Notice that the results in the column below cell D4 change to reflect the new information.

9. Save the workbook.

Two-Variable Table

The Data | Table command can also be used to evaluate the impact of one or more values of two variables in one formula. This is called an equation with two unknowns. When complete, the table is structured as follows:

formula	$value_{b1}$	$value_{b2}$	etc.
$value_{a1}$	$result_{a1,b1}$	$result_{a1,b2}$	
$value_{a2}$	$result_{a2,b1}$	$result_{a2,b2}$	
$value_{a3}$	$result_{a3,b1}$	$result_{a3,b2}$	
etc.			

The top-left cell contains a single formula. Let's determine the results of this formula as two of the variables in the formula change. For instance, you might want to see how the monthly payment changes as a result of different principal amounts and interest rates (see the example that follows). The left column of the table contains a set of values for one of the variables. The top row contains a set of values for the other variable. The results area will contain the result of the formula when the variables are given the different values. Thus, $\text{result}_{a1,b1}$ is the value of the formula when one variable has value_{a1} and the other variable has value_{b1}.

When you construct a two-variable data table, you need enter only the formula and the values. The Data | Table command computes the results.

EXAMPLE

Assume that you want to build a table with columns that contain the monthly payments on various principal amounts at various interest rates for 60 months. The principal amounts are $5,000 to $25,000 in increments of $2,000, and the interest rates are 7.5% to 17.5% in increments of 1.0%. Recall that the Excel function is

PMT(rate,nper,pv,fv,type)

Again, Excel requires cell names in the formula. Assuming that cells X1 and Y1 are vacant, you can use them as the arguments to the function. The Excel formula would then be

=PMT(Y1/12,60,-X1)

In this example, cell X1 is called the column input cell and Y1 is the row input cell.

Now, choose an empty area of the workbook. The area must be 12 columns wide (11 values of *rate* plus 1) and 12 rows deep (11 values of *pv* plus 1). This area is the table range. For this example, use H21:S32 as the table range. Put the PMT( ) formula in cell H21. Use Edit | Fill | Series to fill the range H22:H32 with numbers 5,000, 7,000, ... 25,000. Use Edit | Fill | Series to fill the range I21:S21 with numbers .075, .085, ... .175. Return the cursor to cell H21. Select H21:S32.

Now you can give the Data | Table command. When asked for the row input cell, type or point to Y1. When asked for the column input cell, type or point to X1. Excel calculates the results and places them in cells I22:S32. This operation is illustrated in the following Guided Activity.

GUIDED ACTIVITY 10.7

Creating a Two-Variable Table

In this Guided Activity you create a two-variable data table.

1. If you are not continuing from the previous Guided Activity, load Excel and open DATACOMP.

2. Follow the example discussed above for the Data | Table command to build a table with columns that contain the monthly payments on various principal amounts at various interest rates for 60 months. The principal amounts are $5,000 to $25,000 in increments of $2,000, and the interest rates are 7.5% to 17.5% in increments of 1.0%. Use H21:S32 as the table range.

FIGURE 10.10
A two-variable data table

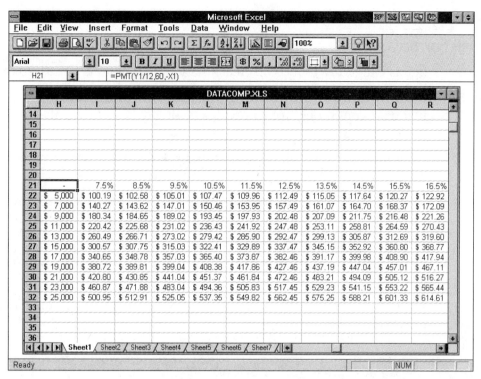

3. You should be able to complete this activity without detailed instructions. After the table is computed, format the data as appropriate. The result should look like Figure 10.10.

4. Save your work. This completes our work with DATACOMP.

Using Array Formulas

To this point, all of the calculations that you have performed in Excel have been single calculations. An *array formula* is a means of performing several calculations at once. In addition, Excel contains several specialized functions that either take arrays as arguments or return arrays as results. To use an array as the argument for a function, select the range where you wish the results to be printed, enter the range where you would normally enter a single value, and press [Ctrl][Shift][Enter]. Excel will place braces { } around each formula in the range to identify it as part of an array.

Suppose you wish to create a square root table for the numbers from 1 to 100. Use the Edit | Fill command to place the values 1 to 100 in A3:A102. Select B3:B102, and type the formula =SQRT(A3:A102) in cell B3; press [Ctrl][Shift][Enter]. Excel will place the results in B3:B102 as an array as illustrated in the next Guided Activity.

GUIDED ACTIVITY 10.8

Using Array Formulas

In this Guided Activity, you create the square root table discussed in the preceding section.

1. If you are continuing from a previous Guided Activity, use the File | New command to bring up a new workbook window.

2. Enter the value 1 in cell A3. Use the Edit | Fill | Series command to place the values 1 to 100 in A3:A102.

3. Select B3:B102. Enter the formula =SQRT(A3:A102) in cell B3. Press . Excel will return the square roots for each number in column A. The formula in each cell will be {=SQRT(A3:A102)}.

4. Format column B to 0.000. You must type this special format into the Format text box.

5. The result should be like Figure 10.11. Save your work with the file name SQRTTABL.XLS.

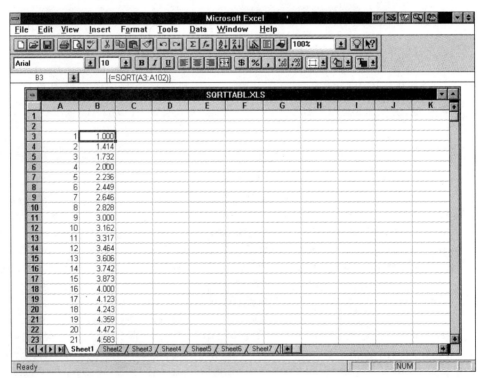

FIGURE 10.11 An array formula

EXERCISE 10.1

Compound Interest Revisited

Look at the situation posed in Application C, "Compound Interest (I)," at the end of Unit 7. Much of the work you accomplished in that application could have been done with Data commands.

1. Starting with a clean workbook, use the Edit | Fill | Series command to enter the dollar amounts in column A and the number of years in row 2. Also, enter the interest rate in cell A1.

2. Select the entire worksheet and use the Format | Cells command to set the format to $#,##0.00; then format A1 and B2:F2 as illustrated in Figure C.1.

3. Develop a formula that you can use in a Data | Table command and place the formula in A2.

4. Use the Data | Table command to calculate the table. Your result should look like Figure C.1, except that the formula in A2 displays a value, probably 0 (zero).

5. Save your work with the filename COMPOX.XLS.

EXERCISE 10.2

A Sales Workbook (V)

Look at the COMPCOST.XLS workbook used in several previous Exercises. Anytime you have the same basic formula copied down a column, you should consider changing the workbook to use the Data | Table command. In this case, you can insert a row before row 12 and enter the formula for Tax in cell D12. (These cell references assume that you moved the table as instructed in step 8 of Exercise 6.1.) Enter the formula for Total in cell E12 and compute the values for rows 13–15 using the Data | Table command. Because this is a small worksheet, you do not gain much using a data table, but consider how useful this would be if you had 100 items on the worksheet.

EXERCISE 10.3

A 401(k) Plan

Many employers offer a 401(k) plan as one of their employee benefits. Simply put, a 401(k) plan allows employees to save a portion of their income for retirement on a before-tax basis, with severe restrictions on their ability to withdraw the funds, and with the understanding that the tax will have to be paid when the funds are withdrawn at retirement. Many employers also offer dollar matching—that is, for every dollar an employee saves, they contribute a dollar.

For the sake of this Exercise, assume that you are an employee of such a company. You are going to create a workbook that will allow you to see the effect of saving money in such a plan. The employer will match dollar-for-dollar up to 6% of your income.

1. Open a new workbook, enter the title `Effect of 401(k) Contributions` in cell A1, and center it across A1:G1.

CHECKPOINT 10B What is the fastest way to center an entry across multiple columns?

2. Enter `Annual Salary` in cell A2 and `35000` in cell B2. For the sake of simplicity, assume a level salary for 30 years. Also, assume that payments into the plan are made by you and your employer once per year, at the end of the year.

3. Enter `Interest Rate` in cell A3 and `6%` in cell B3. Since the interest rate is only a guess, this will allow you (if you wish) to create scenarios with various interest rates and do some simple what-if analysis.

4. Create a series in B6:G6 from 1% to 6%. This will allow you to see the effect of saving different portions of your salary.

5. Create a series from 1 to 30 years in A7:A36.

6. You will use a data table to compute the accumulations. Use the FV( ) function to create a formula in cell A6. Use empty cells (for example, X1 and Y1) for the number of years (column variable) and the percent of contribution (row variable). Remember that the employer is matching your contributions.

7. Use the Data | Table command to compute the table.

8. Adjust column widths and number formats as necessary. If everything is correct, you should arrive at a value of `$332,044.38` in cell G36. (If you arrive at half that amount, remember that the payment equals your contribution *plus* your employer's contribution. Save your work as 401(K).XLS.

9. In reality, you and your employer would probably make contributions each month. Alter the formula in cell B7 so it uses a monthly interest rate, monthly payment, and sets the term to the twelfth month of the year. Copy this formula throughout the appropriate range. The value in cell G36 will be `$351,580.26`, illustrating the increased benefit of monthly payments and compounding. Save this workbook as 401(K)M.XLS.

Review Questions

1. Write formulas for the following functions, which can be used in the Data | Table command. Use cell X1 as the row input cell and cell Y1 as the column input cell.

   *a. The total cost of producing x units, where the total cost is the sum of a constant (fixed) cost of $40,000 and a cost per unit of $69.95.

   b. The amount of a monthly payment on principal of x at y percent per annum interest for three years.

2. You wish to fill a range of cells with a linear series, beginning with cell A1, with the series 0.0, 0.1,...1.0. What do you specify as the:

   *a. Start value?

   b. Step value?

   *c. Stop value?

   d. Range?

Key Terms

Array formula
AutoFill handle
Custom list
Date series

Fill handle
Growth series
Input cell
Linear series

Start value
Step value
Stop value
Trend series

Documentation Research

Referring to the Excel *User's Guide,* find and record the page number of each of the commands discussed in this unit. We recommend that you also write the page number in the margin next to the discussion of the command in the unit.

1. How do you prevent the AutoFill handle from incrementing a series?
2. How can you share a custom AutoFill list with other users?
3. Data l Table—what can you do to edit the individual values in a data table?
4. Data l Table—what is the effect of copying the resulting values of a data table?

Data Selection Operations

This unit deals with those Data commands and functions that are designed to allow rudimentary database management capabilities. With these commands you can sort information, select certain items from a list based on criteria you specify, enter subtotals into a list based on criteria you specify, and compute statistics for a portion of the list.

Learning Objectives

At the completion of this unit you should know

1. definitions of various database terms,
2. how to specify criteria using comparison, computed, and combined methods.

At the completion of this unit you should be able to

1. sort a data range using one or more keys,
2. set databases, criteria, and extract ranges,
3. find records that match specific criteria,
4. extract records that match specific criteria,
5. compute statistics on records that match specific criteria,
6. create a data distribution table using database functions,
7. use a data form to facilitate data entry,
8. create a pivot table.

Important Commands

Data | Filter

Data | Form

Data | PivotTable

Data | Sort

Data | Subtotals

Terminology

Before discussing the commands, we should define a few terms. These definitions are specific to Excel; other database management systems may use some of these terms somewhat differently. A sample database is illustrated in Figure 11.1.[1]

DATABASE A cell range of one or more columns and two or more rows. The top row of an Excel ***database*** contains ***field names***; all other rows contain data. You can specify a database by giving the Insert | Name | Define command and assigning the name "Database" to the specified range. While it is not necessary to do this in order to use

FIGURE 11.1 *A sample database*

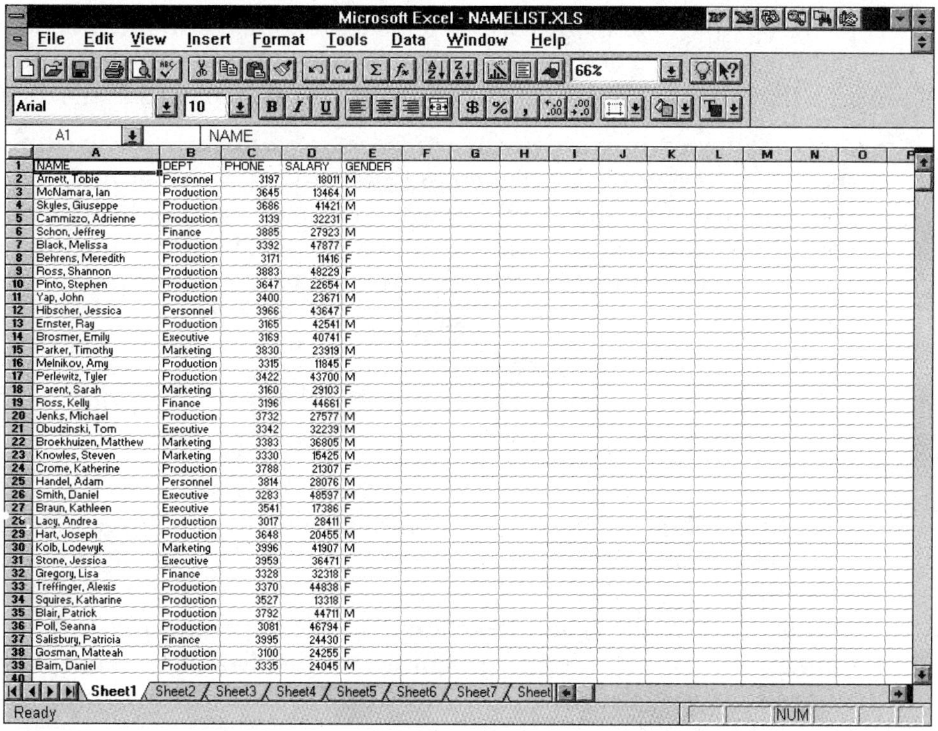

	A	B	C	D	E
1	NAME	DEPT	PHONE	SALARY	GENDER
2	Arnett, Tobie	Personnel	3197	18011	M
3	McNamara, Ian	Production	3645	13464	M
4	Skyles, Giuseppe	Production	3686	41421	M
5	Cammizzo, Adrienne	Production	3139	32231	F
6	Schon, Jeffrey	Finance	3885	27923	M
7	Black, Melissa	Production	3392	47877	F
8	Behrens, Meredith	Production	3171	11416	F
9	Ross, Shannon	Production	3883	48229	F
10	Pinto, Stephen	Production	3647	22654	M
11	Yap, John	Production	3400	23671	M
12	Hibscher, Jessica	Personnel	3966	43647	F
13	Ernster, Ray	Production	3165	42541	M
14	Brosmer, Emily	Executive	3169	40741	F
15	Parker, Timothy	Marketing	3830	23919	M
16	Melnikov, Amy	Production	3315	11845	F
17	Perlewitz, Tyler	Production	3422	43700	M
18	Parent, Sarah	Marketing	3160	29103	F
19	Ross, Kelly	Finance	3196	44661	F
20	Jenks, Michael	Production	3732	27577	M
21	Obudzinski, Tom	Executive	3342	32239	M
22	Broekhuizen, Matthew	Marketing	3383	36805	M
23	Knowles, Steven	Marketing	3330	15425	M
24	Crome, Katherine	Production	3788	21307	F
25	Handel, Adam	Personnel	3814	28076	M
26	Smith, Daniel	Executive	3283	48597	M
27	Braun, Kathleen	Executive	3541	17386	F
28	Lacy, Andrea	Production	3017	28411	F
29	Hart, Joseph	Production	3648	20455	M
30	Kolb, Lodewyk	Marketing	3996	41907	M
31	Stone, Jessica	Executive	3959	36471	F
32	Gregory, Lisa	Finance	3328	32318	F
33	Treffinger, Alexis	Production	3370	44838	F
34	Squires, Katharine	Production	3527	13318	F
35	Blair, Patrick	Production	3792	44711	M
36	Poll, Seanna	Production	3081	46794	F
37	Salisbury, Patricia	Finance	3995	24430	F
38	Gosman, Matteah	Production	3100	24255	F
39	Baim, Daniel	Production	3335	24045	M

1 We changed the zoom ratio to fit the entire database in the figure. (We discuss the View | Zoom command in Unit 12.)

Data commands, Excel will always identify the first row of a range as field names if the range is named "Database." In Figure 11.1, the database is the range A1:E39.

RECORD Each row of data below the first row; a set of information to be processed as a unit. For instance, row 6 contains all information pertaining to Jeffrey Schon: his name, department, phone, salary, and gender.

FIELD Each column of the database. The first row of the column contains field names; subsequent rows contain *fields* within *records*. The field name must be text; all other entries can be text, formulas, or numbers but should be consistent within a field (down a column). In this example, the fields are Name, Dept, Phone, Salary, and Gender.

COMPUTED FIELD Any field that contains formulas or functions is referred to as a *computed field*.

CRITERIA RANGE A named or specified range that contains field names in the first row and criteria in subsequent rows. Field names must match exactly the field names in the input range. *Criteria* can be *comparison*, *computed*, or *combined*. Criteria are used to *filter* a list; that is, to limit the list to those records that meet the criteria. See the section titled "Specification of Criteria" later in this unit.

EXTRACT RANGE Sometimes it is desirable to copy a filtered list to another part of the worksheet. The area that you copy to is known as the *extract range*. To copy all of the fields in the database, make the extract range a single cell. To limit which fields are copied, copy the field names of the fields to be copied into the first row of the extract range. Those fields (columns) whose names do not appear are not copied. The field names that are specified must match exactly the field names in the database range.

SUBTOTAL Frequently, it is desirable to insert *subtotals* in a database. Some database management systems call this *grouping*. Regardless of the terminology, it allows you to easily answer questions like, "How many hamburgers did we serve in May?" or "What is our company's average salary, by gender? by department?" First, sort the database by the field you wish to group. Then, give the Data | Subtotals command, decide what function you wish to use to analyze the subtotal and which field you are going to subtotal, and click OK.

Sorting

The Data | Sort command is used most commonly to sort records (rows) according to one or more *keys* (cell references). The dialog box, illustrated in Figure 11.2, demonstrates the sophistication of the Data | Sort command. Cell A1 was the active cell when we gave the Data | Sort command to capture this illustration. Excel analyzed the cells around cell A1, recognized the first row as field names, recognized that the list to be sorted was in the range A2:E39, selected that range, and allows the user to choose the sort keys by field name, rather than cell reference.

Notice that the sort range selected by Excel is A2:E39, rather than A1:E39. If you had sorted the range including the first row, the field names would be lost somewhere in the database. If the list had not had field names, Excel would have allowed

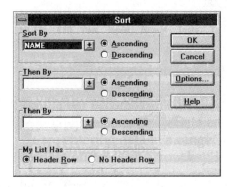

FIGURE 11.2
Data | Sort
dialog box

you to sort the entire range and specify the sort keys by column label. You can also override Excel's analysis of the range by selecting the range you want to sort before giving the Data | Sort command.

To sort the database by name, all you have to do is click OK. To sort the database by another field name, simply select that field name and click OK.

The Then By keys are used to break ties in the Sort By key. They are specified in the same manner as the Sort By key. Be advised that these keys break exact ties only. Numbers that have been rounded for display format might appear to be equal, but not be equal, and would frustrate your attempts to break ties.

If you need to sort by more than three keys, run one sort by the lowest priority key(s) first; then run another sort using the higher priority keys. Using this method, you can run as many sorts as needed to sort by as many keys as needed.

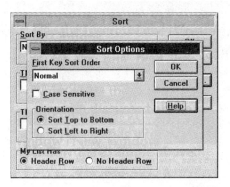

FIGURE 11.3
Data | Sort |
Options
dialog box

To increase the flexibility of the Data | Sort command, Excel provides the Options button. The Sort Options dialog box is illustrated in Figure 11.3. Here you can choose to sort a database by any list in Excel's custom lists (such as Sunday, Monday, Tuesday, and so on) that are used by the AutoFill handle. In this dialog box, you can also make the sort case-sensitive—that is, uppercase letters are sorted before lowercase letters—and you can decide to sort from left to right, instead of from top to bottom.

You can sort any range of cells, regardless of whether Excel recognizes that range as a database. Again, always be careful *not* to include titles or field names as part of the sort range when you are sorting rows (records). If you accidentally include unintentional rows in your sort procedure, simply issue the Edit | Undo Sort command (before doing anything else) and try again.

GUIDED ACTIVITY 11.1

Sorting

In this Guided Activity you sort the data in a workbook.

1. Follow the startup procedure outlined in Unit 1 to load Windows and enter Excel.
2. Open NAMELIST.XLS. This is one of the files that should have been copied to your working data disk in Guided Activity 10.1.
3. Notice that this is the same database discussed in this unit. Do the following to sort the data by salary from highest to lowest. Remember that the sort range does not include row 1.

CHECKPOINT 11A What is the sort range?

   a. Select cell A1.
   b. Give the Data | Sort command.
   c. Click on the Sort By drop-down list arrow. Select SALARY. Select the Descending option button.
   d. Click on OK. After sorting, the workbook should look like Figure 11.4.

5. Save the file.

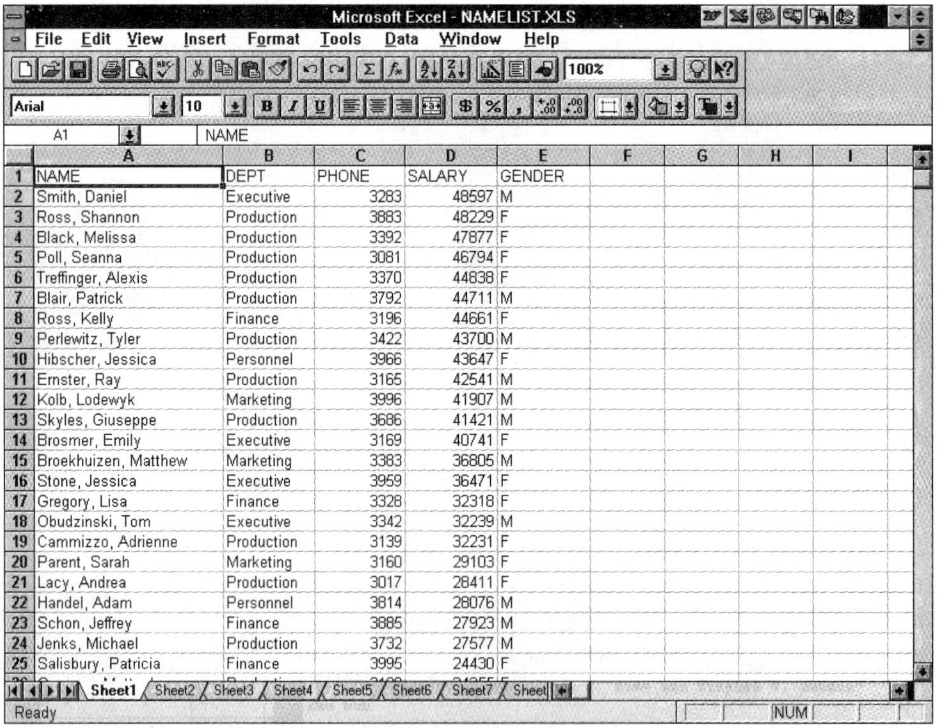

FIGURE 11.4
NAMELIST.XLS after sorting

	A	B	C	D	E
1	NAME	DEPT	PHONE	SALARY	GENDER
2	Smith, Daniel	Executive	3283	48597	M
3	Ross, Shannon	Production	3883	48229	F
4	Black, Melissa	Production	3392	47877	F
5	Poll, Seanna	Production	3081	46794	F
6	Treffinger, Alexis	Production	3370	44838	F
7	Blair, Patrick	Production	3792	44711	M
8	Ross, Kelly	Finance	3196	44661	F
9	Perlewitz, Tyler	Production	3422	43700	M
10	Hibscher, Jessica	Personnel	3966	43647	F
11	Ernster, Ray	Production	3165	42541	M
12	Kolb, Lodewyk	Marketing	3996	41907	M
13	Skyles, Giuseppe	Production	3686	41421	M
14	Brosmer, Emily	Executive	3169	40741	F
15	Broekhuizen, Matthew	Marketing	3383	36805	M
16	Stone, Jessica	Executive	3959	36471	F
17	Gregory, Lisa	Finance	3328	32318	F
18	Obudzinski, Tom	Executive	3342	32239	M
19	Cammizzo, Adrienne	Production	3139	32231	F
20	Parent, Sarah	Marketing	3160	29103	F
21	Lacy, Andrea	Production	3017	28411	F
22	Handel, Adam	Personnel	3814	28076	M
23	Schon, Jeffrey	Finance	3885	27923	M
24	Jenks, Michael	Production	3732	27577	M
25	Salisbury, Patricia	Finance	3995	24430	F

Specification of Criteria

The Data | Filter command, as well as the database statistical functions, depend on criteria for selection of records. Criteria are specified in a *criteria range*, which is an area of the worksheet with one or more field names and one or more criteria. There are three types of criteria: comparison, computed, and combined.

Comparison Criteria

Comparison criteria are used to select records according to a comparison of the data in the record with a criterion. Any criterion contains one or more field names and one or more cells containing data to be compared or computed. Comparison criteria data can be a text string to be matched, a value to be compared, or a wild card character.

A TEXT STRING TO BE MATCHED

For instance, to select all persons in the Production department, you put the field name in one cell, say F1, and the text to be matched in the cell below, which would be F2, as illustrated below. For selection to occur, the text in the database must match the text in the criteria range.

	A	B	C	D	E	F
1	NAME	DEPT	PHONE	SALARY	GENDER	DEPT
2	Smith, Daniel	Executive	3283	48597	M	Production

A VALUE TO BE MATCHED

For instance, to select the person whose phone number is 3885, you put the field name (PHONE) in one cell, say G1, and the value to be matched (3885) in the cell below, which would be G2, as illustrated below. For selection to occur, the value in the database must match the value in the criteria range.

	A	B	C	D	E	F	G
1	NAME	DEPT	PHONE	SALARY	GENDER		PHONE
2	Smith, Daniel	Executive	3283	48597	M		3885

A VALUE TO BE COMPARED

These criteria are used to select records according to the value of a numeric field. Instead of a simple match, however, records are selected if the result of the comparison is true. For instance, to select all persons with salaries exceeding $25,000, you put the field name in one cell, say G1, and >25000 in the cell below, which would be G2, as in the illustration shown here:

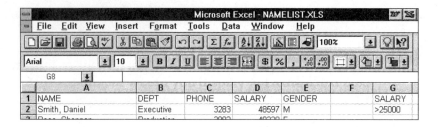

For selection to occur, the value in the database must be greater than 25,000. *Logical operators* are used when comparing value criteria. The six logical operators are as follows:

=   Equal to
<   Less than
<=   Less than or equal to
>   Greater than
>=   Greater than or equal to
<>   Not equal to

WILD CARD CHARACTERS

Excel uses three *wild card characters*:

?   Matches any single character, so that Re?d matches Reed and Reid, but not Reynold.

*   Matches any number of characters in the same position as *, so that P* matches Personnel, Production, and planning (Excel does not consider case in comparison criteria).

~   Matches * and ? that may be located in a *text string*, so that Time~* matches Time* and Time*4 but not Timer.

Excel always assumes that there is an asterisk at the end of text used in comparison criteria, so Rich would match Richard, Richards, Richardson, and Rich's Tire Barn.

The following is an example of a comparison criterion:

	Microsoft Excel - NAMELIST.XLS						
	A	B	C	D	E	F	G
1	NAME	DEPT	PHONE	SALARY	GENDER		DEPT
2	Smith, Daniel	Executive	3283	48597	M		E

Note that the effect of cells G1:G2 is to match all departments with an E as the first letter.

Computed Criteria

A computed criterion is a formula that refers to one or more fields in a database and produces the logical value TRUE or FALSE. The field names entered in the formula must match exactly (except for capitalization) the field names used in the database. The criterion field name must be something other than "Criteria" or a field name of the database. (It can be blank.) Otherwise, Excel will try to interpret the criteria as comparison criteria. Suppose, for example, you need to be able to select the records of all employees whose salaries would exceed $25,000 if they receive a 15% pay increase. The computed criterion would be =(Salary*1.15)>25000. The criterion name might be Raise. This example is illustrated in Guided Activity 11.2. Notice that Excel generates a NAME# error because it does not recognize the field name "Salary." Despite this error message, the criterion still functions correctly.

Computed criteria also give you the chance to create a criterion based on a comparison between two fields. For example, if column F of the database contained a field named Bonus, the formula =bonus>salary would select the records of all employees whose bonus exceeded their salary.

Combined Criteria

The above examples all use a single criterion. It is possible to establish *multiple criteria*, such as *Production Dept and Salary>35000*, by using multiple fields (columns) in the criteria range (F41:G42):

	F	G
41	DEPT	SALARY
42	Production	>35000

It is also possible to establish *alternate criteria*, such as *Production Dept or Salary>35000*, by using multiple rows in the criteria range (F41:G43):

	F	G
41	DEPT	SALARY
42	Production	
43		>35000

When criteria are in more than one column in a given row, a record must pass all criteria to be selected. When the criteria are in more than one row, a record must pass any of the criteria to be selected. Consider this: does your ideal mate need to be rich *and* good-looking (one row), or rich *or* good-looking (two rows)?

Sometimes you want to select records using a criterion such as $20,000 < Salary \leq 30,000$. This requires a criteria range that references Salary twice. (Look ahead to Figure 11.13 to see an example.)

Because the formulas are in the same row, to be selected, a record must have a salary that is both greater than $20,000 and less than or equal to $30,000.

Filtering Records

The Data I Filter commands are used to view only those database records that meet specified criteria.

AutoFilter

Use the Data I Filter I AutoFilter command when you are using simple comparison criteria. You can also use combined criteria if they are in the same field, or if they are of the multiple, rather than the alternate, variety. The AutoFilter command is a toggle command—when the command is on, there is a check mark next to it in the menu structure; when you clear the check mark, the command is off. When you first give the command, Excel places arrows in the cells that contain the field names. The arrows are used to call drop-down list boxes based on the contents of the cells in that field. See Figure 11.5 for an illustration of filtering a list with the AutoFilter command. To complete the filter process, select the desired criteria in one or more of the

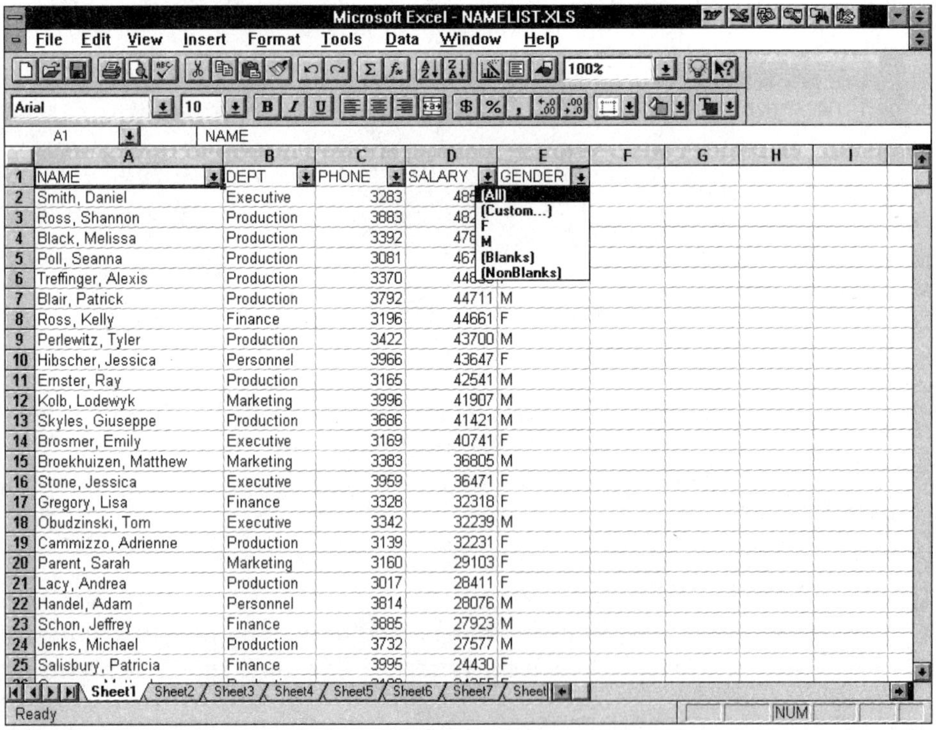

FIGURE 11.5 *Autofiltering a database*

FIGURE 11.6
An autofiltered database

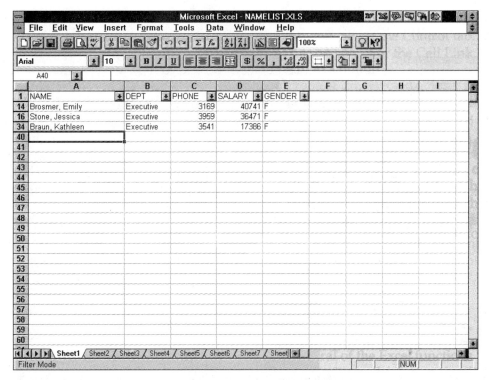

fields of the database. Excel displays those records that meet the criteria and filters out the rest. Suppose you only wanted to view those records for women in the Executive department. Select F in the GENDER drop-down list box and Executive in the DEPT drop-down list box. Figure 11.6 illustrates this filtered list.

CUSTOM CRITERIA

The drop-down list boxes created by the Data | Filter | AutoFilter command contain four entries besides those values contained in the cells in that field: Blanks, Non-Blanks, All, and Custom. Selecting Blanks displays only those records that do not have an entry in this field. Selecting NonBlanks displays only those records that have an entry in this field, including an empty text string (" "). Choosing All removes any filtering based on this field. Choosing Custom displays the dialog box illustrated in Figure 11.7.

FIGURE 11.7
Custom AutoFilter dialog box

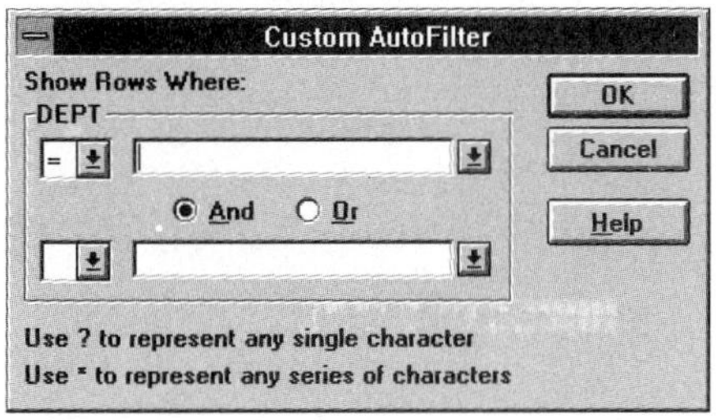

The Custom options greatly increase the flexibility of the AutoFilter command. The drop-down list box containing the equal sign allows you to choose any of the six logical operators, so that you can now create comparison criteria as well as matching criteria. The drop-down text box allows you to type in a criterion that is not an entry in the field, as well as use the wild card characters. Finally, the check boxes allow you to create multiple and alternate criteria on the same field.

Suppose you want to filter the list to only those employees in the Production department who have a salary that is both greater than $20,000 and less than or equal to $30,000. Click the down arrow next to DEPT and select Production. Click the down arrow next to SALARY and select Custom. In the dialog box, select the > sign and type in `20000`. Then select the And check box. Finally, select the <= sign, type in `30000`, and click OK. The filtered database is illustrated in Figure 11.8.

Advanced Filter

The Data | Filter | AutoFilter command is fine as far as it goes, but it is no help if you need to create alternate criteria on more than one field, or use computed criteria, or copy the filtered records to another location on the worksheet, or limit the display to unique records. For these more advanced functions, Excel provides the Data | Filter | Advanced Filter command. The dialog box for this command is illustrated in Figure 11.9.

FIGURE 11.8
A custom autofiltered database

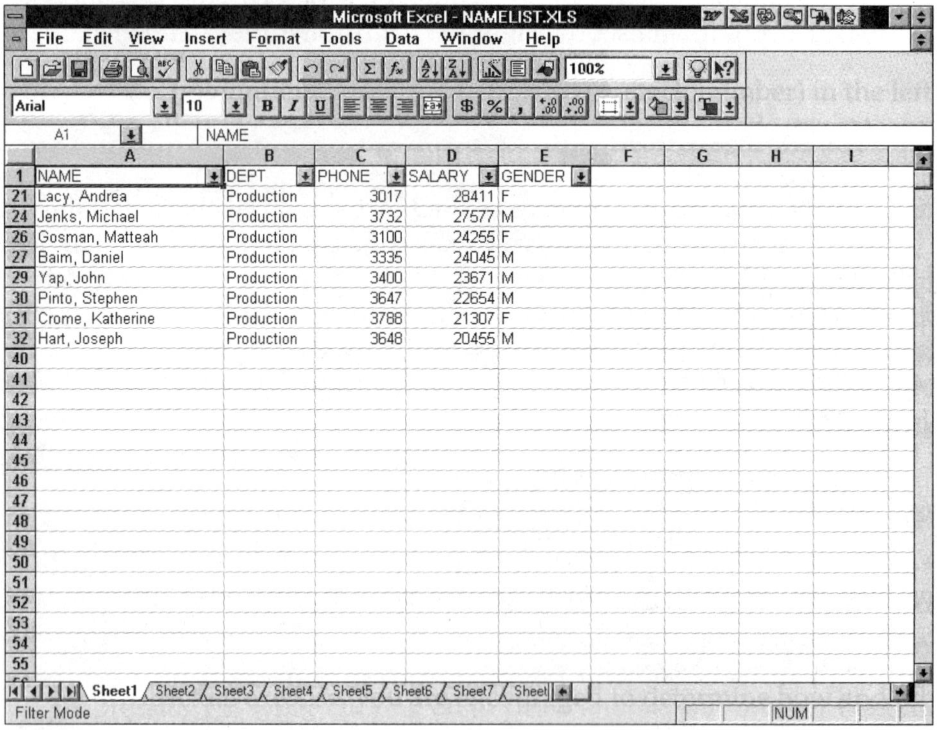
Microsoft Excel - NAMELIST.XLS
File Edit View Insert Format Tools Data Window Help
100%
Arial
10
A1
NAME
A B C D E F G H I
1 NAME DEPT PHONE SALARY GENDER
21 Lacy, Andrea Production 3017 28411 F
24 Jenks, Michael Production 3732 27577 M
26 Gosman, Matteah Production 3100 24255 F
27 Baim, Daniel Production 3335 24045 M
29 Yap, John Production 3400 23671 M
30 Pinto, Stephen Production 3647 22654 M
31 Crome, Katherine Production 3788 21307 F
32 Hart, Joseph Production 3648 20455 M
Sheet1 Sheet2 Sheet3 Sheet4 Sheet5 Sheet6 Sheet7
Filter Mode
NUM

FIGURE 11.9
Data | Filter | Advanced Filter dialog box

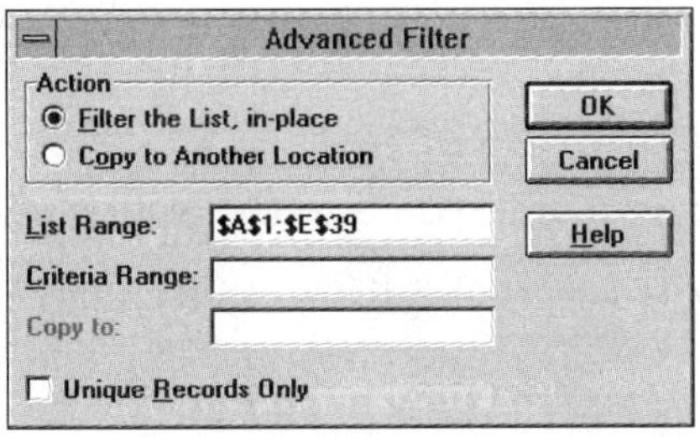

As Figure 11.9 illustrates, the Data | Filter | Advanced Filter command, like most Data commands, will analyze the worksheet and try to determine the range containing the list. You can (or must) make several selections in this dialog box. You can edit the List Range if Excel's analysis is incorrect. You can choose to filter the list in place, or to copy it to an extract range.

If you choose to copy it, you need to enter the reference of the extract range in the Copy to text box. See Figure 11.10 for an example of extract and criteria ranges. Note that these are below the database (A1:E39), that the extract range (A51:C51) contains only three of the field names, and that the criteria range (G51:G52) is based on a comparison of the salary field (>35000).

You must also enter a criteria range. See the earlier section, "Specification of Criteria," for more information on how to specify criteria. Finally, you can choose not to display duplicate records by selecting the Unique Records Only check box.

FIGURE 11.10
Extract and criteria ranges

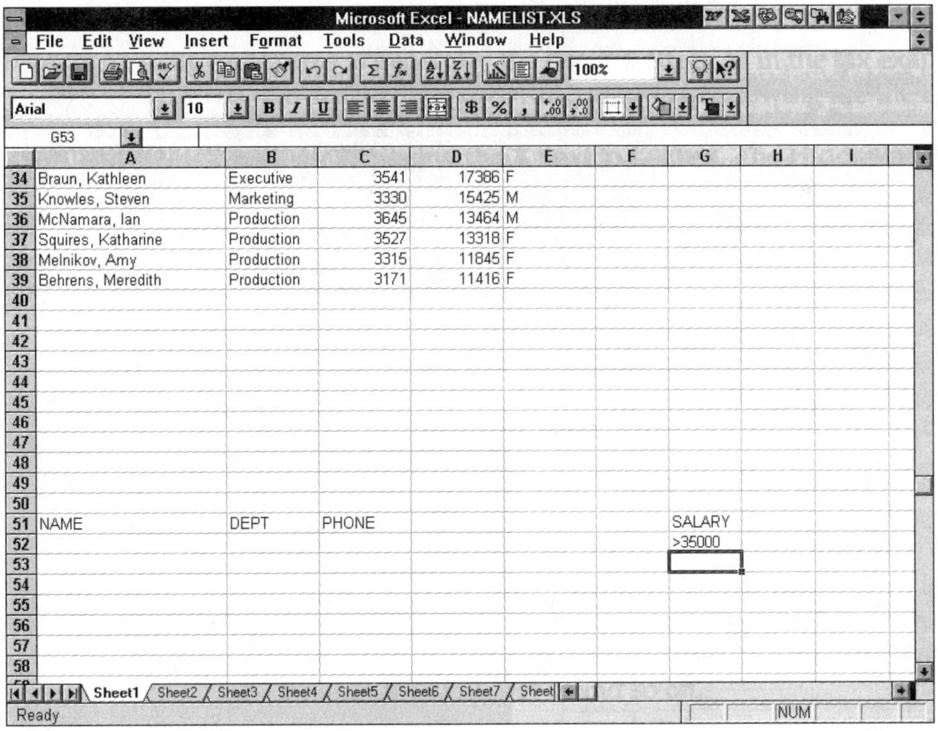

GUIDED ACTIVITY 11.2

Performing Database Operations

In this Guided Activity you use several of the database selection commands.

1. If you are not continuing from the previous Guided Activity, load Excel and open NAMELIST.

2. Select the range A1:E39. Give the Insert | Name | Define command. In the Names in Workbook text box, type Database. Click OK.

3. Using Data | Filter, find all persons who earn more than $35,000.

   a. Give the Data | Filter | AutoFilter command.

   b. Click the arrow next to SALARY and select Custom.

   c. Select the > operator and type in 35000. Click OK. Excel displays only those records that meet the criterion, >35000, as shown in Figure 11.11. Notice that the arrow next to the active criterion changes color, as do the column labels. The status bar lists the number of records that meet the criteria.

CHECKPOINT 11B How many records does Excel display?

   d. Issue the Data | Filter | AutoFilter command to turn off the AutoFilter command and exit filter mode.

4. Using Data | Filter | Advanced Filter, extract the Name, Dept, and Phone of all persons who earn more than $35,000.

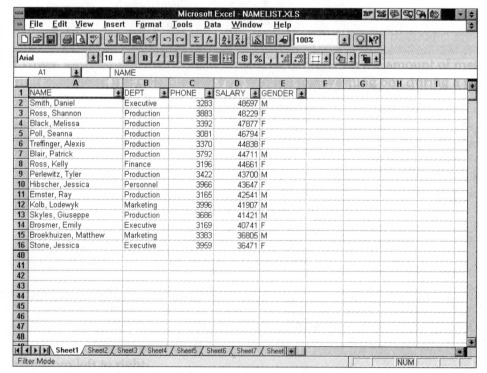

FIGURE 11.11
Results of the Data | Filter | AutoFilter command

a. Before you extract, you must create an extract range. Using the Copy and Paste procedure, copy the first three field names (NAME, DEPT, and PHONE) from the range A1:C1 to the range A51:C51. Using the Copy and Paste procedure ensures that you duplicate the original field names exactly in the output range.

b. Copy the field name in cell D1 to cell G51. In cell G52, enter the criterion >35000. The lower part of your workbook should now look like Figure 11.10.

c. Select any cell in the database and give the Data | Filter | Advanced Filter command. In the dialog box that appears, click Copy to Another Location in the Action group. Click in the Criteria Range text box, then use the pointing method to select the range G51:G52. Click in the Copy to text box and select the range A51:C51. Do not check the Unique Records Only option. Click OK. You should extract 15 records.

5. Change the criterion in G52 to >45000.

6. Follow these procedures to reissue the Data | Filter | Advanced Filter command.

   a. Select a cell somewhere in the database (A1:E39).

   b. Give the Data | Filter | Advanced Filter command. Select Copy to Another Location. Verify the rest of the settings. Click OK. Only four records should be extracted. The lower part of your workbook should look like Figure 11.12.

7. Change the criterion in cell G52 so that all who make less than $20,000 are selected, and extract again.

FIGURE 11.12
Results of the Data | Filter | Advanced Filter command

	A	B	C	D	E	F	G	H	I
34	Braun, Kathleen	Executive	3541	17386	F				
35	Knowles, Steven	Marketing	3330	15425	M				
36	McNamara, Ian	Production	3645	13464	M				
37	Squires, Katharine	Production	3527	13318	F				
38	Melnikov, Amy	Production	3315	11845	F				
39	Behrens, Meredith	Production	3171	11416	F				
40									
41									
42									
43									
44									
45									
46									
47									
48									
49									
50									
51	NAME	DEPT	PHONE				SALARY		
52	Smith, Daniel	Executive	3283				>45000		
53	Ross, Shannon	Production	3883						
54	Black, Melissa	Production	3392						
55	Poll, Seanna	Production	3081						

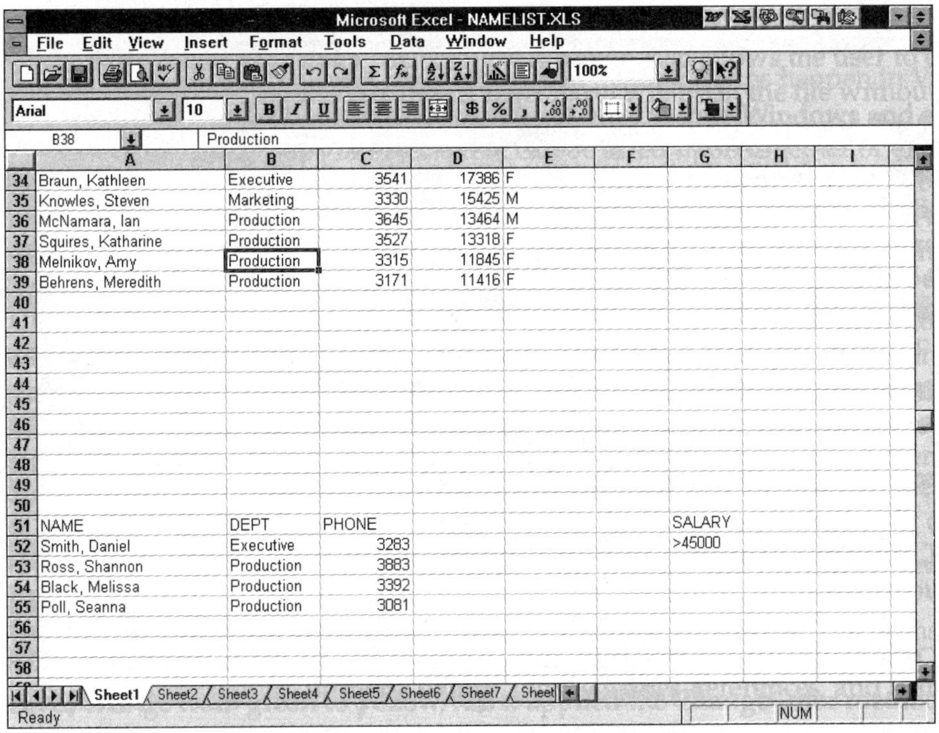

8. Print a copy of the extract range.

9. Type `Raise` in cell G51 and `=salary*1.15>40000` in cell G52, and extract again. (*Note:* Excel will display #NAME? in the cell, but the criterion will still work.) The last name in the extract range should be `Jessica Stone`.

10. Save the workbook. If you must leave the computer, exit Excel and back up your work.

GUIDED ACTIVITY 11.3

Using Combined Criteria

In this Guided Activity you continue to query the NAMELIST file. You use combined criteria to determine who is making more than $20,000 but not more than $30,000 in salary.

1. If you are not continuing from the previous Guided Activity, load Excel and open NAMELIST.

2. Change the criteria range to yield `20,000<Salary<=30,000`:

   a. Enter the text `Low` in cell F51.

   b. Enter the formula `=SALARY>20000` in cell F52.

   c. Enter the text `High` in cell G51.

   d. Enter the formula `=SALARY<=30000`.

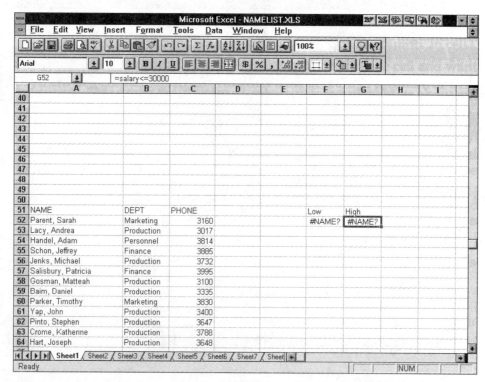

FIGURE 11.13
Results of the Data / Filter / Advanced Filter command using combined criteria

3. Select a cell in the database. Give the Data | Filter | Advanced Filter command. Choose Copy to Another Location. Change the Criteria Range to F51:G52. Click OK. Your workbook should now look like Figure 11.13.

4. Save the file. If you must leave the computer, exit Excel and back up your work.

Creating Subtotals in a Database

The ability to add subtotals to a database allows the user to convert a list of meaningless data into an analysis that can be used to answer specific questions. Among the files you copied from the Student Data Disk in Guided Activity 10.1 is a database of sales information for a national chain of pet stores named Animal House. The file is named PETSALES.XLS. The store has divided its sales into three product lines: rodents, birds, and mammals. The company has four regional salespersons: Eloff, Heredia, Marfori, and Ribeau. The database shows 1996 unit and dollar sales by month, by salesperson, and by product line. There is no exact correlation between unit and dollar sales, because of the mix of sales of different items within the product line, and varying discounts.

Unfortunately, the numbers are useless in their present form. The accountants of the Animal House company need to know which salesperson had the highest dollar sales for the year, and which month had the highest dollar sales. The Data | Subtotals command lets you easily answer these questions. However, before you can effectively use the Data | Subtotals command, you must prepare the database by properly sorting the records. To answer the question of which salesperson had the highest dollar sales for the year, you need to group all the sales for each salesperson together, so you need to sort the database by salesperson.

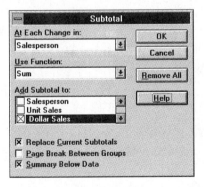

FIGURE 11.14
Data | Subtotals dialog box

Once the database is sorted, you are ready to proceed with the Data | Subtotals command. The dialog box, illustrated in Figure 11.14, allows you to make several decisions:

- Choose which field or fields to group by
- Choose which function to apply, such as sum, count, average, and so on
- Choose which field or fields to subtotal

- Choose whether to replace current subtotals or add another set of subtotals
- Choose whether to insert a page break after subtotals
- Choose whether to have a summary (grand total) at the end

GUIDED ACTIVITY 11.4

Creating Subtotals

In this Guided Activity you generate subtotals in a database.

1. If you are continuing from the previous Guided Activity, close NAMELIST.XLS and open PETSALES.XLS.

2. First, you need to determine the salesperson with the highest sales for the year. Sort the database in ascending order by salesperson.

3. Follow this procedure to give the Data | Subtotals command:

   a. Select a cell in the database range.

   b. Give the Data | Subtotals command. In the dialog box, select Salesperson in the At Each Change in box, select Sum in the Use Function box, and select Dollar Sales in the Add Subtotal to box. Click OK. If you made all the entries correctly, the Eloff total in row 40 should be $780,806.

CHECKPOINT 11C Which salesperson had the highest sales? How much?

4. The second question is which month had the highest dollar sales. Remove the subtotals by giving the Data | Subtotals command and selecting the Remove All button.

5. Re-sort the database in ascending order by month. Click the Options button, and select the list containing the names of the months of the year.

6. Give the Data | Subtotals command again. In the At Each Change in box, select Month; all other settings should be correct. Click OK. If you made the entries correctly, the highest monthly sales should be $318,593 in August.

7. Remove the subtotals by selecting Data | Subtotals and selecting the Remove All button. Save the workbook. If you must leave the computer, back up your work and exit Excel and Windows.

Creating a Pivot Table

One of the primary reasons for working with a database is to "massage" the data to determine answers to specific questions. The Data | Subtotals command discussed in the previous section allows one level of analysis. Most databases will allow you to answer all kinds of statistical questions, if only you know what questions to ask and how to ask them. Excel assists you in this quest with the Data | PivotTable command.

This command creates a table containing the number of instances or other statistics about a particular combination of values. A simple cross tabulation might have two values of each of two fields. One is called the "row category" and the other is called the "column category." The table is structured as follows:

	Val_1 of Col. Cat.	Val_2 of Col. Cat.	Row Total
Val_1 of Row Cat.	$Count_{1/1}$	$Count_{1/2}$	$Count_{1,*}$
Val_2 of Row Cat.	$Count_{2/1}$	$Count_{2/2}$	$Count_{2,*}$
Col. Total	$Count_{*,1}$	$Count_{*,2}$	$Count_{*,*}$ (Grand Total)

$Count_{1/1}$ is the number of records that have $Value_1$ of the row category field and $Value_1$ of the column category field. $Count_{1,*}$ is the number of records that have $Value_1$ of the row category field (any value of the column category field). In addition to counts, you can use Data | PivotTable to compute sums, averages, and several other statistics. More than one field can be used as row or column categories.

EXAMPLE

Consider the questions answered using the subtotals feature: how much did each salesperson sell and how much was sold in each month? To answer those questions, you had to sort the database twice and invoke the Data | Subtotals command twice. The Data | PivotTable command can answer both of those questions at the same time. Look ahead to Figure 11.17 to see the result of the command. Notice that salespersons are listed by column and months are listed by row. At the intersection of a column and row is the amount a salesperson sold that month. At the bottom of the columns are salesperson totals and at the right side of each row are the month totals. You can quickly view this output to determine highest salesperson and highest month. In addition, you can look for consistency—for instance, did the highest salesperson consistently outsell the others or did he have a few good months that put him over the top?

To begin the process of creating a pivot table, place the cell pointer in cell A3, which is the upper-left corner of the data in the PETSALES.XLS worksheet. Then give the Data | PivotTable command and Excel will present a four-step "Wizard" to guide you. The first step is to choose the source of the data. Since your data are on an Excel worksheet, you so indicate and click the Next > button. In step 2, Excel guesses the database range; in this case it correctly chooses A3:E147, and you click Next > to proceed.

Step 3, illustrated in Figure 11.15, is for the selection of which fields are in rows, which in columns, which on pages (allowing a three-dimensional table), and which are in the data area. Normally, row, column, and page fields will contain a limited number of text entries, and data area fields will be numeric data. As Excel instructs, drag field names to the area on the table where you wish them to appear. For this example, drag Salesperson to column and Month to row. Then drag Dollar Sales to the data area. Double-click on the data area to customize that field, as illustrated in Figure 11.16.

FIGURE 11.15
PivotTable Wizard step 3, specifying table layout

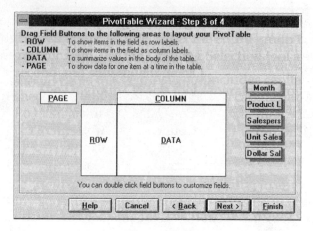

FIGURE 11.16
PivotTable Wizard step 3, customizing the data area

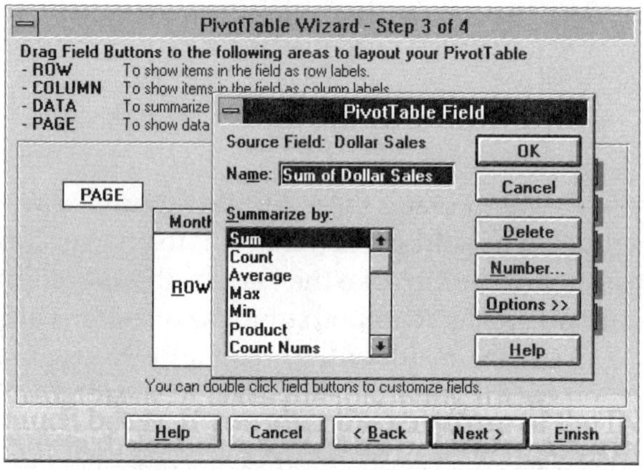

Once you have completed step 3, click Next >. The fourth and final step allows you to specify the starting cell, name, and other options for the table. With the cursor in the PivotTable Starting Cell area, we clicked the tab for Sheet2 (which appeared) and then clicked cell A1. Our resulting table, illustrated in Figure 11.17, occupied Sheet2 cells A1:F15.

If you assign the Product Line field to page, you can view results for each of the product lines individually (see Figure 11.18) or for all product lines at once. To rearrange the placement of data on the table, simply drag the button with a field name to a different location.

Pivot tables have their own special toolbar, which you can see in Figures 11.17 and 11.18. The tools have the following meanings:

 This tool calls the PivotTable Wizard, step 3, allowing you to change the arrangement of the table.

 This tool allows you to change the characteristics of the selected table item. For instance, click a cell in the data area, then click this tool, and you can change from the sum statistic to count, average, and so on.

 These tools allow you to group items (for instance grouping months into seasons), to ungroup them, and to control the amount of detail shown.

 This tool allows you to have page values displayed on separate sheets of the workbook.

FIGURE 11.17 *Result of Data | PivotTable command*

Sum of Dollar Sales	Salesperson				
Month	Eloff	Heredia	Marfori	Ribeau	Grand Total
January	81376	55783	44712	86180	268051
February	86945	67943	70664	88046	313598
March	68483	45723	58059	83098	255363
April	60097	73982	52304	85159	271542
May	43342	70554	63656	80657	258209
June	54595	66541	85843	72455	279434
July	52969	51016	77250	68152	249387
August	74341	76415	72881	94956	318593
September	63363	83761	56657	76484	280265
October	54020	59236	60421	81788	255465
November	64357	48406	63296	102128	278187
December	76918	58799	63802	86931	286450
Grand Total	780806	758159	769545	1006034	3314544

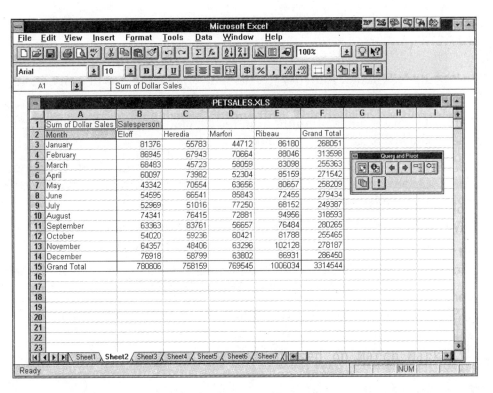

This tool refreshes the data on the table; this step is most useful when the data are drawn from a source such as a database outside of Excel that might change while you are working with the table.

FIGURE 11.18 *Result of Data | PivotTable command with page field*

Product Line	Mammals				
Sum of Dollar Sales	Salesperson				
Month	Eloff	Heredia	Marfori	Ribeau	Grand Total
January	15735	12408	7950	29534	65627
February	24798	14744	20932	41907	102381
March	10248	15812	11214	25482	62756
April	8915	23976	13987	39632	86510
May	7516	16611	15256	29797	69180
June	20511	21811	20331	28579	91232
July	19489	13930	18040	32781	84240
August	15961	14423	12332	36807	79523
September	5920	16430	10060	35344	67754
October	12895	9779	11122	21562	55358
November	9945	6361	16814	42748	75868
December	15150	16321	18823	37154	87448
Grand Total	167083	182606	176861	401327	927877

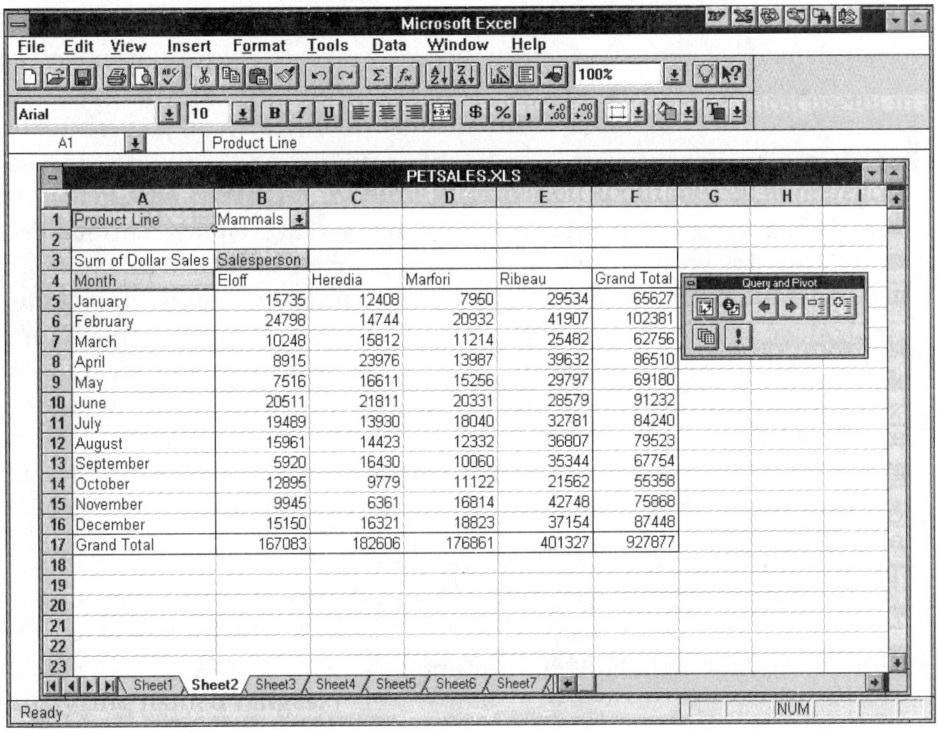

GUIDED ACTIVITY 11.5

Creating a Pivot Table

In this Guided Activity, you develop a pivot table as described in the previous section.

1. If you are not continuing from the previous Guided Activity, start Excel and load the PETSALES.XLS workbook.

2. Select A3 and give the Data | PivotTable command. Excel will present the PivotTable Wizard dialog box. Follow the discussion in the previous section to create a pivot table that looks like Figure 11.17.

3. Click the PivotTable Wizard button illustrated at left and place Product Line as the page field. Your report should now look like Figure 11.18.

4. Select one of the cells in the data area. Then click the PivotTable Field button illustrated at left and change the statistic to maximum.

5. Save the worksheet with the name PETPIVOT.XLS.

Database Statistical Functions

NOTE *The database statistical functions are more complex than the statistical functions discussed earlier in this book. If possible, use the statistical functions (AVERAGE( ), COUNT( ), and so on) rather than the functions discussed below.*

In the following definitions, the *database, field, criteria* (placed between parentheses and separated by commas with no spaces) are the means by which Excel knows which fields (columns) of which records (rows) to average, sum, and so forth.

Database is a range that contains field names and rows of data (records). If the range is named "Database" (or any other defined name), you can reference the range by name. See the discussion of database range in the "Terminology" section at the beginning of this unit. If you wish to perform database functions on more than one range in a worksheet, you can use any range that contains field names in the first row. You may specify the range by a range name or by cell references.

Field identifies the specific field that is summed, averaged, and the like. You can either use a field name enclosed in quotation marks (" ") or a field number. (In NAMELIST, "Name" is field 1, "Dept" is field 2, "Phone" is field 3, "Salary" is field 4, and "Gender" is field 5.) Using the field name is easier. Field numbers are less clear and tend to confuse most Excel users.

Criteria is a named or specified range that contains selection criteria. See the section earlier in this unit titled "Specification of Criteria."

DAVERAGE(database,field,criteria) This returns the average value of the items in the *field* column of *database* range that meet the *criteria*. For example, `=DAVERAGE(Database,"Salary",G1:G2)` averages the values of those cells in the Salary column that meet the criteria established in G1:G2 (this function is discussed in more detail in the "Example" section below).

DCOUNT(database,field,criteria) This returns the number of items that contain numbers in the *field* column of *database* range that meet the *criteria*. For example, =DCOUNT(A1:D40,3,G1:G2) counts the number of cells in the range C2:C40 (column C is the third field) that contain numbers and meet the criteria established in G1:G2.

DCOUNTA(database,*field*,criteria) This returns the number of items that are not blank in the *field* column of *database* range that meet the *criteria*. For example, =DCOUNTA(Database,"Dept",G1:G2) counts the number of cells in the range C2:C40 (column C is the Dept field) that contain data (that is, are not empty) and meet the criteria established in G1:G2. DCOUNT( ) counts only cells that contain numbers; DCOUNTA( ) counts all cells containing any form of data.

DGET(database,field,criteria) This returns the value in the *field* of a single record in the *database* range that meets the *criteria*. This function returns #VALUE! if no record meets the criteria. DGET( ) returns #NUM! if more than one record meets the criteria. For instance, if you put a person's name in the range F5:F6 (enter Name in F5 and the name to be found in F6), the function =DGET(Database,"SALARY",F5:F6) displays the salary for the designated person. If two persons have the same name (which could happen if you use the * wild card character in the criteria or if the database contains a duplicate entry), a #NUM! appears.

DMIN(database,field,criteria) This returns the minimum value in the *field* column of *database* range that meets the *criteria*. For example, =DMIN(Database,4,G1:G2) displays the minimum value of those cells in the range D2:D40 that meet the criteria established in G1:G2.

DMAX(database,field,criteria) This returns the maximum value in the *field* column of *database* range that meets the *criteria*. For example, =DMAX(Database,"PHONE",G1:G2) displays the maximum value of those cells in the Phone column that meet the criteria established in G1:G2.

DSTDEV(database,field,criteria) This returns the sample standard deviation of the items in the *field* column of *database* range that meet the *criteria*. For example, =DSTDEV(Database,"SALARY",G1:G2) displays the standard deviation statistic for those cells in the Salary column that meet the criteria established in G1:G2.

DSTDEVP(database,field,criteria) This returns the population standard deviation of the items in the *field* column of *database* range that meet the *criteria*. For example, =DSTDEVP(Database,"SALARY",G1:G2) displays the standard deviation statistic for those cells in the Salary column that meet the criteria established in G1:G2.

DSUM(database,field,criteria) This returns the sum of the items in the *field* column of *database* range that meet the *criteria*. For example, =DSUM(Database,"SALARY",G1:G2) displays the sum of those cells in the Salary column that meet the criteria established in G1:G2.

DVAR(database,field,criteria) This returns the sample variance of the items in the *field* column of *database* range that meet the *criteria*. For example,

=DVAR(Database,"SALARY",G1:G2) displays the sample variance of those cells in the Salary column that meet the criteria established in G1:G2.

DVARP(database,field,criteria) This returns the population variance of the items in the *field* column of *database* range that meet the *criteria*. For example, =DVARP(Database,"SALARY",G1:G2) displays the population variance of those cells in the Salary column that meet the criteria established in G1:G2.

DPRODUCT(database,field,criteria) This returns the product of the items in the *field* column of *database* range that meet the *criteria*. For example, =DPRODUCT(Database,"SALARY",G1:G2) displays the product of those cells in the Salary column that meet the criteria established in G1:G2.

EXAMPLE

Assume that you have been asked to compute the average salary of all persons in the Executive department. (This example is illustrated in the next Guided Activity.) You use G1:G2 as the criteria range. In cell G1 you put the field name, Dept, and in cell G2 you put the comparison criterion, E. (This criterion would not suffice if the organization had an Ecology department.) You put the formula in cell G7 and text in cells G5 and G6 to identify the value. The appropriate formula is =DAVERAGE(Database,"Salary",G1:G2), which translates to: *Average all numbers in the Salary column in the range named "Database" that meet the criteria specified in range G1:G2, and put the result in this cell.* The result appears instantly. To compute the average salary of all persons in the Finance department, all you have to do is change the text in cell G2 to F or Finance.

GUIDED ACTIVITY 11.6

Using Database Statistical Functions

In this Guided Activity you use database statistical functions in a workbook.

1. If you are not continuing from the previous Guided Activity, load Excel and open NAMELIST.

2. Using DAVERAGE(database,field,criteria), compute the average salary of all persons in the Executive department, as illustrated in Figure 11.19. You will need to change the number format and the column width.

3. Now change the criteria so that the average is of all persons in the Marketing department.

4. Print a copy of the range A1:G40.

5. Save the file. If you must leave the computer, exit Excel and back up your work.

FIGURE 11.19
A database statistical function

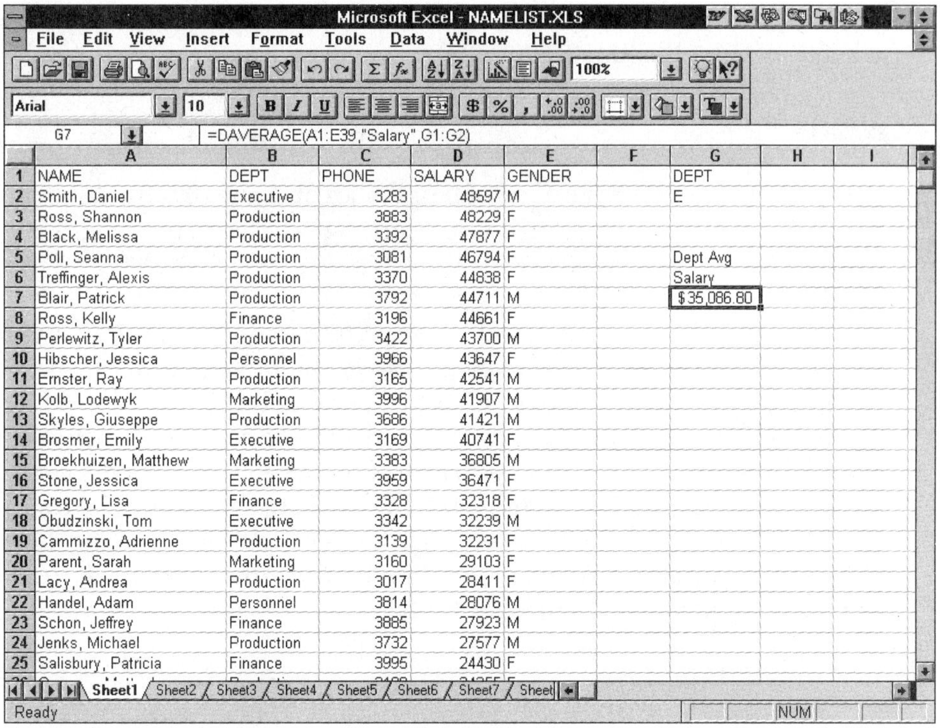

	A	B	C	D	E	F	G	H	I
							=DAVERAGE(A1:E39,"Salary",G1:G2)		
1	NAME	DEPT	PHONE	SALARY	GENDER		DEPT		
2	Smith, Daniel	Executive	3283	48597	M		E		
3	Ross, Shannon	Production	3883	48229	F				
4	Black, Melissa	Production	3392	47877	F				
5	Poll, Seanna	Production	3081	46794	F		Dept Avg		
6	Treffinger, Alexis	Production	3370	44838	F		Salary		
7	Blair, Patrick	Production	3792	44711	M		$35,086.80		
8	Ross, Kelly	Finance	3196	44661	F				
9	Perlewitz, Tyler	Production	3422	43700	M				
10	Hibscher, Jessica	Personnel	3966	43647	F				
11	Ernster, Ray	Production	3165	42541	M				
12	Kolb, Lodewyk	Marketing	3996	41907	M				
13	Skyles, Giuseppe	Production	3686	41421	M				
14	Brosmer, Emily	Executive	3169	40741	F				
15	Broekhuizen, Matthew	Marketing	3383	36805	M				
16	Stone, Jessica	Executive	3959	36471	F				
17	Gregory, Lisa	Finance	3328	32318	F				
18	Obudzinski, Tom	Executive	3342	32239	M				
19	Cammizzo, Adrienne	Production	3139	32231	F				
20	Parent, Sarah	Marketing	3160	29103	F				
21	Lacy, Andrea	Production	3017	28411	F				
22	Handel, Adam	Personnel	3814	28076	M				
23	Schon, Jeffrey	Finance	3885	27923	M				
24	Jenks, Michael	Production	3732	27577	M				
25	Salisbury, Patricia	Finance	3995	24430	F				

A Data Distribution Table

When you ask questions such as "How many people have salaries in the ranges $10,000 to $20,000 and $20,000 to $30,000?", you are asking for a distribution of the raw data. You can use the FREQUENCY(*data_array,bins_array*) function to compute the distribution of values of a range of numbers. When complete, the *data distribution table* is structured as follows:

cutpoint$_1$ count$_1$
cutpoint$_2$ count$_2$
cutpoint$_3$ count$_3$
blank   count$_4$

The left column contains a series of *cutpoints*. This series of values is known as the *bin array*. The right column contains an array function that computes the count of the number of values that are greater than the cutpoint in the row above and less than or equal to the cutpoint in the same row. Thus, count$_1$ is the number of values less than or equal to cutpoint$_1$; count$_2$ is the number of values greater than cutpoint$_1$ and less than or equal to cutpoint$_2$; and so on. Notice that there is one more count than cutpoint. This last count (count$_4$ in this example) contains the number of values greater than the last cutpoint (cutpoint$_3$ in this example).

When you construct a data distribution table, you will need to specify the *data_array* argument (the field of the database that you are counting) and the *bin_array* argument (the series of cutpoints). When you create the data distribution table, you must remember that FREQUENCY( ) is an array function. You must select the cells to the right of the bin array (not forgetting the last row that does not have a cutpoint), enter the FREQUENCY( ) function and arguments, then press Ctrl Shift Enter to actually enter the function.

EXAMPLE

Assume that you have a list of employees and one of the columns is Salary. You want to know how many persons are earning salaries in the ranges $0 to $20,000, greater than $20,000 to $30,000, greater than $30.000 to $40,000, and greater than $40,000.

The salary data are contained in the column range D2:D39. This is part of the database. The first step is to create the bin array. You enter Salary<= in cell G10; this is for information only. Enter cutpoint 20,000 in cell G11, =G11+10000 in cell G12, and =G12+10000 in cell G13. You use formulas to quickly change the set of cutpoints; for example, you could enter 15,000 in cell G11 to create a different distribution. Cell G14 could be blank, but you decide to enter a special formula— =">"&TEXT(G13,"#,##0") —to assist others in understanding the results. [2] Column G now looks like the illustration below. (You might have to use numeric format and alignment commands to duplicate this example.)

	F	G
4		
5		Dept Avg
6		Salary
7		$29,431.80
8		
9		
10		Salary <=
11		20,000
12		30,000
13		40,000
14		> 40,000

You are now ready to enter the FREQUENCY( ) function. Follow the instructions in Guided Activity 11.7 to complete this example.

GUIDED ACTIVITY 11.7

Computing a Data Distribution Table

In this Guided Activity you compute a data distribution table.

1. If you are not continuing from the previous Guided Activity, load Excel and open NAMELIST.

2. Following the discussion in the preceding section, create the bin array.

3. Select the range H11:H14, type =FREQUENCY(, then select the range D2:D39. Type , (a comma), then select the range G11:G14, and press Ctrl Shift Enter. Your screen should look like Figure 11.20.

---

[2] The TEXT( ) function, discussed in Unit 14, is used to combine a numeric entry with a text entry.

FIGURE 11.20
A data distribution table

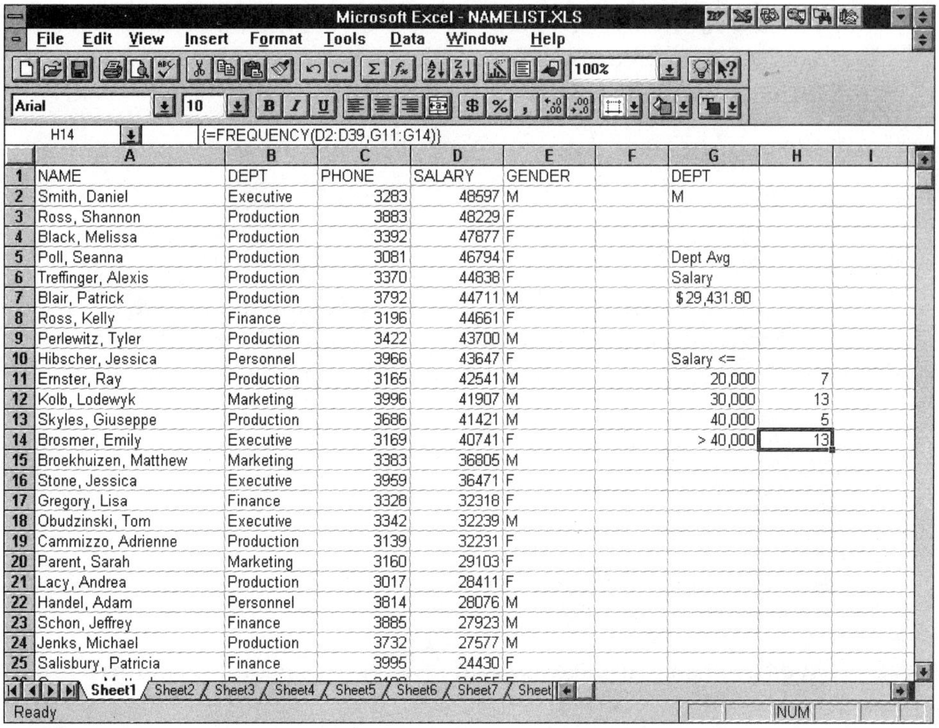

![Figure 11.20 - Excel spreadsheet showing NAMELIST.XLS with columns NAME, DEPT, PHONE, SALARY, GENDER, and a data distribution table with Dept Avg Salary $29,431.80 and Salary <= 20,000: 7; 30,000: 13; 40,000: 5; > 40,000: 13. Formula bar shows {=FREQUENCY(D2:D39,G11:G14)}]

4. Save the workbook.

Using a Data Form

One of the nice features of Excel is its ability to create a *data form* to simplify the input of data into a database. Once you have set the database, issue the Data | Form command to create a form (illustrated in Figure 11.21) containing each of the field names and an entry box for each field. The entry boxes will contain the entries for the first record of the database. Click on the New button to enter new records.

FIGURE 11.21
Data form

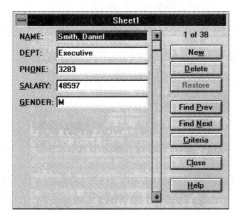

The data form has uses that go beyond making data entry easier. You can also use it to view existing records, delete records, and set criteria. Figure 11.21 illustrates a data form for NAMELIST.

GUIDED ACTIVITY 11.8

Using a Data Form

This Guided Activity examines the uses of the data form. The Personnel department for the company represented by NAMELIST.XLS has made some changes. You have been asked to delete the names of Tom Obudzinski and Andrea Lacy. You have also been asked to insert the information for three new hires:

```
Jokerst, Denise    Executive     3342    $34,159    F
Preston, Pat       Finance       3800    $42,347    F
Homan, Tammy       Production    3017    $26,956    F
```

1. If you are not continuing from the previous Guided Activity, load Excel and open NAMELIST.

2. Give the Data | Form command. Excel displays the data form illustrated in Figure 11.21.

3. To quickly find the record for Tom Obudzinski, click on Criteria and type `Obud` in the Name text box. Click on Find Next.

4. When Tom's record appears, click on the Delete button. Click on OK after receiving the warning message.

5. Repeat this procedure for Andrea Lacy.

6. To insert the new records, click on New. Enter the data for each new hire. Press [Tab] between fields; press [Enter] when the record is complete. If you press [Enter] before the record is complete, simply click the Criteria button, clear any criteria entries, then click on the Find Prev button to back up one record and edit the entry.

7. When the new records are inserted, click on Close to close the data form. Go to cell A38. The new records have been inserted at the end of the database. Save your work as NAMLIST2.XLS.

EXERCISE 11.1

More Database Exercises

In this Exercise, you continue to use the NAMELIST file.

1. If you are not continuing from the previous Guided Activity, load Excel. Open NAMELIST.

2. Sort the database by department in descending order of salary (that is, highest salary at the top of each department). (*Hint*: You need two keys, with the Dept column being the first key.)

3. Determine the maximum, mean (average), and minimum of the salaries in each department.

4. Save your work.

EXERCISE 11.2

The Perfect Job (V)

1. If you are not continuing from the previous Exercise or Guided Activity, follow the startup procedure outlined in Unit 1 to load Windows and enter Excel.

2. Open JOBS.XLS, then do the following steps to further analyze your job prospects.

3. Sort the data in descending order of Salary. Make sure that you include all necessary columns in the sort range.

4. Extract a list of jobs (Company, City, Title, Salary, and Adj. Sal.) for which the adjusted salary is greater than or equal to $23,000.

5. Save the file when you are finished.

EXERCISE 11.3

A Check Register (VI)

1. If you are not continuing from the previous Exercise or Guided Activity, follow the startup procedure outlined in Unit 1 to load Windows and enter Excel.

2. Open the CHECKS.XLS workbook.

3. You have a scholarship that will pay for your living expenses (rent and food). You would like to keep a running total of the checks you have written for those two items. To do so, you must add a Code column that will contain R for reimbursable items and N for others. Put these data in column G.

4. Once the data are coded, you can use a database statistical function to extract the sum of all reimbursable items. Put a criterion in I1:I2 and the function in cell I4.

5. Check your answer by manually adding the amounts of the checks that are reimbursable.

6. Save your work.

EXERCISE 11.4

League Standings (III)

After a period of time, the standings change because teams win and lose games. Enter new won/lost data for your league (or use the Pac-10 data from February 8, 1993, listed below). If you used the correct formulas when you created the LEAGUE.XLS spreadsheet in Unit 6, the new percentages will appear. Sort your data based on conference percentage, with overall percentage used as a tiebreaker. Save your work.

Team	Conference			Overall		
	W	L	PCT.	W	L	PCT.
Arizona	9	0		15	2	
Oregon St.	6	3		10	8	
USC	4	5		11	7	
California	4	5		10	7	
UCLA	4	5		14	7	
Arizona St.	6	3		12	5	
Washington	5	4		11	7	
Washington St.	6	3		12	6	
Stanford	1	8		6	15	
Oregon	0	9		7	14	

EXERCISE 11.5

Business Mileage (VI)

Open the MILES96.XLS workbook. Add the following data and copy the formula in the Miles column that subtracts the reading of the current row from the reading of the row below. *Do not copy this formula to the January 15 row.* Develop a criterion that selects only those records (rows) with business use, and another that selects only those records with pleasure use. Develop two database statistical functions, one that sums all business use miles and another that sums all pleasure use miles. Save your work.

Date	Reading	Use	Miles	Notation
1/11	12795.2	B		Visit Office Showcase (store)
1/12	12863.4	B		Call on Anderson account
1/13	12877.3	B		Deliver blueprints for Devonwood Clubhouse
1/14	12891.8	B		Give talk to Western University Architecture class
1/15	12921.1	P		Family use

EXERCISE 11.6

Things to Do (IV)

Retrieve your TO-DO.XLS spreadsheet and add more entries, without regard to chronological order. As you enter more items, you might note that the dates get out of order. Sort by the date column. Save your work.

EXERCISE 11.7

Software Inventory (I)

1. Open the file SOFTLIST found on your data disk. This file contains a list of common business computer applications, together with their native platform, publisher, and category.

2. Sort the list first by platform, then by publisher, then by category, and finally by title. Save your work as SOFTSORT.XLS.

EXERCISE 11.8

A Statistical Problem

You have a list of 100 numbers. You are being asked to create a formula that will determine how many of the numbers in the list are greater than the average of the list. The formula itself should be self-contained in one cell. There are at least two ways of doing this. One involves a statistical function; the other an array formula. Either solution is quite acceptable. If you use the statistical function, you will need a criteria range on the worksheet.

1. Create a column of 100 random numbers in the range C2:C101. Use the RAND( ) function and then the Copy and Paste Special routine to convert the functions to constant values. Your numbers will be easier to work with if you multiply the result of the RAND( ) function by 1,000 and round it to an integer.

2. Create the required formula in cell A1. If you use the statistical function method, begin the criteria range in cell A3. Also, the statistical function method will require a field name at the top of the list (cell C1). Good luck! Save your solution as PROBLEM.XLS

Review Questions

1. Define the following database terms:
    *a. Database
    b. Field name
    c. Record

*d. Field

e. Criteria range

f. Extract range

2. For this question, assume that your criteria range is K1:K2 and that you are using the NAMELIST.XLS database. To establish each of the criteria listed below, what would you put in cell K1 and what would you put in cell K2?

*a. Select everyone whose last name is Ross.

b. Select everyone whose telephone number is 3883.

*c. Select everyone in the Personnel department.

d. Select those whose salary is less than $20,000.

3. For this question, assume that you are using the NAMELIST.XLS database. To sort by salary, from highest to lowest, what would you specify as:

*a. The sort key

b. The sort order

4. For this question, assume that you are using the NAMELIST.XLS database. The criteria range begins in cell F1. To determine the lowest phone number in the Production department:

*a. What formula would you use?

b. What would be the contents of the criteria range?

Key Terms

Alternate criteria	Cutpoint	Grouping
Bin array	Data distribution table	Key
Combined criteria	Data form	Logical operator
Comparison criteria	Database	Multiple criteria
Computed criteria	Extract range	Record
Computed field	Field	Subtotal
Criteria	Field name	Text string
Criteria range	Filter	Wild card character

Documentation Research

Referring to the Excel *User's Guide*, find and record the page number of each of the commands discussed in this unit. We recommend that you also write the page number in the margin next to the discussion of the command in the unit.

1. Data | Sort—how can you return a list to its original, unsorted state after sorting several times?

2. When evaluating criteria, Excel assumes that there is an asterisk at the end of any text you enter as a criterion. How would you match only those records containing, for example, Smith (not Smithson)?

3. How can you display subtotal rows above the detail data?

APPLICATION

Predicting the Future

In this exercise, you perform data computation and selection operations on an existing database.

1. Start Excel and open PORTFOLI.XLS. This is one of the files you copied to your data disk in Guided Activity 10.1.

2. Note that this workbook is a database with three fields: Name, Act1995, and Pred1996. The entries are names of stock, their 1995 rating, and their 1996 (predicted) rating, respectively. The first 25 rows of the workbook are illustrated in Figure E.1.

3. Create a data distribution table to compute the number of stocks whose 1996 ratings are in each of the following intervals: less than or equal to –250, greater than –250 and less than or equal to 0, greater than 0 and less than or equal to 250, and greater than 250. Start building the table in cell E1.

4. Sort the database in descending order of 1995 ratings. Ensure that the sort range includes all 3 columns (but not the distribution table) and all 37 rows (but not the field names).

5. Print the entire sorted workbook. Circle the name of the stock with the tenth highest rating in 1995.

6. Extract a list of stocks for which the 1996 rating exceeds the 1995 rating. Start the extract range in cell A41.

7. Compute the average 1995 and 1996 ratings of stocks for which the 1996 rating exceeds the 1995 rating. These values should appear in cells E7 and E8.

8. Save your work.

FIGURE E.1
PORTFOLI.XLS workbook

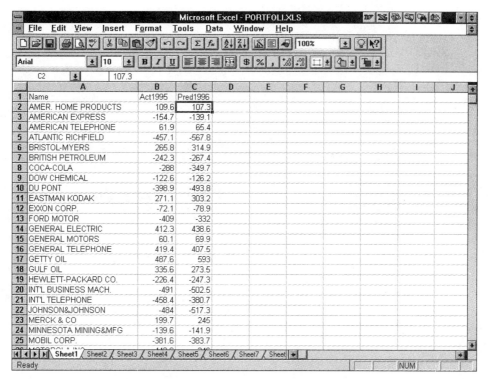

Advanced Windowing and Preference Operations

In this unit you learn about advanced operations available through the View and Window menus and the Tools | Options command. The View menu controls what you see on the screen. The Tools | Options command affects how Excel interacts with the user. The Window menu facilitates dealing with a complex workbook by allowing you to open several windows with different views of the workbook.

Learning Objectives

At the completion of this unit you should know

1. all the display options that are available,
2. what panes and windows are and how they make it easier to use a large workbook,
3. the various toolbars and what tools are available,
4. what cell and workbook protection are and how they facilitate data entry.

At the completion of this unit you should be able to

1. set the Excel options to any of the available choices,
2. use multiple windows and panes to facilitate large workbooks,
3. create and apply range names,
4. suppress the display of zero values,

5. use Undo and Repeat commands,
6. use find and replace procedures,
7. establish protected and hidden cells,
8. place graphic objects on a worksheet,
9. display various toolbars,
10. customize a toolbar,
11. open multiple windows on a workbook,
12. change the zoom ratio of a worksheet,
13. toggle worksheet and workbook protection on and off.

Important Commands

Edit | Find
Edit | Replace
Insert | Name | Apply
Insert | Name | Create
Insert | Name | Define
Tools | Options
Tools | Protection
View | Toolbars
View | Zoom
Window | New Window

Customizing Your Display

The Tools | Options command provides several techniques that you can use to alter the appearance and function of the workbook. The ten tabs in this dialog box allow you to configure Excel to your preferences.

View Tab

The View tab is illustrated in Figure 12.1. You can use the options in this dialog box to control several aspects of the workbook, detailed in the text that follows.

FIGURE 12.1
Tools / Options dialog box, View tab

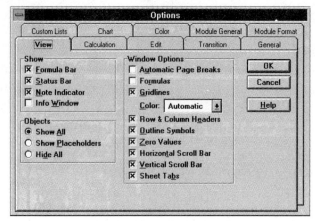

THE SHOW GROUP

The Show group contains four check boxes that allow you to determine whether to display the formula bar, the status bar, the note indicator, or the Info window.

THE OBJECTS GROUP

The Objects group contains three option buttons that determine how Excel will display graphical objects on the worksheet. Depending on the selection chosen, graphical objects (bitmaps, embedded charts, objects drawn with the drawing tools) will either display in their entirety, display as a dashed rectangle (a *placeholder*), or not display at all. These options do not affect the printed workbook. They are provided to increase the speed at which the computer can redraw the screen after data entry. Depending on their complexity, and the type of hardware being used, displaying graphical objects can slow the computer down immensely.

THE WINDOW OPTIONS GROUP

The Window Options group contains nine check boxes and a drop-down list box. The default for all check boxes except Formulas and Automatic Page Breaks is on.

AUTOMATIC PAGE BREAKS When checked, a dashed line appears above and to the left of automatic page breaks. This dashed line is distinguishable from gridlines and from manual page break markers.

FORMULAS When checked, the entries in cells will display as formulas, rather than as the results of formulas.

GRIDLINES When checked, the grid displays on the monitor. When Gridlines is checked on File | Page Setup, this option also controls whether gridlines display in a printout. See the discussion on the File | Page Setup command in Unit 5 for controlling gridline display in a printed workbook.

COLOR This option is completely cosmetic; it allows the user to change the color of the row and column headings and the gridlines. If you select Automatic, Excel defaults to the text color selected in the Windows Control Panel.

ROW & COLUMN HEADERS When checked, the row and column labels display on the monitor. This option does not affect whether these labels display in a printout. See the discussion on the File | Page Setup command in Unit 5 for controlling label display in a printed workbook.

OUTLINE SYMBOLS When checked, the symbols for the outlining procedure display on the monitor above the column labels and to the left of the row labels.

ZERO VALUES When checked, a 0 displays in all cells containing a zero value. When unchecked, any cell containing a zero value is blank.

HORIZONTAL SCROLL BAR When checked, the horizontal scroll bar is displayed at the bottom of the document window.

VERTICAL SCROLL BAR When checked, the vertical scroll bar is displayed at the right side of the document window.

SHEET TABS When checked, the sheet tabs are displayed at the bottom of the document window left of the horizontal scroll bar.

Calculation Tab

The Calculation tab is thoroughly discussed in Unit 7. See that discussion for details concerning this tab.

Edit Tab

The Edit tab, illustrated in Figure 12.2, contains options regarding the editing abilities of the Excel application. The specific options are as follows:

EDIT DIRECTLY IN CELL When checked, allows editing in the cell, as well as in the formula bar.

ALLOW CELL DRAG AND DROP When checked, allows copying and moving via drag and drop.

ALERT BEFORE OVERWRITING CELLS When checked, displays a warning before dropping cells over cells that contain data.

FIGURE 12.2
Tools | Options dialog box, Edit tab

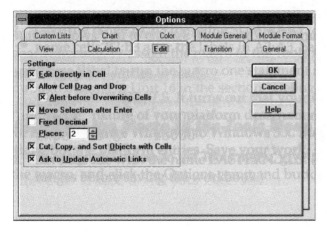

MOVE SELECTION AFTER ENTER When checked, moves the active cell down one row each time the [Enter] key is pressed.

FIXED DECIMAL When checked, causes Excel to automatically place a decimal point at the specified location in any numbers that are entered. For instance, if you enter a 2 in the Places box, and then enter 123 in the workbook, Excel will enter the number 1.23. Entering a negative number in the Places box will cause Excel to embed zeros at the end of entered numbers.

CUT, COPY, AND SORT OBJECTS WITH CELLS When checked, keeps objects with cells when you cut, copy, filter, or sort the cells.

ASK TO UPDATE AUTOMATIC LINKS When checked, displays a dialog box asking if you wish to update links to other documents or applications.

Transition Tab

The selections on the Transition tab, illustrated in Figure 12.3, are designed to help users who are changing from Lotus 1-2-3 to Excel.

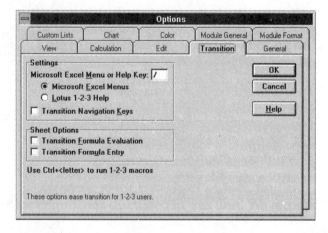

FIGURE 12.3
Tools / Options dialog box, Transition tab

MICROSOFT EXCEL MENU OR HELP KEY Depending on which of the option buttons is selected, the key entered here will either access the Excel menu (like the [Alt] key) or the "Help for Lotus 1-2-3 Users" window.

TRANSITION NAVIGATION KEYS When selected, causes keys like [Home] and [End] to act as they do in Lotus 1-2-3 rather than as they do in Excel. It also causes the ', ", and ^ symbols to act as alignment symbols, as they do in Lotus 1-2-3.

TRANSITION FORMULA EVALUATION When checked, evaluates certain expressions in formulas, such as text strings, Boolean expressions, and database criteria, in the manner used by Lotus 1-2-3.

TRANSITION FORMULA ENTRY When checked, converts formulas entered in the Lotus 1-2-3 syntax into Excel syntax.

General Tab

The General tab, illustrated in Figure 12.4, deals with information regarding the user and the application in general.

FIGURE 12.4
Tools / Options dialog box, General tab

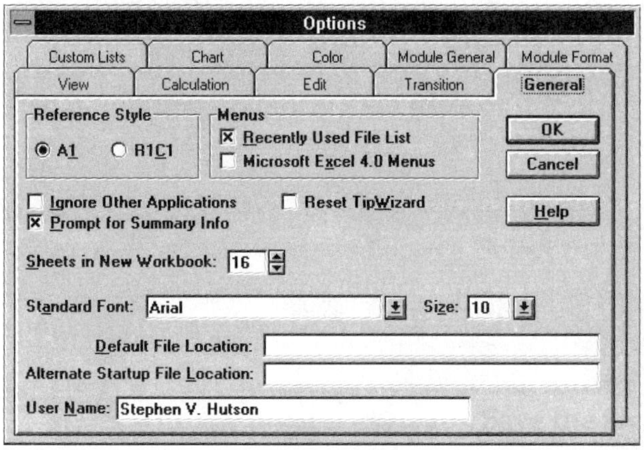

The Reference Style group contains two option buttons. The default, A1, labels columns with letters and rows with numbers. The other choice, R1C1, causes all references to be referred to in the R1C1 style (where the R stands for the number of rows and the C stands for the number of columns).

The Menus group contains two check boxes. The first, Recently Used File List, displays the four documents you most recently saved as commands 1, 2, 3, and 4 in the File menu. The second check box, Microsoft Excel 4.0 Menus, displays the menu structure from the previous version of Excel. The remaining settings in this dialog box are not grouped.

IGNORE OTHER APPLICATIONS When checked, causes Excel to ignore requests from other applications using DDE (Dynamic Data Exchange). We discuss DDE in Unit 13.

PROMPT FOR SUMMARY INFO When checked, causes Excel to display the Summary Info dialog box the first time a file is saved.

RESET TIPWIZARD When checked, allows the TipWizard to display tips you may have already seen.

SHEETS IN NEW WORKBOOK Allows you to specify the default number of worksheets in a new workbook.

STANDARD FONT Allows you to specify the standard font for new sheets and workbooks.

SIZE Allows you to specify the standard font size for new sheets and workbooks.

DEFAULT FILE LOCATION Allows you to specify the primary location where Excel will look for worksheet files.

ALTERNATE STARTUP FILE LOCATION Allows you to specify an additional *startup directory* (in addition to XLSTART). All files located in either XLSTART or the alternate startup directory will be activated each time you enter Excel.

USER NAME Allows you to specify the user name, which is used by the Scenario Manager and the Summary Info dialog box, among other places.

Custom Lists Tab

The Custom Lists tab is discussed fully in Unit 9. See that discussion for details concerning this tab.

Chart Tab

The Chart tab, illustrated in Figure 12.5, contains options that define how Excel will treat specific charting situations.

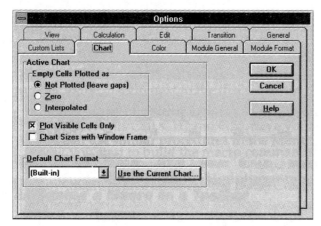

FIGURE 12.5
Tools / Options dialog box, Chart tab

The Active Chart group contains one set of option buttons and two check boxes. All selections made in this group apply only to the active chart. To make these settings the default, create a chart with these settings and make it the default chart format (this procedure is explained shortly).

The group of option buttons labeled "Empty Cells Plotted as" determines how Excel will treat empty cells in a line chart. The first option, Not Plotted, causes gaps to be left in the line, making the line divided. The second option causes empty cells to be plotted as zero, causing the line to plummet to zero for all empty cells. The third option interpolates from the other data in the chart series and calculates an average value for that data point.

The Plot Visible Cells Only check box causes Excel to chart only visible cells when an outline is partially collapsed.

The Chart Sizes with Window Frame check box is equivalent to giving the View I Sized With Window command. It causes the chart to be redrawn to fit the window whenever the window is resized.

The Default Chart Format drop-down list box allows you to select the default for all new charts. The default entries in this list are (Built-in) and Microsoft Excel 4.0. You can use the current chart as a default chart format by clicking on the Use the Current Chart button. Excel will display the Add Custom AutoFormat dialog box illustrated below. Type in a name for the new chart format and click OK.

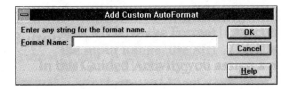

Color Tab

With the Color tab, illustrated in Figure 12.6, you can create a custom color palette or copy colors from another document. The color palette consists of the 56 possible colors that Excel can display and use at one time. If you are printing charts or worksheets on a color printer, this option gives you substantially more flexibility in the creative process.

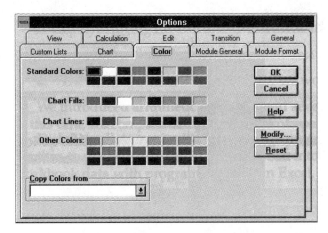

FIGURE 12.6
Tools / Options dialog box, Color tab

Module General Tab

Options in the Module General tab, illustrated in Figure 12.7, allow you to control how Excel runs and displays Visual Basic modules. We discuss Visual Basic and macro modules in detail in Units 15 and 16.

FIGURE 12.7
Tools / Options dialog box, Module General tab

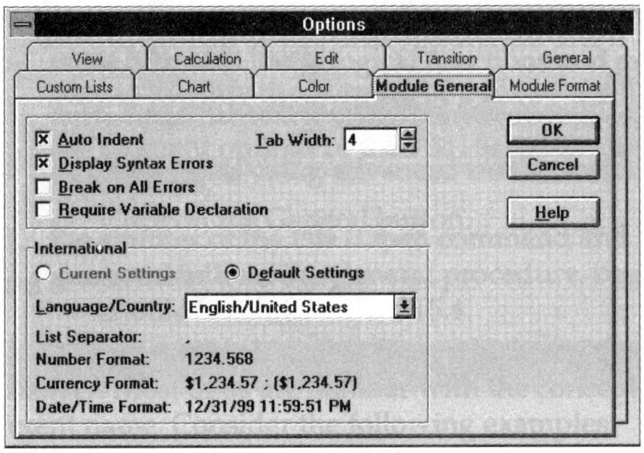

AUTO INDENT When checked, causes Excel to automatically indent certain lines of Visual Basic code.

DISPLAY SYNTAX ERRORS When checked, causes Excel to check the syntax of Visual Basic code and highlight syntax errors.

BREAK ON ALL ERRORS When checked, causes Excel to halt the running of any procedure when an error is encountered.

REQUIRE VARIABLE DECLARATION When checked, Excel requires that all variables be specifically declared before running the procedure. If left unchecked, Excel creates a variable from any unknown word.

TAB WIDTH Determines the number of spaces that lines will be indented.

INTERNATIONAL Allows you to specify the country settings for Visual Basic procedures. It also displays the effect of your choices.

Module Format Tab

The Module Format tab, illustrated in Figure 12.8, allows you to specify the formatting characteristics of Visual Basic (macro) modules.

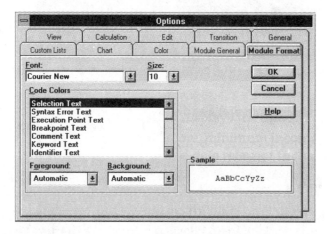

FIGURE 12.8
Tools / Options dialog box, Module Format tab

FONT Allows you to select the font Excel uses in Visual Basic modules.

SIZE Allows you to select the font size Excel uses in Visual Basic modules.

CODE COLORS Allows you to choose various types of text found in Visual Basic modules.

FOREGROUND Allows you to select the foreground color for the selected type of Visual Basic text.

BACKGROUND Allows you to select the background color for the selected type of Visual Basic text.

SAMPLE Displays the effect of your choices.

Document and Cell Protection

You will not be using workbooks long before you realize that you want to protect certain important portions of them from tampering, or even from a careless keystroke that can erase in an instant a formula that took you a long time to perfect. Perhaps you have designed a data entry form for someone else to use, but since he or she may not have your understanding of Excel, you are concerned that entries may be made in the wrong part of the workbook that will destroy your work.[1]

In Excel, the solution to this is called *cell protection*, which comes in two steps: by default, all cells in a new workbook are locked; however, the locking does not actually take effect until the document is protected.

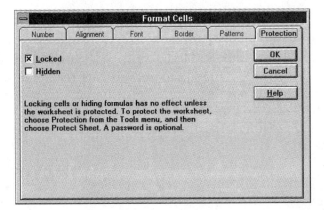

FIGURE 12.9
Format | Cells dialog box, Protection tab

To protect a document, first determine which cells may be changed. Select these cells, issue the Format | Cells command, select the Protection tab (shown in Figure 12.9), and *unlock* them by removing the X next to Locked. The Hidden option allows you to hide the underlying formula from prying eyes. If you select a hidden cell while the document is protected, the formula bar will not display the formula for that cell; it will remain blank.

After you have determined which cells are to be *locked*, which are to be unlocked, and which are to be *hidden*, issue the Tools | Protection | Protect Sheet command. Excel presents the dialog box illustrated in Figure 12.10, where you can decide whether to protect the cell contents, the scenarios, the graphic objects, or any combination of the three.

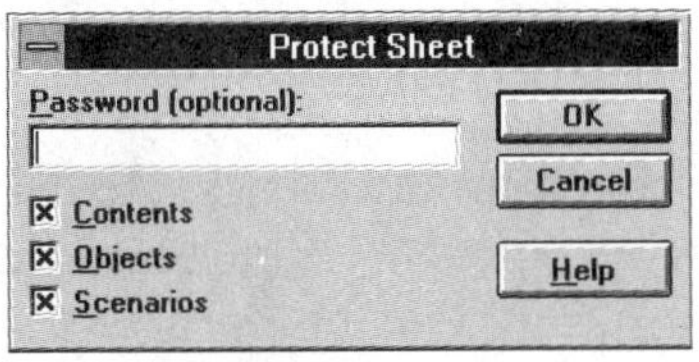

FIGURE 12.10
Tools | Protection | Protect Sheet dialog box

---

1 A backup copy of the workbook file will put a lot of this worry to rest.

You enter a password in the Password box to complete the protection of the workbook. When you enter a password, it does not appear on the screen. Instead, a series of asterisks (*) shows how many characters are in the password. You are then asked to reenter the password, in order to avoid the tragedy of not being able to reach your own data because you accidentally mistyped the password when you assigned it. If you do not enter a password, anyone can issue the Unprotect Sheet command and gain access to the workbook.

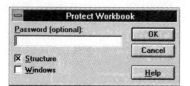

FIGURE 12.11
Tools / Protection / Protect Workbook dialog box

You can also protect the workbook with the Tools | Protection | Protect Workbook command; the dialog box is illustrated in Figure 12.11. Selecting Structure prevents anyone from moving, adding, deleting, hiding, unhiding, or renaming sheets in the workbook. Selecting Windows prevents anyone from moving or resizing windows in the workbook. It also hides the Minimize and Maximize buttons, the Control Menu box, and the window sizing borders. Again, you can assign a password to add an extra level of security.

Using Undo and Repeat

A useful feature of Excel is the ability to reverse an entry—called the Edit | Undo command. With Edit | Undo, you can reverse the most recent entry or the most recent command. Notice that the **Undo** command name changes to reflect the command or entry that will be reversed. It is also important to notice that some commands (Data Extract, for example) cannot be reversed. Depending on the amount of memory in your computer, it is possible that you will see this warning box during a particularly large command operation:

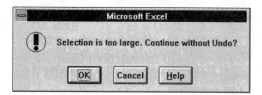

This happens because of the way the Undo command works. Excel always has two versions of the workbook in memory—one before a change and one after a change. When you select the Edit | Undo command, Excel reverts to the version before the change. If the two versions require more memory than is available, Excel sends the warning message. Once you select the Edit | Undo command, the command name changes to Edit | Redo, effectively giving you the opportunity to undo the undo.

There are two ways to use Edit | Undo:

- Use Undo to recover from an incorrect entry. For instance, if you intended to enter a value in cell F89 but entered it in cell F88 instead, invoke Edit | Undo before you make another entry, and the original value is restored to cell F88.

- Use Undo to determine the effect of a change in a value, then restore the data to its original state. For instance, to analyze the effect of different rates of growth for RB Company, first enter 5% in the cell for projected revenue growth, then enter 8% in the same cell. Observe the yearly net income (at 8%). Invoke Edit | Undo and you can see the yearly net income at 5%. You can even look at a graph without losing the ability to switch the numbers.

Occasionally, you wish to repeat a command. Perhaps you have applied number formatting to a range and you wish to apply the same formatting to another range. Like Edit | Undo, the Edit | Repeat command changes its name to reflect the command that will be repeated. To repeat the number formatting command in the example, select the first range, give the Format | Cells command, and apply the desired number formatting. Then select the next range and give the Edit | Repeat Format Cells command. The keyboard shortcut for the Edit | Repeat command is the F4 key. Note that this key does double duty, since it also toggles the cell reference type (from relative to absolute to mixed).

GUIDED ACTIVITY 12.1

Using Undo

In this Guided Activity you use the Undo feature, as discussed in the previous section.

1. Follow the startup procedure outlined in Unit 1 to load Windows and enter Excel.
2. Open RB96PROJ.
3. If cell G5 does not contain the value 5%, enter that number.
4. Give the Window | New Window command to open a second window on the workbook. Click the Column tab—one of the charts you created for the RB Company.
5. Give the Window | Arrange command and select Tiled to view the workbook and the chart on the same screen.
6. Enter the value 8% in cell G5. Note that the chart now reflects greater revenue and gross income.
7. Issue the Edit | Undo Entry command. Note that the entry in cell G5 reverts to 5%.
8. Save your work.

Displaying and Customizing Toolbars

On a couple of different occasions, we have touched on the subject of the toolbars that are included in the Excel package. Excel ships with 13 different toolbars, besides giving the user the ability to customize each toolbar by adding, deleting, or moving tools. Nine of the toolbars are listed in the View | Toolbars dialog box, illustrated in Figure 12.12; scroll down to see the others.

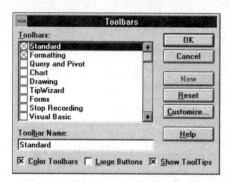

FIGURE 12.12
View | Toolbars dialog box

STANDARD TOOLBAR We discussed these tools in Unit 2 and have been using them throughout this manual.

FORMATTING TOOLBAR Use these tools to quickly access various commands from the Format menu.

QUERY AND PIVOT TOOLBAR Use these tools to query databases and work with pivot tables.

CHART TOOLBAR Use these tools to easily modify Excel charts; the toolbar automatically appears whenever a chart is selected. We discussed this toolbar in Unit 8.

DRAWING TOOLBAR Use these tools to create and modify graphic items on the workbook. We discuss this toolbar in the next section.

TIPWIZARD This opens the TipWizard, where you can view hints about easier ways to use Excel.

FORMS TOOLBAR Use these tools to place controls on worksheets. *Controls* are items like drop-down list boxes and check boxes that are normally found in dialog boxes. We discuss this toolbar later in this unit.

STOP RECORDING TOOLBAR Use this tool to access the Macro Stop Recorder command.

VISUAL BASIC TOOLBAR Use these tools to simplify recording, modifying, and running Visual Basic procedures. We discuss macros in Units 15 and 16.

AUDITING TOOLBAR Use these tools to simplify auditing worksheets. We discussed this toolbar in detail in Unit 9.

WORKGROUP TOOLBAR Use these tools to simplify file sharing in a network environment.

MICROSOFT TOOLBAR Use these tools to start other Microsoft applications easily.

FULL SCREEN TOOLBAR Use this tool to toggle between full screen view and normal view; it displays automatically when you select the View | Full Screen command.

Docking Toolbars

All toolbars are in one of three states: hidden, floating, or docked. When you select a toolbar and choose OK in the View | Toolbars dialog box, the selected toolbar will be unhidden and displayed in its most recent state, either floating or docked. If the toolbar has never been displayed before, it will default to a floating toolbar. A floating toolbar resides on top of the workbook and has a title bar that can be dragged to move the toolbar. Figure 12.13 shows the Standard and Formatting toolbars docked along the top and the Forms toolbar docked along the left side, while the Drawing toolbar is floating. To hide a floating toolbar, either deselect it in the View | Toolbars dialog box, or click the Control Menu box on the toolbar. (In a departure from normal Windows methods, a single click on the Control Menu box, as opposed to the normal double-click, will close a toolbar.)

To dock a floating toolbar, simply drag the toolbar against any of the four sides of the workspace until the outline changes shape, then release the mouse button. If the toolbar contains a wide tool, such as the Font list box or the Style list box, it can only be docked in one of the two horizontal docks at the top and bottom of the Excel window, and not in the vertical docks along the sides. To convert a docked toolbar to a floating toolbar, place the mouse cursor in any blank portion of the toolbar and double-click or drag it toward the center of the screen. To hide a docked toolbar, either make it a floating toolbar and click the Control Menu box, or deselect it in the View | Toolbars dialog box.

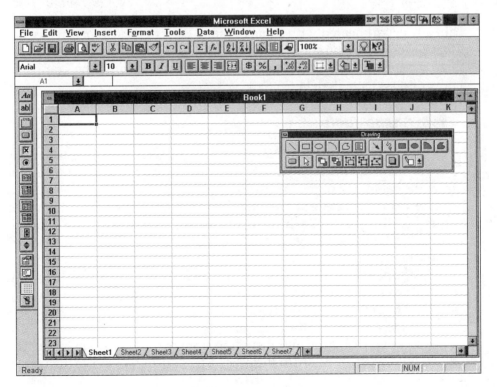

FIGURE 12.13
Excel toolbars

Customizing Toolbars

To customize a toolbar, select Customize from the View | Toolbars dialog box. Excel displays the dialog box illustrated in Figure 12.14. As you select each category, Excel displays the tools that are available in that category. To determine the function of a specific tool, click on it; a brief explanation is displayed at the bottom of the dialog box. To make that tool available on a particular toolbar, drag it to the desired location on the toolbar and release the mouse button.

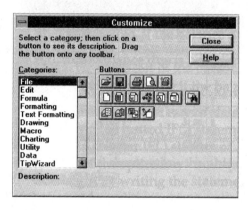

FIGURE 12.14
View | Toolbars Customize dialog box

Graphic Items on the Workbook

Remember from our discussion of toolbars that the tools on the Drawing toolbar are used to create graphic items on worksheets or chart sheets. Perhaps you have already experimented with some of them. Each of these tools creates a graphic item that sits on top of the sheet. Note that these graphic items are not related to the sheet under them; changing the data on the sheet does not alter the graphic objects. We now discuss these in detail.

Plain Shape Tools

Each of the graphical item tools uses the dragging technique with the mouse. To draw a straight line, simply select the Line button and then drag from the beginning of the line to the end.

Select the Rectangle button and then drag from one corner of the rectangle to the other. Holding [Shift] while drawing the rectangle constrains it to a square. The Format | Object command gives you the option of controlling the line and fill patterns for the rectangle.

Select the Ellipse button and then drag from one corner of the imaginary rectangle that would contain the oval to the other. Holding [Shift] while drawing the oval constrains it to a circle. The Format | Object command gives you the option of controlling the line and fill patterns for the oval.

Select the Arc button and then drag from one corner of the imaginary rectangle that would contain the arc to the other. The direction of curve depends on the initial mouse movement. If the first move is left or right, the beginning of the arc will be generally horizontal; if the first move is up or down, the beginning of the arc will be generally vertical. Holding [Shift] while drawing the line constrains the arc to portions of a circle.

Select the Freeform button and then draw whatever shape you desire. For freehand lines, drag the mouse along the desired path. For straight lines, click the mouse button at the two ends of the desired line. The freeform shape is complete when you close the shape by returning to the beginning point.

Select the Text Box button and then drag from one corner of the rectangle to the other. Holding [Shift] while drawing the text box constrains it to a square. Holding [Alt] while drawing the text box restrains it to the gridlines of the workbook. Once the box is drawn, the text box is in edit mode. Begin typing the text to be contained in the box. After you are done typing, you can select the object with the mouse and format both the text and the box with the Format | Object command.

Enhanced Shape Tools

To draw an arrow, select the Arrow button and then drag from the beginning of the line to the end. The distinction is important, because the end of the line contains the arrowhead. Holding [Shift] while drawing the line constrains the line to 45-degree increments.

To draw a freehand line, select the Freehand button and draw the line.

The filled shape tools work exactly like the plain shape tools but they are filled rather than transparent. You can use the Format | Object command to designate a fill pattern and color for each of the filled shapes.

Special Tools

The Create Button tool allows you to create a button on the sheet that can be used to start a macro. (We discuss macros in Units 15 and 16.)

The Drawing Selection tool allows you to select graphic items; this ability will become especially valuable as you begin to use the remainder of the tools in this toolbar. After choosing the Drawing Selection tool, simply click on the border of whatever graphic item you wish to select. To select multiple items, hold the [Shift] key while making the second and subsequent selections.

Working with Graphic Items

If you have experimented with several of the graphic item tools, you may have overlapped some graphic objects. There are four tools (along with the Format | Object command) that help you control the placement of these graphic items.

The Bring to Front tool places a selected graphic item in front of any other graphic items on the workbook.

The Send to Back tool places a selected graphic item behind any other graphic items on the workbook. Note that it still rests on top of the workbook. The only way to view the workbook through a graphic item is to set the graphic item's fill to None with the Format | Object command (or with the Color Palette tool).

The Group Objects tool groups together two or more selected graphic items so that future commands affect the entire group the same way. (To select more than one graphic item, use the Drawing Selection tool and hold down [Shift] while selecting the second and subsequent items.)

The Ungroup Objects tool separates a group of objects into individual items.

The Reshape tool lets you change the shape of a freeform object. Once this tool is activated, it will place a small black box, or handle, at each vertex of the polygon. You can move these vertices, and the lines connected to them, by placing the mouse cursor over them and dragging. You can delete vertices, thus removing details (or complete sides) from a polygon, by pressing the [Ctrl] key and clicking on the handle. Holding the [Alt] key while moving the handle will move it to the nearest cell intersection.

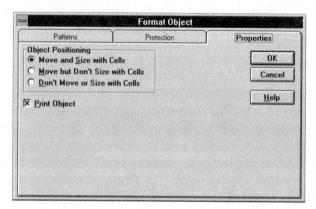

FIGURE 12.15
Format I Object dialog box, Properties tab

The Properties tab of the Format I Object dialog box, illustrated in Figure 12.15, allows you to decide how the graphic items respond to changes in the worksheet cells under them: you can choose to have the graphic items move and resize when the cells underneath are moved or sized; you can decide to have them move without resizing; or you can choose to have them neither resize nor move with the cells beneath. Note that if you select to have the items move and resize, the graphic is tied to the cell, not to the data contained in the cell. The Cut and Paste procedure does not move the graphic item; Insert I Cells, Insert I Rows, Insert I Columns, or Edit I Delete does.

The Drop Shadow Box tool places a shadow box border around a graphic object, a cell, or a group of cells.

The Pattern tool allows you to apply a pattern and a foreground color to a graphic item. The Patterns tab of the Format I Object dialog box allows you to apply a background color, in addition to the pattern and foreground color.

UNIT 12 ADVANCED WINDOWING AND PREFERENCE OPERATIONS

GUIDED ACTIVITY 12.2

Creating an Illustrated Workbook

In this Guided Activity you use the graphic tools to highlight a particular cell entry in a workbook.

1. If you are not continuing from the previous Guided Activity, load Windows, enter Excel, and open RB96PROJ. If you still have two windows open, close the window containing the chart, give the Window | Arrange command, and choose Tiled.

2. Give the View | Toolbars command, select Drawing, and click OK.

3. Use the filled Ellipse button to draw an oval that covers I6:K10. Hold [Alt] to force the oval to the cell boundaries.

4. Give the Format | Object command and select the Patterns tab to set the oval's fill. Click on the Pattern list box. Choose the fourth pattern in the first row. Just for fun, set the foreground color to your favorite color.

5. Next, let's insert some text in the oval.

    a. Use the Text Box button to create a text box inside the oval that ranges from row 7 through row 9. Type the text Based on March Marketing Forecast.

    b. Give the Format | Object command, select the Alignment tab, and select Horizontal Center and Vertical Center.

FIGURE 12.16
RB96OVAL workbook

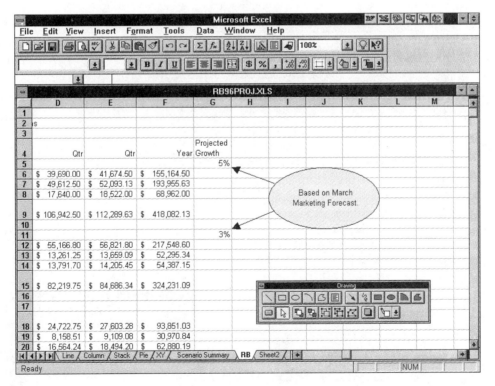

c. Use the Format | Object command to set the text box's border and fill to None. The text appears to be entered in the oval; the text box is invisible.

6. Use the Arrow button to draw two lines extending from the border of the oval to cells G5 and G11. If the arrowheads point at the oval instead of the cells, use Edit | Clear to clear the lines, and draw the lines again, starting at the oval and moving to the cells.

7. Your worksheet should look like Figure 12.16. (You may need to scroll to duplicate the figure exactly.) Save your work as RB96OVAL. Be sure to change the name; you will use RB96PROJ in another Guided Activity.

Using Controls in Worksheets

The Forms toolbar allows you to use the dialog box controls in worksheets. There are two main reasons for wanting to do this: ease of data entry and validation of data entry.

Let us illustrate. Excel is a very powerful and flexible spreadsheet tool, yet one of the first things anyone does with it is to calculate a house payment (or a car payment). We can all remember the time when we even messed that up! However, by using scroll boxes and spinner controls, and then protecting the cells that contain formulas, you can greatly simplify data input and make it nearly impossible to make a mistake. In this section, and in Guided Activity 12.3, you design a bulletproof worksheet that calculates a loan payment.

FIGURE 12.17
Initial CONTROL worksheet

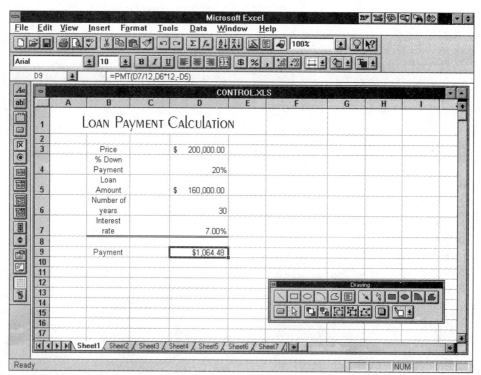

Start with the worksheet illustrated in Figure 12.17. Notice that the Forms toolbar is docked along the left side of the Excel window. The Drawing toolbar is displayed in its floating state in case you need to use the Drawing Selection tool. The heading in row 1 is in a 22-point decorative font and is centered across columns A:E. The width of column B is 10 and the width of column D is 14. The formula in cell D5 is =D3-(D3*D4). You should have no trouble understanding the formula in cell D9.

If you test the formula by changing the price to $100,000, the formula promptly recalculates the payment to $532.24. The only problem with this worksheet is that it is *too* flexible. If you change the interest rate to 200%, it still calculates a payment. To eliminate the possibility of error, you want to limit what can be entered in the cells containing the down payment, interest rate, and years. You want to be able to enter a down payment percentage from 0 to 100% in increments of 5%. You want to be able to enter the life of the loan from 0 to 30 years in increments of 5 years. For these cells, you use a *spinner control*. This is the control with one arrow pointing upward and one pointing downward. When you click on the up arrow, the number gets larger; when you click on the down arrow, the number gets smaller. You want to be able to enter the interest rate from 0 to 25% (may we *never* see 25% interest) in increments of .25%. Since this constitutes over 100 different data points, a spinner would take far too long; instead, you use a scroll bar. A scroll bar is more flexible since it has both an *incremental change* (the amount of change that occurs when you click on the arrows at the ends of the scroll bar) and a *page change* (the amount of change that occurs when you click on the scroll bar.

GUIDED ACTIVITY 12.3

Using Controls in a Worksheet

In this Guided Activity, you create the worksheet illustrated in Figure 12.17 and add controls to make it more reliable.

1. If you are continuing from the previous Guided Activity, close RB96OVAL and open a new workbook. Otherwise, open Excel to get a new workbook.

2. Using the preceding discussion, "Using Controls in Worksheets," as a guide, create the worksheet illustrated in Figure 12.17 and save it as CONTROL.

3. Select the Spinner button on the Forms toolbar and draw a spinner control in the right half of cell E4, like this:

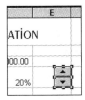

4. Double-click the new spinner control. Excel will display the Format | Object dialog box. Choose the Control tab; change Maximum Value to 100 and Incremental

Change to 5. Click in the Cell Link box and then click on cell H4. (You may have to move the dialog box to reach cell H4.) The dialog box should look like this:

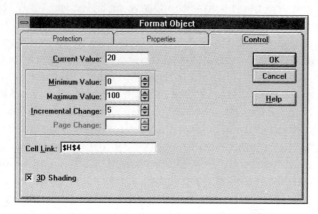

5. When the dialog box is correct, click OK. Click off the spinner control. Now, when you click on the control arrows, you should see the value in cell H4 change in increments of 5. Change the formula in cell D4 to read =H4/100. Now, when you click on the control arrows, the value in cell D4 should change along with cell H4.

6. Repeat the process for the life of the loan (years). Select the Spinner tool and draw a spinner control in the right half of cell E6. Double-click on the spinner to display the Format | Object dialog box. Change Maximum Value to 30, Incremental Change to 5, and the Cell Link to cell H6. Click off the spinner control to activate it. Make sure cell H6 is responding to the movement of the spinner. Then change the formula in cell D6 to =H6.

7. Choose the Scroll Bar tool and draw a scroll bar in the lower half of the range E7:G7. Double-click on the new scroll bar to call the Format | Object dialog box. Since the numbers entered in the Control tab must be integers, multiply everything by 100. Change Maximum Value to 2500, Incremental Change to 25, and the Page Change to 100. Page Change is the amount of change that occurs when the user clicks on the scroll bar between the scroll box and the arrow. Set the Cell Link to cell H7.

8. Click off the scroll bar to activate it and ensure that cell H7 is responding to the scroll bar. Change the formula in cell E7 to =H7/10000. Now you can change the interest rate in increments of 1% by clicking on the scroll bar and change it in increments of .25% by clicking on the arrows.

9. You have accomplished your initial goal of making data entry easier; however, this worksheet is hardly bulletproof. As soon as the user wipes out your formulas by keying in an entry in the range D3:D9, all your work is for nothing. Besides, having the numbers display in column H is not at all cool.

So first, unlock cells D3 and H4:H7. Select the cells, give the command Format | Cells, select the Protection tab, and clear the Locked box.

FIGURE 12.18
CONTROL workbook, complete

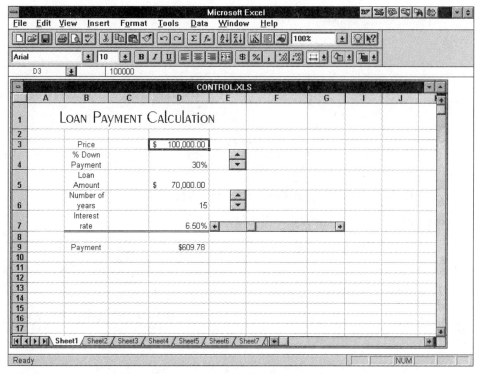

CHECKPOINT 12A Why do you need to unlock cells H4:H7?

10. Next, hide column H. You have already selected cells in column H, so give the command Format | Column | Hide.

11. Finally, lock the worksheet. Give the command Tools | Protection | Protect Sheet and click OK. Clean up the worksheet by hiding the Drawing and Forms toolbars. Your worksheet should look like Figure 12.18. Test the worksheet to ensure that the controls still work and that you cannot make entries in protected cells; then save your work.

Windows and Panes

Window panes and workbook windows provide flexibility as you work with large workbooks.

View | Zoom

Occasionally, you will want to fit more cells on a display, even at the cost of reducing the size of each individual cell. (You needed to do this at the beginning of Unit 11, where you wished to show all 40 rows of a database in one figure.) In other instances, you might wish to enlarge the display to get a clearer view, even though you will not see as many cells at one time. Excel provides the View | Zoom command

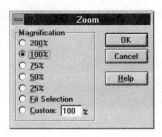

FIGURE 12.19
View | Zoom dialog box

for these situations. The dialog box, illustrated in Figure 12.19, gives you several choices:

200% Doubles the display size of the workbook.

100% Provides the standard display size.

75% Reduces the display size to 75%, thus revealing more cells.

50% Reduces the display size to 50%, thus revealing more cells.

25% Reduces the display size to 25%, thus revealing more cells.

FIT SELECTION Reduces or enlarges the display size as necessary (between 10% and 400%) to fit the selected range in the display area.

CUSTOM Reduces or enlarges the display size to the percentage that you enter (between the limits of 10% and 400%).

Window Panes

Frozen panes are rows or columns of the worksheet that do not move out of sight when you move the active cell down or to the right. When your worksheet is longer than the number of rows your monitor will display, it might be difficult to remember which column is which as you move down the column and the information in the top rows scrolls off the screen. The same problem occurs when the workbook is wider than the number of columns that fit on the screen. The Window | Split command allows you to specify rows and/or columns that remain on the screen. Once you issue the command, use the arrow keys to move the split where you wish to separate the window into *panes*. A very simple shortcut for this command is available to mouse users. There is a solid black bar to the right of the bottom scroll bar and at the top of the right scroll bar. (See Figure 12.20 to locate the split bars.) You can simply drag these split bars to the desired pane separation points.

Once you have split the window into separate panes, you will probably see some cells duplicated in both panes. Issue the Window | Freeze Panes command, and Excel locks the top and left panes into their current position and allows you to scroll the lower-right portion of the workbook. Now, as you move the active cell to a cell that is not on the screen, the frozen panes appear to be fixed and the rest of the screen seems to slide under the frozen panes.

For example, consider the PORTFOLI workbook used in Application E preceding this unit. The column headings are in row 1, and there are over 27 rows in the workbook. As you move to the bottom of the list, the column headings scroll off the screen. To freeze the column headings, do the following:

FIGURE 12.20
Split bars

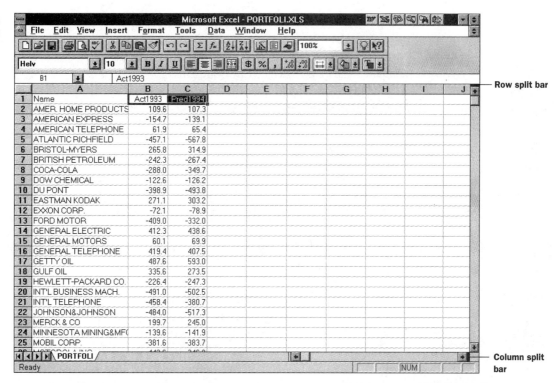

1. Move the horizontal split bar to the gridline between rows 1 and 2.
2. Give the command Window | Freeze Panes, which freezes row 1 in its current position.

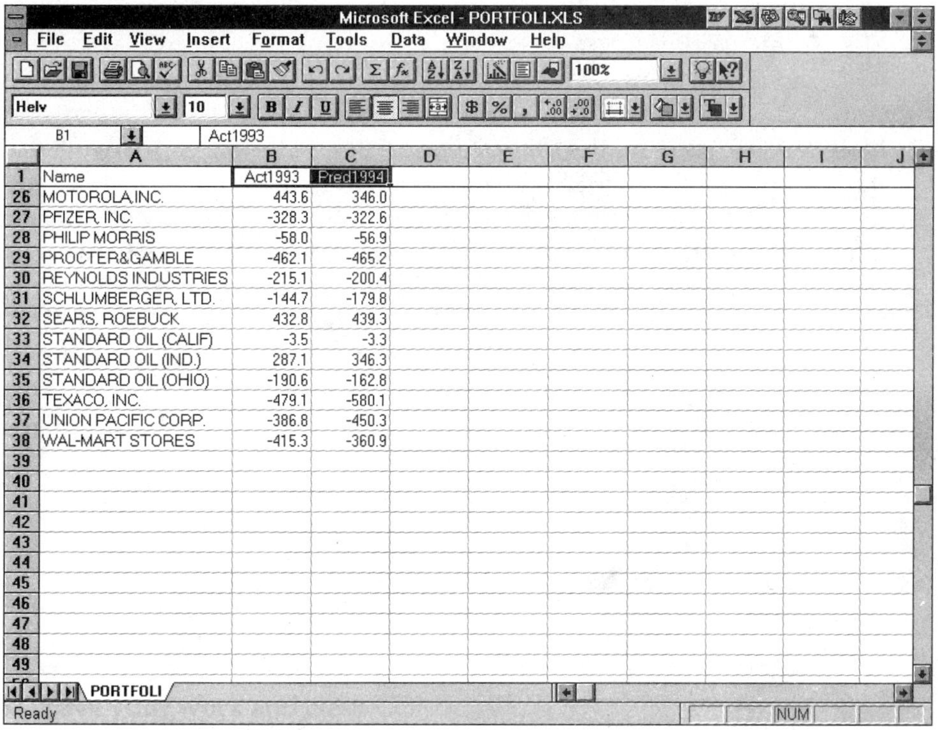

FIGURE 12.21
PORTFOLI.XLS with frozen panes

The PORTFOLI workbook with frozen panes appears in Figure 12.21. Had it been desirable, you could also have created another frozen pane containing columns of data. To remove the frozen panes, give the Window | Unfreeze Panes command, and return the split bars to their original positions.

When you save the file, the frozen panes are saved with it. When you open the file, the frozen panes are still in effect.

Workbook Windows

One of the fundamental benefits of the Windows environment is its ability to have more than one thing happening on the computer screen at a time. For example, in writing this book we have continually had a word processor running in one window and Excel running in another. By sizing the windows properly, we can change from one application to the other simply by clicking the mouse. Alternatively, with each window maximized we can move between applications by pressing the [Alt][Tab] key combination.

Excel provides the same benefit to the spreadsheet program. You have already seen a glimpse of this when you use the Window | Arrange command to view a chart and a worksheet at the same time, or when you open a new workbook for a Guided Activity without first closing the workbook you were using before. But suppose you are working on a very large budget workbook that contains four quarterly budgets and an annual total. You have used your vast wealth of Excel knowledge to design the budget once and copy it four more times to other sheets for the other three quarters and the annual total. But now the workbook contains five sheets. You need to be able to compare one quarter with another or see the effect that changing one quarter's figures has on the annual total.

You can use the Window | New Window command to have two (or more) copies of the same workbook on the screen at the same time. However, they are not both visible, since one is lying on top of the other. Now you can use the Window | Arrange command to see both windows at the same time. Note the title bars: one will have the extension ":1" and the other will have the extension ":2". Two tiled windows are illustrated with the PORTFOLI workbook in Figure 12.22.

Note that since these are both copies of the same workbook, any changes made to one affect the other. If you are using a mouse, you can move between windows by simply clicking the mouse in each window. If you are a keyboard user, you can press [Ctrl][F6] to switch between windows. When you are done using multiple windows, select the Close command from the window's Control menu to close the extra windows.

FIGURE 12.22
PORTFOLI.XLS with two windows

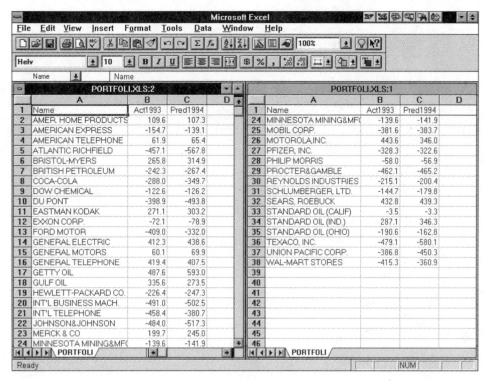

GUIDED ACTIVITY 12.4

Using Workbook Windows and Panes

This Guided Activity requires you to use several of the Window commands in a workbook.

1. If you are not continuing from the previous Guided Activity, load Windows and enter Excel.

2. Open PORTFOLI.

3. Follow the instructions in the previous discussion to make row 1 a frozen pane.

   a. Move the horizontal split bar to the gridline between row 1 and row 2.

   b. Observe the effect, illustrated in Figure 12.23.

   c. Give the Window | Freeze Panes command.

4. Once the frozen pane is set, move the active cell down to cell A38. The screen should look like Figure 12.21.

5. Split the screen vertically:

   a. Give the Window | Unfreeze Panes command.

   b. Move the vertical split bar to the gridline between columns A and B.

   c. Give the Window | Freeze Panes command.

6. Open another window to the PORTFOLI workbook.

FIGURE 12.23
PORTFOLI.XLS with unfrozen panes

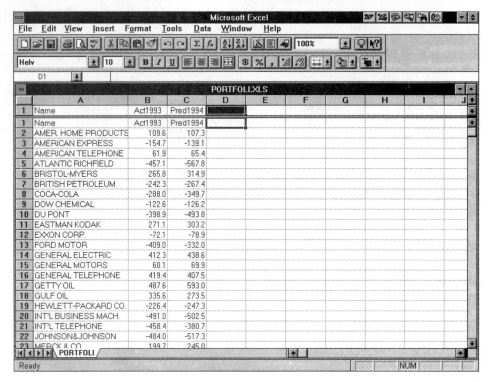

  a. Give the Window | New Window command.
  b. Give the Window | Arrange command, select Tiled, and click OK.
  c. Move the active cell to cell A2 in the active window.
  d. Give the Edit | Clear | Contents command.

CHECKPOINT 12B What was the effect in the inactive window?

  e. Give the Edit | Undo Clear command.

  7. Save the file with the name WINDOWS. Remember to use the File | Save As command to change the file name.

Range Names

We hinted at the virtues of named ranges in Part One. As your workbook grows, it becomes more and more useful to have a quick method of referring to specific portions of the workbook.

For instance, you might have built a workbook to calculate federal income taxes, and have separate areas on your workbook for Form 1040, Schedule A, Schedule D, Form 2441, and so on. As you work on your taxes, you would like some easy way to jump from Form 1040 to Schedule D, and back again. Or you might have built a workbook containing a pet store inventory, grouped into classes such as rodent, bird, fish, and so forth. As you manage your inventory, you would like to be able to write formulas quickly to sum the cost of all the rodents you have in stock.

Your life will be easier if you take the time to create *range names*. It is easier to name ranges as you build the workbook, but ranges can be named at any time.

Assigning Range Names

To name a range, select the range to be named, then give the Insert | Name | Define command. The dialog box illustrated in Figure 12.24 appears. It contains a list of the names already in the workbook and a text box to enter the range to which the name refers (it may suggest a proposed name for the selected range). To accept the suggested name (Excel looks for text in the cells above the range, to the left of the range, and in the upper-left corner of the selection to find a suggested name), simply click on the OK button. To override Excel's suggestion, type your desired name in the Names in Workbook text box and click on OK. Notice that you are not limited to naming only the range that was selected before giving the Insert | Name | Define command. By clicking on the Add button instead of OK, Excel defines the name of the range that was highlighted, but it does not close the dialog box. You can type another name in the Names in Workbook box, highlight the Refers to box, type or point to a range, and click on Add again. You can continue to do this until you have defined all needed range names. Insert | Name | Create can be used to assign names from adjacent cells (see the discussion in the section "Creating Global Range Names" below).

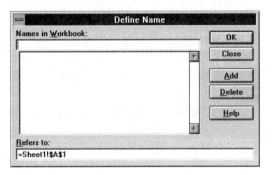

FIGURE 12.24
Insert | Name | Define dialog box

Removing Range Names

You can remove the name from a specific range using the Delete button in the Insert | Name | Define dialog box.

Using Named Ranges in Formulas

Many Excel functions allow the use of range names as arguments. To use a range name as an argument, simply type the range name where you would normally type references. In the following examples, assume that you have named the range Q5:Q20 as WEST.

Unnamed Range	Named Range
IRR(Q5:Q20,0.10)	IRR(WEST,0.10)
SUM(Q5:Q20)	SUM(WEST)
DAVERAGE(Q5:Q20,1,A1:B2)	DAVERAGE(WEST,1,A1:B2)

Using Named Ranges as a Destination

Recall the tax form example. If you name the ranges with names such as FORM1040, SCHEDA, and so on, then it is very easy to jump about. Press [F5] or give the command Edit | Go To, then select the desired range name from the list in the dialog box. The entire range is highlighted and the active cell moves to the upper-left corner of the chosen range. Named ranges also make data entry simpler. Once you go to the named range, the entire range is highlighted, and you can move from one cell to the next by pressing [Tab] or [Enter].

Creating Global Range Names

Most people find it easier to interpret a workbook where the formulas contain descriptive names rather than cell references. However, a large workbook can contain many areas that need to be named and even more formulas where you would need to replace cell references with named ranges.

For this reason, Excel provides the means to create and define all the names needed on a workbook with the Insert | Name | Create command. Figure 12.25 illustrates the HOTEL.XLS workbook that you used in Unit 8. (We have changed the

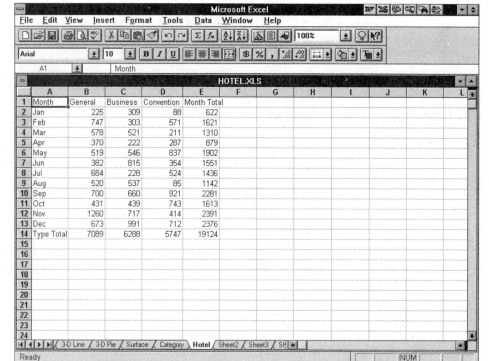

FIGURE 12.25
HOTEL.XLS

FIGURE 12.26
Insert | Name | Create dialog box

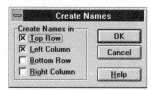

entries in cells E1 and A14.) Select A1:E14 and give the Insert | Name | Create command. Figure 12.26 illustrates the dialog box for this command.

Ensure that Top Row and Left Column are both checked and click on OK.

Excel checks to see where text is located to make a recommendation for the name location in this dialog box. You can override this by simply selecting a different check box. Remember that names must be text, not values or formulas; they cannot look like cell references; and they cannot begin with a number. If the cell in the row or column where Excel is instructed to look for names begins with a number, Excel inserts an _ (underscore) in front of the proposed name.

To see the effect of the Insert | Name | Create command, give the Insert | Name | Define command, which brings up the dialog box illustrated in Figure 12.27. Notice in the Names in Workbook list that there is now a defined name for each row and each column in the selected range.

FIGURE 12.27
Insert | Name | Define dialog box

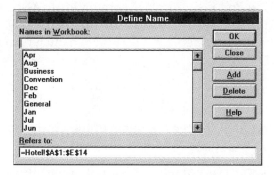

The next step is to convert the cell references in formulas to named ranges. The Insert | Name | Apply command searches all formulas in the selected range and replaces all cell references with their equivalent range names. Give the command Insert | Name | Apply and click on the Options button. You should see the dialog box illustrated in Figure 12.28.

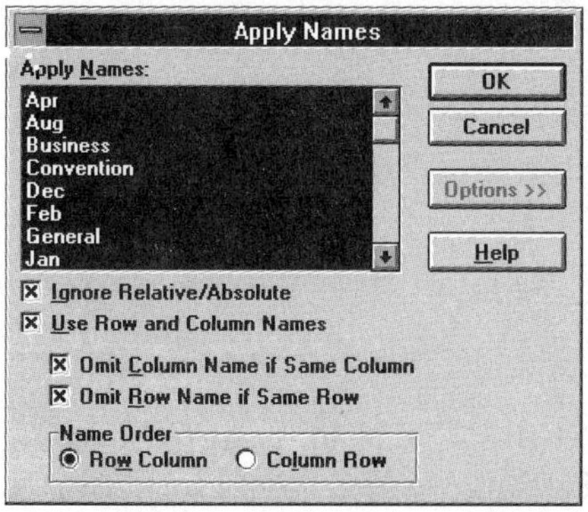

FIGURE 12.28
Insert | Name | Apply dialog box

Select all the names in the list box by holding [Shift] while clicking with the mouse. (All names might already be selected.) Deselect the two check boxes that ask you to omit column or row names (you want to see the full intersection names). The formula for E2 is now =SUM((Jan General):(Jan Convention)). (Remember from Unit 3 that the space is the intersection operator, so that Jan General is the cell where the Jan range intersects the General range.) See the illustration below.

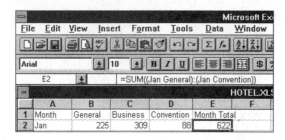

Find and Replace Commands

Excel provides the Edit | Find and Edit | Replace commands to assist you in making changes to a workbook. This feature is similar to the find and replace feature of most word processors. You can find and replace a series of characters in text entries, constant values, or formulas.

NOTE *Be extremely careful about changing constant values; it is very easy to replace numbers you do not intend to replace.*

For instance, you might decide to change the name of the Production department (in the NAMELIST.XLS file) to Operations. To do so, perform the following steps:

1. Select the range B2:B39. (This step is not required, but it limits the search to only the selected range. If only one cell is selected, Excel searches the entire worksheet.)

2. Give the Edit | Replace command. Excel presents the dialog box illustrated in Figure 12.29.

FIGURE 12.29
Edit | Replace dialog box

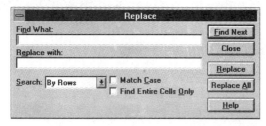

3. Type in the text string to be replaced and the text string to replace it.
4. Click on Match Case if you want Excel to check capitalization.
5. Select Find Entire Cells Only if you want Excel to replace the string only in cells whose entire contents match the Find string. Deselect Find Entire Cells Only if

you want Excel to replace the string in any cells that contain the Find string, even if they contain other text or values.

6. Select By Rows in the Search box if you want Excel to search the range horizontally; select By Columns if you want Excel to search vertically.

7. Click on Replace All if you are confident that Excel will not replace anything you do not want replaced. Click on Find Next if you want to be able to examine the cell containing the string. If you use the Find Next button, you will need to click on Replace in order to actually replace the string.

There are many uses for the search and replace feature. Not only can you replace the contents of a range of text, you can also correct a reference to the wrong cell in a range of formulas. You can change a function—say from PV( ) to FV( )—or you can use the search feature to search a large workbook for every place the PMT( ) function is used.

Example: Using Advanced Windowing Commands

The advanced commands discussed in this unit can be combined to create a useful workbook. For instance, the timekeeper of an organization might wish to build a workbook to record the time worked by each individual in a given week. The Student Data Disk contains the template illustrated in Figure 12.30; the final workbook looks like Figure 12.31.

FIGURE 12.30
TIMEKPR.XLS, as provided on the Student Data Disk

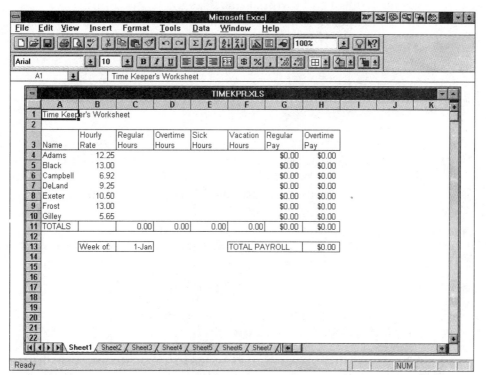

FIGURE 12.31
TIMEKPR2.XLS,
complete

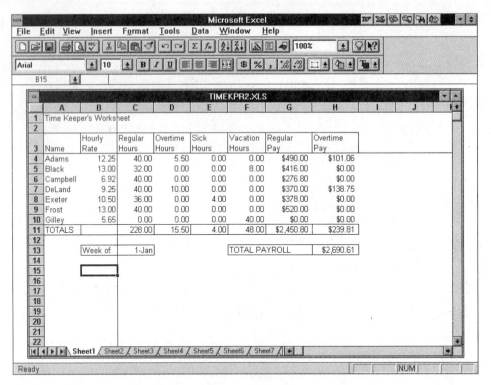

The only things that are input on a weekly basis are the entries in the four Hours columns and the date in row 13. The remainder of the workbook consists of text (such as the names) and formulas (such as the Pay columns).

The timekeeper decides to fix rows 1 through 3 and columns A and B as frozen panes. He splits the window below and to the right of cell B3 and gives the Window | Freeze Panes command.

Example: Global Range Names

The next step is to create named ranges. The first is named Hours and consists of the range C4:F10, the area in which the hours are input. The timekeeper selects the range, issues the command Insert | Name | Define, and enters the name Hours.

Another named range is called Week_of and consists of cell C13, which contains the current week's date. Highlight B13:C13 and give the Insert | Name | Create command. Ensure that Left Column is checked and click on OK.

After the two ranges are named, the timekeeper uses the Format | Cells command to unprotect the cells in the two ranges. For instance, to unprotect the Hours range:

1. Press F5 and select Hours as the destination.

2. Give the Format | Cells command, select the Protection tab, and click on Locked to remove the X and unlock the range. Click on OK.

When both ranges have been unprotected, the timekeeper sets the workbook in the protection-on state with the Tools | Protection | Protect Sheet command. Now the workbook is ready for data entry. To input the Week_of range, changing from the original date to 8-Jan[-96], press [F5], select the desired range name (Week_of), and press [Enter].

The easiest way to change the date entry is to press [F2]. Notice that the Week_of range, which is cell C13, becomes the active cell. Once [F2] is pressed, the cursor in the formula bar becomes an edit cursor. At this point, you can change the arguments to 96,1,8, then press [Enter]. Data entry to the Hours range is similar. *Remember*: when you are entering data in a range, use [Enter] to move downward and [Tab] to move to the right. If you press an arrow key, it will deselect the range.

GUIDED ACTIVITY 12.5

Using Advanced Features

This Guided Activity requires you to use several of the advanced Window commands to complete the examples just discussed.

1. If you are not continuing from the previous Guided Activity load Windows and enter Excel.

2. Open TIMEKPR. Use the arrow keys to move around the workbook, looking at the formulas.

3. Use the Window I Split and Window I Freeze Panes commands to freeze rows 1 to 3 and columns A and B, as in the first example.

4. Use the Insert I Name I Create and Insert I Name I Apply commands to create names in the range A3:H11. Use the discussion in the section "Creating Global Range Names" earlier in this unit as a guide.

5. Next, name the range C4:F10 Hours, and cell C13 Week_of. Follow the second example discussed above.

6. The next step is to unprotect the cells in the ranges Hours and Week_of. Again, follow the example above.

7. Set the worksheet to the protection-on state.

CHECKPOINT 12C What command establishes the protection-on state?

CHECKPOINT 12D If you wish to make a change to a protected cell, what must you do first?

CHECKPOINT 12E Are certain commands unavailable while the workbook is protected? If so, which ones are they? (Look at the menus to determine which, if any, are unavailable.)

8. Using [F5], change the Week_of range to 8-Jan-96 and enter the hours so that your workbook looks like Figure 12.30.

9. Save the result under the name TIMEKPR2.

EXERCISE 12.1

Using Range Names in Formulas

This Exercise provides a simple illustration of how ranges can be named from adjacent labels and how range names can be used in formulas.

1. Follow the startup procedure outlined in Unit 1 to load Windows and enter Excel. If you are continuing from a previous Guided Activity or Exercise and already have a workbook on the screen, use the command File | New to bring up a new workbook.

2. Enter the text Revenue, Expenses, Gross, Taxes, Net down column A, from A2:A6. Use the Insert | Name | Create command to name the adjacent cells in column B (the selection range is A2:B6). In cell C5, enter 42% and name that cell Tax_Rate (include the underscore; Excel does not allow spaces in names).

3. In cell B4, enter the formula =Revenue-Expenses. There are three ways to enter this formula:

   a. Type the range names and operators, =Revenue-Expenses; or

   b. Press [=], give the Insert | Name | Paste command, highlight Revenue, press [Enter], press [-], give the Insert | Name | Paste command, highlight Expenses, and press [Enter] twice; or

   c. Type the formula by pointing or typing the cell reference, =B2-B3, give the Insert | Name | Apply command, and apply the names Revenue and Expenses.

   In any case, the formula is entered as range names, making it easy for you to figure out what you intended when you look at this workbook six months later. In cell B5, enter the formula =Gross*Tax_Rate. In cell B6 enter the formula =Gross-Taxes.

4. Unlock the ranges Revenue, Expenses, and Tax_Rate with the Format | Cells command. Select the entire worksheet and set the number format to #,##0. Format Tax_Rate to 0.0%. Set the worksheet protection on. Take a moment to ponder what you have just created: a simple accounting worksheet with all formulas protected.

5. Test your worksheet by entering various combinations of revenue, expenses, and tax rates. If the tax rate is constant at 42%, which is better: revenue of $10,000 and expenses of $9,000, or revenue of $11,000 and expenses of $9,900?

6. Try to make entries in any protected cell of the workbook. When finished, save your work with the file name TAXPLAN.XLS.

EXERCISE 12.2

The Perfect Job (VI)

1. Close all workbooks. Open JOBS.XLS.
2. Make column A and rows 1:4 frozen panes.
3. Select the chart sheet and use the Window | New Window and Window | Arrange commands to display the graph and columns A:C of the workbook on your screen.
4. Change the salary for the job at Minnie's to $27,000. Note that the graph changes to reflect the changed information.
5. Press Undo ([Ctrl][Z]) to change the salary for the job at Minnie's back to $24,900.
6. Save the file.

EXERCISE 12.3

Search and Replace

1. Open NAMELIST.XLS.
2. Following the example in this unit, change the department title Production to Operations.
3. Save the file.

EXERCISE 12.4

Gas Mileage (IV)

Open GASMILE.XLS. Use a line with an arrowhead, a text box, and a filled oval to highlight the highest MPG value in the workbook. Print a copy and save your work.

EXERCISE 12.5

Software Inventory (II)

Open SOFTLIST.XLS. It turns out that your manager is not satisfied with the "imprecise" nature of your platform designations. Use the find and replace features of Excel to change Windows to Windows 3.x. Make sure that you do not change anything but the platform entries. Save your work.

Review Questions

1. When can you make changes to a protected cell?
*2. What is the normal (default) state of all worksheet cells?
3. What is the normal (default) worksheet protection state?
*4. What effect does the Insert | Name | Apply command have?
5. What is the difference between Insert | Name | Define and Insert | Name | Create?
*6. What key combination do you press to move from one window to another?
*7. What toolbar would you display to create a text box?
8. If a toolbar contains the Style list box, where can you *not* dock it?

Key Terms

Cell protection
Control
Frozen pane
Hidden cell
Incremental change

Locked cell
Page change
Pane
Placeholder
Range names

Spinner control
Startup directory
Undo
Unlock

Documentation Research

Referring to the Excel *User's Guide,* find and record the page number of each of the commands discussed in this unit. We recommend that you also write the page number in the margin next to the discussion of the command in the unit.

1. What happens to an Excel workbook if you minimize it?
2. How do you hide a graphic object?
3. What is the maximum length of a name?
4. How do you insert a space between two tools on a toolbar?

APPLICATION

Spring Break: Florida or Bust

There are no complex commands or formulas in this exercise, nor are there step-by-step instructions. Your task is to build a workbook that contains a cash flow projection and to determine how much money is needed to achieve a desired ending balance.

Your parents, being the frugal sort, have come up with a budget for spring semester that provides for all necessities and a modest amount of fun. What they failed to plan for was your trip to Florida for spring break. Staying on campus in March is no fun, especially when everyone else is in Fort Lauderdale.

Here are your sources of income:

Scholarship	$1,000	paid in January
Parents	$3,000	paid in January
	$500	paid February through June
	$600	additional paid in April
	$300	additional paid in June

The additional amounts are for travel to and from home.

Your budget allows for the following expenses:

Tuition	$2,500	paid in January
Books	$400	paid in January
Room	$275	per month (January through June)
Groceries	$200	per month
Dates	$25	per month
Movies	$20	per month

Sports	$30	per month
Travel to school	$300	in January
Easter travel	$600	in April
Travel to home	$300	in June

This budget is displayed in Figure F.1. You notice that every penny of income is used by the end of June. You need $400 in March for your Florida excursion, and therefore you must get a job. The problem is to figure out how much per month you must earn to keep the balance above zero. Because too much work affects your social and academic life, you must minimize the amount of work in each month. When you save your workbook, name it BUDGET.XLS.

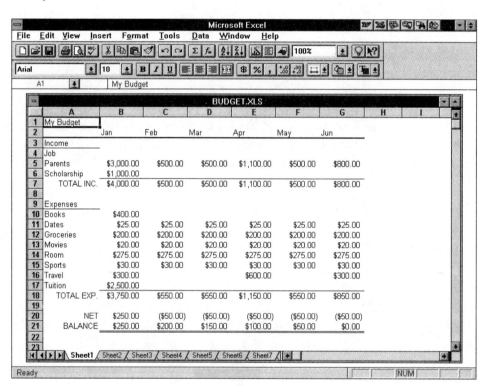

FIGURE F.1
BUDGET.XLS workbook

13 Advanced File Operations and Data Interchange

Disk files allow you to save your work created in one session to be opened in another, to move a portion of one workbook into another workbook, and to share workbook data with programs other than Excel. In this unit we discuss the various types of files and the File commands.

As you become more proficient in using microcomputers, you will learn to use a number of software packages. Someday you will want to take a table created in Excel and put it into a memorandum you are writing with word processing software. Or you might want to extract data from a database file maintained by dBASE IV or a compatible program and use the data in an Excel workbook. This unit introduces the techniques provided by Excel to accomplish data interchange.

Learning Objectives

At the completion of this unit you should know

1. how to identify the purpose of a file by the file extension,
2. the different options of the File | Save As command and when each is most appropriate,
3. the abilities of the File | Open command and how to use it to access data from programs other than Excel.

At the completion of this unit you should be able to

1. link data from two files,
2. import a disk file,
3. use values from other workbooks in the current workbook,
4. create similar workbooks as a workbook,
5. import ASCII data from a .TXT file,
6. export ASCII data to a .TXT file.

Important Commands

Data | Consolidate

Data | Text to Columns

Edit | Links

File | Open

File | Save

File | Save As

File | Save Workspace

Data Disk File Types

Most DOS application programs, including Excel, use the file *extension* to designate the purpose the file serves—that is, the file type. If you are not familiar with the general rules for *file names* and extensions, refer to your Excel *User's Guide* or a DOS manual.

At least four types of files are used by Excel 5 to store data on disks. Files with an .XLS extension contain the workbook itself. Excel workbooks can contain worksheets, chart sheets, macro modules, dialog sheets, and Excel 4 macro sheets. Files with an .XLT extension are templates. Files with an .XLA extension are add-in macros. Files with an .XLW extension are workplace configuration files.

File Commands

The File menu looks like this:

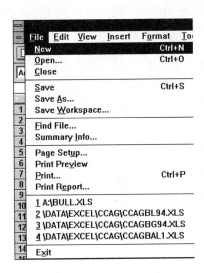

You are already familiar with the File | Save and File | Open commands, which move workbook files to and from disk storage. File | Save assumes an .XLS extension for workbooks, while File | Open defaults to an .XL* extension (that is, the last character can be anything, so long as DOS recognizes it as a file name character). You can also use DOS path names in all File commands that ask for a file name. For example, \BUDGETS\SALES.XLS refers to the file SALES.XLS in the subdirectory BUDGETS. You can either type path names in the list box or use the directory list to select subdirectories and thus build a *path name*.

Moving Data from Memory to Disk

Three commands take data from the current workbook and save it in some form on your data disk or hard disk.

File | Save saves the entire file to disk. All formulas, formats, and settings are saved with the file to a preexisting file name. Use File | Save when you want to save the entire file (the normal case).

File | Save Workspace saves a list of the currently open files to disk. The locations and sizes of each window are also saved. The default extension for File | Save Workspace is .XLW. Workspaces are useful because you can open a workspace, and all associated files will be opened at one time.

File | Save As is the third command that moves data to a disk; it provides several options in how the file can be saved. The dialog box is illustrated in Figure 13.1.

FIGURE 13.1
File | Save As dialog box

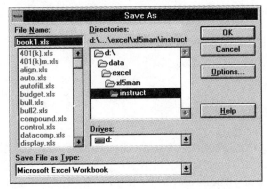

The initial dialog box allows the user to enter a file and path name. This path name can include any disk drive and any directory available to the computer.

FILE FORMAT A quick browse through the Save File as Type drop-down list (Figure 13.2) shows that Excel 5 workbooks can be saved in many different formats for use in other programs. Table 13.1 lists these formats.

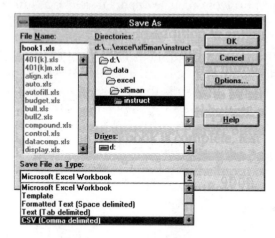

FIGURE 13.2
File | Save As type list

TABLE 13.1
File | Save As formats

EXTENSION	APPLICATION/PROGRAM
CSV	Macintosh, OS/2, or DOS
CSV	Windows, Comma Separated Values
DBF	dBASE (Versions 2.x, 3.x, 4.x)
DIF	Data interchange format—for transfer to VisiCalc
PRN	Formatted text (space-delimited Lotus format)
SLK	Symbolic link (for Multiplan or Excel for Macintosh 1.5 or earlier)
TXT	Text (Macintosh, OS/2, or DOS)
WK1	Lotus 1-2-3 Release 2.x (ALL, FMT)
WK3	Lotus 1-2-3 Release 3.x (FM3)
WKS	Lotus 1-2-3 Release 1.x, Symphony, and early Quattro Pro
WQ1	Quattro Pro for DOS
XLC	Excel Chart (Versions 2.1, 3.0, 4.0)
XLS	Excel (Versions 2.1, 3.0, 4.0)
XLT	Template
XLW	Excel Version 4.0 workbook

This is an impressive list of *file formats* designed to make your Excel workbooks compatible with many different applications. Some of the standards that Excel will save to (DIF, SYLK, and WKS) are almost as old as the PC industry itself. Also, Excel will save to a file format that is compatible with Excel for the Macintosh (another platform) and Excel for OS/2 (another operating system). Obviously, different amounts of information will be saved, depending on the file format chosen. A text format, for example, will only save the characters of the workbook; the columns will be separated by tab stops, and the rows by carriage returns. On the other hand, saving to Excel 2.1 or Lotus's WK1 or WK3 will preserve the spreadsheet characteristics of the file and much of the formatting.

Selecting the Options button in the File I Save As dialog box (Figure 13.3) includes several other possibilities, described next.

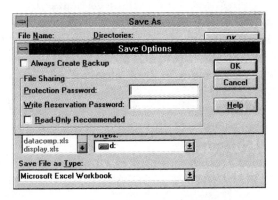

FIGURE 13.3
Save Options dialog box

ALWAYS CREATE BACKUP Selecting this option will rename the existing workbook file with the extension .BAK before saving the new version. This ensures that if something is wrong with the current version, you can step back to the old version and try again.

PROTECTION PASSWORD Selecting this option allows the user to enter a password when saving the file. Excel will not open the file until the user enters the password.

WRITE RESERVATION PASSWORD Selecting this option also allows the user to enter a password when saving the file. In this case, Excel will open the file without the password, but the user must enter the password before saving changes to the file.

READ-ONLY RECOMMENDED Largely for network users, this option is not as stringent as Write Reservation Password. There is no password, but if a user tries to open the document with the Read-Only button unchecked, Excel will display a message stating that the file should be opened as Read-Only unless changes to it need to be saved. The user can then override the message and open the file anyway, or go back and change it to Read-Only.

Moving Data from Disk to Memory

The File I Open command takes data from the disk and loads it into the computer's memory. Excel opens a new workbook window and places the newly opened file into the new window without affecting any existing workbook windows. The only limit to the number of windows that can be opened at one time is the amount of memory (RAM) in the computer.

All formulas, formats, and settings are opened with the file. Use File I Open whenever you want to work on a previously saved workbook.

Other File Management Commands

The File | Close command closes the current document without affecting other open documents or exiting Excel. If there are unsaved changes, Excel presents a dialog box asking if you wish to save changes before closing the file.

The File | Summary Info command allows you to enter information such as Title, Subject, Author, and Keywords for later use in finding files.

The File | Find File command allows you to search a disk for a specific file or for files that meet certain criteria. By clicking on the Advanced Search button, you can search using such criteria as the date the file was last modified, where the file is located in the subdirectory system of the disk, or any of the information in the Summary Info dialog box. You can even look for files that contain a particular text string, but be prepared for a slow process.

The Edit | Links command, although not in the File menu, allows you to manage the links between the current document and other documents that have a DDE or OLE link with them. This command is discussed more fully later in this unit.

Moving and Copying Data from One Workbook to Another

The simplest type of data interchange is copying or cutting data from one workbook and pasting it to another. To accomplish this task, you follow the same Copy and Paste (or Cut and Paste) procedures that you learned in Unit 6. The basic procedure is to give the Edit | Copy (or Edit | Cut) command, then activate a different workbook, then issue the Edit | Paste command. The end result is that data that was contained in one workbook is now contained in another.

By using this procedure, you have not created any link between the two workbooks. The data can be changed in either workbook without affecting the other.

The Edit | Paste Special command provides a way of controlling a data interchange. Suppose you have calculated a loan payment in one cell and want to use the payment as a constant in an amortization table at another location, or in another workbook. Use the Values option of the Edit | Paste Special command to convert the formula to a value. The Formulas option pastes only the formulas (not the formatting) from the copy range. The Formats option pastes only the formatting (not the data) from the copy range. The Transpose option converts rows in the copied range to columns in the pasted range and vice versa. The Skip Blanks option does not paste blank cells; data in the paste range is not overwritten by blank cells in the copy range. The Operation options allow you to perform mathematical operations between the data in the copy range and the data in the paste range.

GUIDED ACTIVITY 13.1

Manipulating Files

In this Guided Activity you use several of the File commands.

1. Load Windows and enter Excel. The data disk should have the workbook files that you created in Unit 7 (RECALC.XLS) and Application C (COMPOUND.XLS).

2. Open RECALC.XLS.

3. Open COMPOUND.XLS and use the Window | Arrange command to see both workbooks.

4. Copy A1:F12 of COMPOUND.XLS into RECALC.XLS.

   Select cell A7 on the RECALC workbook and give the Edit | Paste command.

   Select File | Close to close COMPOUND.XLS. Resize RECALC.XLS to fill the screen. The results should look like Figure 13.4.

5. Notice that the formulas still reflect their original absolute and mixed references. Now you adjust the formulas to account for their new location. Select B9:F18. Replace the formula in cell B9 with =$A9*(1+$A$7)^B$8. Press to copy this formula to the entire range.[1]

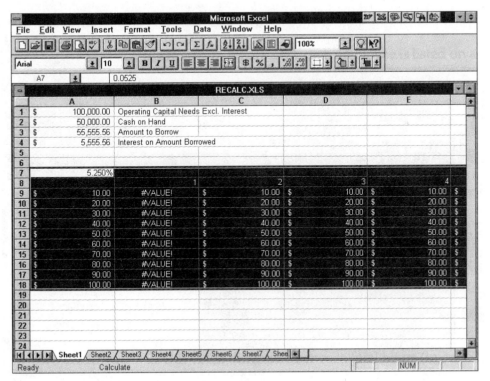

FIGURE 13.4
RECALC.XLS, intermediate

---

[1] Pressing Ctrl Enter is a shortcut that copies a formula entered in one cell of a selected block to all other cells in that block, adjusting relative addresses as necessary.

6. Look at the result of this operation, illustrated below. Use the arrow keys to move around in the area occupied by the cells pasted from COMPOUND.XLS.

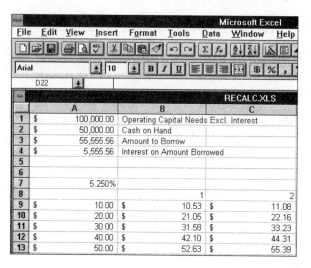

7. Press .

8. Use the File | New command to open a new workbook. Save it with the name EXTRACT.XLS.

9. Copy the range A1:F18 of RECALC.XLS and use the Edit | Paste Special command to copy only the values into EXTRACT.XLS. The result should look like Figure 13.5.

FIGURE 13.5
EXTRACT.XLS, final

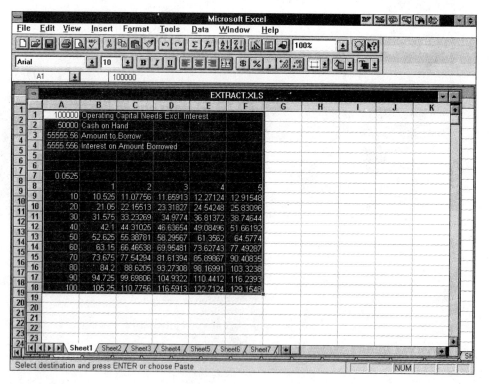

CHECKPOINT 13A What key combination allows you to activate a workbook that is not visible; that is, one on which you cannot click with the mouse?

10. Use the File | Save As command to rename RECALC.XLS with the file name COMBINE.XLS.

11. Examine EXTRACT.XLS. Go to some of the cells that used to have formulas. Are there any formulas left? Why not? Save your work. When you close RECALC.XLS, you may see this dialog box; if so, select No.

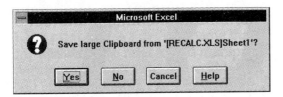

Linking Workbooks by Formula

Excel permits you to refer to values in another workbook when building formulas in the current workbook. This feature is called *linking*. For example, you have a workbook (named INVSTMTS.XLS) in which you keep track of your investments (name, quantity, current market value). One of the cells in that workbook contains the current dollar value of the investments (the sum of quantity times value for all items). This cell is named Cur_Val.

You maintain another workbook (named NETWORTH.XLS) that contains your total net worth—that is, how much your home is worth and the amount of mortgage, your savings and retirement account data, and so on. One of the entries on this second workbook is "Current Value of Investments." To ensure that this figure is up to date whenever you work with NETWORTH.XLS, you create a formula that refers to the Cur_Val range in INVSTMTS.XLS:

```
='[INVSTMTS.XLS]SHEET1'!CUR_VAL
```

Enter it in the cell in NETWORTH.XLS that is supposed to contain the current value of investments. Notice the following about this formula:

- The formula begins with an equal sign
- The workbook name is enclosed in square brackets and includes the extension
- The sheet name follows the workbook name
- The combination of the workbook name and sheet name may be enclosed in single quotation marks (this is not always necessary, but will never cause a problem)
- The combination of the workbook name and sheet name is followed by an exclamation point

- There are no spaces between the workbook name, the sheet name, and the range (cell) name

If INVSTMTS.XLS were on a different disk or directory, the entire path name should be included; for example:

`='[C:\BUDGET\INVSTMTS.XLS]SHEET1'!CUR_VAL`

The easiest way to enter this formula is to use the pointing method. (You learned this method in Unit 3.) To enter the formula, you would open both workbooks, use the Window | Arrange command to see both workbooks, and type =. The workbook is now ready to accept a reference. You would enter the reference by pointing to it. Click on the INVSTMTS.XLS workbook title bar to activate it; then click on the cell named Cur_Val. The reference would be entered in the formula in the NETWORTH.XLS workbook; press [Enter]. The formula is complete.

In Excel terminology, NETWORTH.XLS is a *dependent workbook*—that is, it contains information that depends on another file. INVSTMTS.XLS is a *source workbook*—that is, it contains data that supports a value in another workbook. NETWORTH.XLS and INVSTMTS.XLS are *linked documents*. The reference to INVSTMTS.XLS is an *external reference*. The formula in NETWORTH.XLS is an external reference formula.

If the source workbook and the dependent workbook(s) are in different directories, you should always save all source workbooks before closing the dependent workbook. This ensures that the linking information in the dependent workbook is updated and correct.

You can use a cell reference (such as J35) in the formula, but range names are much better. If you alter the structure of the INVSTMTS.XLS file, the cell reference might change. But the range name would usually continue to be valid, even if it refers to a different cell. If you decide to use cell references, Excel defaults to absolute references.

Whenever you retrieve NETWORTH (unless INVSTMTS is already open), Excel will display a dialog box asking if you wish to update references to unopened documents (INVSTMTS). You should usually answer Yes, which will obtain the current value of the Cur_Val range in INVSTMTS and place that value in the proper place in NETWORTH. If you are operating in a network or multitasking system where it is possible that some other user could change the values in INVSTMTS while you are working in NETWORTH, use the Edit | Links command at regular intervals to retrieve the most recently saved value of Cur_Val.

Linked files have a major advantage over data files that are created using the Copy and Paste procedure. When you paste data, the data in the pasted file reflect the situation at the time the Copy and Paste procedure was initiated. If you subsequently change one of the supporting files, the data in the pasted file are no longer accurate. Linked files always use the most recent data and reflect all changes in the supporting files. The Copy and Paste procedure is somewhat easier to use, however, because large ranges of data can be addressed at once.

GUIDED ACTIVITY 13.2

Linking Workbooks by Formula

In this Guided Activity you will use formulas to link information from two supporting workbooks into a dependent workbook. Suppose that you are responsible for sales reporting for a manufacturing firm. This division has two sales offices—Seattle and Los Angeles. These two departments have turned in the sales reports that are contained in the workbooks SEAREPT.XLS and LAREPT.XLS. You should have copied these files from the Student Data Disk to your working disk in Guided Activity 10.1. Your task is to combine these two workbooks into one consolidated workbook for the Division Manager.

1. If you are not continuing from the previous Guided Activity, load Windows and enter Excel.

2. Open LAREPT.XLS and SEAREPT.XLS.

3. Activate LAREPT.XLS. Use the File | Save As command to change the name to CONSREPT.XLS. Open LAREPT.XLS. You should now have LAREPT.XLS, SEAREPT.XLS, and CONSREPT.XLS open. Use the Tiled option of the Window | Arrange command to see all three workbooks.

4. Activate CONSREPT.XLS. Highlight Los Angeles in cell A1 and change it to Consolidated Total.

5. Select Edit | Delete to remove rows 3 through 8.

CHECKPOINT 13B What is the best way to select an entire row with the mouse? the keyboard?

6. Select cell A2. Change Sales Person to Sales Office. To place the two words on separate lines, press [Alt][Enter] between them. Type Los Angeles in cell A3, Seattle in cell A4, and Total in cell A5.

7. Give the Insert | Name | Define command. Delete the range names LAUNITS and LADOLLARS.

8. Select cell B3. Type =. Activate LAREPT.XLS by clicking on it. Give the Insert | Name | Paste command. Select LAUNITS and click OK. Press [Enter] to complete the formula. Repeat this procedure in cell C3, selecting the range name LADOLLARS this time.

9. Repeat step 8 in the range B4:C4, using the SEAREPT.XLS workbook and selecting the range names SEAUNITS and SEADOLLARS, respectively.

10. Enter the sum functions needed in B5:C5. After formatting, your screen should look similar to Figure 13.6.

11. Save your work.

FIGURE 13.6
Consolidated report, final

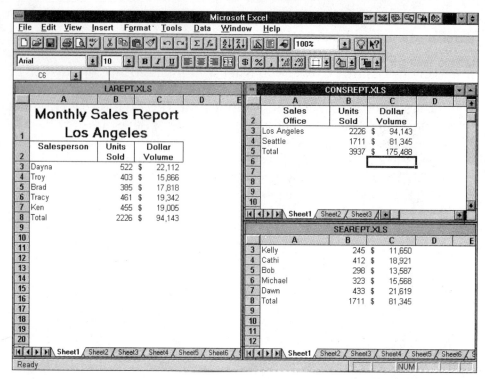

Consolidating Data

The process of combining data from multiple workbooks is called *consolidation*. It is quite important in accounting applications. Data | Consolidate allows you to incorporate data from other Excel workbooks into the current workbook. The Data | Consolidate dialog box is illustrated in Figure 13.7

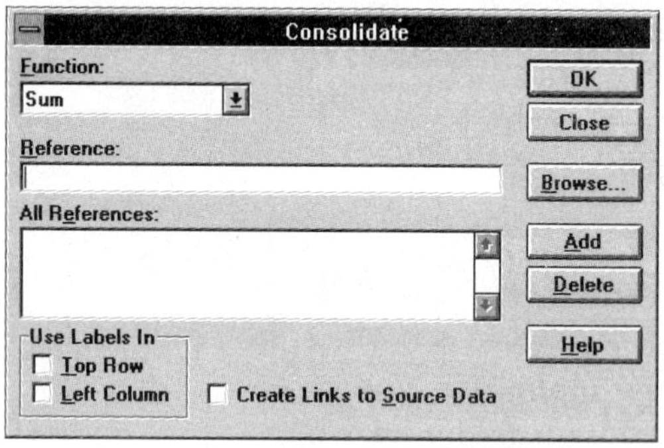

FIGURE 13.7
Data | Consolidate dialog box

First, you need to decide if you are consolidating by position or by category. If each source document has the same categories in the same position (for example, if you are consolidating departmental budgets into a company budget and each department has used the same budget template), you can consolidate by position. If, however, categories of data occupy different locations in different source documents (for example, if revenue occupies column A in one database and column D in another), then you need to consolidate by category. If you are consolidating by category, you must inform Excel whether the category names are in the top row or the left column.

The next step is to select the destination area for the consolidated data. If you will be consolidating by category, the destination area should contain the category titles you are using.

Excel allows you to use 11 different functions to consolidate your data, but defaults to SUM( ). If you need an average, for example, rather than the sum of the data in the source documents, select AVERAGE( ).

Now select the first source area (including the categories, if you are consolidating by category). The easiest way to do this is to have the source document open and select the source area with the mouse. If you do not have a mouse, you can type the external reference. For more information on typing external references, see the section "Linking Workbooks by Formula," earlier in this unit. Once you have entered the reference information, click on the Add button. Continue entering the reference information and clicking on the Add button until you have consolidated all source areas.

The last item in the Data | Consolidate dialog box is the Create Links to Source Data check box. By now, you have probably already figured out that activating this option initiates an active link to the supporting data. If you use this feature, the dependent workbook will change whenever any of the supporting documents changes.

GUIDED ACTIVITY 13.3

Consolidating Data

In this Guided Activity you solve the problem posed in the last Guided Activity, using the Data | Consolidate command. Because of the limitations of the Data | Consolidate command (you must have data locations in the consolidated workbook that correspond to the data locations in the supporting documents), you will make some changes to the source documents.

1. If you are not continuing from the previous Guided Activity, load Windows and enter Excel.

2. Open LAREPT.XLS and SEAREPT.XLS.

   a. Use the File | Save As command to save LAREPT.XLS as LAREPT2.XLS and SEAREPT.XLS as SEAREPT2.XLS.

   b. Use the Edit | Paste Special command to change row 8 of each workbook to values. Then use Edit | Delete to remove rows 3 through 7.

   c. Save both workbooks.

3. Open CONSREPT.XLS. When asked, do not reestablish links.

   a. Use the File | Save As command to change the name to CONREPT2.XLS.

   b. Use Edit | Clear | All to clear B5:C5. Then use Edit | Delete to remove rows 3 and 4. Your screen should now resemble Figure 13.8.

FIGURE 13.8
Preparation to consolidate by position

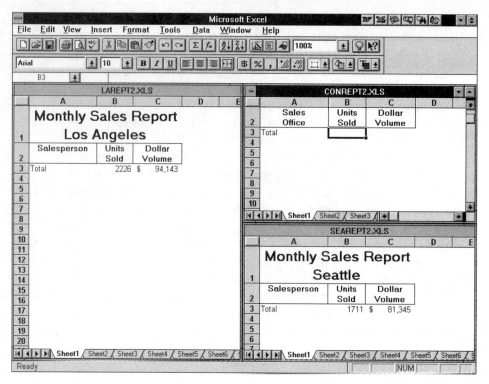

4. You will consolidate these two workbooks by position.

   a. Highlight B3:C3 of CONREPT2.XLS. Give the Data | Consolidate command.

   b. Activate LAREPT2.XLS by clicking on it. Highlight B3:C3. Click on the Add button in the Data | Consolidate dialog box.

   c. Activate SEAREPT2.XLS by clicking on it. Highlight B3:C3. Click on the Add button.

   d. Turn on the Create Links to Source Data button by clicking on it. Click on OK.

5. Excel will consolidate the information from the supporting workbooks into the dependent workbook and outline the dependent workbook.

   a. Close LAREPT2.XLS and SEAREPT2.XLS.

   b. Click on the Expand button, add labels, and format CONREPT2.XLS to look like Figure 13.9.

6. Save your work.

FIGURE 13.9
CONREPT2.XLS
workbook

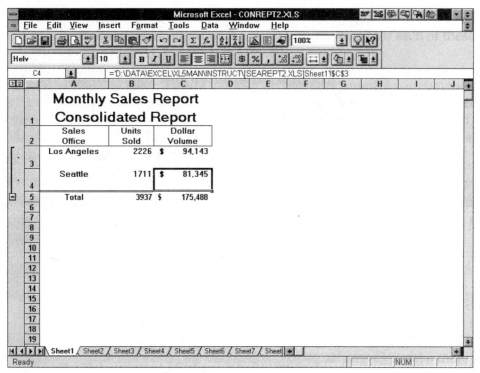

The Workbook as a Consolidation Tool

Since Unit 2, we have been illustrating techniques for storing similar or related data on separate sheets in the same workbook. The workbook is an excellent tool for adding a third dimension to your data analysis. For example, if you are the controller of a company with several divisions, you might be responsible for maintaining the company budget. Such a budget would be arranged by category, by month, by division. The workbook allows you to decide how you want to organize your data. It probably makes sense to place the categories down a column. Then, depending on your needs, you can either place the months along a row and the divisions on different sheets of the workbook (with a company total sheet), or place the divisions along a row and the months on different sheets (with an annual total sheet).

Either way, the workbook gives you a method of creating workbooks with identical structure and similar data in one design step. Remember the RB96PROJ.XLS workbook. Suppose the RB Company has four regional offices in Yuma, Cheyenne, York, and Halifax. Officers need to be able to see the projections for each regional office separately plus a consolidation of the information for the four regions. If you use a workbook for this problem, you will put the four regional projections and the consolidation in five separate sheets of a workbook. Since you have already designed one worksheet for this report, you save the current RB96PROJ worksheet to a new workbook with the name RB96BUDG.XLS and copy the original sheet to four new sheets. To do this, use the Edit I Move or Copy Sheet command and give each sheet a name reflecting its function (for example, Chey, Yuma, York, and Hfax). Then rename the original sheet Total using the Format | Sheet | Rename command.

To gain the benefits of the workgroup, you select multiple sheets before editing. To select consecutive sheets, click on the first sheet tab, hold [Shift], and click on the last sheet in the group. To select nonconsecutive sheets, click on the first sheet tab, hold [Ctrl], and click on the subsequent sheet tabs. Since all five workbooks are part of the group edit, you can select the information that will be identical in each sheet and issue the Edit | Fill | Across Worksheets command. The information will be copied to all selected worksheets. This command functions essentially the same as the other Edit | Fill commands and is much faster than using the Copy and Paste procedure to accomplish the same goal.

Alternatively, you can select multiple sheets and then design a master sheet. As you enter the information in the master sheet, it is automatically copied to the other four sheets in the group. Once you have entered all the information that will be identical for each division, close the group edit by activating a sheet that is not part of the group.

GUIDED ACTIVITY 13.4

Using Workbooks

1. If you are not continuing from the previous Guided Activity, load Windows and enter Excel.

2. Open RB96PROJ.XLS. Select A1:G20 and use Edit | Copy to copy it to the Windows Clipboard. If a dialog box appears asking whether to save a large Clipboard, select Yes. Close RB96PROJ.XLS.

3. Click the New Workbook tool and give the Edit | Paste command. Save the new workbook as RB96BUDG.XLS.

4. West coast data are included in other places, so delete rows 8 and 14. Cell F18 should read $53,115.04. (You will probably have to widen the column to read the number. Don't worry about the other column widths; you will fix that later.) Ensure that the projected growth of revenue (cell G5) is 5% and the projected growth of expenses (G10) is 3%.

5. Create four new sheets following this procedure:

    a. Give the Format | Sheet | Rename command and rename the sheet Total.

CHECKPOINT 13C What is the mouse shortcut to rename a sheet?

   b. Make a copy of the Total sheet by giving the Edit | Move or Copy Sheet command, inserting it before Sheet2, and selecting Create a Copy. Make three more copies of the Total sheet by holding [Ctrl] and dragging the sheet tab to the center of the Sheet2 tab and releasing it. You should now have five copies of the Total sheet named Total, Total(1), through Total(4).

c. Rename Total(1) through Total(4) to Yuma, York, Hfax, and Chey, using the mouse shortcut.

6. Select all five sheets by clicking on Total, then holding [Shift] and clicking on the last of the five worksheets—it should be Chey if you have followed the procedure exactly.

7. Select columns A:G and give the Format | Column | Width command. Enter 11 in the Column Width box and click OK.

8. All five worksheets are currently identical. Deselect the multiple sheet selection by clicking on the Sheet2 tab. Change the four supporting sheets by selecting each in turn and entering the information in this table:

Cell	Yuma	York	Hfax	Chey
C2	Add - Yuma	Add - York	Add - Halifax	Add - Cheyenne
B6	3000	38900	37500	25100
B7	40000	22000	27000	32700
B11	50000	49000	48500	41000
B12	1500	12500	10000	14800
G5	8%	3%	6%	9%
G10	7%	1%	5%	4%

8. Fill in the following information in the Total sheet.

   a. Change the entry in cell C2 to read 1996 Projections - Total.

   b. Use the Edit | Clear | Contents command to erase G4:G10.

   c. Click on cell B6. Enter =sum(, click the Yuma sheet tab, hold [Shift], and click the Chey sheet tab, then select cell B6 and type) (a closing parenthesis). The formula in the Total sheet should read =SUM(Yuma:Chey!B6). The colon following Yuma sets a range across adjacent worksheets in a workbook.

   d. Now use the AutoFill handle to copy cell B6 to cell B7. Use the AutoFill handle again to copy B6:B7 to C6:E7.

   e. Use drag and drop to copy B6:E7 to B11:E12.

   f. Change the column width of column F to 15.

10. Save the file. The Total sheet of your workbook should look like Figure 13.10.

You have now created a Revenue and Expense Projections workbook that links the information from four regional offices into a consolidated total sheet. The consolidated sheet has live links to the four regional reports. If new revenue or expense data are entered into any of the four regional reports, or if any of the projected growth figures change, the consolidated report will immediately reflect the change.

FIGURE 13.10
RB96BUDG.XLS workbook

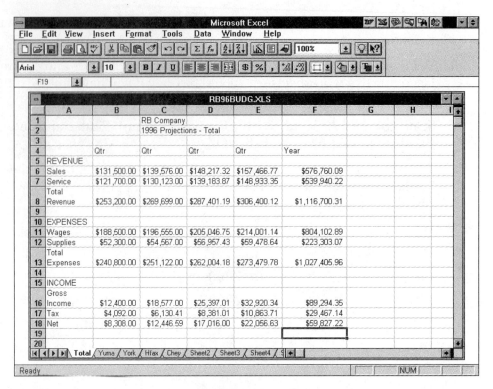

11. To convince yourself that the links work, change the projected revenue growth for York from 3% to 5%. The projected Company Gross should change from $79,095 to $80,800. Change it back to 3% and give the File I Save command to save the workbook.

Exchanging Data with Other Applications

You have seen many ways in which Excel can assist you in manipulating numbers with its date arithmetic, financial functions, data tables, graphics, and so on. However, there are many other personal computer software programs that you might have to operate, and there is a good chance that someday you will want to take data generated elsewhere and insert those data into Excel or to take data from Excel and send them to another application. In the remainder of this unit we discuss methods for *importing* data from other sources into Excel and a method for *exporting* Excel data so that other programs can use them.

The data you wish to manipulate can come from a number of sources:

- Multiplan or some other spreadsheet program, for applications created back in the dark ages before Excel
- Lotus 1-2-3, Quattro Pro, or another "modern" spreadsheet program
- dBASE data files, such as a master accounts or transaction file
- BASIC programs that write sequential files

- WordStar or WordPerfect files; these word processors are also good for entering text and data into sequential files

- The moon, or at least a mainframe computer, via a communications package

The above sources fall into two general categories: *program-specific format* and *ASCII-generic format*. The format determines how you incorporate the file into Excel.

Program-Specific Formats

Most of the database managers and spreadsheet programs use a specialized format for storing data in disk files, with distinctive file extensions (the characters after the period) used to denote the special format. For instance, dBASE IV uses the extension .DBF, the latest release of Lotus 1-2-3 uses .WK4, and Multiplan uses .SLK. A number of programs have the ability to store data in the so-called data interchange format, or .DIF, which was developed by the makers of VisiCalc for transfer of numeric data among programs.

As discussed in the "File Commands" section at the beginning of this unit, the File | Save As command has the ability to transfer data between program-specific formats and Excel workbook formats.[2] Excel can import to the various formats listed in Table 13.1. The program executes the conversion of formats through the Save File as Type button of the File | Save As command (the dialog box was shown previously in Figure 13.2).

Instead of choosing the Microsoft Excel Workbook file format (the default), use the arrow keys to move to the desired file format and then press [Enter] or click on OK. Excel will return you to the main File | Save As dialog box. Notice that the file extension will now match the file extension of the desired format. When you click on OK to save the file, Excel will save the file in the format that you have selected.

Opening a file from a foreign format that Excel can interpret is even easier than saving to a different format. Use the File | Open command as if you were going to open an Excel file. In the File Name text box, change the default file name from `*.XL*` to `*.*` and click on OK. The effect of using the DOS wild card character is to view every file in the selected directory. Then select the file you wish to open and click on OK. If you know the exact extension—for instance, .WK3 for Lotus 1-2-3 Release 3.x and Lotus 1-2-3 for Windows Release 1.x—enter `*.WK3` instead of `*.*`.

If you wish to save the file in Excel format when you are done, follow the procedure earlier in this section. Excel's default is to save the file in the format from which it was opened. In this unit you open a dBASE III[3] .DBF file and save it to an Excel Version 5 (Microsoft Excel workbook) .XLS file.

Since the files to be translated are on the disk in drive A:, you select the `a:` drive in the drive list and `dBASE Files (*.DBF)` in the List Files of Type box. Excel lists all files in the root directory of drive A: that have the .DBF extension (Figure 13.11).

---

[2] If you wish to use an .XLS file from Excel Version 5 with Excel Version 4.0 or earlier, you must first use the File | Save As command to convert it to the Excel Version 4.0, 3.0, or 2.0 format. However, files from older versions of Excel may be opened with the File | Open command directly in Version 5.

[3] dBASE III Plus and dBASE IV use virtually the same file format as dBASE III, so this choice will also translate those dBASE files.

Use the arrow keys or the mouse to select the source file and click on OK. Excel then opens the file. The title bar shows the actual name of the file you opened. Excel converts the file to an Excel format to allow you to edit it in Excel and, unless you instruct differently, will convert it back to its original format when you save the file.

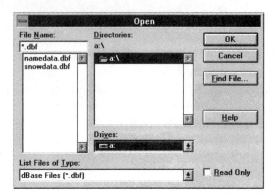

FIGURE 13.11
Opening a dBASE file

Because of differences in the abilities of various formats, you must expect that certain functions and formatting characteristics will not remain true to the original through the conversion process. For example, if you save an Excel 3 workbook with graphic objects and outlining in the Excel 2.1 format, the graphic objects will not be a part of the Excel 2.1 file. The outline will also be lost, although the formatting differences between the various styles will be saved. You can now perform any housecleaning tasks necessary due to the differences between formats; this is much simpler and faster than reentering all the data.

ASCII-Generic Formats

ASCII (pronounced *ass-key*) is the acronym for American Standard Code for Information Interchange. ASCII-generic formatted files are files in which the data are not in a special machine code, but rather in rows and/or columns of plain text. ASCII-generic files are created by BASIC programs as sequential files (but BASIC random access files are not ASCII-generic). WordStar (in the nondocument mode), WordPerfect (using the Text In/Out command), and Word for Windows (using the File | Save As | Text command) create ASCII-generic files. dBASE IV and other database managers can write an ASCII-generic file with commands such as COPY TO...SDF and COPY TO...DELIMITED. Also, anything you receive via modem that is in text and numbers can probably be converted to an ASCII-generic format. Excel generates ASCII-generic files when you use the File | Save As command and choose Text.

Data / Text to Columns and ASCII File Importation

If you wish to import a file containing both text and numbers, give the File | Open command. Excel interprets each line of a text file as a row of the new workbook. To break each line into columns, Excel automatically opens the Text Import Wizard. The dialog box for Step 1 is illustrated in Figure 13.12.

In the Original Data Type group box, select the type of text file you are importing. A delimited file uses a specific character (frequently a tab or a comma) to separate columns. A fixed width file fills each entry with spaces so that each entry in a particular column has the same number of characters. The sample data in the preview box helps you determine which type to choose. The preview in Figure 13.12 is obviously a fixed width file, since the columns line up with one another perfectly, and it contains no characters that might be used as delimiters.

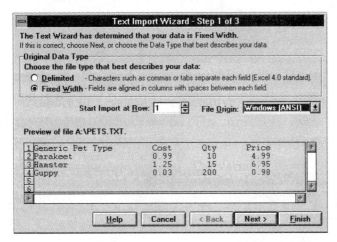

FIGURE 13.12 Text Import Wizard, Step 1

Frequently, text files will begin with a title page or other information that you do not want to import into Excel. The Start Import at Row box gives you the opportunity to leave these rows out of the import process. The File Origin box allows you to select the operating system that created the text file. When you click Next, Excel presents a Step 2 dialog box; the appearance of this dialog box depends on whether you select the Delimited or Fixed Width file type. These dialog boxes are illustrated in Figure 13.13 and 13.14.

The Fixed Width version of the Step 2 dialog box allows you to create, delete, or move *break lines* (the lines that indicate where Excel will create new columns). In Figure 13.13, the break line at column 11 should be moved to column 16, and the break line at column 24 should be deleted.

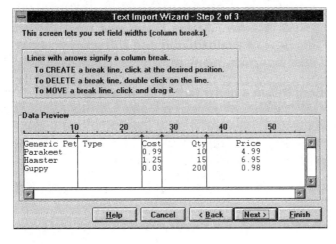

FIGURE 13.13 Text Import Wizard, Step 2, Fixed Width

The Delimited version of the Step 2 dialog box allows you to specify the *delimiter* (the character used to indicate a new column). It also gives you the option of treating consecutive delimiters as a single delimiter. (If a comma is the delimiter, should `James,,Smith` be two columns or three?) In some delimited files,

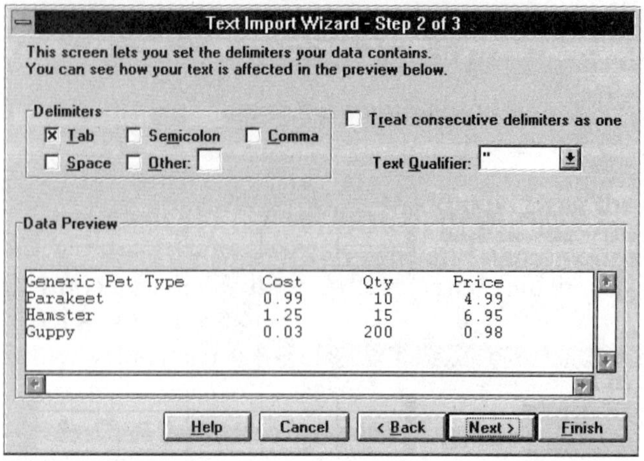

FIGURE 13.14
Text Import Wizard, Step 2, Delimited

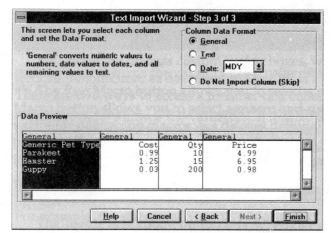

FIGURE 13.15
Text Import Wizard, Step 3

single or double quotation marks are placed around text entries to indicate that they should be treated as text, even if they contain characters that would otherwise be considered delimiters. The Text Qualifier box allows you to specify the text qualifier character. Regardless of which version of the Step 2 dialog box you are using, Excel displays the Step 3 dialog box (illustrated in Figure 13.15) when you click Next.

Step 3 of the Text Import Wizard allows you to make choices about the numeric formatting of individual columns. By default, all columns are formatted as General. If you have a numeric field containing zip codes or telephone numbers, you will probably want to format these as text. Since you will never perform mathematical operations on these fields, they should be treated as text. You also have the option of formatting certain fields as dates, and choosing the date format. Finally, you can choose not to import certain columns.

To open a text file without invoking the Text Import Wizard, hold [Shift] while opening the file. If you do this, Excel will open the file with each line contained in column A (up to the limit of 255 characters per cell) and on a separate row. You can select the rows to be converted to columns, and then choose the Data | Text to Columns command, which opens the Text Wizard. From that point, the procedure is identical to the one we have just described. There is very little to be gained from this, other than understanding the process that takes place.

Say you have a file of inventory data on a disk, with each data line of the file beginning with a text entry followed by three numbers:

```
Generic Pet Type      Cost      Qty      Price
Parakeet              0.99      10       4.99
Hamster               1.25      15       6.95
Guppy                 0.03      200      0.98
```

You wish to bring these data into Excel so that you can calculate how much you have paid for your inventory and how much money you would make if you sell it all. The data are saved in a file named PETS.TXT. You perform this operation in Guided Activity 13.5.

Although the Text Import Wizard might seem difficult, it is by far the easiest way to import tabular ASCII data. On the other hand, when the source of the data can create output in a format that Excel can open directly (see Table 13.1), the Text Import Wizard is not necessary. Both dBASE and Lotus 1-2-3 can write disk files in such formats.

GUIDED ACTIVITY 13.5

Practicing File Import and Export

In this Guided Activity you use several file importing and exporting commands.

1. Check your data disk to ensure that it contains the file PETS.TXT (which should have been copied from the Student Data Disk). Load Windows and enter Excel.

2. PETS.TXT is an ASCII file in tabular form. Use the Text Import Wizard to import the file into your workbook and convert the data to cell entries, as discussed above.

3. Change the column width of column A to 18. Save your file as PETS.XLS.

4. Save your file again as PETS2.PRN. Give the File | Save As command and select Formatted Text (Space delimited) in the Save File as Type box.

5. If you have a word processing package (Notepad or Write, included with Windows, will work fine), use that package to read the file PETS2.PRN. If you do not have a word processor, give the DOS command `type d:pets2.txt` (where *d* is the disk drive letter) to see the result of the export procedure.

Links Between Excel and Other Windows Applications

One of the greatest advantages of the Windows environment is the ability to seamlessly move data between Windows applications. In the following sections we look at two common methods of transferring data—the Windows Clipboard and Object Linking and Embedding, or OLE.

Exchanging Data via the Clipboard

By far the simplest way to exchange data between Windows applications is via the Clipboard. The Clipboard is simply a data storage area, capable of holding text or graphics. The main limitation of the Clipboard is that it can only hold one item of information at a time, although that one item can be very large.

Whether you are aware of it or not, you already have extensive experience with the Clipboard. Anytime you use the Cut and Paste or Copy and Paste procedures, you are using the Clipboard. Anytime a Windows application executes a Cut command or a Copy command, the selected information is either moved or copied to the Clipboard, replacing everything that currently resides there. Anytime a Windows application executes a Paste command, the information contained in the Clipboard is copied to the application.

Pasting information between applications is as simple as giving the Copy command, changing to the second application, and giving the Paste command. Suppose, for example, that you are writing a memo, in Word for Windows, to your manager regarding the recent increase in sales for your company. You have created an excellent chart in Excel that perfectly illustrates your point. When you reach the point in your memo where you wish to insert the chart, click on Excel, or press [Alt][Tab] until Excel is the active application.[4] Open the workbook containing the chart, select the chart,[5] and issue the Edit | Copy command. Then return to Word for Windows and give the Edit | Paste command. The chart will be copied into your memo and can be sized or cropped as needed, using the tools in Word for Windows.

Using OLE with Windows Applications

You have probably already figured out the critical limitation in exchanging data via the Windows Clipboard. Like any pasting operation, the information is static; it is only accurate at the time it is pasted. If the data change later, the memo is out of date and incorrect. If your manager had asked you to submit a copy of that memo on a weekly basis, with the chart included, you would have to do something different.

Object Linking and Embedding (OLE, pronounced *oh-el-ee* or *oh-lay*) is a new standard where *objects*, such as worksheets, charts, or blocks of text, can be either linked or embedded in a document. OLE Version 2.0 is a major step forward in allowing Windows applications to work together and share data. If you create a *linked object* by selecting the Link to File box, it maintains a link to its *source file*; when the source file is changed, the object is automatically changed also. If you double-click on a linked object, the source file is opened in its *native application*, that is, the application that created the source file. You can then modify the source file; the object is also modified through the link.

An *embedded object* may or may not have a source document; it can be created entirely from within the *host application*, that is, the application into which the object is inserted. When you double-click on an embedded object, it is surrounded by a hashed border, and the menu bar and toolbar(s) change to that of the native application—that is, the application used to create the embedded object. The effect is that without leaving Word for Windows, you can create or modify an Excel chart with all the menus and tools that you would have available in Excel. As soon as you deselect the embedded object, the menus and toolbar(s) return to normal.

OLE is accomplished through the Insert | Object command, which has two tabs. The dialog boxes are illustrated in Figures 13.16 and 13.17.

---

4 If Excel is not already running, make Program Manager the active application and start Excel.

5 Keyboard users can select an entire chart by pressing [Esc] to make sure nothing is currently selected and then pressing [→]; mouse users can select an entire chart by clicking anywhere outside the plot area where there is not another item.

FIGURE 13.16
Insert / Object dialog box, Create New tab

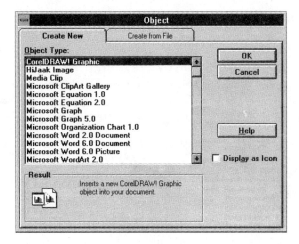

To create a new file, select the Create New tab and select one of the applications from the Object Type list. Anytime you create a new object, it will be an embedded, rather than a linked, object. When you click OK, Excel will draw a box on the worksheet to contain the embedded object. The menu bar and toolbar(s) will change to allow you to create the object. Create the object and click outside the box containing the object, and the Excel menu bar and toolbar(s) will return.

FIGURE 13.17
Insert / Object dialog box, Create from File tab

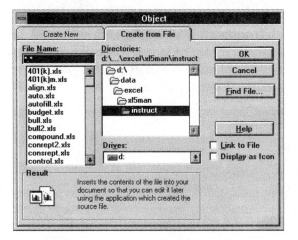

To create an object from an existing source file, select the Create from File tab and select the source file using the familiar Drives, Directories, and File Name boxes. Decide whether you want the file to be linked or embedded; if you wish to establish a link, select the Link to File check box. Select linked objects if you want the file to be updated automatically. Select embedded objects if you want to be able to update the object without leaving Excel. When you click OK, the source file will appear in a box on the worksheet. If both applications support OLE Version 2.0, you can also create an embedded object from an existing file by dragging the object from one application and dropping it in another application.

Updating Remote Links

Once you have established a remote link to another application, Excel gives you a certain amount of control over how the link works and when it is updated. The Edit | Links command provides this control. When you select this command, Excel will present the dialog box illustrated in Figure 13.18. (This particular workbook contains a linked file named SMNET.VSD that was orginally created in Shapeware's Visio application.)

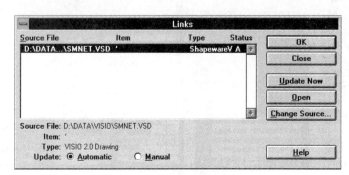

FIGURE 13.18
Edit | Links dialog box

The information list includes the name of the source file, the source of the link (referred to as Item), a description of the source file (referred to as Type), and whether the link is updated automatically or manually (Status). You can change the update status by selecting the Automatic or Manual radio button. You can update the link by selecting the Update Now command button. You can open the source file's native application by selecting the Open command button. You can change the source file by selecting the Change Source command button.

GUIDED ACTIVITY 13.6

Embedding an Object

This Guided Activity is designed to assist those who have access to Word for Windows Version 6.0, a word processor that supports OLE. You will use the procedure described above to create a remote link between Word for Windows and Excel. If you do not have access to Word for Windows (or another Windows word processor that supports OLE), read through this Guided Activity carefully to ensure that you understand the procedure.

1. If you are not continuing from the previous Guided Activity, open Windows and enter Word for Windows.

2. Type a memo to your boss with the text in Figure 13.19. You can use as many features of Word for Windows as you like.

FIGURE 13.19
Memo text

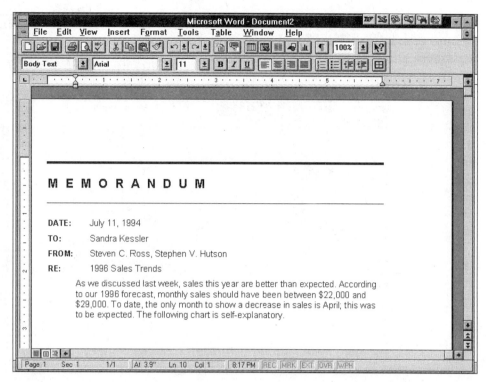

3. Give the Insert | Object command. In the Object dialog box, select Microsoft Excel 5.0 Chart and click OK. The generic chart object shown in Figure 13.20 will display.

FIGURE 13.20
Chart object, step 1

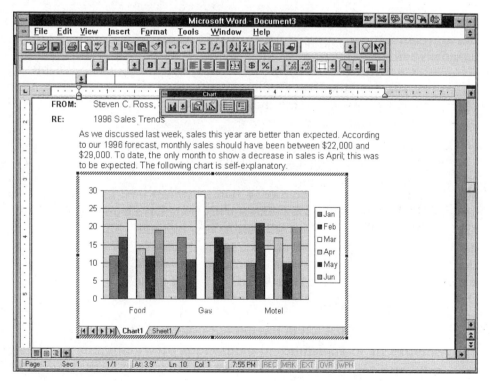

FIGURE 13.21
Chart object, step 2

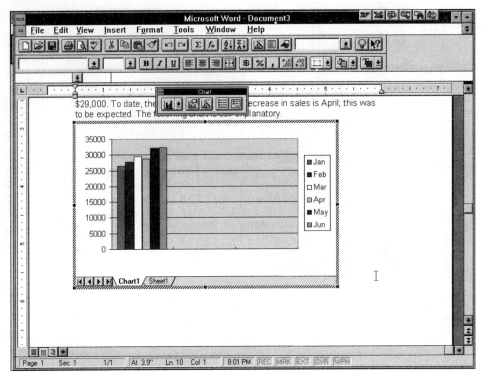

4. Select the Sheet1 tab and enter the following data in the range A2:B8.

Jan	Feb	Mar	Apr	May	June	July
26524	27695	29423	28659	32112	32425	36819

   Your chart should now look like Figure 13.21.

5. Click the ChartWizard tool. (The Chart toolbar should be visible; if it is not, display it using the View | Toolbars command.) Use the ChartWizard to modify the chart settings so that the chart looks like the one in Figure 13.22. (*Hint*: Your data series should be in columns.)

6. Double-click the chart object and select the Sheet1 tab. Change the January sales to 32147. Select the Chart1 tab. Does the link operate correctly? Give the Edit | Undo command.

7. The finished memo should look like Figure 13.22. Save the Word for Windows document with the file name SALESCHT.DOC.

FIGURE 13.22
Chart object, final

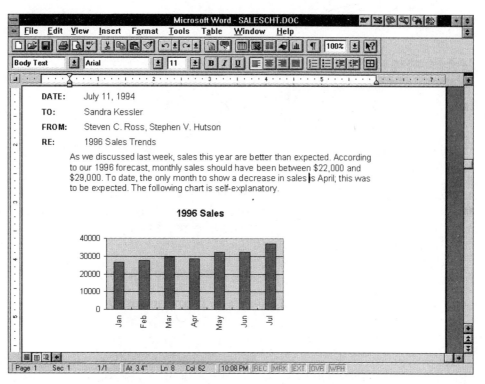

EXERCISE 13.1

Consolidating Data from Two Workbooks

In this Exercise you create two simple workbooks with sales and expenses data, then combine them into a national summary sheet. In practice, the regional workbooks would be much more complex, but this exercise is intended to illustrate the procedure for consolidating data from different workbooks.

1. Starting in cell A1 of a blank workbook, make the following entries:

   ```
   Western Region
   Sales       15000
   Expenses    10000
   ```

2. Give the range B2:B3 the name SUMMARY. Also, use Insert | Name | Create to name cells B2:B3 after the labels in A2:A3. Save the file as WESTERN.XLS.

3. Change the entries to read:

   ```
   Eastern Region
   Sales       17000
   Expenses    13000
   ```

4. Save the file with the name EASTERN.XLS. (You do not have to rename the ranges before saving the workbook.)

5. Change the entries to read:

   ```
   National Summary
   Sales
   Expenses
   NET
   ```

   Note that cells B2 and B3 no longer contain data (clear them with Edit | Clear).

6. Enter the formula =Sales-Expenses in cell B4. Save the file with the name NATIONAL.XLS.

7. Open WESTERN.XLS and EASTERN.XLS. Use the Window | Arrange | Tiled command to see all three workbooks. Make NATIONAL.XLS!B2 the active cell. Use the Data | Consolidate command to consolidate the data from the Sales category in each of the regional workbooks (one at a time). Since you are consolidating by position, you only need to click on the cells containing the data and click on Add. When both have been consolidated, click on OK.

8. To consolidate Expenses, you will consolidate by category.[6] Select NATIONAL.XLS!A3:B3. Give the Data | Consolidate command. Click on Left Column. Place the insertion cursor in the Reference box. If necessary, move the Data | Consolidate dialog box by clicking on the title bar and dragging it. Add the two Expense categories by selecting them (including the category names) and clicking on the Add button. Click on OK.

9. Save the file as NATION2.XLS, then close this workbook (but not WESTERN.XLS nor EASTERN.XLS). The next Exercise links the NATIONAL.XLS workbook to the two regional workbooks.

EXERCISE 13.2

Linking Workbooks

In this Exercise, you link the data from the two regional workbooks into the NATIONAL workbook. You must understand the previous Exercise before attempting this Exercise.

1. If you are not continuing from the previous Exercise, load Excel. Open NATIONAL.XLS.

2. Select NATIONAL.XLS!B2:B3. Give the Data | Consolidate command. You will be consolidating the data by position with the Create Links to Source Data box checked on. Click on the Create Links button. Place the insertion cursor in the Reference box. Select the range B2:B3 on each of the source documents and Add them. Click OK. Click on 2 to expand the outline.

---

[6] In this Exercise, you could either consolidate by position or consolidate by category to accomplish both steps 7 and 8. We used both to illustrate the two kinds of consolidation.

3. Change the values in WESTERN.XLS and EASTERN.XLS. Does the link work properly? Restore WESTERN.XLS and EASTERN.XLS to their original values and save all three files.

EXERCISE 13.3

Snow Data

1. Open the file SNOWDATA.DBF (which you should have copied from the Student Data Disk) to a workbook. Remember to change the File Name text box to either *.* or *.DBF, or you will not be able to find the file.
2. Adjust the column widths so that all field names in row 1 are visible.
3. Using Data commands, determine the average snowfall in each state.
4. Draw a chart on a separate sheet that illustrates the average snowfall in the ten states with the highest averages. Save the file as SNOWDATA.XLS. (Note that this leaves SNOWDATA.DBF unchanged.)

EXERCISE 13.4

Gas Mileage (V)

Open GASMILE.XLS. Open Word for Windows. Open the file EPALTR.DOC, which you should have copied to your working disk in Unit 10. Link the GASMILE.XLS worksheet between the two paragraphs of the letter and print a copy. Save the .DOC file as EPALTR2.

Review Questions

*1. What is the difference between program-specific and ASCII-generic file formats, and how does that difference affect the interchange of data between Excel and other programs?

2. What other applications software programs are available to you? How can you transfer data between them and Excel?

3. What kind of data are contained in files with the following extensions:
   a. .XLS
   *b. .XLT

4. What is necessary in order to establish an OLE link?

Key Terms

ASCII-generic format
Break line
Consolidation
Delimiter
Dependent workbook
Embedded object
Exporting
Extension

External reference
File format
File name
Host application
Importing
Linked document
Linked object
Linking

Native application
Object
Path name
Program-specific format
Source file
Source workbook

Documentation Research

Referring to the Excel *User's Guide,* find and record the page number of each of the commands discussed in this unit. We recommend that you also write the page number in the margin next to the discussion of the command in the unit.

1. How can you cause Excel to automatically open a file when the program is loaded?

2. What is DDE?

3. How many source areas can the Data | Consolidate command use?

Advanced Functions

We introduced arithmetic operators and several of the Excel functions in Unit 3. In this unit, we complete the presentation of operators and functions by discussing lookup tables, string expressions, logical expressions, and advanced mathematical functions.

Learning Objectives

At the completion of this unit you should know

1. the full range of workbook functions available in Excel Version 5.

At the completion of this unit you should be able to

1. design a lookup table,
2. use the lookup functions to extract data from the table,
3. write formulas using logical functions and expressions,
4. write formulas using string functions and expressions,
5. write formulas using advanced mathematical functions.

Lookup Tables

A *lookup table* is a table from which you draw information based on an *index number*. Most of us are familiar with the concept of such a table, perhaps with a different name. Consider the following examples:

Grades

0 to 69	=	F
70 to 76	=	D
77 to 84	=	C
85 to 92	=	B
93 to 100	=	A

Taxes

If taxable income is over:	but not over:	tax is:	of the amount over:
0	3,400	0	
3,400	5,500	11%	3,400
5,500	7,600	231 + 12%	5,500
7,600	11,900	483 + 14%	7,600

Sales

Stock No.	Description	Cost	Price
10005	93 Geo Metro	4,037	6,600
10115	94 Pont. Gran Prix	7,632	9,590
11250	94 Buick LeSabre	8,546	10,950

Each of these examples has a few characteristics in common:

- An index (minimum score, minimum income, stock number) in the left-hand column allows us to find data relevant to that index (grade, tax rate, cost, price).
- There are no duplicate index values.
- The table is sorted in ascending index value order.

We can use the VLOOKUP(lookup_value,table_array,col_index_num) function to extract data from the preceding tables. *Lookup_value* is the compare value for which you are finding data. *Table_array* is the entire range containing compare values, column headings, and data. *Table_array* can be a named or specified (by cell references) range. *Col_index_num* is the column number in which you will locate the data. Assume that we have put a tax table in range A7:C10 named TABLEY. *Col_index_num* is the number of columns to the right of the index column (*Col_index_num* for the index column is 1 [one]).

A workbook with this example appears in Figure 14.1. The formula in cell B3 is the key to the workbook; that formula is

```
=VLOOKUP(Income,tabley,2)+(VLOOKUP(Income,tabley,3)*(Income-VLOOKUP(Income,tabley,1)))
```

For intellectual exercise, you are encouraged to determine how and why this formula works.

FIGURE 14.1
INC_TAX.XLS workbook

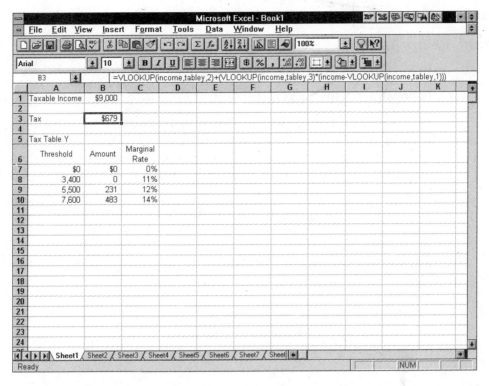

Where the *lookup_value* argument is not matched exactly, the row chosen by VLOOKUP( ) is the last row in which the *index* (left) column value is less than the *index* argument value. This is generally the desired effect, as in the tax example.

VLOOKUP( ) is one of several choice functions. The following are the most commonly used choice functions (recall that the arguments in italics are optional).

CHOOSE(index_num,value1,*value2*...*value13*) Select value: if *index_num* = 0, then the cell containing this function displays #VALUE!; if *index_num* = 1, then the cell displays value1; and so forth. *Index_num* and *value1* ... *value13* can be constants, other cell addresses, or functions.

HLOOKUP(lookup_value,table_array,row_index_num) Table lookup with index row: this function is used to select a value from a table based on the *lookup_value*.

VLOOKUP(lookup_value,table_array,col_index_num) Table lookup with index column.

INDEX(reference,row_num,column_num,*area_num*) Value of cell at intersection: this yields the value of the cell in *reference*, *row_num* rows from the top, *column_num* columns from the left. For instance, =INDEX(A1:C9,1,1) returns the value of cell A1, while the result of =INDEX(A1:C9,K3,J9) depends on the values of cells K3 and J9 as well as the values in the range A1:C9. An *area_num* argument can be used if the *reference* is composed of a multiple selection. The first area of a multiple range selected is number 1, the second is number 2, and so on.

GUIDED ACTIVITY 14.1

Building a Lookup Table

In this Guided Activity you build a lookup table.

1. Follow the startup procedure outlined in Unit 1 to load Windows and enter Excel.

2. Build the tax example lookup table discussed above. The workbook should look like Figure 14.1. In addition to entering the text, values, and VLOOKUP( ) formula, you must also adjust the width of column A, name two ranges (INCOME and TABLEY), format several numbers, and change the alignment on some cells.

CHECKPOINT 14A How do you cause the numbers to be aligned on the right side when some are formatted as currency and others are not?

3. Once the workbook is complete, test the function by entering the following numbers in cell B1. Check the function by computing the tax by hand.

   5700   3400   9000

4. Save your work with the file name INC_TAX.XLS.

Logical Expressions

Logical expressions are cell entries combining logical functions and logical operators. Logical expressions are used when the value to be assigned to a cell is dependent on the value of one or more other cells.

There are several situations in which logical functions are necessary. For instance, a merchant might keep a list of credit accounts on a workbook. One of the columns is the balance due on the account and another is the minimum payment. The minimum payment is one of the following:

- The balance due, if the balance due is less than $20
- $20, if the balance due is between $20 and $200
- 10% of the balance due if the balance due is over $200

As another example, consider the payroll of a small manufacturer. Most employees are paid overtime at the rate of 1.5 times their hourly wage if they work more than 40 hours per week. A few employees, in exempt status, are not eligible for overtime regardless of how many hours they work.

We use these two examples to illustrate the use of logical operators and functions; but first, we present lists of the operators and functions.

Logical Operators

The *logical operators* are as follows. If you recall from our discussion of the order of evaluation in Unit 3, these comparison operators are at the bottom of the order of evaluation, with all of them at the same level. Therefore, they will be evaluated from left to right.

=	Equal to
<	Less than
<=	Less than or equal to
>	Greater than
>=	Greater than or equal to
<>	Not equal to

Special Functions

Excel provides the following four special functions for logical expressions.

NA( ) Not available; sets the value of the cell to #NA!. This function takes no argument.

AND(logical1,logical2...logical30) Logical "AND"; returns the value TRUE if all arguments are true; returns the value FALSE if one or more arguments are false.

OR(logical1,logical2...logical30) Logical "OR"; returns the value TRUE if one or more arguments are true; returns the value FALSE if all arguments are false.

NOT(logical) Logical "NOT"; reverses the value of the argument; returns the value TRUE if the argument is false; returns the value FALSE if the argument is true.

Logical Functions

The following logical functions deal with results that can be categorized as true or false.

FALSE( ) Returns the value FALSE (or 0 [zero]).

TRUE( ) Returns the value TRUE (or 1 [one]).

IF(logical_test,value_if_true,value_if_false) If the *logical_test* argument is true, returns the *value_if_true* argument (or TRUE if the *value_if_true* argument is omitted); if the *logical_test* argument is false, returns the *value_if_false* argument (or FALSE if the *value_if_false* argument is omitted).

ISNUMBER(value) Returns the value TRUE if *value* refers to a number.

ISREF(value) Returns the value TRUE if *value* refers to a reference. =ISREF(A1:C9) always returns the value TRUE because A1:C9 is a legitimate range reference. =ISREF(SALES) returns the value TRUE if there is a range with the name SALES in the current workbook. =ISREF(WESTERN.XLS!EXPENSES) is true if there is a range named EXPENSES in the workbook WESTERN.XLS.

ISTEXT(value) Returns the value TRUE if *value* refers to text.

ISBLANK(value) Returns the value TRUE if *value* refers to an empty cell.

ISNONTEXT(value) Returns the value TRUE if *value* refers to anything other than text (including error values, numeric values, logical values, references, and blank cells).

ISLOGICAL(value) Returns the value TRUE if *value* refers to a logical value (TRUE or FALSE). Note that *value* can be a logical statement that evaluates to TRUE or FALSE, such as =A1>100.

ISNA(value) Returns the value TRUE if *value* refers to the error value #NA!.

ISERR(value) Returns the value TRUE if *value* refers to any error value other than #NA!.

ISERROR(value) Returns the value TRUE if *value* refers to any error value (#NA!, #VALUE!, #REF!, #DIV/0!, #NUM!, #NAME?, or #NULL!).

Excel considers any value that is not equal to zero to be TRUE. The value zero and any formula that yields the result zero is FALSE. An IF( ) statement might look like =IF(a1,b1,c1), which would return the value of cell B1 if cell A1<>0, and the value of cell C1 if cell A1 = 0.

Another possible IF statement would be =IF(a1>a2,b1,c1), which returns the value of cell B1 if A1>A2; otherwise, it takes the value of cell C1.

The following are examples of cell entries using logical operators and special and logical functions.

=IF(A1>0,A5,NA( ))	Yields the value of cell A5 if cell A1 is greater than 0; otherwise is #NA!.
=IF(ISERROR(C9),A5,0)	Yields the value of cell A5 if cell C9 is an error value; otherwise is 0 (zero).
=IF(AND(A2=A8,A3=A9),TRUE( ),NA( ))	Yields the value TRUE (1) if both A2 = A8 and A3 = A9; otherwise is #NA! Because of the order of precedence, the arguments are evaluated first, then the function AND( ) is evaluated.

When writing complex expressions such as these, it is a good idea to test them with dummy data before entrusting the fortunes of the company to your ability to think logically.

Examples

The two situations outlined earlier, overtime and minimum payment, are evaluated here.

Overtime

Consider the payroll of a small manufacturer. Most employees are paid overtime at the rate of 1.5 times their hourly wage if they work more than 40 hours per week.

FIGURE 14.2
OVERTIME.XLS
workbook

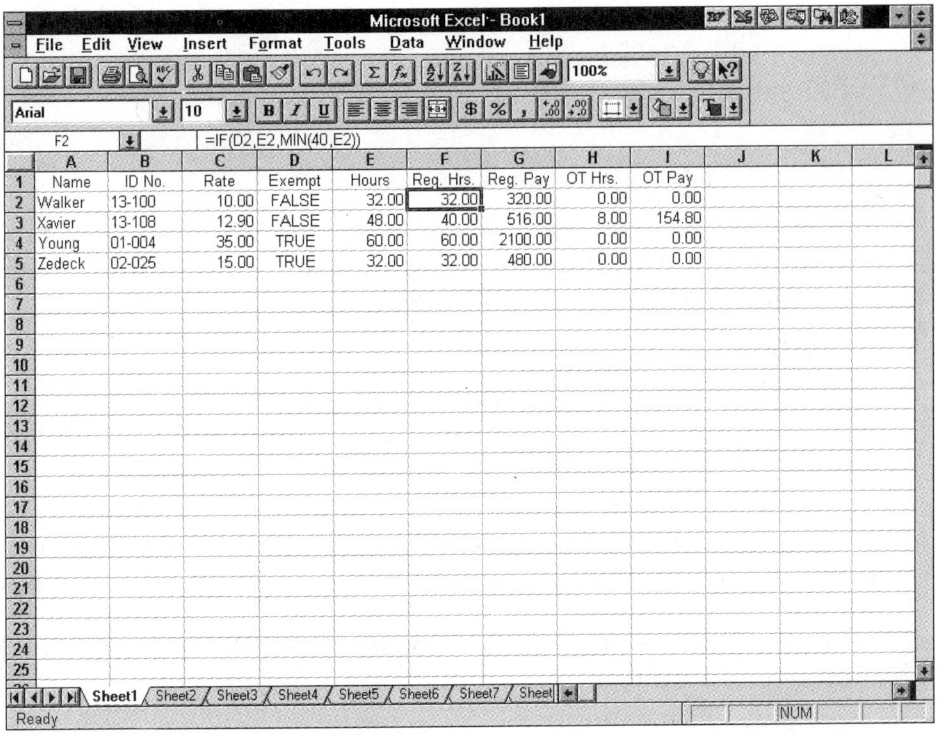

	A	B	C	D	E	F	G	H	I
1	Name	ID No.	Rate	Exempt	Hours	Reg. Hrs.	Reg. Pay	OT Hrs.	OT Pay
2	Walker	13-100	10.00	FALSE	32.00	32.00	320.00	0.00	0.00
3	Xavier	13-108	12.90	FALSE	48.00	40.00	516.00	8.00	154.80
4	Young	01-004	35.00	TRUE	60.00	60.00	2100.00	0.00	0.00
5	Zedeck	02-025	15.00	TRUE	32.00	32.00	480.00	0.00	0.00

F2: =IF(D2,E2,MIN(40,E2))

A few employees, with exempt status, are not eligible for overtime regardless of how many hours they work.

In the workbook illustrated in Figure 14.2, each employee is listed on a separate row. Name and ID number are in columns A and B, the hourly rate is in column C, the exempt status is in column D, and the total hours worked are in column E. (*Note:* This is not the same as the timekeeper's workbook discussed in Unit 11.) Columns A and B are text, columns C and E are values, column D is a series of TRUE (for exempt) and FALSE (for nonexempt) entries.

The number of regular hours is computed in column F and the pay for those hours in column G. The number of overtime hours, if any, is computed in column H, and the overtime pay, for those who are not exempt, is computed in column I. The following entries would be made in row 2, the first row of data:

- In cell F2: =IF(D2,E2,MIN(40,E2)). This translates as follows: If the employee is an exempt employee—that is, cell D2 is TRUE( )—then all hours (in cell E2) are regular hours. If the employee is nonexempt, then the number of regular hours is 40 hours or the number of hours worked, whichever is less.

- In cell G2: =C2*F2. This is the hourly rate times the number of regular hours worked.

- In cell H2: =E2-F2. This is the difference between total hours (in cell E2) and those hours that are regular hours. For exempt employees and those nonexempt employees who work 40 hours or less, this is 0 (zero).

- In cell I2: =1.5*C2*H2. This is 1.5 times the hourly rate times the number of overtime hours.

Corresponding entries would be made in the remaining rows of the workbook. The key to this application is column F. Study the formula carefully. This example is incorporated in Guided Activity 14.2, which follows this section.

Minimum Payment

Recall the merchant who keeps a list of credit accounts on a workbook. In column B is the balance due on the account and in column C is the minimum payment. The minimum payment is one of the following:

- The balance due, if the balance due is less than $20
- $20, if the balance due is between $20 and $200
- 10% of the balance due if the balance due is over $200

Assume that the first row of data is row 2. When there are three choices, as above, you usually need nested IF( ) statements—that is, one IF( ) statement contained as an argument to another IF( ) statement. The trick to building this logic is to momentarily ignore one of the options.

You begin by writing the statement that accomplishes the first condition and part of the second condition:

```
=IF(B2<20,B2,20)
```

Then you include that expression as the false condition argument in an IF( ) statement dealing with the second and third conditions:

```
=IF(B2>200,.10*B2,IF(B2<20,B2,20))
```

This can be read as: *If the value of cell B2 (the balance due) is greater than 200, then display 10% of cell B2; otherwise, if the value of cell B2 is less than 20, display cell B2; otherwise display 20.*

GUIDED ACTIVITY 14.2

Using Logical Functions

In this Guided Activity you use logical functions.

1. If you are not continuing from the previous Guided Activity, load Excel. If you are continuing from the previous Guided Activity, use the File | New command to get a clean workbook.

2. Build a workbook like that illustrated in Figure 14.2:

    a. Center-align the text entries in row 1.

    b. Before making the entries in column B, select the entire column, give the Format | Cells command, select the Number tab, and choose Text.

    c. The entries in columns A and B are text, those in columns C and E (below row 1) are values, and those in column D are either TRUE( ) or FALSE( ).

d. Enter the formulas discussed in the preceding section in F2:I2. If you do not obtain the results illustrated in Figure 14.2, carefully check your work.

e. The formulas can be copied to the range F3:I5.

f. Format numeric entries to match the illustration. The completed workbook should look like Figure 14.2.

3. Save this workbook with the name OVERTIME.XLS.

String Reference, Manipulation, and Functions

The ability to refer to and manipulate text (strings) in functions allows you to develop more sophisticated workbooks. A logical formula can return a string. The text contents of a cell can be referred to by another cell. Text can be entered as usual in cells, but text used in a formula must be entered as a *literal string*—enclosed in double quotation marks (" "). Two text entries are combined (concatenated) with the & operator. For instance, if cell A1 contains the text United Consolidated Industries and cell F9 contains the text Overdrawn (there is a space before the word "Overdrawn"), then

- The cell entry =A1 displays the contents of cell A1—United Consolidated Industries—in the current cell.

- The cell entry =A1&F9 yields United Consolidated Industries Overdrawn

- The cell entry =A1&" Ltd." yields United Consolidated Industries Ltd.

- The entry =IF(J1>K1,J1-K1,F9) yields the difference if cell J1 is greater than cell K1; otherwise, it yields Overdrawn

This feature permits you to use the same workbook to analyze a different company by simply changing the contents of cell A1, which changes the result displayed by all cells that reference cell A1. The following functions are provided to further enhance the use of string data.

CHAR(number) Returns the character whose ANSI (American National Standards Institute) value is *number*. This is often used to create characters that are not directly accessible on the keyboard. For instance, =CHAR(189) displays ½ on the screen.[1]

CLEAN(text) Removes all nonprintable characters from *text*. These control characters are not usable by many printers or other applications.

CODE(text) Returns the ANSI value of the first character in *text*.

---

1 As a Windows application, Excel selects characters from the ANSI code chart. These characters differ from the extended character set built into the IBM PC and compatibles.

DOLLAR(number,*decimals*) Formats *number* to currency format, and then converts it to text. If the *decimals* argument is omitted, it is assumed to be 2.

EXACT(text1,text2) Returns the value TRUE if *text1* and *text2* are an exact equivalence, where exact equivalence includes capitalization. Use of the = operator also checks for equivalence, but ignores capitalization. For instance, if cell C35 contains `Polish` and cell J35 contains `polish`, then `=IF(C35=J35,TRUE( ),FALSE( ))` is TRUE, while `=EXACT(C35,J35)` is FALSE.

FIND(find_text,within_text,start_at_num) Returns a number that corresponds to the location of *find_text* in *within_text*. This is used to determine the position of the *find_text* in *within_text*, starting with the character at *start_at_num*. FIND( ) returns the #VALUE! error value if *find_text* is not located in *within_text*, if *start_at_num* is less than or equal to zero, or if *start_at_num* is greater than the length of *within_text*.

FIXED(number,*decimals*) Rounds *number* to *decimals* number of decimal places, formats *number* to include commas, and converts *number* to text. If *decimals* is omitted, it is assumed to be 2.

LEFT(text,num_chars) Returns the first (leftmost) *num_chars* characters in *text*. If *num_chars* is omitted, it is assumed to be 1.

LEN(text) Returns the number of characters in *text*.

LOWER(text) Converts *text* to lowercase and displays the result. It could be used before an EXACT comparison. Following the above example, `=EXACT(LOWER(C35),J35)` is TRUE.

MID(text,start_num,num_chars) Returns a portion of *text*, starting at *start_num*, proceeding for *num_chars* characters.

N(value) Converts *value* to a number. If *value* is a number, it retains the value of the number. If *value* is a date, it returns the serial number of that date. If *value* is a logical value of TRUE, it returns the value of 1. If *value* is anything else, it returns a value of 0 (zero). This function is rarely needed, since Excel automatically converts values as necessary, but it allows compatibility with other spreadsheet programs.

PROPER(text) Converts *text* to proper capitalization. This capitalizes the first letter of each word in *text* and converts all other letters to lowercase. Excel assumes that a new word begins after each space or punctuation mark. See the example in the REPT( ) function discussion below.

REPLACE(old_text,start_num,num_chars,new_text) Replaces text in *old_text* with *new_text*, beginning at *start_num*, continuing for *num_chars* characters.

REPT(text,number_times) Repeats *text number_times* times. For example: `=PROPER("SHE LOVES YOU, "&(REPT("YEAH ",3)))` yields She Loves You, Yeah Yeah Yeah. (Note the space after "YEAH" in the formula.)

RIGHT(text,*num_chars*) Returns last (rightmost) *num_chars* characters in *text*. If *num_chars* is omitted, it is assumed to be 1.

T(value) Returns the text referred to by *value*. Excel automatically converts values to text as needed; this function is available to provide compatibility with other spreadsheet programs.

TEXT(value,value_format) Formats *value* to *value_format* and converts it to text. The *value_format* argument needs to placed in double quotation marks (" ").

TRIM(text) Removes excess spaces. This removes leading and trailing space characters and converts multiple embedded spaces to single spaces.

UPPER(text) Converts *text* to uppercase and displays the result.

VALUE(text) Converts *text* to a value. Excel automatically converts text to values as necessary; this function is available to provide compatibility with other spreadsheet programs.

Cell and Range Reference Functions

The functions in this group are used to determine information about the cells and ranges of a workbook. In general, their use is beyond the scope of this manual.

ADDRESS(row_num,column_num,*abs_num,a1,sheet_text*) Creates a cell address as a text entry from the values of *row_num* and *column_num*. These arguments would usually be cell references. If *abs_num* is 1 (the default), the cell reference is absolute. If *abs_num* is 4, the cell reference is relative. Other values of *abs_num* create mixed cell references (see the discussion of the ADDRESS( ) function in the Excel Help facility for the complete list). The *a1* argument determines whether the reference is in A1 style (the default) or R1C1 style. The *sheet_text* argument allows the entry of the name of an external workbook or macro sheet.

AREAS(reference) Returns the number of areas in *reference;* most useful in analyzing named ranges containing a multiple selection.

CELL(info_type,*reference*) Returns information about the cell at *reference*. If *reference* is omitted, it is assumed to be the active cell. The types of information can include contents of cell, numeric format, protection status, and several others. Consult the Excel Help facility for more information and a list of all the attributes.

COLUMN(reference) Returns the number of columns in *reference;* most useful when used with named ranges.

INDIRECT(ref_text,*a1*) Returns the content of the cell referenced by the cell at *ref_text*. This allows one cell to reference another cell that contains a value. For instance, if cell F9 contains the label entry K9 and cell K9 contains the value 100, then a cell containing the function INDIRECT(F9) would also display the value 100. The *a1* argument is a logical value (TRUE or FALSE) that determines if *ref_text* is an A1 (TRUE) type reference or an R1C1 (FALSE) type reference. If omitted, *a1* is assumed to be TRUE.

ROWS(reference) Returns the number of rows in *reference;* again, most useful when analyzing named ranges.

TYPE(value) Returns a code describing the data type of *value*. Type 1 is a number; type 64 is an array. For a complete list, consult the description of TYPE( ) in the Excel Help facility.

Advanced Mathematical Functions

Excel provides a number of functions oriented to engineering and other nonbusiness mathematical applications. Some of them are listed here, should you have use for them in your academic or professional life.[2]

The terms in parentheses that follow a function are called arguments of the function. In the examples below, *number* can be a cell, a constant value, a formula, or another function. For instance, `=ABS(number)` could be either `=ABS(A10)`, `=ABS(5029)`, `=ABS(A10-B12)`, or `=ABS(TAN(G9))`.

ABS(number) Absolute value of *number*.

ACOS(number) Arc cosine of *number*, the angle in radians whose cosine is *number*. If *number* is not between −1 and +1, the value is #NUM!. To convert radians to degrees, use the DEGREES( ) function; for example, if cell H8 contains a cosine, then the angle in degrees is determined by the function `=DEGREES(ACOS(H8))`.

ASIN(number) Arc sine of *number*, the angle in radians whose sine is *number*. If *number* is not between −1 and +1, the value is #NUM!. To convert radians to degrees, use the DEGREES( ) function; see ACOS( ), above, for an example.

ATAN(number) Arc tangent of *number*, the angle in radians whose tangent is *number*. To convert radians to degrees, use the DEGREES( ) function; see ACOS( ), above, for an example.

ATAN2(x_num,y_num) Arc tangent of *y_num/x_num*, the angle in radians whose tangent is *y_num/x_num*. See the Excel Help facility for the distinction between this and ATAN( ). To convert radians to degrees, use the DEGREES( ) function; see ACOS( ), above, for an example.

COS(number) Cosine of *number* in radians. To convert degrees to radians, use the RADIANS( ) function; for example, if cell G12 has a number in degrees, then the function is `=COS(RADIANS(G12))`.

DEGREES(number) Converts radians to degrees.

EXP(number) Returns *e* raised to the power of *number*.

FACT(number) Returns the factorial (1×2×3…*number*) of *number*.

INT(number) Integer part of *number*. The cell entry `=INT(2.95)` yields the value 2. The cell entry `=INT(-2.95)` yields the value -3.

LN(number) Natural logarithm ($\log_e$) of *number*.

---

[2] A complete list of Excel 5 functions is included in Appendix B, along with a brief explanation of each.

LOG(number,base) Log$_{base}$ of *number*.

LOG10(number) Returns the base-10 logarithm of *number*.

MOD(number,divisor) *Number* mod *divisor*. Modular part (remainder) of *number/divisor*. The cell entry =MOD(6,4) yields the value 2.

PI( ) π is 3.14159265358979324.

RADIANS(number) Converts degrees to radians.

RAND( ) Generates a random number between 0 and 1.

ROUND(number,num_digits) Rounds *number* to *num_digits* decimal places.

SIGN(number) Returns the sign of *number*.

SIN(number) Sine of *number* in radians. To convert degrees to radians, use the RADIANS( ) function; see COS( ), above, for an example.

SQRT(number) Square root of *number*.

TAN(NUMBER) Tangent of *number* in radians. To convert degrees to radians, use the RADIANS( ) function; see COS( ), above, for an example.

TRUNC(number,num_digits) Truncates *number* to an integer. INT( ) and TRUNC( ) are similar in that they both truncate a number to an integer; they are different in how they treat negative numbers. INT( ) rounds down to the lower number (=INT(-2.95) yields -3); TRUNC( ) simply truncates the decimal portion of the number (=TRUNC(-2.95) yields -2).

Matrix Functions

The following functions deal with matrices.

MDETERM(array) Returns the determinant of a matrix *array*.

MINVERSE(array) Returns the inverse of a matrix *array*.

MMULT(array1,array2) Returns the product of two matrices, *array1* and *array2*.

SUMPRODUCT(array1,array2,...) Returns the sum of the crossproducts of matrices *array1* and *array2*.

TRANSPOSE(array) Returns the transpose of a matrix *array*.

Advanced Statistical Functions

The following functions deal with advanced statistical concepts such as regression and trends. These functions accept arrays as arguments and return arrays.

GROWTH(known_y's,known_x's,new_x's,const) Fits an exponential curve to the *known_y's* and *known_x's* and then returns new *y* coordinates that correspond to the *new_x's* array.

LINEST(known_y's,known_x's,const,stats) Calculates a straight line that corresponds to the *known_y's* and *known_x's*, and then returns an array that describes the line.

LOGEST(known_y's,known_x's,const,stat) Fits an exponential curve to the *known_y's* and *known_x's* and then returns an array that describes the curve.

TREND(known_y's,known_x's,new_x's,const) Fits a straight line to the *known_y's* and *known_x's* and then returns new *y* coordinates that correspond to the *new_x's* array.

EXERCISE 14.1

Assigning Grades

In this Exercise you construct a simple workbook that looks up a string value.

1. Start with a clear workbook.

2. Build a workbook with a lookup table for the assignment of grades, using the cutoff values at the beginning of the unit. Put the table in cells J1:K5. Assign the name CUTOFF to the table range.

3. Enter the following data in A1:B5:

Name	Score
John	92
Paul	73
George	88
Ringo	77

4. In cell C1, enter the label Grade. In cell C2, enter a lookup function that computes John's grade based on his score. For the range in the function, use CUTOFF. Once the function is working properly (you might test it by changing John's grade to a different number, but remember to change it back to the original 92), copy the formula to the other students. You should have their grades instantly.

5. Save your work with the file name GRADES.XLS.

EXERCISE 14.2

Computing Minimum Payments

In this Exercise you construct a simple workbook that uses a logical formula to compute a minimum payment due.

1. Start with a clear workbook.

2. Make the following entries in A1:C4:

Name	Bal Due	Min Pay
Jones	255	
Smith	15	
Kaczmierk	145	

3. Following the discussion in the "Minimum Payment" section in this unit, create a logical function that computes the minimum payment for each of these. (Develop the function in cell C2; copy it to C3:C4.)

4. Save this workbook with the name MINPAY.XLS.

EXERCISE 14.3

Catch the Wave

Both engineers and surfers think that one of the most beautiful shapes in the world is the sine wave: a plot of the values of the sine function. In this Exercise you compute a table of values and chart a sine wave. When you save the files, use the name SINEWAVE.XLS.

1. Start with a clear workbook.

2. Use the Edit | Fill | Series command to create a series of values, starting in cell A2 and proceeding down column A, that start with -4π, increase in steps of $\pi/20$, and stop at $4\pi+.01$ (because of rounding errors, a "fudge factor" of .01 is needed). (*Hint*: To calculate the step and stop values, use the PI( ) function in D1:D2 and then type the answer in the dialog box. Widen column D to get a more precise answer.)

3. Enter the function =SIN(A2) in cell B2.

4. Use the Data | Table command to compute the remaining values. The table range is from cell A2 to cell B162, and the column input cell is cell A2. Set the format of columns A and B to 0.00.

5. Graph the result using an XY graph. For a smoother line, set the format to lines only (not symbols). (*Hint*: Use the Format | Selected Object command to remove the markers.)

*= If (C12 <= 21500, C12 * 15%, If (And (C12 > 21500, C12 < 50000), 3232 + (C12 - 21500) * 28%, If (C12 >= 50000, Don't use the Ez Form, Dummy!)))*

EXERCISE 14.4

Form 1040EZ (V)

The tax tables of Form 1040EZ are based on a formula that calculates the tax to the nearest dollar of the dollar amount in the middle of each range. In prose, the formula reads like this: *If the taxable income is less than or equal to $21,500, the tax is 15% of the taxable income; if the taxable income is greater than $21,500 but less than $50,000, the tax is $3,232 plus 28% of the amount that taxable income exceeds $21,500.*

Open 1040EZ.XLS and convert the prose description to an Excel formula and enter the formula in cell C17. This formula will calculate the tax exactly for taxable income at the midpoints of each of the ranges in the tax table, and will be within $7 of the correct amount anywhere within a range. It is useful to enter formulas to compute taxes because they are quicker than looking up and entering the value. Save your work.

EXERCISE 14.5

Dice (I)

Ask anyone under the age of 16 the primary purpose of a personal computer and you will discover that it is an excellent platform for games. In this Exercise, you will teach Excel to play craps—well, at least to roll dice.

1. In cell A1, create a formula that will generate a random integer between 1 and 6. Recall that RAND( ) generates a random number between 0 and 1. You will need to use a ROUND( ) function. Test your formula by pressing [F9] about a dozen times. If your formula generates a 0 or a 7, go back and correct it. When it is correct, copy the formula to cell A2.

2. You now have all you need to roll a pair of dice, but, as any entertainment programmer knows, you have to have good graphics to sell those games. While Excel's graphics abilities are limited, we can at least represent a pair of dice.

    a. Change the height of rows 5, 6, and 7 to 40. Place a border around the range A5:C7. This will be the first die. Place another border around E5:G7 to create the second die. Select A5:G7 and center all entries both horizontally and vertically. Click the Bold tool. Turn the gridlines off.

    b. Think about the appearance of each face of a die; there are seven possible places for a spot on the die. In our first range, the spots are at cells A5, C5, A6, B6, C6, A7, and C7.

    c. There are always spots at cells A5 and C7 if the number rolled is higher than 1. In prose, the formula is: *If the number rolled is greater than one, place an X; otherwise leave it blank.* (Recall that the X is a text string; it must be surrounded by quotation marks.) Convert this to an Excel formula and enter it in cells A5 and C7.

    d. There are spots at cells C5 and A7 if the number rolled is a 4, 5, or 6. In prose, the formula is: *If the number rolled is greater than or equal to four, place an X; otherwise leave it blank.* Convert this to an Excel formula and enter it in cells C5 and A7.

    e. There are spots at cells A6 and C6 only if a 6 is rolled. In prose, the formula is: *If the number rolled is equal to six, place an X; otherwise leave it blank.* Convert this to an Excel formula and enter it in cells A6 and C6.

    f. There is a spot at cell B6 if the number rolled is a 1, 3, or 5. In prose, the formula is: *If the number rolled is odd, place an X; otherwise leave it blank.* Convert this to an Excel formula and enter it in cell B6.

3. Once you are sure the formulas are correct (make sure all references are absolute), copy them to E5:G7. Use the Edit|Replace command in the range E5:G7 to replace $A$1 with $A$2. Now test your work again; you "roll the dice" by pressing [F9]. Do this until you are satisfied that the graphic dice properly represent the numbers created by your random generator.

4. Hide rows 1 and 2. You no longer need to see the numbers, and furthermore they detract from the romance of what you have created. Save your work as DICE.XLS.

Review Questions

*1. Cells H19 and J19 contain two numbers. Write a logical formula that yields -1 if cell H19 is not greater than cell J19, +1 otherwise.

2. Cell K9 contains a number. Write a logical formula that yields 100 if cell K9 is greater than zero, 0 (zero) if cell K9 equals zero, and #NA! if cell K9 is less than zero. (*Hint*: The formula has one IF( ) contained within another IF( ).)

Key Terms

Index number
Literal string
Logical operators
Lookup table

Documentation Research

Referring to the Excel *User's Guide*, find and record the page number of each of the commands discussed in this unit. We recommend that you also write the page number in the margin next to the discussion of the command in the unit.

1. How can you limit a lookup table to the exact values in the lookup value list?

15 Macro Commands and Customization

By now, you most likely are impressed, as you have worked your way through this volume, by the versatility that Excel provides. There are dozens of uses for Excel, whether you require it for mathematics, science, business, or the home. Well, hang on tight. With the versatility offered by macros, you can add to or even completely obliterate the existing menus and write your own. If Excel does not provide the functions you need, you can write custom functions to add to the function list built into Excel. You can write automatic macros that run every time you open Excel…or run every time you open a particular workbook…or run every time you close a particular workbook. You can write macros that guarantee that you will produce work with the same quality and the same appearance time after time. *This* is versatility!

Learning Objectives

At the completion of this unit you should know

1. the uses of macros,
2. the meanings of the various terms for object-oriented programming.

At the completion of this unit you should be able to

1. record a macro for repeated data entry,
2. record a macro for repeated command execution,
3. edit a macro with the recorder,
4. edit a macro manually,

5. assign a macro to a button,
6. assign a macro to a menu item,
7. assign a macro to a toolbar,
8. create a global macro,
9. create a user-defined command.

Important Commands

Tools | Assign Macro

Tools | Macro

Tools | Menu Editor

Tools | Record Macro

Macro Commands

Excel currently maintains two methods of creating macros—the Excel Version 4.0 macro language, which is essentially a group of specialized functions that provide rudimentary programming, and Visual Basic for Applications, Excel edition, which is a version of Visual Basic designed exclusively for Excel and other Windows applications. In this manual, we will deal only with Visual Basic, since Microsoft has stated that they will not continue to update the Excel Version 4.0 macro language after this version of Excel. However, you will find as you continue through this unit and the next, that there are much better reasons for learning Visual Basic for Applications. For the purposes of this manual, we will use the term Visual Basic to refer to Visual Basic for Applications.

One excellent reason to focus on Visual Basic for Applications is that its programming language, Visual Basic, has become popular because it is highly robust (that is, it can be used to accomplish very involved tasks) and easy to learn. Visual Basic, itself, is founded on BASIC, a programming language that many of you may have experienced. The "Visual" in Visual Basic indicates that much of the design work (such as designing dialog boxes) is done by dragging items onto a grid, rather than calculating pixels and memory locations. Recall in Guided Activity 12.3 that you created a worksheet with controls to simplify data entry and eliminate the possibility of error. That was actually an introduction to Visual Basic, and that is much the type of thing you will be doing in this unit and the next.

Recording Macros

The simplest method of creating a macro is to record it. The Tools | Record Macro | Record New Macro command provides an easy method of recording a series of keystrokes or mouse actions to replay later on another worksheet or at another location on the same worksheet. Excel opens a new macro module and presents a dialog box asking if you wish to name the range containing the macro "Macro1." You can (and should) change the name to one that will help you to remember what the macro accomplishes.

It is important to understand the difference between a macro module and a macro. A *macro* is a series of statements on a macro sheet; you cannot record or enter a macro on a worksheet. A *macro module* can contain many macros. The *macro name* is contained in the first line of the macro that begins with the word Sub.

Once you give the Tools | Record Macro | Record New Macro command and name the macro, every keystroke and every mouse action is recorded by the *Macro Recorder*. However, there is an exception to that rule: in order for the action to be recorded, it must end in a command or an entry action (such as pressing [Enter] or an arrow key).

For example, suppose you select a range on the workbook, then realize you have selected the wrong range, reselect, and then give the Format | Column | Width command. Excel only records the second selection and the command. Since the first selection did not end in a command, it was a nonaction as far as the Macro Recorder is concerned.

Likewise, if you make an error in typing, press [Backspace] to back up to the error, correct it, and press [Enter], the Macro Recorder does not record the incorrect typing, since it no longer exists at the time [Enter] was pressed. However, if you complete a command before realizing a mistake, the Macro Recorder records both the error and the correction. Suppose you give the Format | Cells command to change the size of a font, realize after looking at it that you do not want it that way, and then give the Edit | Undo command to return it to its original state. Excel records both the incorrect command and the Edit | Undo command.

GUIDED ACTIVITY 15.1

Recording a Macro

Suppose you are making a workbook and you must enter the text "General Fiduciary" in several places on that workbook. You decide to use a macro to save some typing.

1. Follow the startup procedure outlined in Unit 1 to load Windows and enter Excel.

2. Select cell A1. Give the Tools | Record Macro | Record New Macro command. Excel opens a new module and presents this dialog box (we selected the Options button to show you the entire dialog box):

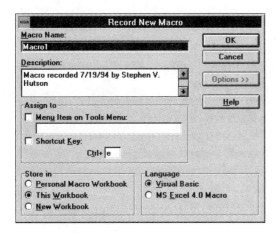

In the dialog box, name the macro General. Make the shortcut key a capital G (shortcut keys are case-sensitive). Click OK. The Stop Macro button will display on your screen.

3. Type the following in A1: General Fiduciary. Press Enter.

4. Click the Stop Macro button.

5. Go to wherever you want "General Fiduciary" to appear—say, to cell D1.

6. Give the command Tools | Macro, then select General and click Run. The text will appear in the cell. You can use the shortcut keys to reduce the number of keystrokes. Move to another cell on the workbook, say, D5. Press Ctrl Shift G. You can now move to other places and put "General Fiduciary" in those places by pressing Ctrl Shift G.

7. Use the Window | New Window and the Window | Arrange | Tiled commands to look at the module and the worksheet together. Resize the windows manually so you can see all of the text of the macro. It should look like Figure 15.1.

8. Save the workbook as RECORDER.XLS.

The Visual Basic Toolbar

Notice, in Figure 15.1, that when a macro module is the active sheet, the Visual Basic toolbar is displayed (unless you have closed it). This toolbar contains several buttons that will make your work with macros easier. Let's examine the available tools.

The Insert Module button inserts a module sheet before the current sheet.

The Menu Editor button calls the Menu Editor dialog box. We explain the Menu Editor later in this unit. The Object Browser button calls the Object Browser dialog box. The Object Browser allows you to examine the various objects in Visual Basic and their methods and properties. We discuss objects, methods, and properties later in this unit.

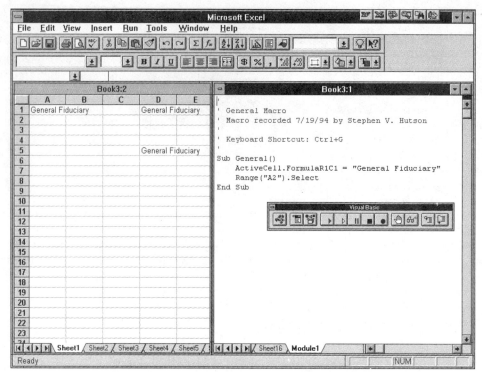

FIGURE 15.1
RECORDER.XLS workbook, step 1

The Run Macro button allows you to select a macro and execute it. The Step Macro button allows you to select a macro and run it one line at a time. This button is useful for debugging macros; we discuss debugging in Unit 16. The Resume Macro button allows you to continue a paused macro at the point where it was paused. The Stop Macro button allows you to stop running a macro, or to stop the Macro Recorder.

The Record Macro button allows you to start the Macro Recorder.

The Toggle Breakpoint button sets or removes breakpoints. Breakpoints are a tool for debugging macros. The Instant Watch button displays the value of an expression; this is another tool for debugging.

The Step Into button allows you to step through the currently active procedure one line at a time. If the procedure calls another procedure, it steps through that procedure one line at a time also. The Step Over button is similar, until the currently active procedure calls another procedure. At that point, it executes the called procedure as a complete unit.

Editing with the Recorder

Before we proceed any further, let's analyze the macro you recorded. Notice that there are a total of ten lines of code—six comment lines (that start with an apostrophe) and four command lines. The comment lines include the macro name (General Macro), the creation information line (Macro recorded by ...), and the keyboard shortcut (Ctrl+G). The first command line takes the form `Sub Macro_Name( )` and will begin each macro. One of the conventions that Visual Basic inherits from BASIC is that each procedure is a *subroutine*, that is, a series of statements that can be used by other procedures. So the first line does double duty: it indicates the beginning of a subroutine and names it as well. The last command line, `End Sub`, will end each macro. The two middle lines do all the work.

Generally, it is easiest to read Visual Basic statements from right to left. You can interpret the second command line as *Enter "General Fiduciary" as the formula in the active cell*. The next line interprets as *Select the cell range, A2*. The third line appears because the Move Selection after Enter box in the Edit tab of the Tools | Options dialog box is selected by default. Therefore, when you pressed [Enter] after typing in `General Fiduciary`, the Macro Recorder recognized two actions, the Formula action and the Select action. We recommend you turn off Move Selection after Enter before recording any more macros.

For the macro in the previous example to be of much use, you need to be able to format the column to properly display the text that you have entered. Since you did not include this step when you created the macro, you need to edit the macro. There are two ways to edit a macro—direct editing or recording. You shall do both as a part of Guided Activity 15.2. First, select the line with the Select action and delete it. The easiest way to do this is to place the mouse cursor at the beginning of the line, drag across the line to select it, and press [Del]. You should now have a blank line; press [Del] again to remove the blank line.

Next, you need to add lines using the Macro Recorder. To accomplish this, first select the spot where you wish to add lines; since you wish to add them just before the End Sub statement, you are already in the correct position. Next, give the Tools | Record Macro | Mark Position for Recording command, which allows you to direct Excel where to begin recording on the module.

The Tools | Record Macro | Record at Mark command signals Excel when you are ready to start recording. The selection mode of the Macro Recorder can be either absolute or relative. That is, when a macro selects a range, it can either select the same range that was selected when the macro was recorded (absolute mode, the default setting) or it can select a range based on movement from the active cell (relative mode).

Relative Recording

The Tools | Record Macro | Use Relative References command changes the selection mode of the Recorder from absolute to relative. This command is a toggle; when there is a check mark next to the command name, the Recorder is in relative mode; when the check mark is absent, it is in absolute mode. The Recorder frequently uses R1C1 (row 1; column 1) style references. After the Tools | Record Macro | Use Relative References command is invoked, the Recorder registers all selections in terms of relative positions. For instance, the reference R[2]C[-3] is interpreted as *two rows down and three columns left*.

GUIDED ACTIVITY 15.2

Editing a Macro with the Recorder

1. If you are not continuing from the previous Guided Activity, load Windows and enter Excel.

2. Open RECORDER.XLS. You should have saved the workbook with two tiled windows open. In Window 2 (the one with the worksheet) select Sheet2.

3. Select cell A1 in Sheet2. Press [Ctrl][Shift][G]. You should see `General Fiduciary` appear in cell A1.

4. Following the instructions previously given, delete line 9 of the macro.

5. With the cursor immediately before the End Sub statement, give the Tools | Record Macro | Mark Position for Recording command.

6. Select cell A1 in Sheet2. Give the Tools | Record Macro | Record at Mark command.

7. Make the formatting more appropriate for a column header.

    a. Use the Format | Column | Width command to widen the cell to 18. Do not use the mouse shortcut, as this will produce a different statement.

    b. Click on the Center button.

    c. Click on the Bold button.

8. Click the Stop Macro button. Your screen should be similar to Figure 15.2.

9. Try using the [Ctrl][Shift][G] shortcut on different cells in Sheet2.

10. Save the workbook.

GUIDED ACTIVITY 15.3

More Editing by Recording

This Guided Activity gives you more experience in recording command macros. You also see how cursor movement and functions are dealt with in a macro. You will need to create a new General Fiduciary report each day. This report needs the current date, and the cell containing the date should be named DATE_CELL. It also needs your name as the submitter.

1. If you are not continuing from the previous Guided Activity, load Windows and enter Excel. Open RECORDER.XLS.

2. Activate the module. Ensure that the cursor is immediately before the End Sub statement and give the Tools | Record Macro | Mark Position for Recording command.

3. Select cell A1 in Sheet2. Ensure that the Tools | Record Macro | Use Relative References command is selected. Give the Tools | Record Macro | Record at Mark command.

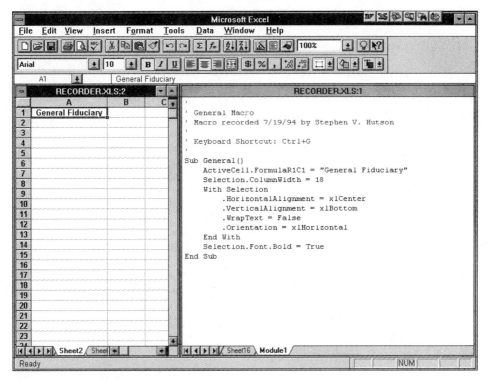

FIGURE 15.2
RECORDER.XLS workbook, step 2

4. Enter the date:

   a. Make D1 the active cell.

   b. Give the command Insert | Function. Select the TODAY( ) function.

   c. Format the cell to d-mmm-yy. Change the column width to 10.

   d. Give the command Insert | Name | Define. Enter DATE_CELL in the Names in Workbook box.

5. Enter your name:

   a. Make A2 the active cell.

   b. Enter Submitted by: (your name)

6. Click the Stop Macro button. Your results should be very similar to Figure 15.3 (except that we changed the shape of the Visual Basic toolbar to prevent it from obscuring any of the lines of code).

7. To fully test your work, select Sheet3, cell A1, and press [Ctrl][Shift][G]. All entries and formatting should automatically appear. Save the workbook.

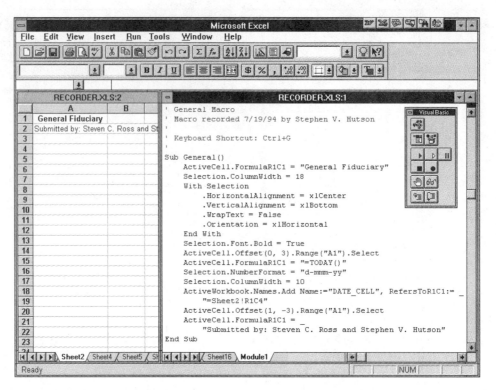

FIGURE 15.3
RECORDER.XLS,
step 3

Analyzing Macro Statements

There are several benefits to using the Macro Recorder to create your initial macros:

- You can begin creating useful macros almost immediately with minimal training.

- The Macro Recorder can do the bulk work of creating your macros, minimizing the amount of time that you must spend typing.

- You can analyze the recorded macros to gain an understanding of the syntax and construction of the Visual Basic language.

Let's take advantage of the last of these benefits as we continue to analyze the statements that were appended in Guided Activities 15.2 and 15.3.

Before we actually look at the effects of the lines, let's notice some formatting. Recall that, in Unit 12, we looked at the various tabs of the Tools | Options dialog box. Two of these tabs were the Module General and the Module Format tabs. The Module Format tab determines the text formatting for module sheets in a workbook. If you have left the defaults alone, comment text is in green on your monitor, and *keywords* are in blue. Keywords are words that have a reserved meaning in the Visual Basic language, such as True, False, Sub, With, and so on. Also notice the settings that begin with the letters "xl"; these are *built-in constants*. The "xl" reminds you that they are part of the Excel application, as opposed to constants that you will create in later procedures, which you will begin with the letters "my". The meanings and effects of these constants should be obvious from their names.

The group of lines that begins with `With Selection` and ends with `End With` are the result of choosing the Center button to set the alignment to center. The With and End With statements are Visual Basic's method of applying several properties to one object. This group of commands could be read, *For the active selection, set the horizontal alignment to center, the vertical alignment to bottom, the wrap text to false, and the orientation to horizontal.* The obvious question here is that we only changed one setting, so why do we have four statements. The answer is that the Center button is a shortcut for giving the Format | Cells command, selecting the Alignment tab, and selecting Horizontal Center without changing any other settings. The Macro Recorder, by default, creates a statement for each setting on each selected tab of the dialog box. Had you given the Format | Cells command and also changed the font before leaving the Format | Cells dialog box, you would have added another ten statements to the With/End With statement. You will use this information as you manually edit the macro in Guided Activity 15.4.

The statement `ActiveCell.Offset(0, 3).Range("A1").Select` can be interpreted as *Select as the new active cell the cell that is three columns to the right and in the same row as the current active cell.* This is the Macro Recorder's method of moving the active selection when in relative recording mode, known as the Offset method. In effect, it creates a worksheet within the worksheet and sets the new cell A1 (the active cell) to the location determined by the Offset method.

There are several other ways to select a cell or range of cells in Visual Basic, although the one used by the Macro Recorder is best for selecting a relative reference. One of the alternatives for absolute referencing is the Cells method, which would take the form `Cells(1,4).Select`. This statement can be interpreted as *Select the cell in the first row and the fourth column.* To select a range of cells, say A1:D3, using absolute referencing, use the Range method, which would take the form `Range(Cells(1, 1), Cells(3, 4)).Select`. You can interpret this as *Select the range beginning with the cell in the first row and first column, and ending with the cell in the third row and the fourth column.*

The statement `ActiveCell.FormulaR1C1 = "=TODAY()"` can be interpreted as *Insert the formula =TODAY( ) in the active cell.* The Macro Recorder uses the FormulaR1C1 property, rather than the Formula property, which shows its tendency toward the R1C1 reference convention. Either reference convention would accomplish the same task.

The statement `ActiveWorkbook.Names.Add Name:="DATE_CELL", RefersToR1C1:= "=Sheet2!R1C4"` can be interpreted as *Insert the name DATE_CELL into the collection of names in the active workbook and make the name refer to cell D1 of Sheet2.* Notice that we omitted the underscore following RefersToR1C1:=, which informs Visual Basic that the code on the next line is actually a continuation of the same statement. However, you now can see a problem that wasn't noticeable when you ran the macro to test it. The Insert | Name | Define command is always going to refer to cell D1 on Sheet2, when you want it to refer to cell D1 on the current sheet. You can change this by deleting the `Sheet2!` portion of the statement.

You should be able to decipher the rest of the statements of this procedure. They are either straightforward applications of commands, or are extremely similar to statements that we decoded for you.

GUIDED ACTIVITY 15.4

Manually Editing a Macro

In this Guided Activity, you manually edit the macro according to the discussion in the "Analyzing Macro Statements" section.

1. If you are not continuing from the previous Guided Activity, load Windows and enter Excel. Open RECORDER.XLS.

2. Activate the module. Place the cursor immediately after the 18 in the `Selection.ColumnWidth = 18` statement. Press [Enter].

3. Type the statement `Selection.RowHeight = 36`.

4. Change the vertical alignment to center by changing the constant `xlBottom` to `xlCenter` in the line `.VerticalAlignment = xlBottom`.

5. Delete the lines `.WrapText = False` and `.Orientation = xlHorizontal`.

6. In the line `ActiveWorkbook.Names.Add Name:="DATE_CELL", RefersToR1C1:= "=Sheet2!R1C4"`, delete `Sheet2!`. Be sure to leave the equal sign!

7. Select Sheet4 and run the macro again. Your worksheet should now look like Figure 15.4. Press [F5] and select DATE_CELL to verify that the DATE_CELL name was properly applied this time. (You should go to Sheet4!D1.) Save your work and back it up.

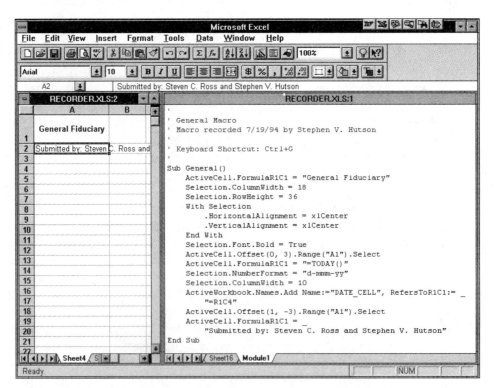

FIGURE 15.4
RECORDER.XLS, step 4

Running Command Macros

You have already seen how to run a macro by assigning a *shortcut key* combination (Ctrl + a letter key, a–z or A–Z). You can also run a command macro by:

- Invoking the Tools | Macro command, selecting the macro name and selecting Run
- Assigning the macro to a button or other graphical object
- Making the macro an automatic macro
- Assigning the macro to the Tools menu
- Assigning the macro to a custom menu item and adding the item to a menu
- Assigning the macro to a toolbar

The Tools | Macro Command

The Tools | Macro command is one way of executing a command macro. When you give the Tools | Macro command, Excel presents this dialog box:

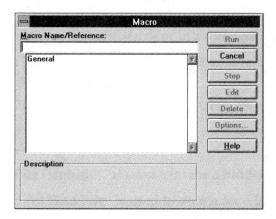

The Macro Name/Reference box contains a list of all the macro names on any module sheets. The command buttons in this dialog box allow you to run, edit, step through, delete, or change the options of a selected macro. The Options command button allows you to change the creation information line, change (or assign) the keyboard shortcut, or assign the macro to the Tools menu. The Step command button will cause Excel to run the macro one statement at a time. (We discuss stepping through macros in Unit 16 in the section "Debugging Macros.")

Assigning the Macro to the Tools Menu

To assign the macro to the Tools menu, give the Tools | Macro command, select the macro, and click the Options command button. You will see this dialog box:

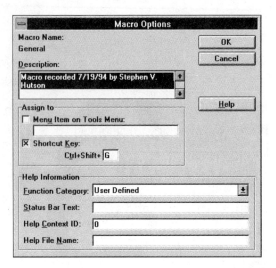

Select the Menu Item on Tools Menu check box and type the command name in the text box as you wish it to appear on the menu. Click OK and you will return to the Macro dialog box. When you click Close, the menu item will appear just as you typed it.

Assigning the Macro to a Button

In Unit 12 we briefly examined the buttons in the Drawing toolbar. One of these is the Create Button tool, which is designed to draw a button on the screen, and then assign a macro to the button. Then, when you click on the button, Excel runs the macro assigned to that button.

To use this feature, select the Create Button tool from the Drawing toolbar. Draw the button on the screen using the procedures you learned in Unit 12 in the section "Graphic Items on the Worksheet." Excel will present the Assign Macro dialog box:

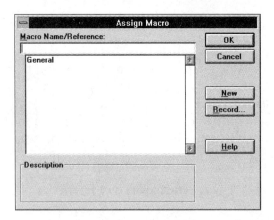

Select the desired macro from the Macro Name/Reference box. Then, while the button is still selected (the handles are still surrounding the button), highlight the text inside the button by dragging the mouse over it, and type the desired text on the button. You can also format the text while the text is highlighted. Once you click away from the button, you deselect it; then anytime you place the mouse cursor over the button, it will take the shape of a hand with the index finger extended. Pressing the mouse button will execute the assigned macro, rather than selecting the button.

If you later decide to change the shape or text on the button, press `Ctrl` while moving the mouse cursor over the button, and click to select it. The `Ctrl` key will change the pointer from execute mode to select mode.

You can assign a macro to any graphical object on the screen, whether you created it with the graphical item tools or imported it from another program. For example, you might create a logo in Paintbrush, copy it to the Clipboard, and paste it into place in the workbook. Once the item is in place, select the item and give the Tools | Assign Macro command. Once you issue this command, Excel presents the Assign Macro dialog box illustrated above. Select the macro from the Macro Name/Reference box. Now when the mouse cursor passes over the graphical object, it will change to the shape of a hand. If you press the mouse button, the macro will run.

Creating Automatic Macros

Another method of executing a macro is to instruct Excel to automatically run the macro whenever a predefined event occurs. To create an *automatic macro* that runs whenever a particular workbook is opened, name the subroutine Auto_Open; to create an automatic macro that runs whenever the workbook is closed, name the subroutine Auto_Close. You can only have one Auto_Open and one Auto_Close procedure in a workbook. To prevent an automatic macro from running when the workbook is opened or closed, hold `Shift` while choosing OK in the File Open or File Close dialog box.

While not truly automatic, there are several procedures, called *OnEvent procedures*, or *event handlers*, that you can use in a macro to run another macro when a particular event occurs, such as an error, the activation of a worksheet, or a particular time interval. (These are discussed in more detail in Unit 16.)

Assigning a Macro to a Command

Another method of running a macro is to assign the macro to a custom command and assign the command to a menu bar. In Excel terminology, a command is referred to as a *menu item*. To create a custom menu item, select Tools | Menu Editor when a Visual Basic module is active. Excel will display the dialog box in Figure 15.5.

To add the new menu item, follow these steps:

1. Select from the Menu Bars box the menu bar you wish to change. Excel currently ships with four menu bars—Worksheet, Chart, No Documents Open, and Visual Basic Module. The Menu Editor also enables you to modify any of the three groups of shortcut menus.

2. In the Menus box, select the menu to which you wish to add the new menu item.

3. Select from the Menu Items box the item above which you would like to place the new menu item.

4. Click the Insert button.

FIGURE 15.5
Menu Editor dialog box

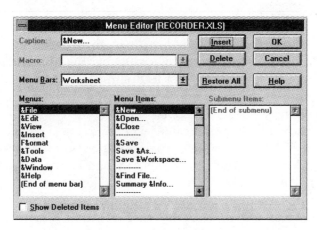

5. In the Caption box, type the name of the new menu item. Place an ampersand (&) in front of the character that will be the *accelerator key*. An accelerator key is the key that you press to give the command once the menu is selected. Ensure that the accelerator key is unique in that menu.

6. In the Macro box, select the macro you wish the new menu item to execute. Click OK.

You can use similar procedures in the Menu Editor to create new menus or even new menu bars.

Assigning a Macro to a Toolbar

The last method of executing a macro is to assign it to a toolbar. To assign a macro to a toolbar, give the View | Toolbars command and select Customize. In the Categories list, select Custom. You may have to remove a tool from the toolbar in order to make room. To remove a tool, select it and drag it off the toolbar. Select a new tool from the Custom list and drag it to the desired location on the toolbar. Excel will display the Assign Macro dialog box, as shown here:

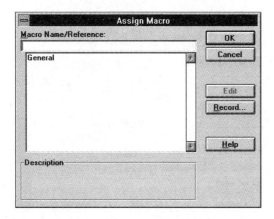

Select the desired macro and click OK.

GUIDED ACTIVITY 15.5

Creating a Button-Operated Macro

In this Guided Activity you assign a macro to a button.

1. If you are not continuing from the previous Guided Activity, load Windows and enter Excel.

2. Open RECORDER.XLS. In the worksheet window, select Sheet5.

3. Draw the button on the screen.

   a. Display the Drawing toolbar. Click on the Create Button tool.

   b. Hold down [Alt] while you start in the upper-left corner of cell A1 and drag to the lower-right corner of that cell. Holding [Alt] causes the button to align exactly with cell borders.

   c. Release [Alt] and the mouse button. Excel presents this dialog box:

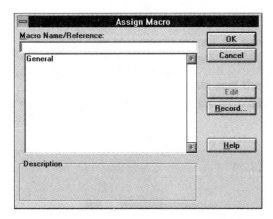

   d. Highlight General. Click OK.

4. Change the text on the button.

   a. Highlight the text Button 1 by dragging over it.

   b. Type General. Click anywhere on the workbook away from the button.

5. Now test your work.

   a. Close the Drawing toolbar and maximize the window containing Sheet5.

   b. Highlight cell E1.

   c. Click on the General button.

   d. Excel follows the General procedure, beginning in cell E1. Your workbook should look like Figure 15.4.

6. Restore the window containing Sheet5 to its original size. Save the workbook.

GUIDED ACTIVITY 15.6

Creating a New Menu Item

1. If you are not continuing from the previous Guided Activity, load Windows and enter Excel.
2. Open RECORDER.XLS. Activate the window containing the module.
3. Select Menu Editor from the Tools menu.
4. Follow the discussion in the section "Assigning a Macro to a Command" to create a command named Title on the Insert menu.
5. Now test your work. Select Cell A1 of Sheet6 and give the Insert | Title command.
6. Save your work. Close RECORDER.XLS.

User-Defined Commands

One use of Visual Basic is to create user-defined commands that meet specific needs. For example, a common feature of many spreadsheet programs is a command that converts formulas to values. In Excel, you can do this, but you must first give the Edit | Copy command, then the Edit | Paste Special command, then select Values and click OK. It would be nice to be able to do all of this with one command. You create this command in Guided Activity 15.7.

Global Macros

Until now, all the macros you have created have been stored in the workbook, making them available only when that workbook is open. However, some macros, such as the user-defined commands discussed in the previous section, would be useful anytime, and should be available anytime Excel is open. Excel allows you to accomplish this with the Personal Macro Workbook. When you choose to record a new macro, Excel presents the Record New Macro dialog box. Click the Options button and it looks like this:

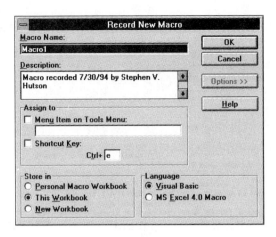

If you select Personal Macro Workbook in the Store in group of option buttons, Excel will place your new macro in a hidden workbook named PERSONAL.XLS. This workbook is opened every time you open Excel, but it is hidden, so that it does not get in the way. Because it is always open, the macros in it are always available. To edit a macro in PERSONAL.XLS, give the Window I Unhide command and select PERSONAL.XLS.

GUIDED ACTIVITY 15.7

Creating a User-Defined Command

In this Guided Activity you create a user-defined command and store that command in the Personal Macro Workbook.

1. If you are not continuing from the previous Guided Activity, load Windows and enter Excel. If you are continuing, click the New Workbook tool to get a clear workbook.

2. Give the Tools I Record Macro I Record New Macro command. Name the macro ConvertToValues. Click the Options button. Select Personal Macro Workbook. When your dialog box looks like this, click OK:

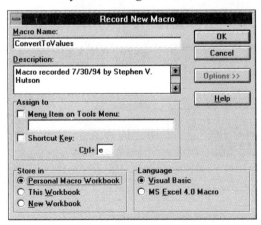

3. Give the Edit | Copy command. Give the Edit | Paste Special command. Select Values. Click OK. Press [Esc] to cancel the copy marquee.

4. Click the Stop Macro button.

5. Now, assign the tool to the Standard toolbar.

   a. Give the View | Toolbars command.

   b. Select Customize.

   c. Drag the TipWizard tool off the toolbar.

   d. Select the Custom group.

   e. Drag the tool with the happy face to the Standard toolbar and place it between the Format Painter button and the Undo button.

   f. In the Assign Macro dialog box, select PERSONAL.XLS!ConvertToValues and click OK.

   g. In the Customize dialog box, click Close.

6. Next, add status bar text to your macro.

   a. Give the Window | Unhide command. Select PERSONAL.XLS.

   b. Give the Tools | Macro command. Select ConvertToValues. Click the Options button.

   c. In the Status Bar Text field, type `Converts formulas to values`. Click OK.

   d. In the Macro dialog box, click Close. Give the Window | Hide command.

7. Close the active workbook without saving. Click the New Workbook tool for a new workbook.

8. In cell A1, enter the formula =5+5. You should see the formula in the formula bar and the result in the cell. Click the Custom tool. As you rest the mouse cursor on the tool, notice the help text in the status bar. The formula bar entry should now be 10.

9. Close the active workbook without saving. Unless you are continuing on to the Exercises, exit Excel, then exit Windows to the operating system.

Visual Basic Terminology

Visual Basic is an *object-oriented programming* language. Rather than focusing on a series of instructions, object-oriented programming (OOP) recognizes that each item in an application is an *object* that can be manipulated. Anyone who tries to explain object-oriented programming ends up using some analogy, so why should we be any different?

Consider your local park. There are several objects that make the park what it is—trees, paths, swing sets, and so on. Each object has properties that define its nature. Some properties can only be recognized; others can be changed. For example, you could change the surface property of a path from dirt to concrete. Furthermore, the objects belong to classes; for example, the trees either belong to the deciduous or conifer class. Objects also belong to collections; a play area may contain several swing sets. It is a collection of the swing set object. However, each swing set is itself a collection of the swing object. A method is one means you might use to change an object; for instance, you might apply the AddSlide method to a swing set to add a slide.

As in our analogy, each object in Excel, be it a chart, a range, a button, a window, or any other object, has *properties*. For example, among the dozens of properties of a range are formula, font, number format, and row height. We used the ActiveCell property of the Worksheet object (the Worksheet object is understood, rather than specified) in the statement `ActiveCell.Offset(0, 3).Range("A1").Select` to select a new active cell. Properties can be either read-only or read-write. For example, ActiveCell is a read-only property; it is used to determine a starting place for the Offset method. On the other hand, ColumnWidth is a read-write property, so the statement `Selection.ColumnWidth = 18` simply sets a new value for the ColumnWidth property of any columns in the Selection object.

Objects are said to be in the same *class* if they have the same list of properties, even if the values of those properties are different. For example, HiLo lines and Uplines (used in charts) are in the same class, since they each have the same properties.

Methods are another means of effecting changes to objects. The statement `ActiveCell.Offset(0, 3).Range("A1").Select` uses the Offset method to define a new Range object. Once the range is created, it uses the Select method to select it. Methods are the most common way of making things happen in Visual Basic.

Collections are groups of objects that can be acted upon together or alone, depending upon the circumstances. When you add a worksheet to a workbook, you are actually adding it to the Worksheets collection, which is a collection of Worksheet objects. Collection names can generally be differentiated from the objects in the collection by the plural name.

A *procedure* is a statement or series of statements that performs an action. *Functions* in Visual Basic are used much as they are in Excel—to input values and return calculated results. Functions are different from procedures in that they do not perform actions. They can be either built-in or custom-defined. You will create a custom-defined function in Unit 16.

Visual Basic Help

If you are like most people, your head is spinning about now. The terms above are all new, rather confusing, and frequently overlapping. For example, if a tree's leaves change from green to yellow, has it applied the ChangeColor method, or did it change its LeafColor property from green to yellow? Don't despair; there is help available (literally). Give the Help | Contents command and select Programming with Visual Basic. From here, you can select Using Visual Basic, which contains examples on getting started, running Visual Basic, debugging, and optimizing. The Programming Language Summary contains an alphabetical list of all objects, methods, properties, functions, statements, and keywords in Visual Basic. Best of all, if you select an object, you can get a list of the applicable properties and methods for that object. If you select a property or method, there is a listing of all objects to which that property or method applies. Finally, the Visual Basic Reference contains a Reference Information section with a glossary, a discussion of error types, and other valuable information. We encourage you to use the Help facility freely as you complete this unit and Unit 16.

EXERCISE 15.1

Running Macros

In this Exercise you create a button-operated macro that formats selected text as bold and centered with an outline border.

1. If you are not continuing from the previous Guided Activity, load Windows and enter Excel. Open a blank workbook.

2. Give the Tools | Macro Record | Record New Macro command and name the macro Heading. Make sure that the macro is stored in this workbook and not in the Personal Macro Workbook. Record a macro that gives the Format | Cells command and sets Alignment (Horizontal) to Center selection, sets Font to Bold, and sets Border to Outline. Click the Stop Macro button.

3. Draw a button on the workbook that occupies the space H1:H2. Assign the Heading macro to the button. Type the text `Heading` on the button. In cell G1, type `To format a range as headings, select the range and press this button`. Right-align this text.

4. Test your work by entering some text or values in several cells, selecting the cells, and clicking on the button. Your final result should look something like Figure 15.6. Save your file with the name BUTTON.XLS before closing it.

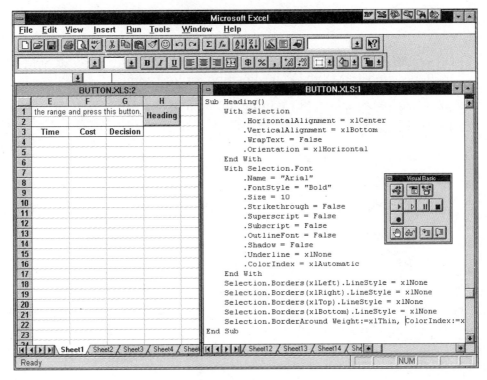

FIGURE 15.6
BUTTON.XLS workbook

EXERCISE 15.2

Transpose Command

Write a macro to create a user-defined command that transposes rows and columns in one step. Store the command in the PERSONAL.XLS workbook. Assign the command to a menu item named Transpose on the Edit menu. Test your work with ranges that have more rows than columns and more columns than rows.

EXERCISE 15.3

Business Mileage (VII)

Open the MILES96.XLS workbook. Write a macro that will take a user to the range necessary to make another entry. Ensure that the macro copies formulas to the new row and updates the database statistical function with the new information. Save your work.

EXERCISE 15.4

Dice (II)

Open the DICE.XLS workbook. Write a macro that "rolls the dice" and assign it to a button labeled Roll. Store the macro in the DICE.XLS workbook. Save your work.

Review Questions

*1. What is the difference between Tools | Record Macro | Record at Mark and Tools | Record Macro | Mark Position for Recording?

2. Name two methods for editing an existing macro.

*3. Name five methods for executing a macro.

4. Give an example of each of the following:
   a. Object
   b. Method
   c. Property
   d. Collection
   e. Function

*5. How many shortcut key combinations are possible in one workbook?

Key Terms

Accelerator key
Automatic macro
Built-in constant
Class
Collection
Event handler
Function
Keyword

Macro
Macro module
Macro name
Macro Recorder
Menu item
Method
Object

Object-oriented
   programming
OnEvent procedure
Procedure
Property
Shortcut key
Subroutine

Documentation Research

Referring to the Excel *User's Guide* and the *Visual Basic User's Guide*, find and record the page number of each of the commands discussed in this unit. We recommend that you also write the page number in the margin next to the discussion of the command in this unit.

1. How do you delete a menu item from a menu? Can you delete built-in menu items?

2. How do you create a separator line between menu items using the Menu Editor?

3. In which directory is the PERSONAL.XLS workbook stored?

16 Visual Basic Programming

In Unit 15 you recorded several macros that were designed to simplify repetitive entries and procedures; however, much more sophistication is possible with macros. A series of macro programming functions is available. With these, it is possible to write your own menus and to use conditional logic to determine workbook operations. The *Visual Basic User's Guide* contains an extensive discussion of programming with Visual Basic. The discussion that follows provides only an overview of what Visual Basic can accomplish. If you wish to take full advantage of Excel macros, consult the *User's Guide* and *Visual Basic User's Guide*. Examples of programming with macros are presented later in this unit and in Application G, which follows.

In this unit, we examine those Visual Basic functions that perform actions, customize the program, control the flow of the macro itself, deal with text files, and return values to the macro.

Learning Objectives

At the completion of this unit you should know

1. the different types of Visual Basic functions that are available,
2. the control structures available in Visual Basic programming,
3. the purpose and usage of variables in Visual Basic programming.

At the completion of this unit you should be able to

1. program a simple Visual Basic procedure that uses branching and loops and interacts with the user,

2. declare a variable,
3. use break mode to debug a procedure that does not work as expected,
4. write a custom dialog box,
5. write a custom function.

Using Control Structures in a Procedure

Control structures are fundamental to any programming language. They generally solve one of two problems—decision making and controlling repetitions.

Making Decisions in a Procedure

Recall the statistical problem from Exercise 11.8. Concisely stated, you have an array of numbers and you need to determine how many of the numbers are greater than the average of all the numbers in the array. Suppose that, instead of counting the numbers greater than the average, you need to highlight them by changing the font color. As you arrive at each cell, you need to make a decision. If the number is greater than the average, you want to change the color; if it is not, you wish to leave it alone.

Almost universally, programming languages refer to this as an If-Then procedure, or *branching*. It is one of the fundamental building blocks of programming. In Visual Basic, it takes the following form:

```
If conditionA Then
    Statements to execute if conditionA is true
ElseIf conditionB Then
    Statements to execute if conditionB is true
ElseIf conditionC Then
    Statements to execute if conditionC is true
Else
    Statements to execute if all conditions are false
End If
```

There are several things to note about the above structure. First, only the If statement and the End If statement are required. Next, note that the Then keyword is on the same line as If and is only separated from the condition by a space. Also note that the statements are always indented to highlight the If-Then procedure. Finally, note that the order of the conditions is crucial to making the correct decision. *ConditionA* must be the most stringent condition; if it is met, the statements associated with it are executed, the End If statement is executed and the decision is complete. If, and only if, *conditionA* is false, Visual Basic checks for *conditionB*; if *conditionB* is true, the statements associated with it are executed, the End If statement is executed, and the decision is complete (and so on for *conditionC*, etc.). Finally, if none of the conditions are true, the statements associated with the Else statement are executed, the End If statement is executed, and the decision is complete.

Controlling Repetition in a Procedure

One of the things that computers do best is repetitive tasks; this ability is called *looping*. It is only effective, however, if you are able to stop the loop when it is no longer needed. If you fail to provide a proper exit for the loop, you refer to that as an *infinite loop*; that is, the computer continues to loop until the program is broken[1] or the power is shut off. Visual Basic provides two looping mechanisms—the Do-Loop and the For-Next loop.

The Do-Loop takes the form:

```
Do Until condition
     Statements to be executed within loop
Loop
```

The Until keyword provides the break for the loop. The *condition* is checked before each loop is performed; when it becomes true, the statements associated with the loop are not executed and the loop is ended.

Again, recalling the statistical problem from Exercise 11.8, the array of values was in a column. The statements inside the loop would check the value of the current cell, compare it to the average of the values in the array, format the cell with a new foreground color if necessary, then move down to the next cell. When the last cell is reached, the next cell down would be blank, which would be the condition that would end the loop. The Do statement would take the form `Do Until ActiveCell = ""`.

The second looping mechanism in Visual Basic is the For-Next loop. It takes the form:

```
For i = 1 to number
     Statements to be executed within loop
Next i
```

In this scenario, *i* is a variable; we discuss declaring variables in the next section. *Number* is the number of times you want to execute the loop. The Next *i* statement adds 1 to the value of *i* and checks if it is greater than *number*. If it is not, it returns control to the For statement; if it is, it ends the loop and executes the next statement in the procedure.

Recalling the statistical problem from Exercise 11.8, you know that there are 100 numbers in the column. In this case, the For statement would take the form `For i = 1 to 100`. As before, the statements inside the loop would check the value of the current cell, compare it to the average of the values in the array, format the cell with a new foreground color if necessary, then move down to the next cell. At the

---

[1] In DOS and Windows operating systems, pressing Ctrl Break will normally break an infinite loop.

conclusion of each loop, the Next *i* statement adds 1 to the value of *i* and repeats the loop. When the last cell is reached, the value of *i* would be 100 and the loop would end.

Variables in Visual Basic

A *variable*, in programming parlance, is a storage location for a value that may or may not change. The value can be a number, text, or an object. The various data types allowed in Visual Basic are listed in Table 16.1.

TABLE 16.1 Visual Basic data types

DATA TYPE	STORAGE SIZE	EXPLANATION
Boolean	2 bytes	True or False
Integer	2 bytes	–32,768 through 32,767—no decimals
Long (long integer)	4 bytes	–2,147,483,648 through 2,147,483,647—no decimals
Single (single-precision floating-point)	4 bytes	–3.402823E38 through –1.401298E–45 for negative values; 1.401298E–45 through 3.402856E38 for positive values
Double (double-precision floating-point)	8 bytes	–1.79769313486232E308 through –4.94065645841247E–324 for negative values; 4.94065645841247E–324 through 1.79769313486232E308 for positive values
Currency	8 bytes	–922,337,203,685,477.5808 through 922,337,203,685,477.5807
Date	8 bytes	January 1, 0100 through December 31, 9999
String	1 byte per character	0 through 65,535
Object	4 bytes	Any object reference
Variant	Varies	Any numeric value up to the range of a double-precision floating-point, or text
User-defined	Varies	Depends on the fundamental data type

There are two schools of thought with regard to *declaring variables*. (Declaring a variable is the process by which you define the variable and make it available to the procedure.) Some argue that there is no point in declaring a variable; if a procedure contains a word that the programming language does not recognize, it should automatically assume that the unrecognized word is a variable. Others argue that explicit declaration prevents typographical errors from introducing errors into programs. Visual Basic lets you choose by selecting or clearing the Require Variable Declaration box on the Module General tab of the Tools | Options dialog box. We tend toward the latter argument, especially with new programmers. A variable declaration takes the form `Dim myVariable as data_type`.

Put some thought into choosing the appropriate data types when declaring variables. There are two possible errors. If you declare all variables as a variant (the data type with the most latitude), the value stored by the variable will never exceed the capabilities of the data type; however, you will needlessly consume memory and delay procedures if a more restrictive data type is adequate. Alternatively, if the data stored by the variable exceeds the capacity of the data type, the best you can hope for is an error message. Far worse, there is the possibility that the procedure will appear to run correctly, but return incorrect solutions.

Our next concern is *initializing variables*. Initialization is the (optional) process of assigning an initial value to the variable. The keyword Let is used to assign a value to a variable and takes the form `Let myVariable = value`. This is such a common operation that the keyword can be omitted, as in the form `myVariable = value`. Whenever the keyword is omitted in initializing a variable, Let is assumed.

Another keyword, Set, can be used to assign a cell's value to a variable, as in the form `Set myVariable = ActiveSheet.Cells(1, 1)`. Notice that when using this keyword, the variable must be of the object data type. The advantage of the Set keyword is that, if the cell's value changes, the variable's value changes with it.

In Guided Activity 16.1, you are going to want to initialize a variable as the average of a named range. Each of Excel's worksheet functions can be accessed in a Visual Basic module as a method of the Application object. This takes the form `Application.Function_Name(arguments)`. Named ranges can be accessed as arguments of the range object. This takes the form `Range("range_name")`. Finally, you are going to want to execute one macro from another; to do this, simply enter the macro name on a line of the procedure.

GUIDED ACTIVITY 16.1

A Statistical Problem Revisited

In this Guided Activity, you will re-create the scenario from Exercise 11.8, that is, a column of 100 random numbers between 1 and 1,000. Then you will write a Visual Basic procedure (macro) that examines those numbers and changes the font color of all cells whose value is greater than the average of the numbers. As you write this procedure, make sure you understand how the control structures (branching and looping) work.

1. Follow the startup procedure outlined in Unit 1 to load Windows and enter Excel.

2. Create a column of 100 random numbers in the range C2:C101 by following this procedure:

    a. Select Cell C2. Enter the formula =ROUND(1000*RAND(),0).

    b. Use the AutoFill handle to copy the formula to the range C2:C101.

    c. With the range C2:C101 still selected, use the Copy and Paste Special Values procedure to convert these formulas to values. (If you have completed Guided Activity 15.7, you can click the button with the happy face to accomplish this task. If not, we leave it to you to remember the Copy and Paste Special procedure.)

   d. Give the Insert | Name | Define command and name the range C2:C101 List.

3. Before you begin to create the procedure, give the Tools | Options command, select the Module General tab, and select the Require Variable Declaration box.

4. The best way to begin the process of creating the procedure is to record the action that will be carried out if the tests are met.

   a. Select cell C2. Give the Tools | Record Macro | Record New Macro command.

   b. Name the macro ChangeColor. Click the Options button and ensure that the macro is stored in this workbook.

   c. Give the Format | Cells command, select the Font tab, and change the font color to red.

   d. Click the Stop Macro button.

   e. You have now recorded a macro that changes the font color. However, that may not be appropriate for the value in cell C2. Give the Format | Cells command again and change the font color back to Automatic.

   f. Select the Module1 tab. Give the Window | New Window command. Select the Sheet1 tab. Give the Window | Arrange command and choose Tiled. Save your work as PROBLEM2.XLS. Your screen should look similar to Figure 16.1.

5. Next, you create the control procedure:

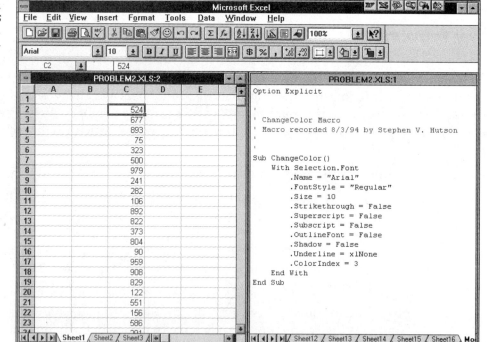

FIGURE 16.1 PROBLEM2.XLS workbook, step 1

a. Activate the Module1 sheet. Place the cursor right after the End Sub statement. Press Enter twice.

b. Enter the comment statements:

```
'
' CheckCell Macro
' Created by your_name on date
'
```

c. Name the procedure and declare the variables:

```
Sub CheckCell()
Blank line
Dim myCounter as Integer
Dim myAverage as Single
Let myAverage = Application.Average(Range("List"))
Blank line
```

d. Save your work. Enter the counter loop. It should move down one cell at a time, until the active cell is blank.

```
Do Until ActiveCell = ""
Selection.Offset(1, 0).Range("A1").Select
Loop
```

e. Save your work. Enter the checking routine. It should occur inside the loop, before the `Selection.Offset` statement.

```
If ActiveCell > myAverage Then
    ChangeColor
End If
```

6. Compare your procedure to the one in Figure 16.2. (We changed window sizes in the figure so you could see the entire CheckCell procedure.) Notice how the lines are indented to call attention to branches and loops. When your procedure is the same as the figure, you are ready to test. Select cell C2 of Sheet1 and give the Tools | Macro command, select CheckCell, and click the Run button. Check your work by entering the average of List in a cell and comparing random cells to the calculated average.

7. Save your work. Close the PROBLEM2.XLS workbook.

Custom Functions

While Excel has a very complete set of built-in functions, you will occasionally find that you are reusing the same set of calculations on an ongoing basis. In this case, it would be more convenient to define a function that performs these calculations in one step. Visual Basic provides this capability in the *custom function*.

Suppose, for example, that you are responsible for the payroll of an automobile dealership who pays their salespeople on commission. The commission structure is

FIGURE 16.2
PROBLEM2.XLS workbook, complete

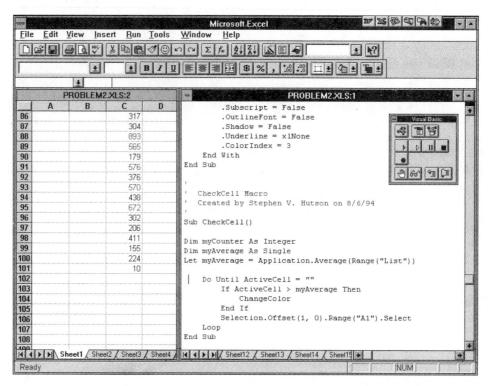

as follows: if a salesperson's monthly sales are at least $500,000, the commission is 25% of net sales (gross sales less the total cost of automobiles sold); for sales of at least $350,000, the commission is 20% of net sales; for sales of at least $200,000, the commission is 15% of net sales; for sales under $200,000, the commission is 10% of net sales (and the salesperson should start looking for another line of work). While a lookup table might work for this, you would have to frequently re-create it, so you decide to create a custom function named Commission. The Commission function will take two arguments—GrossSales and TotalCost.

There is a fundamental difference between a function and a procedure—a function returns a value; a procedure performs an action. Creating functions is similar to creating Visual Basic procedures and differs in only three areas. Functions are enclosed with the keywords Function and End Function, rather than Sub and End Sub. The second difference is that a function has arguments. This takes the form `Function Function_Name(Argument1,Argument2,etc.)`. The final difference is that a function has an assignment statement in which the function name is assigned a value (referred to as the ***return value***). This takes the form `Function_Name = expression`, where *expression* is a formula defining the return value of the function.

GUIDED ACTIVITY 16.2

Defining a Custom Function

In this Guided Activity you create the custom function defined in the previous section.

1. If you are not continuing from the previous Guided Activity, use the startup procedure to open Excel. If you are continuing, click the New Workbook tool to open a clear workbook.

2. Insert a module sheet before Sheet1. In a real-life situation, you might prefer to create this function on the Personal Macro Workbook, making it available to all workbooks.

3. Create the required function, following this procedure:

    a. Enter the comment lines:

    ```
    '
    ' Commission Function
    ' Created by your_name on date
    '
    Blank line
    ```

    b. Define the function and declare the variables:

    ```
    Function Commission(GrossSales, TotalCost)
    Blank line
    NetSales As Long
    NetSales = GrossSales - TotalCost
    Blank line
    ```

    c. Create the branches and assignment statements, and end the function:

    ```
    If GrossSales >= 500000 Then
         Commission = NetSales * 0.25
    ElseIf GrossSales >= 350000 Then
         Commission = NetSales * 0.2
    ElseIf GrossSales >= 200000 Then
         Commission = NetSales * 0.15
    Else
         Commission = NetSales * 0.1
    End If
    Blank line
    End Function
    ```

4. When your custom function looks like Figure 16.3, save your work as COMMISH.XLS. Test your function on Sheet1 by entering gross sales, total cost, and the commission formula (=Commission(B1,B2)) in the range B1:B3. Enter the proper labels in A1:A3. Try several combinations of gross sales and total cost to verify that the formula works properly.

CHECKPOINT 16A What happens if the total cost exceeds the gross sales?

5. Oops! Labor laws will not allow your company to pay a negative commission. You must revise your function to return a value of 0 if net sales is a negative number. Try to do this yourself; if you need assistance, look at Figure 16.4.

6. Save your work and close COMMISH.XLS.

418 PART THREE ADVANCED WORKSHEET AND DATABASE OPERATIONS

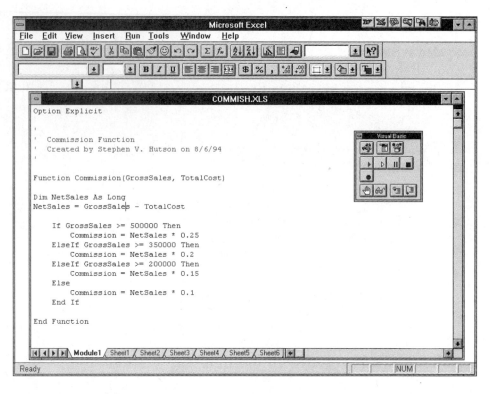

FIGURE 16.3
COMMISH.XLS workbook, step 1

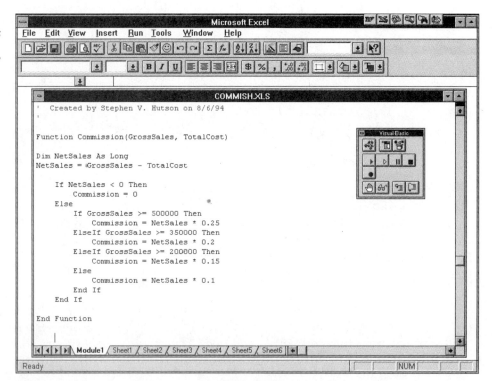

FIGURE 16.4
COMMISH.XLS workbook, complete

Interactive Procedures

The procedures you have written so far are interesting, but they lack a very important ingredient—none of them allow the user to have any input. In order to be truly useful, most procedures will have to allow the user to input certain information.

In this section, you develop the first of two simple examples of macro programming. The first example prompts the user for input of a series of numbers needed to complete a financial statement. The second example illustrates custom dialog boxes and the menu-editing capability of macro programming.

In many situations, persons who are not very familiar with Excel are asked to enter data into the program. This process is much easier, and less error-prone, if macro commands are used to manage the interaction between the user and the program. In this example, you develop a series of macro commands that prompt the user for specific values and then store the results in a workbook. This macro executes automatically when the workbook is opened.

As with any programming assignment, it is useful to begin by laying out the steps to be accomplished. With Excel this can often be done by an experienced user (you!) going through the process on a workbook, carefully recording the steps taken. Since an *experienced* person "knows" where to move the active cell and how to enter a particular number, you need to develop a program instruction to aid the *inexperienced* user. Begin by developing a simple workbook, shown in Figure 16.5.

Once the workbook is constructed, you determine what essential acts are to be performed by the user. In this case, you decide that the active cell should move to each of the input cells, which are A1, B5..B6, B10..B14, and C18. (These cells are unprotected. All other cells contain formulas or constant text information and are

FIGURE 16.5
SERVICE.XLS
workbook
Sheet1

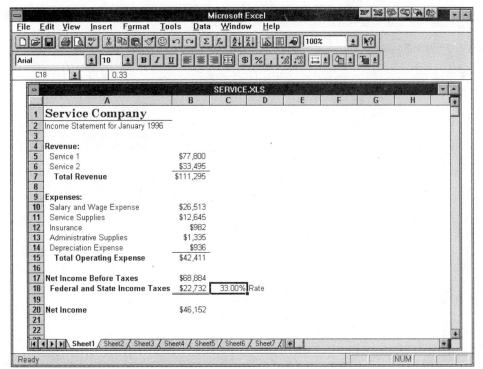

protected.) As the active cell moves, the user should be prompted for the appropriate information, and that information should be stored in the proper cell.

The easiest way to start this macro is to record the bulk of it. You can then edit where necessary to insert prompts and clean up the difference between the way you record and the way you want the macro to run. Since it is important to simplify what the end user will have to do, the macro will be designed to run automatically when the user opens the workbook SERVICE.XLS. For this to work, the macro must have the name Auto_Open. Now, every time SERVICE.XLS is opened, the macro Auto_Open will be executed.

Since Excel only records an action when it is complete, you will enter the values shown in Figure 16.5. You will later edit these ActiveCell.Formula statements to include InputBox functions. Once you have entered the tax rate in cell C18, you click the Stop Macro button. The screen should look like Figure 16.6.

Now it is time to begin editing the macro. The Range.Select statements select the various cells and ranges where you wish to make entries. To protect your macro from errors, it is necessary to insert another Range.Select statement immediately after the Sub Auto_Open( ) statement:

```
Range("A1").Select
```

This statement ensures that regardless of where the active cell was the last time SERVICE.XLS was saved, you will begin your entries in cell A1. Notice that the reference is in A1 format as an absolute reference. The quotation marks indicate that it is a text entry.

The ActiveCell.FormulaR1C1 statements actually make the entries. These are the statements you need to edit. For instance, the statement in cell B3 should read:

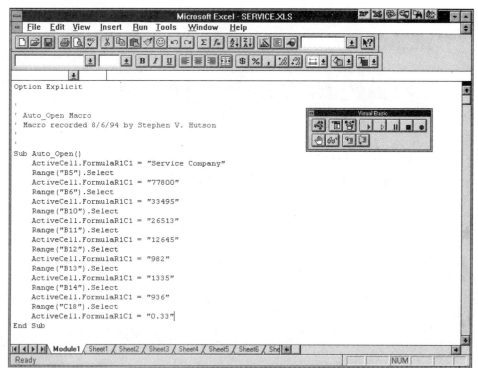

FIGURE 16.6
SERVICE.XLS macro module, step 1

```
ActiveCell.FormulaR1C1 = InputBox("What is the name of the company?","Company Name")
```

Notice that the InputBox( ) function is the value of the Formula property. Any value returned by InputBox( ) is entered into the cell by the Formula property. The InputBox( ) function has seven arguments—the first is required and the last six are optional. It takes the form InputBox(prompt,title,default,xpos,ypos,helpfile,context). The *prompt* argument is the text in the dialog box (note that it is a text string enclosed in quotation marks). The *title* argument, also a text string, gives a title to the dialog box. The *default* argument determines the return value of the function if the user selects OK without making an entry in the dialog box. The *xpos* and *ypos* arguments determine the location of the upper-left corner of the dialog box; if omitted, the dialog box is centered on the screen. The *helpfile* and *context* arguments allow you to attach a help file to the dialog box. After you have edited all the ActiveCell.Formula statements, the finished macro should look like Figure 16.7.

GUIDED ACTIVITY 16.3

Creating an Interactive Procedure

In this Guided Activity you develop a workbook that uses interactive procedures to control input.

1. Create the workbook in Figure 16.5, and add the macro program for input shown in Figure 16.7.

FIGURE 16.7
SERVICE.XLS macro module, complete

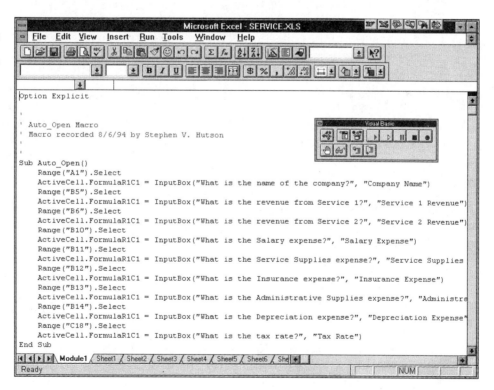

a. You should be able to determine what formulas are in the workbook by looking at Figure 16.5 (a real-life situation; often you will be given a finished product and asked to duplicate it with Excel). Read the discussion in the previous section carefully to determine which cells are for data entry and which contain formulas. Use Tools and Format menu commands to enhance the appearance of the workbook. Drag the Module1 sheet in front of Sheet1.

b. Start the Macro Recorder, and name your macro Auto_Open. Then enter the data in cell A1 and in the appropriate cells in columns B and C. The recorded statements are illustrated in Figure 16.6.

c. Edit the macro statements as illustrated in Figure 16.7.

d. Test the macro by reentering the data illustrated in Figure 16.5.

2. When everything works, save the workbook as SERVICE.XLS. Test the Auto_Open function by closing the workbook, and then reopening it. The macro should execute automatically. Enter any data you wish for testing purposes; then close SERVICE.XLS without saving it.

Collections Revisited

Before we can discuss custom dialog boxes, we need to review the concept of collections. A collection, as discussed in Unit 15, is a group of the same type of item. There are two ways to access a member of a collection. The first is to use an index number. For example, the statement `DialogSheets(1).Show` would display the first dialog sheet in the collection of dialog sheets (generally, the workbook). You can change the index number of an item in a collection by relocating it. For example, if you place Sheet16 at the front of a workbook, you could activate it with the statement `Sheets(1).Activate`.

The other method of accessing an item in a collection is to use the item's name. For example, the statement `Sheets("January").Activate` would activate a worksheet named January. Note that the sheet name is a text string, and must be enclosed in quotation marks.

Custom Dialog Boxes and Menu Items

You can extend the above example by providing the user with a new menu item to complete all the changes. Contrary to how we have normally operated in this book, we discuss here more *what* can be done, rather than *how* to do it, as this is a rather complex task. The principles that we apply to create a custom menu item can be followed to create an entire menu (such as the Edit menu) as well as an entire menu bar.

The first step in creating this new menu item is to create the dialog box that the menu command will call. To do this, we inserted a macro dialog (Dialog1) in front of Module1 and created edit boxes for each item that needs to be entered. We use the Edit Box button, the Label button, and the Group Box button. After creating a couple

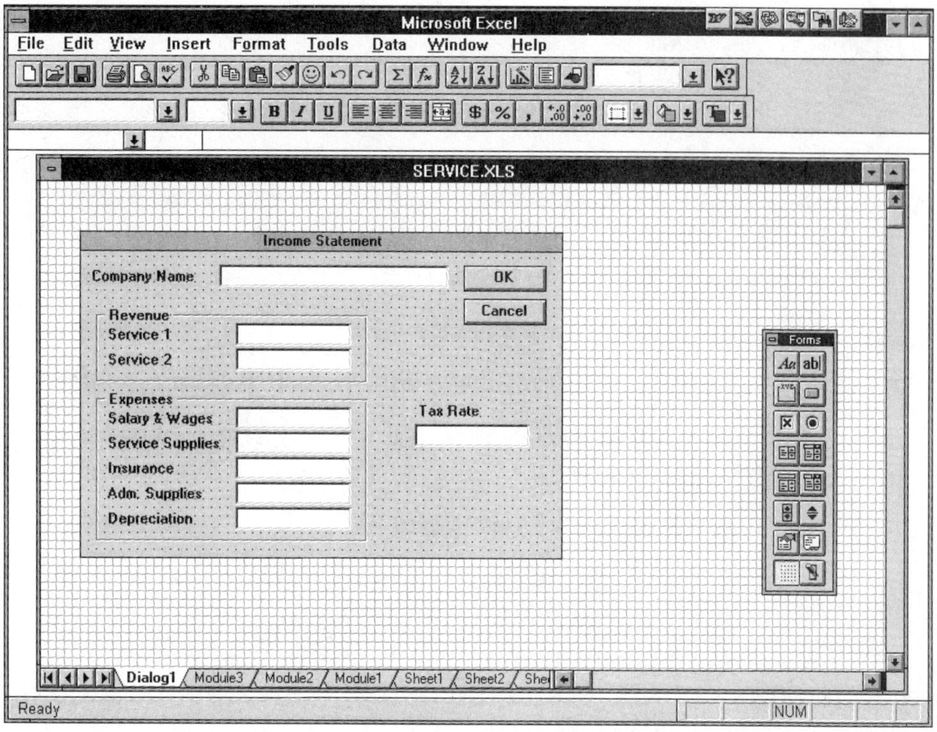

FIGURE 16.8
SERVICE.XLS
workbook,
Dialog1

of edit boxes, we selected them (along with the labels) by dragging a marquee around them. We then copied them by holding [Ctrl] and dragging them to their new location, and edited the labels. When the dialog box was complete, we gave the Tools | Tab Order command to ensure that the edit boxes were in the correct order, and at the top of the Tab Order list. If you need to, review the section "Using Controls in Worksheets" in Unit 12 for a refresher on the various tools and their uses. You can see the finished dialog box in Figure 16.8.

Now that you have a dialog box, you need to be able to display it. After the user enters the information, you then need to be able to read the data from it and transfer it to the appropriate cells on the worksheet. Visual Basic procedures can handle both of these requirements. Rather than dispose of the Auto_Open macro we wrote for SERVICE.XLS, we inserted a new macro module (Module2) in front of Module1 and copied the procedure to it as a skeleton for our next procedure. We then renamed Auto_Open to Phase_One, so that it would not continue to execute automatically. We also inserted a third macro module (Module3) in front of Module2 for another series of procedures. Let's examine each of the routines needed to complete this exercise. Figure 16.9 illustrates the ShowDialog and ReadDialog procedures.

The ShowDialog procedure actually accomplishes three tasks. The first line *initializes* the dialog box; that is, it resets the value of each edit box to an empty text string in order to prevent values from its last use being carried over to its next use. The second line actually displays the dialog box. The last line is executed when the user dismisses the dialog box, either by selecting the OK or Cancel button. The last line calls the ReadDialog procedure.

The ReadDialog procedure should look very familiar. It is based largely on the old Auto_Open procedure. It moves the active cell through the nine cells that need

FIGURE 16.9
SERVICE.XLS
workbook,
Module2

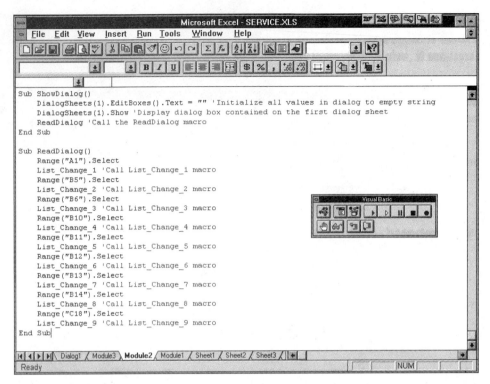

to be changed. However, rather than displaying an input box, it calls a procedure from Module3 that is associated with the list box for that cell. Once it executes the procedure for the active cell, control of the procedure is returned to ReadDialog, where the process begins all over again.

Module3 contains a snippet of code for each edit box in the dialog box. A portion of this module is illustrated in Figure 16.10. These procedures assign the text string of the current edit box to a variable named CurVal, then activate the worksheet containing the income statement, then assign the value of the variable to the active cell, already established by the ReadDialog procedure.

There are a couple of interesting things about the List_Change procedures. First, we only wrote one procedure, then shamelessly made eight copies of the procedure, and edited and renamed each one to refer to the correct edit box. Also, notice that the CurVal variable is declared outside any procedure. This makes it a *module-level variable*, that is, it is available to any procedure in that module. Until now, we have always declared variables within a procedure, making the variable a *local variable*, available only to that procedure. Visual Basic has a third type of variable, the *public variable*, which is available to all procedures and is declared with the keyword Public, rather than Dim. This property of availability of variables is called the *scope* of the variable.

The complete procedure is as follows: the ShowDialog procedure initializes and displays the dialog box. When the user dismisses the dialog box, the ShowDialog procedure then calls the ReadDialog procedure. The ReadDialog procedure activates cell A1 and calls List_Change_1, which copies the contents of the first edit box in the collection to cell A1. Control is then returned to the ReadDialog procedure, which moves to cell B5 and calls List_Change_2, and so on.

FIGURE 16.10
SERVICE.XLS
workbook,
Module3

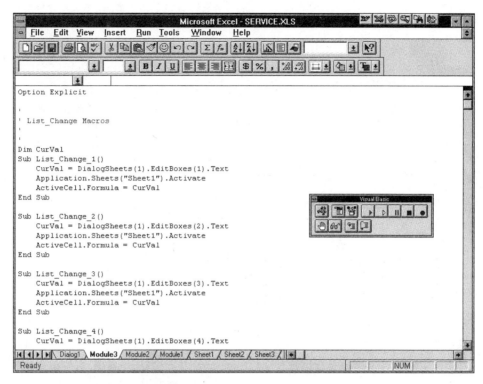

Now that you have a fully functional dialog box, you need a menu item to give your procedure the feel of a "real" command. Use the Tools | Menu Editor command to create a new menu item on the Insert menu that calls the ShowDialog routine.

GUIDED ACTIVITY 16.4

Enhancing an Interactive Procedure

In this Guided Activity, you will follow the instructions in the preceding sections to create a custom dialog box, enter the code to display and read it, then create a menu item to call the entire procedure.

1. If you are not continuing from the previous Guided Activity, use the startup procedure to open Excel. Open SERVICE.XLS.

2. Insert a macro dialog in front of Module1. Follow the instructions in the previous section to design a dialog box similar to the one in Figure 16.8.

3. Save your work.

    a. Insert a new macro module in front of Module2.

    b. Copy the Auto_Open procedure to Module2.

    c. Rename the Auto_Open procedure on Module1 to Phase_One.

    d. Rename the Auto_Open procedure on Module2 to ReadDialog and edit the procedure so that it is identical to Figure 16.9.

e. Add the ShowDialog procedure illustrated in Figure 16.9.

4. Save your work. Insert a new macro module in front of Module2. Follow the instructions in the previous section to create the List_Change procedures illustrated in Figure 16.10.

5. Save your work. Select Module2 and give the Tools | Menu Editor command. Insert an item named New En&try at the end of the Insert menu to call the ShowDialog macro. The dialog box should look like this:

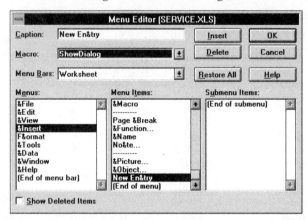

6. Select OK. Save your work. Test your work by giving the Insert | New Entry command. You should see the Income Statement dialog box. Enter the data shown in this illustration:

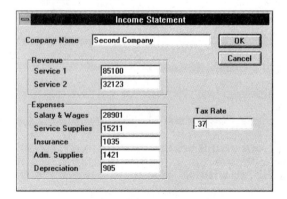

7. Select OK. The data should appear in the correct locations on Sheet1. If the data are in the wrong locations, go back and check the tab order of the list boxes in Dialog1. When it is complete, save your work.

Debugging Macros

Like any other computer programming endeavor, creating workbooks with macros requires careful thought and extreme precision. Most of the macro programming exercises in this book give you complete and exact texts for the macros, and you might think that accomplishing those exercises would be a simple typing exercise. Even the best typists make mistakes, however, and those mistakes yield macros that do not operate properly. Also, even the best programmers write programs that act differently than they expected.

Visual Basic has several valuable tools to locate problems in procedures. Due to space limitations, we only discuss two of these here—break mode and watch expressions. If you wish more information, the Visual Basic Help facility has more than a dozen excellent articles under the heading "Debugging"

Determining where errors lie in programs and removing those errors is called *debugging* (removing the bugs). Before you can begin debugging, you need to understand the various types of errors that can creep into a program. The first is called a *syntax error*; this type of error involves a misuse of the programming language, a misspelling, an omitted keyword (such as an If without a Then or an End If), incorrect punctuation, and so on. Visual Basic will usually inform you of these errors, either when you leave the line, or when you attempt to execute the procedure. The second error type is the *run-time error*. This type of error generally occurs when a program attempts to modify an object that cannot occur in the current context, such as a graphical object that does not exist on the current sheet. Visual Basic will inform you of run-time errors when you try to execute the procedure. Usually, the solution to a run-time error is doing more preparatory work (creating the graphical object, for example) or changing the context (for example, activating the proper sheet). The third, and perhaps most frustrating, error type is the *logic error*. Logic errors do not usually generate error messages; everything seems to work the way it is supposed to, but the procedure yields incorrect results.

The first step in debugging is to check all entries for typographical errors and to go through the instructions to ensure that you did not skip a step. If you cannot find the problem this way, then perhaps you can discover the problem by watching the program execute. One of the best aids for debugging is the ability to have the program execute instructions one step at a time. Visual Basic refers to this as *break mode*. There are several ways to enter break mode. Visual Basic will enter break mode automatically when it encounters a run-time error. You can enter break mode manually by entering a line with the statement Stop. The Stop statement pauses the procedure and places it in break mode. Another way to enter break mode is to select a line and click the Toggle Breakpoints button on the Visual Basic toolbar. Visual Basic will enter break mode before executing the line designated as a breakpoint.

Occasionally, you will encounter an error that only occurs under certain conditions, for example, when a variable reaches a certain number. To isolate such an error, use a *watch expression*. A watch expression can be used to determine the value of an expression at certain points in your procedure, or to enter break mode when an expression reaches a certain value.

EXERCISE 16.1

A Check Register (VII)

Create a macro for data entry. The macro should accept input, add that input to the bottom of the list of checks, format value entries, and update the balance, distribution table, and sum of reimbursable items.

EXERCISE 16.2

Business Mileage (VIII)

Open the file MILES96.XLS. Create a menu item on the Edit menu labeled New Entry that will activate the macro created in Exercise 15.3. Save your work.

EXERCISE 16.3

Form 1040EZ (VI)

Open the file 1040EZ.XLS. Create a custom function named Tax( ) and use it to replace the formula in cell C17. Save your work.

Review Questions

*1. Name two different kinds of loops and explain the differences.

2. When would you use a branch statement in a macro? What statement would you use?

3. List three differences between a procedure and a function.

*4. What is the purpose of initializing a dialog box?

5. Name two tools available in Visual Basic to debug procedures.

Key Terms

Branching	Initialize (dialog boxes)	Return value
Break mode	Initializing variables	Run-time error
Control structure	Local variable	Scope
Custom function	Logic error	Syntax error
Debugging	Looping	Variable
Declaring variables	Module-level variable	Watch expression
Infinite loop	Public variable	

Documentation Research

Using the *Visual Basic User's Guide*, find and record the page number of each of the commands and functions discussed in this unit. We recommend that you also write the page number in the margin next to the discussion of the command in the unit.

1. How does Visual Basic react when two variables have the same name?
2. What branching statement is available in Visual Basic, besides If-Then?

APPLICATION G
Poor Richard's (III)

In this Application, you make modifications to the workbook you created in Applications A and B. This requires you to use many of the commands and concepts discussed in Part Three of this book. You enter a formula containing a lookup table reference, name several ranges, establish workbook titles, use query commands, and write several macro commands.

For most people, creation of a complex, sophisticated workbook such as this one is an iterative, trial-and-error process. The discussion that follows leads you through the steps in developing this workbook.

Our desire was to build a workbook that would be fairly foolproof. When the workbook is retrieved, it should present the user (a car salesperson, not a computer operator) with three buttons: Select a car, Analyze the purchase, and Exit.

To simplify the process further, the workbook should contain a list of the inventory and automatically fill in the Dealer Cost and List Price cells, as well as display a description of the car.

1. Load Windows and enter Excel. Open the AUTO.XLS workbook you edited in Application B.

2. The first step is to build a table with the inventory list. Follow the example provided in Figure G.1.

   a. Insert two rows above row 1.

   b. Column I: Set the width to 12. Bold the entry in I4. Center all entries in the column.

   c. Column J: Set the width to 30. Bold and center the entry in J4.

d. Column K: Set the width to 12. Bold and center the entry in K4. Format all numbers in the column to #,##0.

   e. Column L: Set the width to 13. Bold and center the entry in L4. Format data as in column K.

   f. Enter the data as shown in Figure G.1.

3. When the Inventory table is complete, name the range I5:L12 as INVENTORY. Do not include row 4 in the named range. Save your work (continue to use AUTO.XLS as the file name).

4. At this point, split panes between rows 4 and 5 and freeze panes. Your screen should look like Figure G.1.

5. Move the cells containing Sales Tax Rate, Finance A.P.R., and Number of Payments to E18:G20. (You can see where these end up if you look ahead to Figure G.2.)

6. Define the following names:

A26	Dialog
C6	Case
C10	Trade_In_Value
C11	Trade_In_Allowance
G20	Months
J5:J12	Description

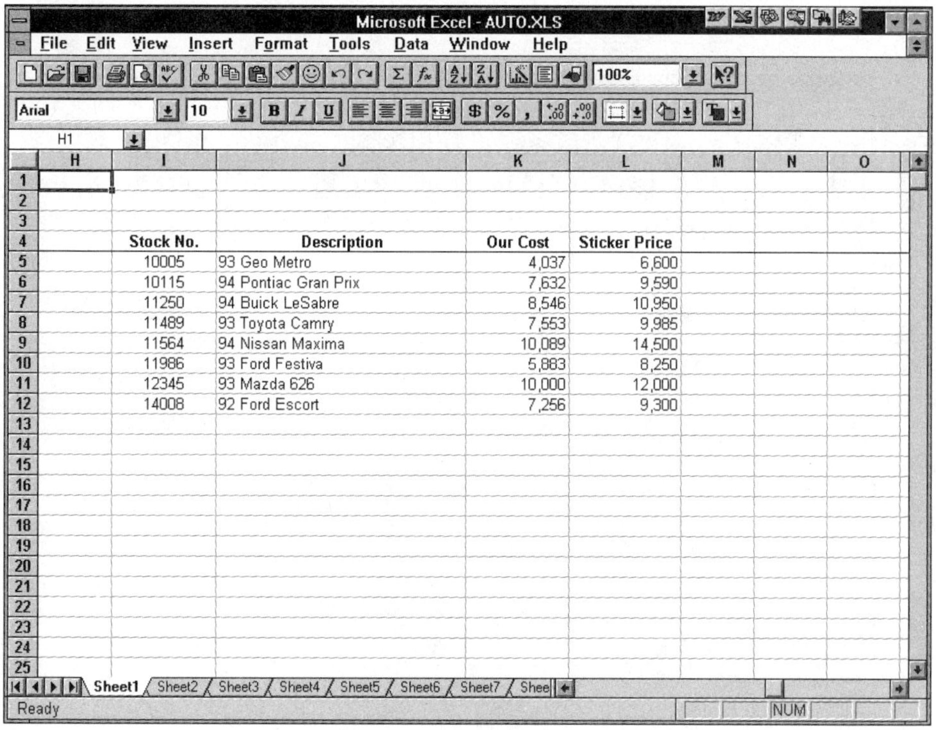

FIGURE G.1
The Inventory section (Note: Costs and prices are wild guesses.)

	Stock No.	Description	Our Cost	Sticker Price
5	10005	93 Geo Metro	4,037	6,600
6	10115	94 Pontiac Gran Prix	7,632	9,590
7	11250	94 Buick LeSabre	8,546	10,950
8	11489	93 Toyota Camry	7,553	9,985
9	11564	94 Nissan Maxima	10,089	14,500
10	11986	93 Ford Festiva	5,883	8,250
11	12345	93 Mazda 626	10,000	12,000
12	14008	92 Ford Escort	7,256	9,300

7. Now you use a lookup function. Note that the Dealer Cost figure is in the third column of Inventory. Go to cell C7. Enter the following function:

   =VLOOKUP(CASE,INVENTORY,3)

   Convince yourself that this works by changing the stock number (cell C6) a few times and watch the Dealer Cost change. Convince yourself that it does not work perfectly by entering a bogus stock number, such as 11000. We fix that later. When you have had enough fun, put stock number 12345 in cell C6.

8. Enter a similar function in cell C8 to read the List Price from the INVENTORY range. (You can copy the function from cell C7, then change the offset, then negate the number by placing a hyphen in front of the function and enclosing the function in parentheses.)

9. Enter a similar function in cell E6 to read the Description.

10. Set the width of column C to 12 and column D to 14 and change the width of column H so the inventory list is not visible (on our system, we made column H quite a bit wider). The Analysis portion of the workbook should now look like Figure G.2.

11. Unprotect cells C10, C11, and G20. Save your work.

12. Now you start to build the macro commands.

    a. Give the Insert | Macro | Module command.

    b. You need a dialog box to display the automobile descriptions. Give the Insert | Macro | Dialog command.

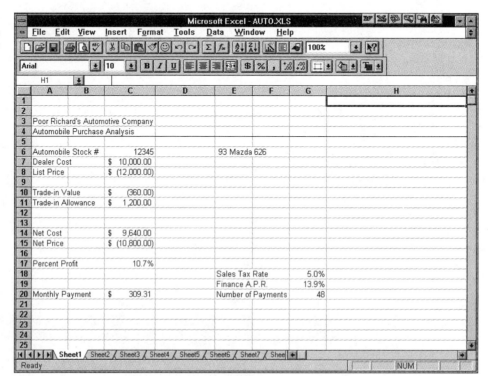

FIGURE G.2 The Analysis section

c. The only control in the dialog box will be a list box. With the list box selected, give the Format | Object command. Select the Control tab. For the Input Range, use `AUT.XLS!Description`. For the Cell Link, use `AUTO.XLS!Dialog`.

d. Change the dialog caption to `Auto Selection`.

e. Change the formula in cell E6 to read `=INDEX(Description,Dialog)`.

f. Change the formula in cell C6 to read `=INDEX(INVENTORY,Dialog,1)`. Your dialog sheet should look like Figure G.3.

13. Activate the macro module. You need to write a SelectAuto, an Analyze, and an Exit procedure. The object of the SelectAuto macro is to display the dialog box, allowing the user to choose an automobile from the Inventory list and place the stock number of the chosen vehicle in cell C6 of the workbook. The link between the dialog box and cell C6 accomplishes much of this work. The complete macro is displayed in Figure G.4, and is discussed in step 15.

14. Let us examine the SelectAuto macro in detail:

    a. The first statement in cell A2 turns off workbook protection. Some of the commands will not work while protection is on.

    b. The next two statements sort the Inventory list by stock number. This protects the macro from someone who might change the order of the Inventory list by mistake.

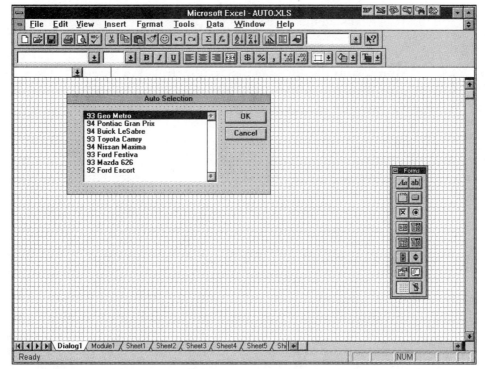

FIGURE G.3
Dialog sheet

FIGURE G.4
SelectAuto procedure

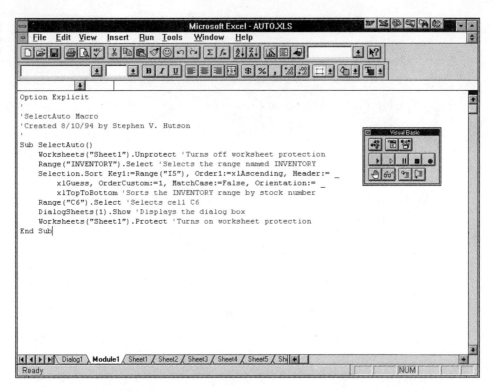

c. The next statement selects cell C6. Basically, you do this so that the INVENTORY range will not still be selected when the user returns to the worksheet.

d. The next statement displays the dialog box.

e. The last statement turns workbook protection back on.

15. The purpose of the Analyze macro (illustrated in Figure G.5) is to allow the user to enter the trade-in value, the trade-in allowance, and the number of payments, and to enter those numbers in the respective cells. The first statement selects the Months cell. The next statement creates an input box and enters the result in the current cell. The fourth statement is new; the InputBox( ) function can only return text. You need to multiply the output of this function by –1 to get a negative number. Therefore, we used the InputBox *method* instead of the InputBox *function*. The InputBox method applies only to the Application object, but allows the programmer to specify the type of return value. As entered, this statement requires a numeric return value.

16. The purpose of the ExitApp macro is to save the workbook and then exit the program.

17. Now let's return to Sheet1 to complete the final steps. Draw a button over the range A1:B2. Assign the SelectAuto macro to the button, and change the text on the button to `Select`. Remember: if you deselect the button, you can reselect it by pressing [Ctrl] while clicking on it. Draw another button over the range D1:D2. Assign the Analyze macro to the button, and change the text to `Analyze`. Draw

FIGURE G.5
The Analyze and ExitApp macros

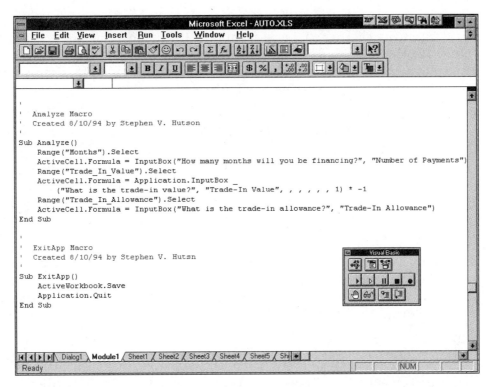

```
' Analyze Macro
' Created 8/10/94 by Stephen V. Hutson
'
Sub Analyze()
    Range("Months").Select
    ActiveCell.Formula = InputBox("How many months will you be financing?", "Number of Payments")
    Range("Trade_In_Value").Select
    ActiveCell.Formula = Application.InputBox _
        ("What is the trade-in value?", "Trade-In Value", , , , , 1) * -1
    Range("Trade_In_Allowance").Select
    ActiveCell.Formula = InputBox("What is the trade-in allowance?", "Trade-In Allowance")
End Sub

' ExitApp Macro
' Created 8/10/94 by Stephen V. Hutsn
'
Sub ExitApp()
    ActiveWorkbook.Save
    Application.Quit
End Sub
```

a third button over the range F1:G2. Assign the ExitApp macro to the button, and change the text on the button to Exit. The worksheet should look like Figure G.6. Save the workbook.

FIGURE G.6
AUTO.XLS workbook, complete

	A	B	C	D	E	F	G	H
1	Select			Analyze		Exit		
2								
3	Poor Richard's Automotive Company							
4	Automobile Purchase Analysis							
5								
6	Automobile Stock #		10115		94 Pontiac Gran Prix			
7	Dealer Cost		$ 7,632.00					
8	List Price		$ (9,590.00)					
9								
10	Trade-in Value		$ (450.00)					
11	Trade-in Allowance		$ 1,500.00					
12								
13								
14	Net Cost		$ 7,182.00					
15	Net Price		$ (8,090.00)					
16								
17	Percent Profit		11.2%					
18					Sales Tax Rate		5.0%	
19					Finance A.P.R.		13.9%	
20	Monthly Payment		$ 197.21		Number of Payments		60	

18. The workbook should now be ready for the execution of the macros. Start the macro by clicking on the Select button. If you have entered everything properly, you should see a dialog box like that shown in Figure G.7. Use the arrow keys to highlight each of the choices. The next several paragraphs discuss what should happen as you execute each of the macros. Read the descriptions and test your work.

19. Consider what happens when the Select button is pressed. Excel presents the dialog box in Figure G.7. When the user selects an automobile, the dialog box returns a value corresponding to the car's position in the list to the Dialog cell. This is converted to a stock number that is entered in the Case cell and a description that is entered into cell E6. When the user dismisses the dialog box by pressing either the OK or Cancel button, protection is turned back on and the procedure is complete.

20. Things are less complex when the Analyze button is pressed. Excel highlights the Months cell and presents the Input box. The ActiveCell.Formula statement places the value returned by InputBox( ) in the Months cell. The same basic procedure is followed for the Trade_In_Value cell and the Trade_In_Allowance cell.

21. The Exit button saves the current workbook (AUTO.XLS) and exits Excel.

22. Test the macro by selecting the 1994 Nissan Maxima. Then analyze the transaction by entering a Trade-In Value of $1,000 and a Trade-In Allowance of $1,500. You should show a Percent Profit of 30.1% (Poor Richard will be *very* pleased) and a monthly payment of $372.32 for 48 months.

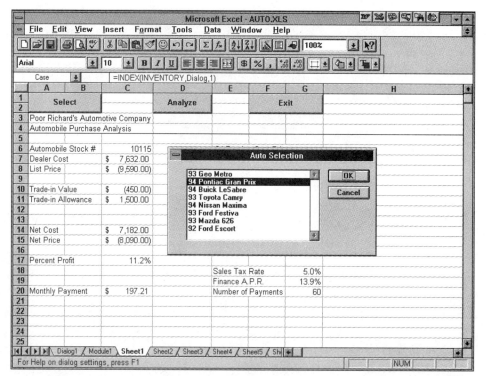

FIGURE G.7 The Auto Selection dialog box

23. Finally, press the Exit button.

24. The final test is to open Excel, give the File | Open AUTO.XLS command, and see that the workbook was saved before exiting.

APPENDIX A
Answers

Answers to Checkpoints

1A. Press [Ctrl][Home] or [End][Home] to quickly return to cell A1.

1B. The window is the same size as it was when Excel was first opened.

1C. If you are using Windows 3.1, the size should be 15,872 bytes.

2A. Make a cell the active cell by clicking on it with the mouse or pressing the arrow keys until it is highlighted.

2B. Your disk should now contain the files BULL.XLS and BULL2.XLS.

3A. Invoke File | Save As, then type FUNCTION, and press [Enter].

4A. You can either choose Cells from the Format menu, or right-click the range and choose Format Cells from the shortcut menu.

4B. The date entries will be different because they reflect the dates when each of us did the work.

4C. The [Ctrl][Shift][End] key combination selects all cells in the range between the active selection and the lower-right corner of the data block.

5A. The printout differs in that each cell containing a formula now displays the formula rather than the result of the formula.

6A. The formulas differ in that they refer to different cell references. They are similar in that they refer to cells that are in the same relative position to the cell containing the formula.

6B. The formulas refer to different cells, but in all cases the formulas refer to the cell immediately to the right.

6C. It still sums B6:B7 and does not include the inserted cell, B8.

6D. With the mouse, click on the column label. From the keyboard, select a cell in the column and press [Ctrl][Spacebar].

7A. =D8*(1+$G$5)

7B. Cell A3 is a function of cell A4, and A4 is a function of A3.

8A. A4:E4 contains the category names; column A contains the data series names for the legend; row 9 contains the total revenues; row 15 contains the total expenses; row 18 contains the difference, the gross profit.

8B. Hold the [Ctrl] key and drag the sheet tab to the center of the next tab to the right.

9A. The entry in cell B12 applies to all lines and must be referenced absolutely by all of the formulas that will be copied from E5. The entry in cell B9 is the total of all lines, and must also be referenced absolutely by those formulas.

9B. Give the View | Toolbars command and select Auditing.

10A =125*X1 and =200*X1

10B Click the Center Across Columns button on the toolbar.

11A A2:E39

11B 15 of 38 records found

11C Ribeau, with $1,006,034

12A The cells in H4:H7 are modified by the controls; if they are not unlocked, the controls will be unable to change their value.

12B When the formula was cleared in the active window, it was also cleared in the inactive window.

12C Tools | Protection | Protect Sheet

12D Unprotect the sheet.

12E In fact, most commands are unavailable while the sheet is protected. The entire Format menu and most of the Edit, Insert, and Data menus are not available.

13A Press [Ctrl][F6] to activate the next workbook.

13B Mouse users can select an entire row by clicking on the row label. Keyboard users can select an entire row by placing the active cell in that row and pressing [Shift][Spacebar].

13C Double-click on the sheet tab and enter a name in the dialog box.

14A To align a combination of currency and noncurrency numeric formats, select the format #,##0.00_) for the noncurrency numbers.

16A Commission( ) returns a negative number.

Answers to Review Questions

1-1c. The [F5] key is the Go To key. It opens a dialog box allowing you to move directly to another location on the worksheet.

1-1e. The [PgUp] key scrolls the worksheet upwards one screen at a time.

1-1h. In edit mode, the [Backspace] key deletes either the highlighted character(s) or the character to the left of the cursor.

1-2b. The mouse cursor takes the shape of a pointer when it is on the menu bar, one of the toolbars, the title bar, or one of the scroll bars.

1-2c. The mouse cursor takes the shape of a cross when it is on the worksheet.

1-2e. The mouse cursor takes the shape of a double arrow when it is on a window border.

1-3b. The scroll bar rapidly brings different parts of the worksheet into view.

1-3d. The Minimize button reduces the window to an icon at the bottom of the screen.

1-3e. The Maximize button expands the window to fill the screen.

2-1. A cell is the building block of a worksheet.

2-3. A cell's reference is the combination of the column letter and the row number.

2-6. The pointing method is a method for entering cell formulas by moving the cell pointer to cells to be included in the formula instead of entering the cell address.

2-8. Move to the cell, type `General Generators`, then press [Enter].

2-10. Move to cell B6 and press [=], [←], [↓], [Enter].

2-12. Press [Alt][F], [O], type `assets`, and press [Enter].

3-1. The order of precedence is the order in which the elements of a formula are evaluated.

3-2b. The formula that will compute the absolute value of the difference is `=ABS(D5-D6)`.

3-3. The formula that will compute the monthly payment is `=PMT(F9/12,60,-F8)`.

4-1b. The entry `d` displays a single-digit numeric day in a date format; the entry `dd` would force a 0 in front of the first nine days of the month; the entry `ddd` would display an abbreviation of the day's name; the entry `dddd` would display the entire day's name.

4-1d. The entry `a` displays a time value in 12-hour format followed by an `a` to identify AM.

4-1e. The @ sign acts as a text placeholder; any text entered in the cell is placed at the location of the @.

4-3. Select the entire worksheet by clicking on the Select All button, give the Format | Cells command, and select the Number tab.

4-5. Select a cell and give the Insert | Row command; Excel will insert a row above the row containing the selected cell.

4-8. Select the range, give the Format | Cells command, and select the Alignment tab.

4-10. Give the Format | Style command, select the desired style name, and click OK.

5-1. A print area is a defined name that refers to the portion of the worksheet that you wish to print.

6-2. They change to reflect the new positions of the cells.

6-3. They do not change.

6-6. Use Edit | Copy to duplicate a formula, number, or text.

6-8. All, Formulas, Values, Formats, Notes, Arithmetic Operations, Skip Blanks, and Transpose

7-2. Use mixed or absolute references when the row, column, or cell reference must not change.

7-4. Absolute cell references do not change.

7-7. Cells are calculated such that all cells referenced by a given cell are calculated prior to the given cell being calculated.

7-9a. =down-1 + left-1

7-12. Tools | Options

8-1. The 15 basic chart types are area chart, bar chart, column chart, line chart, pie chart, doughnut chart, radar chart, XY (scatter) chart, combination chart, 3-D area chart, 3-D bar chart, 3-D column chart, 3-D line chart, 3-D pie chart, and 3-D surface chart.

8-2b. The line chart is usually used to show trends.

8-2d. Use stacked bar charts for totals.

8-2e. Use XY charts to show the relationship between two numeric scales.

9-2. The target cell must contain a formula that refers, directly or indirectly, to the changing cell(s).

10-1a. The formula is =40000+69.95*X1.

10-2a. The start value is 0.

10-2c. The stop value is 1.

11-1a. A database is a cell range of one or more columns and two or more rows. The top row of a database contains field names; all other rows contain data.

11-1d. A field is each column of the database.

11-2a. The criteria are K1: Name K2: Ross.

11-2c. The criteria are K1: Dept K2: Personnel.

11-3a. The sort key is Salary.

11-4a. The formula is =DMIN(A1:E39,2,F1:F2).

12-2. Worksheet cells are locked but not hidden.

12-4. It applies all defined names to all formulas in the selection (or the worksheet if only one cell is selected).

12-6. [Ctrl][F6]

12-7. The Drawing toolbar

13-1. ASCII-generic files contain only letters, numbers, and basic punctuation. Excel can open them and manipulate them as text files. Program-specific file formats contain other characters in a language specific to that application. Excel can only open and manipulate them if a filter for that particular format is included in its programming.

13-3b. The .XLT extension signifies a template file.

14-1. The formula is =IF(H19,-1,1).

15-1. Tools | Record Macro | Mark Position for Recording determines where the next recording will take place. Tools | Record Macro | Record at Mark starts the Macro Recorder at that location.

15-3. Assign it to a menu item, a button or graphical object, or a toolbar. Use a shortcut key. Use the Run selection from the Tools | Macro command.

15-5. 26 lowercase letters and 26 uppercase letters for a total of 52

16-1. The For-Next loop loops until a counter (variable) reaches a certain number. The Do-Loop loops until a condition is met (an expression that yields the value True).

16-4. The purpose of initializing a dialog box is to prevent the value returned by its last use from being carried over to its next use.

APPENDIX B
Excel Version 5 Functions

This appendix contains a reference to all functions available on Excel Version 5 worksheets arranged according to their primary use: mathematical, financial, logical, and so on. Some of the functions are illustrated in the units of this book; for more information on others, you will need to refer to the Help facility in the Excel program.

Mathematical Functions

ABS(number)   Absolute value of *number*.

ACOS(number)   Arc cosine of *number*, the angle in radians whose cosine is *number*. If *number* is not between –1 and +1, the value is #NUM! To convert radians to degrees, use the DEGREES( ) function; for example, if cell H8 contains a cosine, then the angle in degrees is determined by the function =DEGREES(ACOS(H8)).

ACOSH(number)   Inverse hyperbolic cosine of *number*.

ASIN(number)   Arc sine of *number*, the angle in radians whose sine is *number*. If *number* is not between –1 and +1, the value is #NUM! To convert radians to degrees, use the DEGREES( ) function.

ASINH(number)   Inverse hyperbolic sine of *number*.

ATAN(number)   Arc tangent of *number*, the angle in radians whose tangent is *number*. To convert radians to degrees, use the DEGREES( ) function.

ATAN2(x_num,y_num)   Arc tangent of the *x* and *y* coordinates, *x_num* and *y_num*, the angle in radians whose tangent is *y_num/x_num*. To convert radians to degrees, use the DEGREES( ) function.

ATANH(number)   Inverse hyperbolic tangent of *number*.

CEILING(number,significance) Rounds *number* away from zero to nearest multiple of *significance*.

COMBIN(number,number_chosen) Number of combinations in *number* containing *number_chosen* objects.

COS(number) Cosine of *number* in radians. To convert degrees to radians, use the RADIANS( ) function; for example, if cell G12 has a number in degrees, then the function is =COS(RADIANS(G12)).

COSH(number) Hyperbolic cosine of *number*.

COUNTIF(range,criteria) Counts the number of nonblank cells in *range* that meet the given *criteria*.

DEGREES(number) Converts radians to degrees.

EVEN(number) Rounds *number* away from zero to the nearest even integer.

EXP(number) Returns *e* (2.71828182845904) raised to the power of *number*.

FACT(number) Returns the factorial (1×2×3... *number*) of *number*.

FACTDOUBLE(number) Returns the double factorial of *number*.

FLOOR(number,significance) Rounds *number* away from zero to the nearest multiple of *significance*.

GCD(number1,number2,...) Returns the greatest common divisor of two or more integers.

INT(number) Returns the integer part of *number*.

LCM(number1,number2,...) Returns the least common multiple of two or more integers.

LN(number) $\log_e$ of *number*.

LOG(number,base) $\log_{base}$ of *number*.

LOG10(number) Returns the base-10 logarithm of *number*.

MOD(number,divisor) *Number* mod *divisor*: modular part (remainder) of *number/divisor*.

MROUND(number,multiple) Returns *number* rounded to *multiple*.

MULTINOMIAL(number1,number2,...) Returns the ratio of the factorial of *numbers* to the product of factorials.

ODD(number) Returns *number* rounded up to the nearest odd integer.

PI( ) π is 3.14159265358979324.

POWER(number,power) Returns the value of *number* raised to the power of *power*.

PRODUCT(number1,number2,...) Returns the product of *numbers*.

QUOTIENT(numerator,denominator) Returns the value *numerator/denominator*.

RADIANS(number) Converts degrees to radians.

RAND( ) Random number between 0 and 1.

RANDBETWEEN(bottom,top) Random number between *bottom* and *top*.

ROMAN(number,*form*) Converts Arabic *number* to a Roman numeral, as text. *Form* is an optional argument that determines the type of Roman numeral generated.

ROUND(number,num_digits) Rounds *number* to *num_digits* decimal places.

ROUNDDOWN(number,num_digits) Rounds *number* down to *num_digits* decimal places (toward zero).

ROUNDUP(number,num_digits) Rounds *number* up to *num_digits* decimal places (away from zero).

SERIESSUM(x,n,m,coefficients) Returns the sum of a power series.

SIGN(number) Returns the sign of *number*.

SIN(number) Sine of *number* in radians. To convert radians to degrees, use the DEGREES( ) function.

SINH(number) Hyperbolic sine of *number*.

SQRT(number) Square root of *number*.

SQRTPI(number) Square root of (*number*×π).

SUM(number1,*number2*,...) Sum of *numbers*.

SUMIF(range,criteria,*sum_range*) Adds the cells in *sum_range* that correspond to the cells in *range* that meet the given *criteria*. If *sum_range* is not specified, it adds the cells in *range* that meet the given *criteria*.

SUMSQ(number1,*number2*,...) Sum of the squares of *numbers*.

SUMX2MY2(array_x,array_y) Sum of the difference of the squares of corresponding values of *array_x* and *array_y*.

SUMX2PY2(array_x,array_y) Sum of the sum of the squares of corresponding values of *array_x* and *array_y*.

SUMXMY2(array_x,array_y) Sum of the squares of the differences of corresponding values of *array_x* and *array_y*.

TAN(number) Tangent of *number* in radians. To convert radians to degrees, use the DEGREES( ) function.

TANH(number) Hyperbolic tangent of *number*.

TRUNC(number,*num_digits*) Truncates *number* to an integer.

Financial Functions

ACCRINT(issue,first_interest,settlement,coupon,*par*,frequency,*basis*) Accrued interest for a security that pays periodic interest.

ACCRINTM(issue,settlement,rate,*par*,*basis*) Accrued interest for a security that pays interest at maturity.

AMORDEGRC(cost,date_purchased,first_period,salvage,period,rate,basis) Depreciation for each accounting period.

AMORLINC(cost,date_purchased,first_period,salvage,period,rate,basis) Depreciation for each accounting period.

COUPDAYBS(settlement,maturity,frequency,*basis*) Number of days from the beginning of the coupon period to the settlement date.

COUPDAYS(settlement,maturity,frequency,*basis*) Number of days in the coupon period that contains the settlement date.

COUPDAYSNC(settlement,maturity,frequency,*basis*) Number of days from the settlement date to the next coupon date.

COUPNCD(settlement,maturity,frequency,*basis*) The next coupon date after the settlement date.

COUPNUM(settlement,maturity,frequency,*basis*) Number of coupons payable between the settlement date and the maturity date.

COUPPCD(settlement,maturity,frequency,*basis*) Previous coupon date before the settlement date.

CUMIPMT(rate,nper,pv,start_period,end_period,type) Cumulative interest paid between two periods.

CUMPRINC(rate,nper,pv,start_period,end_period,type) Cumulative principal paid on a loan between two periods.

DB(cost,salvage,life,period,*month*) Fixed-declining balance depreciation.

DDB(cost,salvage,life,period,*factor*) Double-declining balance depreciation, the depreciation amount in a specific *period,* given the initial *cost, salvage* value, and *life* of the item. *Factor* is the rate at which the balance declines; if omitted, Excel will assume it to be 2, thus using the double-declining balance method.

DISC(settlement,maturity,pr,redemption,*basis*) Discount rate for a security.

DOLLARDE(fractional_dollar,fraction) Converts a dollar amount, expressed as a fraction, into a dollar amount, expressed as a decimal.

DOLLARFR(decimal_dollar,fraction) Converts a dollar amount, expressed as a decimal, into a dollar amount, expressed as a fraction.

DURATION(settlement,maturity,coupon,yld,frequency,*basis*) The Macauley duration for an assumed par value of $100.

EFFECT(nominal_rate,npery) Effective annual interest rate.

FV(rate,nper,pmt,*pv,type*) Future value of an ordinary annuity with payments of *pmt* at the end of each period, at a per-period interest rate of *rate*, for *nper* periods. *Pv* is the present value that a series of future payments is worth now; if omitted, it is assumed to be 0. *Type* is a code to indicate whether the payments are due at the end of the period (0) or the beginning of the period (1); the default is 0.

FVSCHEDULE(principal,schedule) Future value of an initial principal after applying a series of compound interest rates.

INTRATE(settlement,maturity,investment,redemption,*basis*) Interest rate for a fully invested security.

IPMT(rate,per,nper,pv,*fv,type*) Interest payment for an investment for a given period.

IRR(values,*guess*) Internal rate of return of *values*, the series of cash flows in the range. If *guess* is omitted, Excel will use 0.10 as *guess*.

MDURATION(settlement,maturity,coupon,yld,frequency,*basis*) The Macauley modified duration for a security with an assumed rate of $100.

MIRR(values,finance_rate,reinvest_year) The internal rate of return where positive and negative cash flows are financed at different rates.

NOMINAL(effect_rate,npery) Annual nominal interest rate.

NPER(rate,pmt,pv,*fv,type*) Number of periods, the number of payments necessary to achieve the present value *pv* (or the future value *fv*), given the payment *pmt* and interest *rate*.

NPV(rate,value1,...) Net present value of the series of cash flows in the *values*, discounted at *rate* interest rate.

ODDFPRICE(settlement,maturity,issue,first_coupon,rate,yld,redemption,frequency,*basis*) Price per $100 face value of a security with an odd first period.

ODDFYIELD(settlement,maturity,issue,first_coupon,rate,pr,redemption,frequency,*basis*) Yield of a security with an odd first period.

ODDLPRICE(settlement,maturity,last_coupon,rate,yld,redemption,frequency,*basis*) Price per $100 face value of a security with an odd last period.

ODDLYIELD(settlement,maturity,last_coupon,rate,pr,redemption,frequency,*basis*) Yield of a security with an odd last period.

PMT(rate,nper,pv,*fv,type*) Payment on a loan of principal *pv* at a per-period interest rate of *rate*, for *nper* periods.

PPMT(rate,per,nper,pv,*fv,type*) Returns the payment on the principal of a loan of principal *pv* at a per-period interest rate of *rate*, for *nper* periods.

PRICE(settlement,maturity,rate,yld,redemption,frequency,*basis*) Price per $100 face value of a security that pays periodic interest.

PRICEDISC(settlement,maturity,discount,redemption,*basis*) Price per $100 face value of a discounted security.

PRICEMAT(settlement,maturity,issue,rate,yld,*basis*) Price per $100 face value of a security that pays interest at maturity.

PV(rate,nper,pmt,*fv*,*type*) Present value of an ordinary annuity at a per-period interest rate of *rate* with *nper* payments of *pmt* at the end of each period (*type* = 0) or the beginning of each period (*type* = 1).

RATE(nper,pmt,pv,*fv*,*type*,*guess*) Interest rate if a loan of principal *pv* is paid in payments of *pmt* for *nper* periods.

RECEIVED(settlement,maturity,investment,discount,*basis*) Amount received at maturity for a fully invested security.

SLN(cost,salvage,life) Straight-line depreciation, which is the same amount for each period, given the initial *cost, salvage* value, and *life* of the item.

SYD(cost,salvage,life,per) Sum-of-the-years' digits depreciation, for a specified *per*, given the initial *cost, salvage* value, and *life* of the item.

TBILLEQ(settlement,maturity,discount) Bond-equivalent yield for a Treasury bill.

TBILLPRICE(settlement,maturity,discount) Price per $100 face value for a Treasury bill.

TBILLYIELD(settlement,maturity,pr) Yield for a Treasury bill.

VDB(cost,salvage,life,start_period,end_period,*factor*,*no_switch*) Variable-declining balance depreciation, the depreciation amount in a specific period, given the initial *cost*, *salvage* value, and *life* of the item.

XIRR(values,dates,*guess*) Internal rate of return for a series of cash flows that is not necessarily periodic.

XNPV(rate,values,dates) Net present value for a schedule of cash flows that is not necessarily periodic.

YIELD(settlement,maturity,rate,pr,redemption,frequency,*basis*) Yield on a security that pays periodic interest.

YIELDDISC(settlement,maturity,pr,redemption,*basis*) Annual yield for a discounted security.

YIELDMAT(settlement,maturity,issue,rate,pr,*basis*) Annual yield of a security that pays interest at maturity.

Date and Time Functions

DATE(year,month,day) Serial number of a given date.

DATEVALUE(date_text) String to date, converts a string to a serial date number.

DAY(serial_number) Day of the month of the given date.

DAYS360(start_date,end_date,*method*) Difference in dates using a 360-day year (that is, 12 months, each with 30 days). *Method* is a logical value determining whether or not Excel should use the European method of calculating days.

EDATE(start_date,months) Serial number of the date that is *months* before or after *start_date*.

EOMONTH(start_date,months) Serial number of the last day of the month that is *months* before or after *start_date*.

HOUR(serial_number) Hour value of time number.

MINUTE(serial_number) Minute value of time number.

MONTH(serial_number) Month number of the given date.

NETWORKDAYS(start_date,end_date,*holidays*) Number of whole workdays between *start_date* and *end_date*. The result excludes the number of dates included in the optional *holidays* argument.

NOW( ) Current system date and time.

SECOND(serial_number) Second value of time number.

TIME(hour,minute,second) Serial time number, computes the time number of the arguments.

TIMEVALUE(time_text) String to time, converts a string to a serial time number.

TODAY( ) Current system date.

WEEKDAY(serial_number,*return_type*) Day of the week of *serial_number*. *Return_type* is a number representing the system used to return the number.

WORKDAY(start_date,days,*holidays*) The serial number of the date *days* before or after *start_date*. The result excludes the number of dates included in the optional *holidays* argument.

YEAR(serial_number) Year number of the given date.

YEARFRAC(start_date,end_date,*basis*) The year fraction representing the number of whole days between *start_date* and *end_date*.

Statistical Functions

AVEDEV(number1,*number2*,...) The average of the absolute deviations of *numbers* from their means.

AVERAGE(number1,*number2*,...) The average value of the items in the list.

BETADIST(x,alpha,beta,A,B) The cumulative beta probability density.

BETAINV(probability,alpha,beta,A,B) The inverse of the cumulative beta probability density.

BINOMDIST(number_s,trials,probability_s,cumulative) The individual term binomial distribution.

CHIDIST(x,degrees_freedom) The one-tailed probability of the chi-squared distribution.

CHIINV(probability,degrees_freedom) The inverse of the chi-squared distribution.

CHITEST(actual_range,expected_range) The test for independence.

CONFIDENCE(alpha,standard_dev,size) The confidence interval for a population.

CORREL(array1,array2) The correlation coefficient between two data sets.

COUNT(value1,*value2*,...) The number of numeric values in the list. Only numeric values in a range count.

COUNTA(value1,*value2*,...) The number of values in the list. Every nonblank cell in a range counts, whether it contains a value or text.

COVAR(value1,*value2*,...) The covariance, the average of the products of paired deviations.

CRITBINOM(trials,probability_s,alpha) The smallest value for which the cumulative binomial distribution is less than or equal to a criterion value.

DEVSQ(number1,*number2*,...) The sum of squares of deviations.

EXPONDIST(x,lambda,cumulative) The exponential distribution.

FDIST(x,degrees_freedom1,degrees_freedom2) The F probability distribution.

FINV(probability,degrees_freedom1,degrees_freedom2) The inverse of the F probability distribution.

FISHER(x) The Fisher transformation.

FISHERINV(y) The inverse of the Fisher transformation.

FORECAST(x,known_y's,known_x's) Returns a value along a linear trend.

FREQUENCY(data_array,bins_array) Returns the frequency distribution as a vertical array.

FTEST(array1,array2) The result of an F-test.

GAMMADIST(x,alpha,beta,cumulative) The gamma distribution.

GAMMAINV(probability,alpha,beta) The inverse of the gamma cumulative distribution.

GAMMALN(x) The natural logarithm of the gamma function.

GEOMEAN(number1,*number2*,...) The geometric mean.

GROWTH(known_y's,*known_x's,new_x's,const*) Fits an exponential curve to the *known_y's* and *known_x's* and then returns new *y* coordinates that correspond to the *new_x's* array.

HARMEAN(number1,*number2*,...) The harmonic mean.

HYPGEOMDIST(sample_s,number_sample,population_s,number_population) The hypergeometric distribution.

INTERCEPT(known_y's,known_x's) The intercept of the linear regression line.

KURT(number1,*number2*,...) The kurtosis of a data set.

LARGE(array,k) Returns the *k*th largest value in *array*.

LINEST(known_y's,*known_x's,const,stats*) Calculates a straight line that corresponds to the *known_y's* and *known_x's*, and then returns an array that describes the line.

LOGEST(known_y's,*known_x's,const,stat*) Fits an exponential curve to the *known_y's* and *known_x's*, and then returns an array that describes the curve.

LOGINV(probability,mean,standard_dev) The inverse of the lognormal distribution.

LOGNORMDIST(x,mean,standard_dev) The lognormal distribution.

MAX(number1,*number2*,...) The maximum value in the list.

MEDIAN(number1,*number2*,...) The median of *numbers*.

MIN(number1,*number2*,...) The minimum value in the list.

MODE(number1,*number2*,...) The mode (most common value) of *numbers*.

NEGBINOMDIST(number_f,number_s,probability_s) The negative binomial distribution.

NORMDIST(x,mean,standard_dev,cumulative) The normal cumulative distribution.

NORMINV(probability,mean,standard_dev) The inverse of the normal cumulative distribution.

NORMSDIST(z) The standard normal cumulative distribution.

NORMSINV(probability) The inverse of the standard normal cumulative distribution.

PEARSON(array1,array2) The Pearson product moment correlation coefficient.

PERCENTILE(array,k) Returns the *k*th percentile of values in *array*.

PERCENTRANK(array,x,*significance*) The percentage rank of *x* in *array*.

PERMUT(number,number_chosen) The number of permutations for a given number of objects.

POISSON(x,mean,cumulative) The Poisson probability distribution.

PROB(x_range,prob_range,lower_limit,*upper_limit*) The probability that values in a range fall between two limits.

QUARTILE(array,quart) The quartile of a data set.

RANK(number,ref,*order*) The rank of a number in a list of numbers.

RSQ(known_y's,known_x's) The r^2 value of the linear regression line.

SKEW(number1,*number2*,...) The skewness of a distribution.

SLOPE(known_y's,known_x's) The slope of the linear regression line.

SMALL(array,k) Returns the kth smallest value in *array*.

STANDARDIZE(x,mean,standard_dev) Returns a normalized value.

STDEV(number1,*number2*,...) The standard deviation of the items in the list. STDEV( ) assumes that its arguments are a sample of the population.

STDEVP(number1,*number2*,...) The sample standard deviation of the items in the list. STDEVP( ) assumes that its arguments compose the entire population.

STEYX(known_y's,known_x's) The standard error of the predicted y value for each x in the regression.

TDIST(x,degrees_freedom,tails) The Student's t-distribution.

TINV(probability,degrees_freedom) The inverse of the Student's t-distribution.

TREND(known_y's,*known_x's,new_x's,const*) Fits a straight line to the *known_y's* and *known_x's*, and then returns new y coordinates that correspond to the *new_x's* array.

TRIMMEAN(array,percent) The mean of the interior of a data set.

TTEST(array1,array2,tails,type) The probability associated with a Student's t-test.

VAR(number1,*number2*,...) The variance of the items in the list. VAR( ) assumes that its arguments are a sample of the population.

VARP(number1,*number2*,...) The sample variance of the items in the list. VARP( ) assumes that its arguments compose the entire population.

WEIBULL(x,alpha,beta,cumulative) The Weibull distribution.

ZTEST(array,x,sigma) The two-tailed P-value of a z-test.

Database and List Management Functions

DAVERAGE(database,field,criteria) The average value of the items in *field* column of *database* range that meet the *criteria*.

DCOUNT(database,*field*,criteria) The number of items that contain numbers in the *field* column of *database* range that meet the *criteria*.

DCOUNTA(database,field,criteria) The number of items that are not blank in the *field* column of *database* range that meet the *criteria*.

DGET(database,field,criteria) The value in the *field* of a single record in the *database* range that meets the *criteria*.

DMAX(database,field,criteria) The maximum value in the *field* column of *database* range that meets the *criteria*.

DMIN(database,field,criteria) The minimum value in the *field* column of *database* range that meets the *criteria*.

DPRODUCT(database,field,criteria) The product of the items in the *field* column of *database* range that meet the *criteria*.

DSTDEV(database,field,criteria) The standard deviation based on a sample of a population in the *field* column of *database* range that meet the *criteria*.

DSTDEVP(database,field,criteria) The standard deviation based on the entire population in the *field* column of *database* range that meet the *criteria*.

DSUM(database,field,criteria) The sum of the items in the *field* column of *database* range that meet the *criteria*.

DVAR(database,field,criteria) The variance based on a sample of a population in the *field* column of *database* range that meet the *criteria*.

DVARP(database,field,criteria) The variance based on the entire population in the *field* column of *database* range that meet the *criteria*.

SQLREQUEST(connection_string,*output_ref*,*driver_prompt*,query_text, *column_names_logical*) Connects with an external database source, runs a query, and returns the result as an array.

SUBTOTAL(function_num,ref) This function returns a subtotal in a list or database.

Choice Functions

CHOOSE(index_num,value1,*value2*,...*value13*) Select value: if *index_num* = 0, then the cell containing this function displays #VALUE!; if *index_num* = 1, then the cell displays value1; and so forth. *Index_num* and *value1...value13* can be constants, other cell addresses, or functions.

HLOOKUP(lookup_value,table_array,row_index_num,*range_lookup*) Table lookup with index row: this is used to select a value from a table based on the *lookup_value*. If *range_lookup* is FALSE, HLOOKUP( ) will look for an approximate match; otherwise (if *range_lookup* is TRUE or omitted), it requires an exact match.

INDEX(reference,row_num,column_num,*area_num*) Value of cell at intersection: this yields the value of the cell in *reference*, *row_num* rows from the top, *column_num* columns from the left.

INDEX(array,*row_num*,*col_num*) Value of an element in an array.

LOOKUP(lookup_value,lookup_vector,result_vector)

LOOKUP(lookup_value,array) Looks up values in a vector or an array.

MATCH(lookup_value,lookup_array,*match_type*) Looks up values in a vector or an array.

VLOOKUP(lookup_value,table_array,col_index_num) Table lookup with index column. If *range_lookup* is FALSE, VLOOKUP( ) will look for an approximate match; otherwise (if *range_lookup* is TRUE or omitted), it requires an exact match.

Logical Functions

AND(logical1,*logical2*,...*logical30*) Logical "AND"; returns the value TRUE if all arguments are true; returns the value FALSE if one or more arguments are false.

FALSE( ) Returns the value FALSE (or 0 [zero]).

IF(logical_test,*value_if_true*,*value_if_false*) If the *logical_test* argument is true, returns the *value_if_true* argument (or TRUE if the *value_if_true* argument is omitted); if the *logical_test* argument is false, returns the *value_if_false* argument (or FALSE if the *value_if_false* argument is omitted).

ISBLANK(value) Returns the value TRUE if *value* refers to an empty cell.

ISERR(value) Returns the value TRUE if *value* refers to any error value other than #NA!

ISERROR(value) Returns the value TRUE if *value* refers to any error value (#NA!, #VALUE!, #REF!, #DIV/0!, #NUM!, #NAME?, or #NULL!).

ISEVEN(number) Returns the value TRUE if *number* refers to an even number.

ISLOGICAL(value) Returns the value TRUE if *value* refers to a logical value (TRUE or FALSE).

ISNA(value) Returns the value TRUE if *value* refers to the error value #NA!

ISNONTEXT(value) Returns the value TRUE if *value* refers to anything other than text (including error values, numeric values, logical values, references, and blank cells).

ISNUMBER(value) Returns the value TRUE if *value* refers to a number.

ISODD(number) Returns the value TRUE if *number* refers to an odd number.

ISREF(value) Returns the value TRUE if *value* refers to a reference.

ISTEXT(value) Returns the value TRUE if *value* refers to text.

NA( ) Not available; sets the value of the cell to #NA! This function takes no argument.

NOT(logical) Logical "NOT"; reverses the value of the argument; returns the value TRUE if the argument is false; returns the value FALSE if the argument is true.

OR(logical1,*logical2*,...*logical30*) Logical "OR"; returns the value TRUE if one or more arguments are true; returns the value FALSE if all arguments are false.

TRUE( ) Returns the value TRUE (or 1 [one]).

Matrix Functions

MDETERM(array) Returns the determinant of a matrix *array*.

MINVERSE(array) Returns the inverse of a matrix *array*.

MMULT(array1,array2) Returns the product of two matrices, *array1* and *array2*.

SUMPRODUCT(array1,array2,...) Returns the sum of the crossproducts of matrices *array1* and *array2*.

TRANSPOSE(array) Returns the transpose of a matrix *array*.

Text String Manipulation Functions

CHAR(number) Returns the character specified by the code *number*.

CLEAN(text) Removes all nonprintable characters from *text*. These control characters are not usable by many printers or other applications.

CODE(text) Returns the ANSI value of first character in *text*.

CONCATENATE(text1,*text2*,...*text30*) Joins multiple text strings into one string.

DOLLAR(number,*decimals*) Formats *number* to currency format, and then converts it to text. If the *decimals* argument is omitted, it is assumed to be 2.

EXACT(text1,text2) Returns the value TRUE if *text1* and *text2* are an exact equivalence, where exact equivalence includes capitalization.

FIND(find_text,within_text,*start_at_num*) Returns a number that corresponds to the location of *find_text* in *within_text*.

FIXED(number,*decimals*,no_commas) Rounds *number* to *decimals* number of decimal places, formats *number* to include commas, and converts *number* to text. If *decimals* is omitted, it is assumed to be 2.

LEFT(text,*num_chars*) Returns the first (left-most) *num_chars* characters in *text*. If *num_chars* is omitted, it is assumed to be 1.

LEN(text) Returns the number of characters in *text*.

LOWER(text) Converts *text* to lowercase and displays the result.

MID(text,start_num,num_chars) Returns a portion of *text*, starting at *start_num*, proceeding for *num_chars* characters.

N(value) Converts *value* to a number. If *value* is a number, it retains the value of the number. If *value* is a date, it returns the serial number of that date. If *value* is a logical value of TRUE, it returns the value of 1. If *value* is anything else, it returns a value of 0 (zero).

PROPER(text) Converts *text* to proper capitalization. This capitalizes the first letter of each word in *text*, and converts all other letters to lowercase. Excel assumes a new word begins after each space or punctuation mark.

REPLACE(old_text,start_num,num_chars,new_text) Replaces text in *old_text* with *new_text*, beginning at *start_num*, continuing for *num_chars* characters.

REPT(text,number_times) Repeats *text number_times* times.

RIGHT(text,*num_chars*) Returns last (right-most) *num_chars* characters in *text*. If *num_chars* is omitted, it is assumed to be 1.

SEARCH(find_text,within_text,*start_num*) Finds *find_text* within *within_text*.

SUBSTITUTE(text,old_text,new_text,*instance_num*) Substitutes *old_text* with *new_text* within *text*.

T(value) Returns the text referred to by *value*.

TEXT(value,*format_text*) Formats *value* to *format_text*, and converts it to text. The *format_text* argument must be placed in double quotation marks ("…").

TRIM(text) Removes excess spaces. This removes leading and trailing space characters and converts multiple embedded spaces to single spaces.

UPPER(text) Converts *text* to uppercase and displays the result.

VALUE(text) Converts *text* to a value.

Cell and Range Reference Functions

ADDRESS(row_num,column_num,*abs_num,a1,sheet_text*) Creates a cell address as a text entry from the values of *row_num* and *column_num*. These arguments would usually be cell references. If *abs_num* is 1 (the default), the cell reference is absolute. If *abs_num* is 4, the cell reference is relative. Other values of *abs_num* create mixed cell references (see the Help screen for the complete list). The *a1* argument determines whether the reference is in A1 style (the default) or R1C1 style. The *sheet_text* argument allows the entry of the name of an external worksheet or macro sheet.

AREAS(reference) Returns the number of areas in *reference*; most useful in analyzing named ranges containing a multiple selection.

CELL(info_type,*reference*) Returns information about the cell at *reference*. If *reference* is omitted, it is assumed to be the active cell.

COLUMN(reference) Returns the number of columns in *reference*; most useful when used with named ranges.

COLUMNS(array) Returns the number of columns in *array*.

COUNTBLANK(range) Returns the number of blank cells in *range*.

ERROR.TYPE(error_val) Returns a number corresponding to an error type.

INDIRECT(ref_text,*a1*) Returns the content of cell referenced by cell at *ref_text*. This allows one cell to reference another cell that contains a value. The *a1* argument is a logical value (TRUE or FALSE) that determines if *ref_text* is an A1 (TRUE) reference or an R1C1 (FALSE) reference. If omitted, *a1* is assumed to be TRUE.

INFO(type_text) Returns information about the current operating environment.

OFFSET(reference,rows,cols,*height,width*) Returns a reference offset from a given reference.

ROW(reference) Returns the row number of *reference*.

ROWS(reference) Returns the number of rows in *reference*; again, most useful when analyzing named ranges.

SERIES(*name_ref,categories*,values,plot_order) Represents a data series in the active chart. This function is used only on charts.

TYPE(value) Returns a code describing the data type of *value*.

Engineering Functions

BESSELI(x,n) The modified Bessel function $I_n(x)$.

BESSELJ(x,n) The Bessel function $J_n(x)$.

BESSELK(x,n) The modified Bessel function $K_n(x)$.

BESSELY(x,n) The modified Bessel function $Y_n(x)$.

BIN2DEC(number) Converts a binary *number* (base-2) to a decimal (base-10).

BIN2HEX(number,*places*) Converts a binary *number* to a hexadecimal (base-16).

BIN2OCT(number,*places*) Converts a binary *number* to an octal (base-8).

COMPLEX(real_num,i_num,*suffix*) Converts real and imaginary coefficients into a complex number.

CONVERT(number,from_unit,to_unit) Converts a number from one system of measurement to another.

DEC2BIN(number,*places*) Converts a decimal *number* to a binary.

DEC2HEX(number,*places*) Converts a decimal *number* to a hexadecimal.

DEC2OCT(number,*places*) Converts a decimal *number* to an octal.

DEGREES(angle_in_radians) Converts *angle_in_radians* to degrees.

DELTA(number1,number2) Tests whether *number1* and *number2* are equal.

ERF(lower_limit,upper_limit) Returns the error function.

ERFC(x) Returns the complementary error function.

GESTEP(number,step) Tests whether *number* is higher than a threshold value *step*.

HEX2BIN(number,places) Converts a hexadecimal *number* to a binary.

HEX2DEC(number) Converts a hexadecimal *number* to a decimal.

HEX2OCT(number,places) Converts a hexadecimal *number* to an octal.

IMABS(inumber) Returns the absolute value of *inumber* (a complex number).

IMAGINARY(inumber) Returns the imaginary coefficient of *inumber*.

IMARGUMENT(inumber) Returns the argument θ, an angle expressed in radians.

IMCONJUGATE(inumber) Returns the complex conjugate of *inumber*.

IMCOS(inumber) Returns the cosine of *inumber*.

IMDIV(inumber1,inumber2) Returns the quotient of *inumber1* and *inumber2*.

IMEXP(inumber) Returns the exponential of *inumber*.

IMLN(inumber) Returns the natural logarithm of *inumber*.

IMLOG10(inumber) Returns the base-10 logarithm of *inumber*.

IMLOG2(inumber) Returns the base-2 logarithm of *inumber*.

IMPOWER(inumber,number) Returns *inumber* raised to the *number* power.

IMPRODUCT(inumber1,inumber2) Returns the product of *inumber1* and *inumber2*.

IMREAL(inumber) Returns the real coefficient of *inumber*.

IMSIN(inumber) Returns the sine of *inumber*.

IMSQRT(inumber) Returns the square root of *inumber*.

IMSUB(inumber1,inumber2) Returns the difference of *inumber1* and *inumber2*.

IMSUM(inumber1,inumber2,inumber3,...) Returns the sum of *inumbers*.

OCT2BIN(number,places) Converts an octal *number* to a binary.

OCT2DEC(number) Converts an octal *number* to a decimal.

OCT2HEX(number,places) Converts an octal *number* to a hexadecimal.

RADIANS(angle_in_degrees) Converts *angle_in_degrees* to radians.

SQRTPI(number) Returns the square root of ($number \times \pi$).

DDE/External Functions

CALL(register_id,*argument1*,...)

CALL(module_text,procedure,type_text,*argument1*,...)

CALL(file_text,resource,type_text,*argument1*,...) Calls a procedure in a dynamic link library (DLL) or code resource.

REGISTER.ID(module_text,procedure,*type_text*) Returns the register ID of a dynamic link library (DLL) or other code resource that has been previously registered.

SQLREQUEST(connection_string,*output_ref*,*driver_prompt*,query_text, *column_names_logical*) Connects with an external database source, runs a query, and returns the result as an array.

APPENDIX C
Excel Version 5 Commands

This appendix contains a list of the commands of Excel Version 5 in the order they appear on the Excel menus. For more information, consult the body of this module and the Excel *User's Guide*.

Application Control Menu

Restore is used to restore the active window to its former size and location.

Move is used to reposition the active window or an open dialog box that has a Control menu.

Size is used to change the size of the active window.

Minimize is used to reduce the active window to an icon at the bottom of the screen.

Maximize is used to enlarge the active window to fill the screen.

Close is used to close the active window or an open dialog box that has a Control menu.

Switch To is used to list all currently open applications and activate the one you select.

Document Control Menu

Restore is used to restore the active window to its former size and location.

Move is used to reposition the active window or an open dialog box that has a Control menu.

Size is used to change the size of the active window.

Minimize is used to reduce the active window to an icon at the bottom of the screen.

Maximize is used to enlarge the active window to fill the screen.

Close is used to close the active window or an open dialog box that has a Control menu.

Next Window is used to activate the next window of the current document.

File Menu

File | New is used to create a new workbook.

File | Open is used to open an existing workbook.

File | Close is used to close all windows of the active workbook.

File | Save is used to save changes made to the active workbook.

File | Save As is used to save a new workbook or a new version of an existing workbook in the file format and with the file name you specify. It is also used for saving a file on a different drive or in a different directory.

File | Save Workspace is used to save the current open workbooks and their size and position on the screen.

File | Macro*[1] is used to open, run, or edit an existing macro.

File | Record New Macro* is used to create a new macro sheet and start recording your actions as a macro.

File | Unhide* is used to make a hidden window visible.

File | Find File is used to search for a file.

File | Summary Info is used to open the Summary Info window for the open workbook.

File | Page Setup is used to control the appearance of items such as headers, footers, and margins on the document's printed pages.

File | Print Preview is used to display the document's pages so that you can see how they will look when printed.

File | Print is used to print the active document.

File | Print Report is used to print a report.

File | 1,2,3,4 is used to list the last four files you opened.

File | Exit is used to end your Excel session.

---

[1] Commands marked with an * are available only on the Null menu, that is, when there is no active workbook.

Edit Menu

Edit | Undo is used to reverse certain commands or actions.

Edit | Repeat is used to repeat the last command you chose.

Edit | Cut is used to remove the selection and place it onto the Clipboard.

Edit | Copy is used to copy the selection and place it onto the Clipboard.

Edit | Copy Button Image is used to copy the picture on the selected tool and place it onto the Clipboard. This command appears only when the Customize dialog box or the Toolbars dialog box is open.

Edit | Copy Picture is used to copy a picture of the current selection and place it onto the Clipboard. This command appears only when you hold down [Shift] and select the Edit menu.

Edit | Paste is used to paste the Clipboard contents into a workbook, group, or chart or into the formula bar.

Edit | Paste Button Image is used to paste the picture from the Clipboard onto the selected tool. This command appears only when the Customize dialog box or the Toolbars dialog box is open.

Edit | Paste Picture is used to paste a picture from the Clipboard into an Excel document. This command appears only when you hold down [Shift] and select the Edit menu.

Edit | Paste Special is used to paste selected attributes of copied cells into the current selection.

Edit | Paste Picture Link is used to paste a picture from the Clipboard into an Excel document and create a link between the picture and the document from which it came. This command appears only when you hold down [Shift] and select the Edit menu.

Edit | Fill | Down is used to copy the contents and formats of cells in the top row of a selected range into the remaining cells in the selection.

Edit | Fill | Right is used to copy the contents and formats of cells in the left column of a selected range into the remaining cells in the selection.

Edit | Fill | Up is used to copy the contents and formats of cells in the bottom row of a selected range into the remaining cells in the selection.

Edit | Fill | Left is used to copy the contents and formats of cells in the right column of a selected range into the remaining cells in the selection.

Edit | Fill | Across Worksheets is used to enter the contents of the active sheet's selection into the same area on all selected sheets.

Edit | Fill | Series is used to create a series of numbers on the worksheet.

Edit | Fill | Justify is used to take the text contained in its left column and distribute it evenly throughout the selected range.

Edit | Clear is used to remove the data, formats, or both from selected workbook cells. If the active document is a chart, it removes chart data series or formats.

Edit | Delete is used to remove selected cells from a workbook and move the surrounding cells to fill the space.

Edit | Delete Sheet is used to remove selected sheets from a workbook.

Edit | Move or Copy Sheet is used to move or copy selected sheets within a workbook or between workbooks.

Edit | Find is used to search selected cells or the entire workbook for specified characters and select the first cell containing those characters.

Edit | Replace is used to find and replace characters in selected cells or on the entire workbook.

Edit | Go To is used to select cell references or named areas you specify.

Edit | Links is used to open linked documents or change links.

Edit | Objects is used to edit the selected object.

View Menu

View | Formula Bar is used to display the formula bar.

View | Status Bar is used to display the status bar.

View | Toolbars is used to customize or display the various toolbars.

View | Full Screen is used to display the worksheet in full screen mode. In effect, full screen hides everything but the worksheet, the menu bar, the sheet tabs, and the scroll bars.

View | Sized with Window is used to cause a chart to change size with its window. This command is only available on a chart sheet or when a chart is selected.

View | Zoom is used to change the scale at which you view the workbook.

View | View Manager is used to define or display a named view.

Insert Menu (Workbook)

Insert | Cells is used to insert a range of cells equivalent in size and shape to the selected range, and to move the surrounding cells to accommodate the inserted range.

Insert | Copied Cells (or **Cut Cells**) is used to insert a new range of cells and paste the contents of the Clipboard into the inserted range. This command is available only immediately following the use of Edit | Cut or Edit | Copy.

Insert | Rows is used to insert the number of rows equivalent to the number of rows in the current selection.

Insert | Columns is used to insert the number of columns equivalent to the number of columns in the current selection.

Insert | Worksheet is used to insert the number of sheets in the workbook equivalent to the number of sheets in the current selection.

Insert | Chart | On This Sheet is used to insert a chart based on the current selection as an embedded chart on the current sheet.

Insert | Chart | As New Sheet is used to insert a chart based on the current selection as a new chart sheet in the current workbook.

Insert | Macro | Module is used to insert a macro module sheet in the current workbook.

Insert | Macro | Dialog is used to insert a macro dialog sheet in the current workbook.

Insert | Macro | MS Excel 4.0 Macro is used to insert an Excel Version 4-style macro sheet in the current workbook.

Insert | Object inserts a new OLE object in the current document.

Insert | Page Break is used to set manual page breaks for a printed worksheet.

Insert | Remove Page Break is used to remove manual page breaks for a printed worksheet. Insert | Remove Page Break replaces Insert | Set Page Break when the active cell is below or to the right of a manual page break or when the entire workbook is selected.

Insert | Function is used to open the Function Wizard.

Insert | Name | Define is used to create a name for a cell range, value, or formula.

Insert | Name | Paste is used to insert the selected name into the formula bar.

Insert | Name | Create is used to create names from the text in the top, bottom, left-most, or right-most cells of a selected cell range and apply them to the rows and columns of the selected cell range.

Insert | Name | Apply is used to search formulas in selected cells and replace cell references with the names defined for them.

Insert | Note is used to add, delete, edit, or view notes for specific cells on the active workbook.

Insert | Picture is used to insert a picture in the active worksheet.

Insert | Object is used to insert an embedded object (OLE) in the active worksheet.

Format Menu (Workbook)

Format | Cells is used to change various display settings of the selected cells.

Format | Object is used to set various properties of the selected object(s). This command replaces Format | Cells when an object or group of objects is selected.

Format | Row | Height is used to change the height of selected rows.

Format | Row | AutoFit is used to automatically change the height of selected rows to the height of the tallest entry in the selection.

Format | Row | Hide is used to change the height of selected rows to zero.

Format | Row | Unhide is used to restore the height of hidden rows in the selection.

Format | Column | Width is used to change the width of selected columns.

Format | Column | AutoFit Selection is used to automatically change the width of selected columns to the width of the widest entry in each column.

Format | Column | Hide is used to change the width of selected columns to zero.

Format | Column | Unhide is used to restore the width of hidden columns in the selection.

Format | Column | Standard Width is used to change the standard width for all columns in the worksheet.

Format | Sheet | Rename is used to change the name of the current worksheet.

Format | Sheet | Hide is used to hide the current worksheet.

Format | Sheet | Unhide is used to unhide any hidden worksheets in the selection.

Format | AutoFormat is used to apply a built-in table format to the selected range.

Format | Style is used to define and apply cell styles.

Format | Placement | Bring to Front is used to place selected objects in front of all other objects.

Format | Placement | Send to Back is used to place selected objects behind all other objects.

Format | Placement | Group is used to group several objects into a single object.

Format | Placement | Ungroup is used to ungroup previously selected objects into individual objects. This command replaces Group when a group of objects is selected.

Tools Menu

Tools | Spelling is used to check the spelling in the current worksheet.

Tools | Auditing | Trace Precedents is used to create arrows on the screen showing the cells that the formula in the current cell refers to (precedents).

Tools | Auditing | Trace Dependents is used to create arrows on the screen showing the cells containing formulas that refer to the current cell (dependents).

Tools | Auditing | Trace Error is used to create arrows on the screen showing the cells containing formulas that are causing an error in the current cell.

Tools | Auditing | Remove All Arrows is used to remove the arrows created by the other Tools | Auditing commands.

Tools | Auditing | Show Auditing Toolbar is used to display the Auditing toolbar.

Tools | Goal Seek is used to vary the value in a specified cell until a formula dependent on that cell reaches the desired value.

Tools | Scenarios is used to manage the different scenarios of a what-if analysis model.

Tools | Solver is used to start the Solver, which finds optimal solutions to problems with multiple variables.

Tools | Protection | Protect Sheet is used to turn on a worksheet's contents, objects, and scenarios protection.

Tools | Protection | Protect Workbook is used to turn on a workbook's structure and window protection.

Tools | Protection | Unprotect Sheet is used to turn off a worksheet's contents, objects, and scenarios protection. It replaces Tools | Protection | Protect Sheet when protection has been turned on.

Tools | Protection | Unprotect Workbook is used to turn off a workbook's structure and window protection. It replaces Tools | Protection | Protect Workbook when protection has been turned on.

Tools | Add-Ins is used to install or uninstall add-in macros.

Tools | Macro is used to open, run, or edit a macro.

Tools | Record Macro | Record New Macro is used to open a macro module if necessary and record your actions as a macro.

Tools | Record Macro | Stop Recording is used to end macro recording. This command replaces Tools | Record Macro | Record New Macro during the recording of a macro.

Tools | Record Macro | Use Relative References is used to instruct the macro recorder to record selections as relative references.

Tools | Record Macro | Use Absolute References is used to instruct the macro recorder to record selections as absolute references.

Tools | Record Macro | Mark Position for Recording is used to define the position on your macro module as the location for future recordings.

Help | Technical Support is used to view details regarding support services available from Microsoft.

Help | About Microsoft Excel is used to display the version number of Excel that you are using and other information about the computer system on which you are running Excel.

Insert Menu (Chart)

Insert | Titles is used to put a title on a chart or attach text to a chart object.

Insert | Data Labels is used to put a label on each data point in a chart.

Insert | Legend is used to add a legend to the active chart.

Insert | Axes is used to control whether axes are visible on the active chart.

Insert | Gridlines is used to control whether gridlines are visible on the active chart.

Insert | Picture is used to insert a picture on the active chart.

Insert | Trendline is used to insert trendlines on the active chart.

Insert | Error Bars is used to insert error bars on the active chart.

Insert | New Data is used to add data to a data series on the active chart.

Insert | Worksheet is used to insert a sheet in the current workbook.

Insert | Chart | On This Sheet is used to insert a chart based on the current selection as an embedded chart on the current sheet.

Insert | Chart | As New Sheet is used to insert a chart based on the current selection as a new chart sheet in the current workbook.

Insert | Macro | Module is used to insert a macro module sheet in the current workbook.

Insert | Macro | Dialog is used to insert a macro dialog sheet in the current workbook.

Insert | Macro | MS Excel 4.0 Macro is used to insert an Excel Version 4-style macro sheet in the current workbook.

Format Menu (Chart)

Format | Selected Object is used to change the appearance of the selected chart object.

Format | Sheet | Rename is used to change the name of the current chart sheet.

Format | Sheet | Hide is used to hide the current chart sheet.

Format | Sheet | Unhide is used to unhide the current chart sheet.

Format | Chart Type is used to change the type of chart.

Format | AutoFormat is used to apply one of Excel's predefined chart types to the current chart.

Format | 3-D View is used to change the view on a 3-D chart.

Format | Placement | Bring to Front is used to move a selected chart object to the top layer.

Format | Placement | Send to Back is used to move a selected chart object to the bottom layer.

Format | Placement | Group is used to group the selected chart objects.

Format | 1, 2, 3 is used to format the data series in a chart by group.

Info Menu

The Info menu appears on the menu bar when you select the Info Window check box in the Tools | Options dialog box. It controls which information about the active cell is displayed in the Info window. Each option corresponds to a unique item of information.

Info | Cell is used to display the cell's reference.

Info | Formula is used to display the contents of the cell.

Info | Value is used to display the value in the cell in General format.

Info | Format is used to display the number format, alignment, font, borders, and shading of the cell.

Info | Protection is used to display the protection status of the cell.

Info | Names is used to display the names that include references to the cell.

Info | Precedents is used to display a dialog box containing two options: Direct Only displays only the direct precedents that the cell refers to. All Levels displays both direct and indirect precedents that the cell refers to.

Info | Dependents is used to display a dialog box containing two options: Direct Only displays only the direct dependents that refer to the cell. All Levels displays both direct and indirect dependents that refer to the cell.

Info | Note is used to display the cell note.

Index

NUMBERS AND SYMBOLS

! symbol, 205
(pound) sign, 44
#NULL!, 45
#REF!, 45
& (ampersand) character, 126
& (concatenation) operator, 66
< (less than sign), 270
<= (less than or equal to sign), 270
> (greater than sign), 270
>= (greater than or equal to sign), 270
= (equal sign), 44, 69
?, 270
~, 270
100% stacked column chart, 190
1040EZ.XLS, 59, 88, 118, 133, 428
12-hour clock, 103
24-hour clock, 103
3-D area chart, 197
3-D bar chart, 198
3-D column chart, 198
3-D floor, 204
3-D line chart, 198
3-D pie chart, 199
3-D surface chart, 199
3-D walls, 204
401(k) Plan exercise, 261
401(K).XLS, 262
401(K)M.XLS, 262

A

A4 paper size, 128
ABS( ), 70
Absolute cell reference, 167–168
Absolute value, 70
Accelerator key, 400
Accounting format, 100
Accounting underlining, 105
Active cell, 7, 18, 21
Active window, 13
Add-in manager, 39
Addition, 65
Alignment tab, 103
Alternate criteria, 271
Always Create Backup, 41
Annotations, 66
Annual interest rate, 72
Annuity, 71

Appearance, workbook, 100
    See also Formatting
Application object, 413
Application window, 11
Arc button, 312
Area charts, 193
Arguments, 32, 69
Arithmetic operators, 65
Arranging windows, 202
Array formula, 259
Arrow, 10, 204, 211
    button, 313
    tool, 211
ASCII-generic format, 355
Assigning Grades exercise, 382
Auditing
    toolbar, 310
    workbook, 39
Auto Outline, 157
AUTO.XLS, 93, 135, 430
Auto_Open, 420
AutoFill, 241
    handle, 151, 250, 267
AUTOFILL.XLS, 252–253
AutoFilter command, 272
AutoFit, 108
    Selection, 109
AutoFormat, 111
Automatic
    border, 208
    chart, 186
    fill, 208
    macro, 397
    page breaks, 127, 300
    recalculation, 45, 173
    scale, 209
AutoSum button, 35, 70
Average value, 76
AVERAGE( ), 76
Axes, 204

B

B5 paper size, 128
Background color, 208
Backup, 53
    methods, 53
Bar charts, 193
BASIC, 387
Best case assumptions, 230
Big Picture, 156
Bin array, 287
Binding, 229
Block, 95
Boilerplate, 110
BOOK1.XLS, 49
Border, 10, 13–14, 37, 208
    tab, 106
Branching, 410
    See also If statement
Break
    lines, 357
    mode, 427
Bring to Front tool, 313
BUDGET.XLS, 336
Buford Fencing Company exercises, 89, 118, 134
BUFORD.XLS, 90, 118, 134
Built-in constants, 394
BULL.XLS, 49, 131
BULL2.XLS, 55
Business Mileage exercises, 58, 88, 118, 133, 163, 292, 407, 428
BUTTON.XLS, 406

C

Calculation tab, 301
Cancel button, 37
Caps Lock, 38
Case sensitive, 267

Cash flows, 70
Catch the Wave exercise, 383
Category, 200
    axis, 200
    names, 200
Cell, 32, 95
    mode, 10
    Note window, 66
    protection, 307
    references, 33
    selection, 96
    shortcut menu, 99, 103
Center Across Columns tool, 36
Center Across Selection, 104
Center alignment, 103
Centering, document, 125
Changing cell, 227
Chart, 185
    definition, 190
    export, 211
    formats, 205
    menu bar, 189–190
    series assigment, 201
    tab, 211, 304
    toolbar, 310
Charting State Sales Data exercise, 218
ChartWizard, 36, 185, 187, 201
Check box, 12, 15, 17
Check Register exercises, 58, 88, 117, 133, 162, 291, 428
CHECKS.XLS, 58, 88, 117, 133, 162, 291
Circular reference, 173
Class, 405
Clear Contents, 99
Click, 9, 12
Clipboard, 8, 211, 359
Collapse button, 157
Collections, 422, 405
Colon, 96
Color
    palette, 102, 305
    tab, 305
Column, 33, 95
    charts, 186, 190, 193, 213
    deletion, 99
    input cell, 258
    insertion, 100
    labels, 301
    selection, 96
Columnwise order of recalculation, 172
    See also Recalculation
Combination chart, 197
Combined criteria, 266
    See also Criteria
Command button, 12, 15, 17
Comment lines, 390
Comments, 66
COMMISH.XLS, 417
Comparison, 65
    criteria, 266, 269
COMPCOST.XLS, 161, 180, 219, 236, 261
Complete
    column, 95
    row, 95
Compound Interest application, 182–183
Compound Interest Revisited exercise, 261
COMPOUND.XLS, 182, 343
Compounding, 73
COMPOX.XLS, 261
Computed criteria, 266, 271
    See also Criteria
Computed field, 266
Computing Minimum Payments exercise, 382
Concatenation, 65
Conditional values, 102
CONREPT2.XLS, 349
Consolidating Data from Two Workbooks exercise, 365

Consolidation, 348
CONSREPT.XLS, 347
Constant values, 43
Constraints, 226
    See also Sensitivity analysis
Control menu, 10, 13, 16
Control Panel, 16, 300
Control structures, 410
CONTROL.XLS, 317
Controls, 310
Copy, 139
    area, 139
    button, 143
    Copy and Paste operation, 139
    Copy and Paste Special Values procedure, 244
    general rules for, 149
COUNT( ), 76
COUNTA( ), 85
Crawling border, 151
Create Button tool, 313, 398
Criteria, 266
    range, 266, 269, 275
Cross, 10, 16
Crosshairs, 10
[Ctrl][Enter], 145
[Ctrl][F6], 203
Currency
    button, 36
    format, 101
Current date, 74
Current time, 74
Custom
    dialog box, 422
    footer, 126
    format characters, 101
    function, 415
    header, 126
    lists, 251
    tab, 304

CUSTOM.DIC, 223
Customizing toolbars, 312
Cut and Paste operation, 150
Cutpoints, 287

D

Data Disk, copying, 245
Data
    distribution table, 287
    form, 289
    input, 97
    labels, 206
    marker, 200
    points, 200, 206
    series, 191, 200, 204
    series name, 191, 200
    table, 255
    types, 412
Data | Consolidate command, 348
Data | Filter commands, 272, 275
Data | Form command, 289
Data | Group and Outline, 157
Data | PivotTable command, 280
Data | Sort command, 266
Data | Subtotals command, 279
Data | Table command, 255
Data | Text to Columns command, 358
Database, 265
    entry form, 39
    menu, 39
    statistical functions, 284
DATACOMP.XLS, 247
Date and Currency Formats exercise, 116
Date
    format, 101
    functions, 74
    series, 242
series type, 241
DATE( ), 74

DATEVALUE( ), 74
DAVERAGE( ), 284
Day
    abbreviation, 102
    name, 102
    of the month, 75
    of the week, 75
DAY( ), 75
DAYS360( ), 75
DB( ), 73
dBase, 340
DCOUNT( ), 285
DCOUNTA( ), 285
DDB( ), 73
DDE, 303
Debugging macros, 427
Decision variable, 227
Declaring variables, 412
Delimiter, 357
Demote, 157
Dependent workbook, 346
Dependents, 233
Depreciation, 73
DGET( ), 285
Dialog box, 11, 14
Dice exercises, 384, 407
DICE.XLS, 407
Difference in dates, 75
Dim keyword, 412, 424
Directories, 22
    pane, 23
Discontinuous ranges, 97
Disks, 53
DISPLAY, 178
Divide by 0 (zero), 45
DMAX( ), 285
DMIN( ), 285
Do-Loop, 411
Docked toolbars, 311
Document window, 11

DOS, 28
Dots per inch, 129
Double-click, 9
Double-declining balance depreciation, 73
Doughnut chart, 195
DPRODUCT( ), 286
Drag, 9
Drag and drop, 150, 301
Dragging, 150
Drawing
    Selection tool, 313
    tool, 211
    toolbar, 36, 211, 310, 312, 317
Drive window, 26
Drop lines, 204
Drop Shadow Box tool, 314
Drop-down list box, 12
DSTDEV( ), 285
DSTDEVP( ), 285
DSUM( ), 285
DVAR( ), 285
DVARP( ), 286
Dynamic Data Exchange, 303

E

EASTERN.XLS, 365
Edit menu, 39, 98
Edit mode, 10, 37, 45
Edit tab, 301
Edit | Clear commands, 99, 251, 316, 324
Edit | Copy command, 35, 139, 211
Edit | Cut command, 35, 150
Edit | Delete command, 99, 251
Edit | Fill commands, 145, 241, 251, 352
Edit | Find, 328
Edit | Go To, 98, 326
Edit | Links command, 342
Edit | Paste command, 35, 139, 211

Edit | Paste Special command, 35, 153, 244, 342
Edit | Redo, 308
Edit | Replace, 328
Edit | Undo commands, 267, 308
Ellipse button, 312
Ellipsis, 14
Else statement, 411
    See also If statement
Embedded chart, 187, 189
Embedded object, 360
End If statement, 410
    See also If statement
Enter button, 37
EPALTR.DOC, 367
Equal to, 270
Equations with one unknown, 255
Event handlers, 399
Excel commands, 39
Expand button, 157
Exploded segment, 216
Exponential curve, 241
Exporting data, 354
Extension, 41, 338
External reference, 205, 346
Extract range, 266, 275
EXTRACT.XLS, 344

F

F4, 170
F9, 173
Field, 266
    names, 265
File folder, 23
File formats, 340
File list, 42
File Manager, 22, 53, 55
File menu, 39–40, 339
File name, 40, 338
File pane, 23
File | Create Directory, 55
File | Exit, 42
File | New, 35
File | Open, 35, 42
File | Page Setup, 122, 211, 217, 300
File | Print, 35, 122, 129
File | Print Preview, 35, 129, 217
File | Save, 35, 42, 51
File | Save As, 40
File | Save Workspace command, 339
Files, 22
Fill, 208
    alignment, 103
    handle, 250
    pattern, 207–208
Filter, 39, 266
Financial functions, 70
Find, 39
Finding an Interest Rate exercise, 235
Finding files, 342
Fixed-declining balance depreciation, 73
Floating toolbars, 311
Font, 36
    size, 36, 105
    style, 105
    tab, 105
    underline, 105
Footers, 126
For-Next loop, 411
Foreground color, 208
Form 1040EZ exercises, 59, 88, 118, 133, 383, 428
Format, 24
Format menu, 39, 100, 190
Format Painter button, 35
Format | AutoFormat, 111
Format | Cells commands, 36, 100, 103, 112, 307, 330

Format | Chart Type, 185, 188, 190, 204, 212–213
Format | Column commands, 108, 113, 319
Format | Object command, 313
Format | Row, 108
Format | Selected Object commands, 207–218
Format | Style, 109
FORMATS.XLS, 114
Formatting, 22
    toolbar, 36, 310
Forms toolbar, 310, 316–317
Formula, 32, 44, 97, 300
Formula bar, 37, 47, 51, 300
Fraction format, 101
Freeform button, 313
Freehand button, 313
FREQUENCY( ), 287
Frozen panes, 320
Full Screen toolbar, 311
Function Wizard, 35, 76
    button, 76
    dialog box, 76
FUNCTION.XLS, 85
Functions, 69, 405
Future value, 71
FV( ), 71

G

Gap Width, 191
Gas Mileage exercises, 163, 180, 219, 333, 367
GASMILE.XLS, 164, 180, 219, 333, 367
General
    alignment, 103
    format, 101
    macro, 389
    tab, 303
Goal seeking, 39
GOAL.XLS, 225, 235

GRADES.XLS, 382
Graphic
    format, 207
    items, 36, 205
    objects, 300
Greater than or equal to, 270
Gridlines, 204, 207, 300
    printing, 123
Group Objects tool, 314
Grouping, 266
Growth
    series, 241
    type, 241
GROWTH( ) function, 241

H

Handles, 204
Harold's G.P.A. exercise, 56
HAROLD.XLS, 57, 132
Headers, 126
Heads-up computing, 40
Help
    Context-Sensitive, 36
    menu, 39
    window, 78
Help | Contents command, 406
Hi-lo lines, 204
Hidden
    cells, 307
    toolbars, 311
Hierarchy of operations, 64
Host application, 360
Hotel Manager application, 221
HOTEL.XLS, 203, 221
Hour
    entry, 102
    value, 75
HOUR( ), 75
Hourglass, 10

I

I-beam, 10
If statement, 410
Importing data, 354
In-cell editing, 301
INC_TAX.XLS, 372
Incremental change, 317
Index number, 369
Infinite loop, 411
Info window, 300
Initializing
    dialog box, 423
    variables, 413
Input cell, 255
InputBox function, 420
Insert command, 100
Insert menu, 39, 99, 116, 190, 206
Insert Module button, 389
Insert | Axes command, 206
Insert | Cells command, 99, 251
Insert | Chart command, 185, 190, 201, 203
Insert | Columns command, 99
Insert | Copied Cells command, 154
Insert | Data Labels command, 206
Insert | Gridlines command, 207
Insert | Legend command, 206
Insert | Name commands, 97, 265, 325, 327
Insert | New Data command, 205
Insert | Note command, 66
Insert | Object command, 360
Insert | Page Break command, 127
Insert | Picture, 207
Insert | Rows command, 99
Insert | Titles, 206, 217
Insert | Worksheet command, 99
Instant Watch button, 390
INT( ), 70
Integer, 70
Interactive procedures, 419

Interest rate, 72
    converting annual to monthly, 72
Internal rate of return, 71
IPMT( ), 82
IRR( ), 71
Iterations, 174

J

JOBS workbook, 57, 117, 161, 219
JOBS.XLS, 291, 333
Justify alignment, 103

K

Keyboard, 12, 23
Keyboard shortcut, 17
Keypad, 7
Keys, 266
Keywords, 394

L

Landscape orientation, 124, 128
LAREPT.XLS, 347
LAREPT2.XLS, 349
LEAGUE, 162
League Standings exercises, 162, 219, 292
LEAGUE.XLS, 219, 292
Left alignment, 103
Legal-sized paper, 128
Legend, 200, 204, 213
Let keyword, 413
Letter-sized paper, 128
Level button, 157
Line button, 312
Line charts, 193, 194, 212, 304
Line definition, 209
Linear series, 241
Linear type, 241

Linked
    documents, 346
    object, 360
    paste, 154
Linking, 345
Linking Workbooks exercise, 366
List box, 15, 17
Literal string, 66, 377
Local variable, 424
Locked cells, 307
Logarithmic scale, 210
Logic error, 427
Logical
    expressions, 372
    operators, 270, 372
Lookup table, 369
Looping, 411
Lottery Winner exercise, 87
LOTTERY.XLS, 87
Lotus 1-2-3, 39, 302, 340

M

Macintosh, 340
Macro, 387
    dialog, 422
    module, 388
    name, 388
    recorder, 39, 388
Major tick mark, 209
Manual
    page breaks, 127
    recalculation, 173
Margin settings, 125
MARINA.XLS, 237–238
Marker definition, 209
Marquee, 139
Mathematical functions, 69
MAX( ), 76
Maximize button, 10, 20

Maximum value, 76, 209–210
Menu, 34, 39
    bar, 34
    Editor button, 389
    item, 399
Methods, 405
Microsoft, 32, 34
    Office Manager, 33
    toolbar, 310
MILES96.XLS, 58, 88, 118, 133, 163, 292, 407, 428
MIN( ), 76
Minimize button, 10, 14
Minimize command, 17
Minimum value, 76, 209–210
Minor tick mark, 209
MINPAY.XLS, 383
Minute
    entry, 102
    value, 75
MINUTE( ), 75
Mixed cell reference, 167–168
MOD( ), 70
Modular part, 70
Module
    Format tab, 306
    General tab, 305
Module-level variable, 424
Month abbreviation, 102
Month
    name, 102
    number, 75
MONTH( ), 75
Monthly
    interest rate, 72
    payments, 72
More Database Exercises exercise, 290
More Fun with Functions exercise, 86
MOREFORM.XLS, 117
MOREFUNC.XLS, 87

Most likely assumptions, 230
Mouse, 8, 23
Move command, 16
Moving between windows, 203
Multiplan, 39, 340
Multiple
   copies, 154
   criteria, 271
   sheets, 52, 98
Multiplication, 65

N

Named ranges, 97, 324
NAMELIST.XLS, 268, 290, 333
NAMLIST2.XLS, 290
NATIONAL.XLS, 366
Native application, 360
Natural order of recalculation, 172
Negation, 65
Net present value, 71
Normal Font, 106
Not equal to, 270
Note, 99
   indicator, 66, 300
   printing, 123
NOW( ), 74
NPER( ), 72–73
NPV( ), 71
Num Lock, 38
Number
   as text, 43
   format, 100
   format codes, 101
   of cells, 76
   of payments, 72
   of periods, 72–73
   series, 241
   tab, 100, 112

Numeric
   day entry, 102
   entry display, 103
   format examples, 103
   month entry, 102

O

Object, 360, 404
Object Browser button, 389
Object Linking and Embedding, 360
Object-oriented programming, 404
Objective, 227
OLE, 360
OnEvent procedures, 399
Operands, 64
OPERATOR.XLS, 69
Operators, 64
Optional numeric entry, 101
Order of precedence, 64
Orientation alignment, 104
OS/2, 341
Outline, 157
Outlining, 301
Overflow values, 44
Overlap, 191
OVERTIME.XLS, 377

P

Page break, 127, 280
Page change, 317
Page Order, 123
Page Setup, 122
Panes, 320
Paper
   orientation, 128
   size, 125, 128
Partial
   column, 95

Partial (continued)
  row, 95
Password, 41–42
  protection, 341
  write reservation, 341
Paste, 139
  area, 139
  button, 144
  link, 154
Path name, 339
Pattern tool, 314
Patterns tab, 107
Payment on a loan, 72
Percentage format, 101
Perfect Job exercises, 57, 117, 161, 219, 291, 333
Periodic interest, 73
Personal dictionary, 223
PERSONAL.XLS, 407
PETS.TXT, 359
PETS.XLS, 359
PETS2.PRN, 359
PETSALES.XLS, 280
Picture file, 207
Pie chart, 194, 213
Pivot Table Wizard, 39, 280
Placeholder, 300
Places Rated Almanac, 161
Pleasant Cove Marina exercises, 236, 238
Plot area, 204
PMT( ), 72, 258
Point-and-click, 10, 12, 22
Pointing method, 44
Poor Richard's applications, 92–93, 135, 430
PORTFOLI.XLS, 296, 323
Portrait orientation, 124, 128
Precedents, 233
Precision as Displayed, 177
Present value, 71
Preview Picture, 207

Primary axis, 192
Print
  area, 122
  Preview, 129
  quality, 125
  titles, 123
Printer resolution, 129
Printer Setup, 127
Printing, 51
Printing a Header exercise, 132
PROBLEM.XLS, 293
PROBLEM2.XLS, 415
Procedure, 405
Program group, 11, 17
Program Manager, 11, 13–14, 16
Program-specific format, 355
Programming Language Summary, 406
Programming with Visual Basic, 406
Promote, 157
Properties, 405
Properties tab, 314
Protection, 97
  password, 341
  tab, 107
Public
  keyword, 424
  variable, 424
PV( ), 71

Q

Query and Pivot toolbar, 310

R

R1C1 style, 303
R1C1 style references, 391
Radar chart, 195
Radio button, 12

Range, 4, 95
  data entry, 98
  names, 325
  protection, 97
  selection, 96
  specification, 96
  deselection, 98
Rate, 72
RATE( ), 72–73
RB Company, 309
RB96BUDG.XLS, 352
RB96MID.XLS, 156
RB96PROJ.XLS, 140, 171, 212, 216, 230, 309, 315
Read-only, 41, 341
RECALC.XLS, 176, 343
Recalculation, 45, 172
Record Macro button, 390
RECORDER.XLS, 389
Records, 266
Rectangle button, 312
Reference section, 37
Relative cell reference, 167–168
Remainder, 70
Rename Sheet dialog box, 52
Repeat tool, 35
Repetition, 410
REPORT.XLT, 115
Require Variable Declaration box, 412
Required numeric entry, 101
Reshape tool, 314
Restore button, 10, 15, 20
Resume Macro button, 390
Return value, 416
Ribbon chart, 198
Right alignment, 103
Right-click, 9
Round, 70
ROUND( ), 70

Row, 33, 95
  deletion, 99
  input cell, 258
  insertion, 100
  labels, 301
  selection, 96
Rowwise order of recalculation, 172
Run Macro button, 390
Run-time error, 427
Running Macros exercise, 406

S

Sales by State exercise, 178
Sales Workbook exercises, 160, 180, 219, 261, 236
SALESCHT.DOC, 364
Scale, 206, 209
Scaling, 124
Scatter chart, 196
Scenario, 230
  management, 39
  Manager, 230
Scientific
  format, 101
  notation, 102
Scope, variable, 424
Scroll
  bar, 11, 15, 19, 301, 317
  box, 11, 16, 316
  Lock key, 38
Search and Replace exercise, 333
SEAREPT.XLS, 347
SEAREPT2.XLS, 349
Second entry, 103
Second value, 75
SECOND( ), 75
Secondary axis, 192, 206
Select All button, 96
Selecting chart items, 204

INDEX

Send to Back tool, 313
Sensitivity analysis, 152
Serial date number, 74
Serial number of a given date, 74
Serial time number, 75
Series formulas, 205
SERIES( ), 205
SERVICE.XLS, 422, 425
Set keyword, 413
Sheet, 33
    insertion, 100
    tab, 20, 52, 301
    selection, 98
SHIRT.XLS, 228
Shortcut
    key, 397
    menus, 43
Simultaneous equations, 174
SINEWAVE.XLS, 383
Size command, 16
Sizing mode, 10
SLN( ), 73
SLSTREND.XLS, 250
Smoothed line, 209
Snow Data exercise, 367
SOFTLIST.XLS, 333
SOFTSORT.XLS, 293
Software Inventory exercises, 293, 333
Solver, 39, 226
Sort, 39
Source
    file, 360
    workbook, 346
Spell checker, 39, 223
Spelling, 35
Spinner control, 316, 317
Spreadsheet, 32
Spring Break: Florida or Bust application, 335
SQRTTABL.XLS, 260

Stacked
    column chart, 190
    line charts, 193
Standard
    toolbar, 310
    underlining, 105
    Width, 109
Start value, 241
Startup directory, 303
Statistical functions, 75
Statistical Problem exercise, 293
Status bar, 38, 300
Step Into button, 390
Step Macro button, 390
Step Over button, 390
Step value, 241
Stop Macro button, 390
Stop Recording toolbar, 310
Stop statement, 427
Stop value, 241
Straight-line depreciation, 73
Strikethrough, 105
String to date, 74
String to time, 75
Strings, 66
Student Data Disk, 245, 329
Style, 109
    apply, 110
    creating by example, 110
    define, 109
    merge, 110
Subdirectory specification, 40
Subroutine, 391
Subscript, 105
Subtotal, 39
Subtotals, 266, 279
Sum, 70
Sum of the crossproducts, 76
Sum of the products, 76
SUM( ), 70

Sum-of-the-years' digits depreciation, 73
Summary Info, 303, 342
    dialog box, 49
SUMPRODUCT( ), 76
Superscript, 105
Surface chart, 199
SYD( ), 73
Syntax error, 306, 427

T

Target cell, 227
Task List, 55
TAXPLAN.XLS, 332
Template, 110
Text, 66, 204
    box, 12, 15, 17, 36
    box button, 313
    entries, 32, 43
    format, 101
    Import Wizard, 357
    items, 205
    joining, 65
    string, 102
Then keyword, 410
Things to Do exercises, 60, 118, 133, 293
Thousands separator, 101
Three-dimensional ranges, 98
Tick mark labels, 210
Tiled windows, 322
Time format, 101
Time functions, 74
TIME( ), 75
TIMEKPR.XLS, 331
TIMEKPR2.XLS, 331
TIMEVALUE( ), 75
TipWizard, 36, 303, 310
Title bar, 10, 13, 33, 49
TO-DO.XLS, 60, 118, 133, 293
TODAY( ), 74

Toggle Breakpoints button, 390, 427
Toolbars, 34, 311
Tools menu, 39
Tools | Auditing commands, 232–233
Tools | Goal Seek command, 224
Tools | Macro command, 397
Tools | Options command, 106, 130, 174, 251, 299
Tools | Protection commands, 307, 308, 319
Tools | Protection | Protect Sheet command, 330
Tools | Record Macro commands, 387, 391
Tools | Scenarios command, 230
Tools | Solver command, 226
Tools | Spelling command, 223
Tools | Tab Order command, 423
ToolTips, 34
Tracing arrows, 232
Transition tab, 302
Transpose, 154
Transpose Command exercise, 407
Trend
    calculation, 241
    series, 242
TREND( ) function, 241, 251
Tutorial, 39

U

Unattached text, 211
Undo, 308
Ungroup Objects tool, 314
Unique Records Only, 275
Unknown numeric entry, 101
Unlock, 307
Using Range Names in Formulas exercise, 332
Using Visual Basic, 406

V

Value, 32
Value axis, 200
Variable, 306, 412
Variable declining balance depreciation, 74
VDB( ), 74
Vertical alignment, 104
View
    Manager, 39
    menu, 39
    tab, 299
View | Full Screen, 311
View | Toolbars command, 233, 310–311, 315, 400
View | Zoom command, 319
Visual Basic, 305, 310, 387
    for Applications, Excel edition, 387
    Reference, 406
    toolbar, 310, 389
    User's Guide, 409
VLOOKUP( ), 370

W

Watch expression, 427
WEEKDAY( ), 75
WESTERN.XLS, 365
WESTREG.XLS, 179, 218
What-if analyses, 255
Wild card characters, 270
Window, 10, 322
    menu, 39
Window | Arrange command, 202, 205, 309, 315, 322
Window | Freeze Panes command, 320
Window | New Window command, 202, 309, 322
Window | Split command, 320
Window | Tile command, 54–55
Windows, 8, 11, 16, 105, 211
Windows Clipboard, 139
Word for Windows, 211
Workbook, 20, 31–32, 35, 351
    appearance, 100
    file, 32, 49
    window, 18, 21
Workgroup toolbar, 310
Worksheet, 32, 95, 185
    menu bar, 189–190
    selection, 96
    structure, 232
Worst case assumptions, 230
Wrap Text, 103
Write reservation password, 341
Write-protect, 54
WYSIWYG (what you see is what you get), 129

X

X-axis, 196, 210
XLS extension, 40
XY chart, 196, 215

Y

Y scale, 218
Y-axis, 196, 210, 213, 218
Year
    entry, 102
    number, 75
YEAR( ), 75

Z

Z-axis, 197
Zero values, 301
Zoom, 36
    tool, 203

Notes

Notes

Notes

Notes

Notes

Quick Reference

This card lists commonly used Excel 5 commands. See Appendix C of this manual for a complete list.

Microsoft Excel 5

File Menu	Purpose
File	Close	Close the active document
File	Exit	End your Excel session
File	New	Create a new document
File	Open	Open an existing document
File	Page Setup	Control the appearance of printed pages
File	Print	Print the active document
File	Print Preview	Preview the printed pages
File	Save	Save changes to the active document
File	Save As	Save the active document with a new file name

Edit Menu	Purpose
Edit	Clear	Delete data from cells
Edit	Copy	Copy the selection to the Clipboard
Edit	Cut	Move the selection to the Clipboard
Edit	Delete	Remove selected cells
Edit	Find	Find cells containing search characters
Edit	Paste	Paste the Clipboard contents
Edit	Repeat	Repeat the last command you chose
Edit	Replace	Replace characters with other characters
Edit	Undo	Reverse certain commands or actions

View Menu	Purpose
View	Toolbars	Hide or display various toolbars
View	Zoom	Change the display size of the worksheet

Insert Menu	Purpose
Insert	Cells	Insert a range of cells
Insert	Chart	Insert a chart

Insert Menu	Purpose
Insert | Columns	Insert a range of cells
Insert | Function	Open the Function Wizard
Insert | Macro	Insert a macro sheet
Insert | Name	Insert a name
Insert | Page Break	Insert a page break in a printout
Insert | Rows	Insert a range of cells
Insert | Worksheet	Insert a new worksheet

Format Menu	Purpose
Format | Cells	Set the display of numbers
Format | Column	Change the width of selected columns
Format | Row	Change the height of selected rows
Format | Sheet	Rename or hide/unhide worksheets

Tools Menu	Purpose
Tools | Auditing	Map the structure of a worksheet
Tools | Options	Control option affecting the Excel application
Tools | Protection	Protect/unprotect a worksheet or workbook
Tools | Record Macro	Create/play macros
Tools | Solver	Solve goal-seeking problems
Tools | Spelling	Spell check a workbook

Data Menu	Purpose
Data | Filter	Filter records from a database
Data | Form	Display a database form
Data | PivotTable	Create a pivot table from a database
Data | Sort	Rearrange a selection
Data | Table	Create a data table

Window Menu	Purpose
Window | Arrange	Arrange the open windows
Window | New Window	Open an additional window

Help Menu	Purpose
Help | Contents	Display the Help table of contents
Help | Search for Help on	Search the Help index for keywords